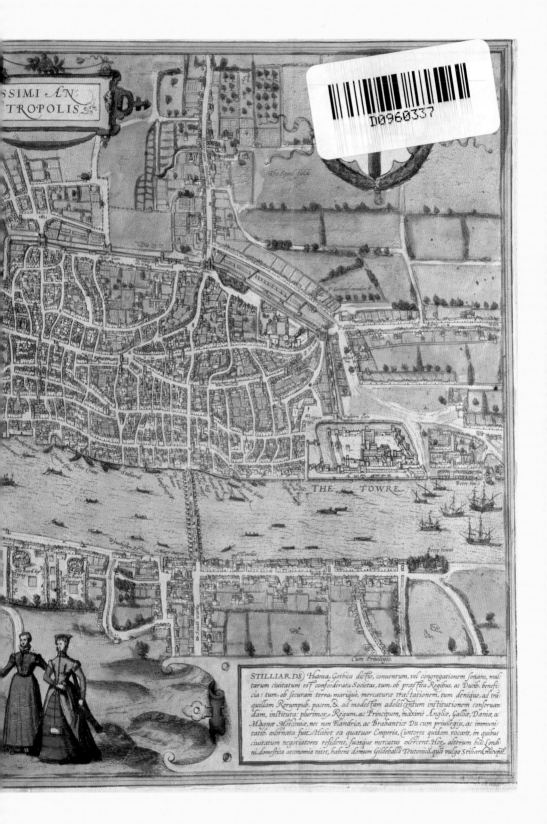

SSIMI AN:
TROPOLIS

The Spol felo

Moore gates

Gerhard swaders

Postern Gate

THE TOWRE

Beere howse

Beere howse

Cum Priuilegio.

STILLIARDS) Hansa, Gothica dictio, conuentum, vel congregationem sonans, multarum ciuitatum est confœderata Societas, tum ob præstita Regibus, ac Ducib. beneficia: tum ob securam terra marique, mercaturæ tractationem, tum denique, ad tranquillam Rerumpub. pacem, & ad modestam adolescentum institutionem conseruandam, instituta: plurimor. Regum, ac Principum, maximè Angliæ, Galliæ, Daniæ, ac Magnæ Moscouiæ, nec non Flandriæ, ac Brabantiæ Du cum priuilegijs, ac immunitatib. exornata fuit. Habet ea quatuor Emporia, Cuntores quidam vocant, in quibus ciuitatum negotiatores resident, suosque mercatus exercent. Hor. alterum scil. Londini, domestica oeconomia nitet, habens domum Gildehalla Teutonica, quã vulgo Stiliard, nuncupat.

ELIZABETH'S
LONDON

To the Reader

Divers writers of histories write diversely ... For though it be written homely, yet it is not (as I trust) written untruly. And in histories the chief thing that is to be desired is truth. Wherefore, if thou find that in it, I beseech thee, wink at small faults, or at the least, let the consideration of my well meaning drown them.

John Stow

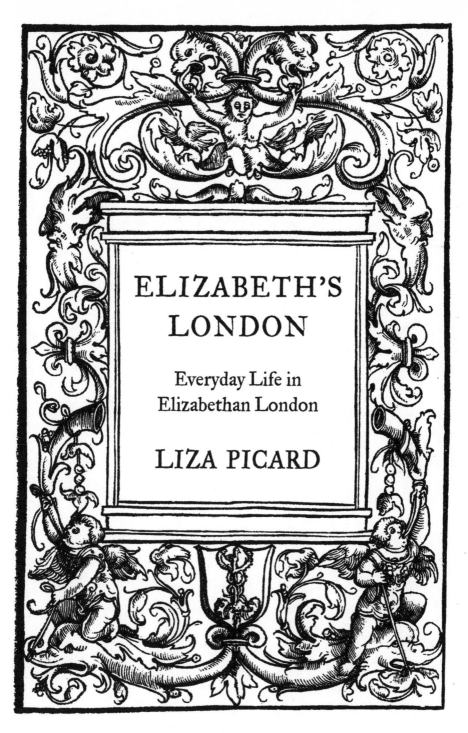

ELIZABETH'S LONDON

Everyday Life in
Elizabethan London

LIZA PICARD

Weidenfeld & Nicolson
LONDON

First published in Great Britain in 2003 by
Weidenfeld & Nicolson

A CIP catalogue record for this book is
available from the British Library.

ISBN 0 297 60729 4

Typeset by Selwood Systems,
Midsomer Norton

Printed in Great Britain by Butler & Tanner Ltd,
Frome and London

Weidenfeld & Nicolson
The Orion Publishing Group Ltd
Orion House
5 Upper Saint Martin's Lane
London WC2H 9EA

Contents

PART TWO: THE PEOPLE

List of illustrations

The author and publisher are grateful to the following for permission to reproduce illustrations: AKG London, 1, 2, 28; Bridgeman Art Library, 3, 4, 5, 10, 23, 25, 37, 40, 42, 44, 45 and the endpaper map; Folger Shakespeare Library, 8, 15, 16; Museum of London, 9, 17; Guildhall Library, Corporation of London, 11, 13, 43; V&A Picture Library, 12; Wellcome Library, London, 18, 19, 20, 21, 41; Pepys Library, Magdalene College, Cambridge, 26, 27; by kind permission from *Reading Tudor and Stuart Handwriting* by Lionel Munby, published by Phillimore & Co. Ltd, Chichester, West Sussex, for the British Association of Local History, 29, 31; photo by John Tramper, 1998, of *The Merchant of Venice* at the Globe Theatre, 30; Getty Images, 33; National Portrait Gallery, London, 34; by kind permission of the Duke of Buccleuch and Queensberry from his Collection at Boughton House, Northamptonshire, 35, 36; British Museum, 38.

Preface

You only have to open Samuel Pepy's *Diary* and you are back in the London of Charles II. A hundred years later, Dr Johnson is pontificating and Hogarth is painting, and again, you can easily imagine that time. But to go back to the days of the first Queen Elizabeth needs more effort. Her own appearance is familiar, from the many portraits which she authorised, to keep her image before her public. As she aged, her portraits became less and less like her, but the idea behind them remained the same – a gorgeously dressed queenly icon. The members of her Court look out from their portraits, some so lifelike that they could be the commercial barons and top civil servants of nowadays, in fancy dress. But they were a tiny section of society. Where can we find the ordinary people?

When I began this book I found them elusive. There was no diarist who conveniently covered the period. There are few buildings surviving, especially in London. Artefacts and clothes from the time are rare. How could the life of Londoners during Elizabeth's long reign, 1558–1603, be evoked ?

The first man I turned to was John Stow. He lived in London all his life, 1525–1605. His father and grandfather had been Londoners too. He belonged to the Merchant Taylors' livery company, who clearly thought him a worthwhile member, whatever his merits as a tailor, because he was given a pension in 1578 so that he could devote all his time to his historical research. He published his *Survey of London* in 1598, when he was over 70.[1] It is a meticulous account of the London he knew, based on his own perambulations and on records he had seen and collected over the years. He looked back to the 1300s as if they were yesterday. The only caveat I would enter for a modern reader is that he dealt with London ward by ward: if at all possible, have a map of the wards by you as you read.

William Harrison, 1535–93, wrote a *Description of England* for inclusion in Holinshed's *Chronicles* in 1587.[2] It contains many references to London, as well as generalities about England and its laws, customs, etc. Just occasionally one is aware of a possible tendency to pad the book out – was he paid by the thousand words?

I found, as I delved deeper, more diaries than I had originally expected, but of course they were kept by moderately prosperous men – none was kept by a poor man or by a woman. Some were travel journals kept by foreign visitors. A young Venetian merchant Alessandro Magno arrived in London in August 1562. He knew no English, but he had an acute eye, and the account of his seven-week stay is factual and fascinating.[3] Emmanuel van Meteren, another merchant, this time Dutch, had lived all his life, 1558–1612, in England; he wrote a description of it in 1599.[4] A Dutch physician, Levinus Lemnius, came to see his son, who was practising as a physician in London, in 1560, and wrote very favourable 'Notes on England'.[5] Samuel Kielchil spent more than two months in England in 1585, possibly influenced by the English habit of kissing visitors, 'even foreigners'.[6] London was on the route of educational tours by young Germans, who found Protestant England more congenial than Catholic Italy. Frederick, Duke of Würtemberg, arrived in 1592. He – or his secretary – wrote a detailed description of London, as well as Oxford and Cambridge, no doubt for home consumption to show how profitably he had spent his time.[7] Paul Hentzner came over in the suite of a young Silesian noble in the summer of 1598, and was startled by Queen Elizabeth's 'uncovered bosom'.[8] Thomas Platter arrived from Basle in 1599 and conscientiously did the tourist sites.[9]

Elizabeth's astrologer, Dr Dee, recorded in his diaries many domestic details as well as his success, or otherwise, in summoning spirits.[10] Another astrologer, Simon Forman, ran a thriving medical practice. His habit of keeping notes on his patients, deplored by the College of Physicians, provides a treasure-trove for historians.[11] Thomas Wythorne was born in Somerset in 1528. His efforts to find himself a rich wife in London while evading the attentions of marriage-bent widows, as recorded in his diary, could happen to any young man.[12] Henry Machyn's *Diary* is a much more serious matter. His business was the provision of funeral furnishings. Few sights delighted him more than a properly organised funeral, but he found time to record much of the daily life of London.[13] Richard Stoneley was a Treasury official, whose manuscript diary happened to be included in the vast mass of papers left by Lord Burghley. It attracted the notice of an antiquarian with a magpie mind, Francis Douce, who copied in his own handwriting the passages that intrigued him: mostly notes of expenses, including the cost of a short spell in prison while Stoneley's official accounts were sorted out. Fortunately Douce's handwriting is for the most part legible.[14]

Accounts may sound formidably dry, but they can provide a vivid objective picture. The prosperity of the great livery companies, shown in their accounts, made them sitting ducks for the Queen's constant demands for revenue.[15] Probate inventories of the possessions of the rich, such as the Earls of Leicester and Bedford, throw a narrow but dazzling light on their lives.[16] At the other end of the scale, the churchwardens of each parish painstakingly recorded every sum spent or received, such as the bellringers' pay for ringing the bells of Lambeth Church whenever the Queen chose to pass by on the river.[17] A laborious search of the records kept by clerks and officials, and administrative proclamations and statutes, produced occasional rewards, such as the irate woman screaming rude words at her neighbour across the yard, which were carefully noted in a court record.

Elizabethan Londoners' ambivalence about foreigners gave rise to periodic checks on them to see exactly what they were doing and how many of them there were. An astonishing amount of information was recorded – the names, ages, occupations and places of birth of all foreign household members in London, including servants and apprentices. In those respects we know much more about foreign immigrants than about native-born Londoners. Here I relied principally on the scholarship of Irene Scouloudi, who edited the 1593 Return of Strangers.[18] Another meticulous work of research enables the reader to visualise each building in a group of inner London parishes, and trace its history from the Great Fire of 1666 back to the thirteenth century.[19]

Shakespeare arrived in about 1580, half way through Elizabeth's reign, but there were earlier playwrights and poets, from whose works an image of London life can sometimes be inferred, if only by noting the things they took for granted. Another set of writers was invaluable – the ultra-Puritans, who disapproved of almost everything. Foremost among them was Phillip Stubbes, whose descriptions of contemporary dress enable us to see it in every shocking detail.[20]

At an early stage I decided that as much as possible I would quote verbatim from the contemporary documents I was using, which evoke those times more vividly, to me, than the most scholarly or the most imaginative accounts based on them. I hope you agree. I have in places punctuated the excerpts I have used, to make them easier to read, and I have used modern spelling. Where the sense needed the addition of a word or two I have added them in square brackets. I should perhaps say at this stage that I consistently, and sometimes inaccurately, refer to Elizabeth's chief minister William Cecil as Burghley. This is the name by which he is best known to us, and it would be, I thought, needlessly pettifogging to signal the exact date, 1571, when Elizabeth made him an earl.

I knew I needed help this time, and I had the sense to ask for it. In that way I met many delightful people who wear their immense knowledge lightly, and unstintingly share it with an amateur making clumsy and, I am sure, badly timed, enquiries. Jenny Tiramani, Master of Design of the New Globe Theatre, found time in an appallingly busy day to talk to me about making Elizabethan costumes. Nick Humphrey took me round his new British Galleries in the V. & A. and explained them so that I saw them with new eyes. Gill Saunders, of the Prints and Drawings Department there, showed me fascinating survivals of wallpaper which I would never have seen without her. The staff of the London Metropolitan Archives were as always endearingly enthusiastic and brilliantly helpful. Heather Creaton and Olwen Mihill of the Centre for Metropolitan Studies in the Institute of Historical Research did not mind at all that I didn't even know what I was looking for, and directed me to all kinds of treasures. I spent a happy day with Marion Rea, archivist of Bart's, looking at the hospital's amazingly complete early records, and two more days in Horley reading the early records of Christ's Hospital with the help of its archivist, Rona Mitchell. Irene Gilchrist and her staff at the Guildhall Library were as unfailingly helpful as I have always found them. The staff of the British Library patiently saw me through my difficulties with their computerised catalogue.

In Oxford I have been privileged to learn from Professor Catherine Duncan-Jones, Dr Marjory Pelling, Dr Barbara Harvey and Dr Lucy Wooding. The last piece of research I undertook was a boat trip from Gravesend up the Thames as far as Lambeth, with that unique source of riverine experience and knowledge Captain Potter, of MV *Princess Pocahontas*. The fact that the trip was entirely pleasurable does not disqualify it from being work. But the star of this list has to be Ms Lawik, who deals with requests by country readers for books from the London Library, that astonishing institution. Not only did she see that whatever I asked for arrived, but also she helped constructively with suggestions, and it was always a delight to talk to her.

From time to time I flagged, or panicked, or both simultaneously, but I knew that I could rely on the wisdom and encouragement of my editor, Benjamin Buchan, in whom I am very fortunate. My other unfailing sources of support have been my friend Henrietta Wilson of Gray's Inn, who has sheltered and refreshed me in all the ways a friend can do, and, as always, my dear son John. Now I can add his wonderful wife Natasha. Their daughter Rosa is a bit too young to do more than crow with laughter, understandably, at the sight of me. Lastly I thank once again my kind neighbour Peter Stalker, without whom much of this book would have disappeared several times.

Liza Picard
Oxford
December 2002

Prologue

Everyone knows what Elizabeth herself looked like – or, at least, what her public image looked like – but how relevant was that, to the life of the average woman? Did the man in the street really wear those amazing upholstered knickers, or were they just a Court fashion? Who were these 'average' women and 'men in the street' anyway? How did they live, and love, and have children, and go about their businesses?

The recent history of England

Henry VIII had six wives. That is sometimes all that people know about him. He was Elizabeth's father. What about her grandfather, Henry VII? It seems reasonable to start with him. After all, most people can remember at least one grandparent.

The Wars of the Roses had been bloody and miserable, not deserving their fragrant name, which was thought up by Sir Walter Scott. Bickering between rival aspirants to power dragged on for 30 years, ending in 1485 with the Battle of Bosworth, when Richard III was killed by the army led by Henry Tudor, an obscure Welshman with a shaky claim to the legitimate succession. As Henry VII he managed to wean his subjects away from the habit of war, in favour of peace and prosperity. By 1501 he had made England sufficiently important on the European stage for the Spanish monarchs to send their daughter Katherine to marry his eldest son Arthur. Arthur died, however, a few months later. His brother Henry succeeded to the throne in 1509, aged eighteen. He was the ideal Renaissance man.

Henry's matrimonial ventures were sometimes dictated by his heart, when he fell in love – again – and sometimes by his head, as when he decided that it made good political sense for him to marry Katherine of Aragon, his brother's widow. This needed permission from the Pope. Marrying your deceased brother's wife did not become legal until the twentieth century. Katherine and Henry duly married, in 1509, but poor Katherine let him down by producing only a daughter, in 1516, after a series of miscarriages and stillbirths. The succession would be safer in the hands of a son, and anyway Henry was in love. He applied to the Pope again, to release him from the marriage that the Pope had sanctioned. He expected that his application would be granted without difficulty: after all, he had written a fulsome pamphlet in defence of the Papacy in 1521, for which the Pope had bestowed on him the title of Defender of the Faith. But he found that this time the current Pope, fortified by the power of Spain, was not so amenable. Henry's determination to get rid of Katherine resulted in a permanent rift with the Church of Rome and the genesis of the Church of England. In the end an English court gave Henry a controversial decree of annulment in 1533. Katherine stayed on in England until her death in 1536. Her daughter, Mary, was brought up as a devout Catholic.

The next queen, Anne Boleyn, had a daughter by Henry in 1533. This was a severe disappointment to Henry, who longed for a son, but at least he gave her his mother's name, Elizabeth. Whatever Anne's private morals – and Henry later said she was a whore so that he could have her executed in 1536 and move on to his next conquest – she was a well-educated Renaissance lady, and her daughter was brought up in the same climate. In 1537 Henry's third wife, Jane Seymour, produced the longed-for male heir, Edward. He was reared in the Protestant faith. Under the terms of Henry's will he took precedence over both his sisters, and succeeded to the throne on Henry's death in 1547. He died of tuberculosis six years later. Just before he died he and his advisers tried to prevent Mary from succeeding, by interposing the unfortunate Lady Jane Grey. She had some claim to the throne and, more importantly, she was a Protestant. England, especially the provinces, did not care for this manoeuvre. Mary was acclaimed as the rightful queen in 1553. Jane was executed a few months later.

Mary had led a secluded and devout life. It was clear to her that her religious duty obliged her to marry a Catholic and have his children, so securing the succession to her throne in a Catholic dynasty. The obvious choice was Philip, the son and heir of the Holy Roman Emperor. Philip arrived in England in 1554, and Mary pathetically fell deeply in love with him, a passion that was not reciprocated. She was convinced she could still have a child by him, despite her age, 38. The short time Philip could spare Mary from his other duties (he became King of Spain two years after becoming king consort of England) was not long enough for her to achieve pregnancy. She even announced the glad news that she was with child, but the swelling in her abdomen was a cancerous tumour from which she died, in 1558.

Mary's devotion to her mother's faith led her to extreme measures. Her father had banished the monastic orders. She invited some of them to return, and retrieved some of their property for them. To save the souls of the heretic English, and in their true interests, as she saw them, she burned about 300 of their bodies. Perhaps all that she achieved was to water the Church of England with the blood of martyrs.

Elizabeth's accession in 1558 was welcomed with rejoicing. Since her father's death she had lived quietly and circumspectly, careful to avoid any appearance of courting popular sympathy. People still remembered the civil war. In his old age John Stow told how he had talked with old men who remembered Richard III, who had died in 1485 in the last battle of the war. No one wanted war again, even though the new sovereign was, unfortunately, female.

Elizabeth was 25 when she came to the throne, and 70 when she died in 1603. She never married, and she died a virgin. She used her matrimonial possibilities as a counter in European diplomacy, and an inducement to her supporters at home to spend their lives and wealth in her service. She was beautiful, as a young woman, and could assume the appearance of beauty when she was old. She was learned and accomplished, speaking several languages fluently. She was superlatively eloquent in English. Above all, she was an unbeatable politician, seeming to bend to popular opinion where necessary but following her own line even when it seemed circuitous to the onlooker. She spent money when she had to, but much preferred other people to foot the bill. By the time she died, the southern part of this small offshore island had become a world power.

During her reign some things, naturally, changed. Elizabeth had played her cards so wisely during her sister's Spanish marriage that

Philip became the first of her suitors, and they might have lived happily ever after if Elizabeth had not put English religious and political freedom, and her own independence, above wedded bliss. In thirty years, Philip changed from affectionate brother-in-law to public enemy number one, who dispatched the Armada.

Elizabeth had to resile from the generous religious toleration that she had promised at the beginning of her reign, because of persistent disaffection fomented by foreign Catholic powers, coming to a head when Mary Queen of Scots was implicated in plots to displace Elizabeth and take the English throne herself. By 1587 Elizabeth had no choice but to order her execution. London rejoiced, but religious toleration suffered. Some regretted the passing of the old Catholic religion of her sister Mary, or the new Protestantism of her brother Edward. In general, most people seem to have acquiesced in Elizabeth's religious settlement with sighs of relief.

The history of London[1]

The site of the city of Londinium was inevitable once the Romans' invasion strategy had been decided, in AD 43. To reach the shires north of the river, they had to cross the Thames. The most efficient way was to bridge it, and the best place to do so was where there was a narrow spit of hard ground in the surrounding marshes, on the north bank of the river, and a smaller outcrop opposite it, which meant that a bridge could be built to carry the army over to the north bank. The Romans built their capital city there, and constructed a road network from Exeter to the Scottish border, centred on Londinium.

The site of the bridge had another advantage. The river was still tidal there. As long as a channel was kept clear by dredging, sea-going ships could unload trade goods and army *matériel* at the extensive wharves that the Romans built, and load the cargoes of slaves, tin and lead which Britain produced.

After the Romans left, in 410, their city mouldered, but successive waves of invaders never totally destroyed it. In 604 the Anglo-Saxons used the site of a Roman temple to Diana, within the walls, to build a cathedral dedicated to St Paul. West of London there was another outcrop of hard gravel at Thorney Island. Edward the

Confessor (who ruled 1042–66) decided to build himself a palace there, thus initiating the two-centre conurbation, London and Westminster, that has characterised the metropolitan area ever since. Edward also founded there a magnificent minster or cathedral, in the Norman style familiar to him from years of living in France. He died just before the Normans arrived, in 1066.

The Roman city was still worth salvaging. The Normans fortified the river crossing by a massive keep beside the north end of the bridge. In 1087 the Anglo-Saxon cathedral within the walls was destroyed by fire. The Normans rebuilt it using stone imported from France.

The effective administrative system of parishes and wards which was already in place was formalised. Many parish churches date from this time. Religious communities began to congregate in London, funnelling the wealth contributed by the faithful into abbeys and convents. They often chose sites at the edge of the built-up area, but still within the Roman walls. The increasing prosperity of London was, however, brutally halted in 1349 by the Black Death, a virulent epidemic of plague, which killed half the population of England and left many empty spaces in London.

Nobles began to find it convenient to have London bases near the royal Court in Westminster, as well as their territorial seats, since disputes could no longer be settled by war. As manufactures and import and export trading grew, merchants set up commodity exchanges, and built themselves comfortable houses in the City. There was a thriving market for construction skills, and for workers in luxury and service trades, all of whom had to find roofs over their heads, and markets supplying their everyday needs.

By the sixteenth century the monastic orders had acquired enormous wealth. Once Henry VIII broke with Rome he dissolved the orders, appropriated their possessions and sold off or gave away their lands. As he disposed of property after property, between 1536 and 1540, London became a vast building site. This turmoil of redevelopment was still going strong at the end of the century.

By the middle of the sixteenth century, the population of England was probably about 3 million, increasing to over 4 million by the end of the century. London had begun its inexorable growth, rising from about 120,000 in mid-century to 200,000 in 1600.[2] The authorities did not think this was a good thing, and periodically tried to persuade the nobles to go home to their country houses, and the merchants and others to stop building new houses in London. But as a policy, it did not work. Building went on.

... *as the Elizabethans saw it*

To be respectable, a city had to be old. John Stow, that devoted historian of London, began his *Survey of London* thus:

> As the Roman writers, to glorify the city of Rome, derive the original thereof from gods and demi-gods, by the Trojan progeny, so Geoffrey of Monmouth, the Welsh historian, deduceth the foundation of this famous city of London, for the greater glory thereof and emulation of Rome, from the very same original. For he reporteth that Brute, lineally descended from the demi-god Aeneas, the son of Venus, daughter of Jupiter, about the year of the world 2855, and 1108 before the nativity of Christ, built this city ...

Here Stow coughs slightly, and excuses his colleague: 'antiquity is pardonable, and hath a special privilege ... to make the first foundation of cities more honourable, more sacred, and, as it were, of greater majesty'. He himself prefers the surer ground of Julius Caesar. He takes his readers methodically through the Romans and the Saxons, and then breaks off to look at the 'Wall about the City of London'. But he does bring London history up to date – he was writing in 1598 – with reasonable accuracy, despite his regret, as an antiquarian, for so much that had gone.

Historians of the time had to tread fairly carefully when they got to recent events. By then England was safely out of the bosom of the evil Papacy, where it had rested comfortably for so many centuries, and the Tudor dynasty was firmly settled on the throne. But one never knew whether a careless word might be misinterpreted and have to be explained away. So perhaps it was wise to focus on the Trojans, whose wars and heroes could not upset the most tender conscience.

Definitions

We think of London as the metropolis that has recently acquired a mayor of its own: the vast sea of bricks and mortar, with occasional green patches, that stretches out of sight from the top of the London Eye, with a population of seven million people, not counting commuters. In this book, I use 'London' to mean the two cities of London and Westminster, with adjacent built-up areas along the banks of the river. By 'the City' I mean the area of one square mile within the Roman walls, with the outlying developments round the walls, and the parish of Southwark across the Bridge: the territory within the jurisdiction of the Lord Mayor of the City of London.

Part One

THE PLACE

It is high tide. The river laps at its shores, rocking the swans, and the ships waiting for daylight. Ropes tap, timbers creak, a bird calls. Moonlight silvers the Tower of London and gleams on the water, save for the shadow cast by the Bridge. Sleepy sounds come from sheep waiting in Southwark for the Bridge gate to open. Someone is playing a lute by an open window in one of the houses on the Bridge, and singing a love song. The City crouches close to the water. A bull roars and stamps its feet, in its stall on the south bank. On the north bank, the great mansions show a few lights in their windows, and there are flickering torches at one jetty, waiting for the master of the house to come home from a night's revels. The sky begins to colour and the stars are less bright. Smoke rises from the chimneys. London is awake.

CHAPTER I

The River

T hames, the most famous river of this island, beginneth a little above a village called Winchcombe, in Oxfordshire, and still increasing, passeth first by the University of Oxford, and so with a marvellous quiet course to London, and thence breaketh into the French ocean by main tides, which twice in twenty four hours' space doth ebb and flow more than sixty miles in length, to the great commodity of travellers …

So said that devoted London supporter John Stow.[1] The Thames drove some poets to verse:

> Thou stately stream that with the swelling tide
> 'Gainst London walls incessantly dost beat
> Thou Thames, I say, where barge and boat do ride,
> And snow-white swans do fish for needful meat …

And so on. The poet, George Turberville, is asking the river not to be beastly to his loved one when she embarks on it, by weltering up and surging in wrathful wise as rivers sometimes do, but just to stay in its normal channel and 'in wonted gulf to glide'; a very practical suggestion.[2] Edmund Spenser went in for a more rhapsodic approach. To cure his irritation at having got nowhere at Court, he

> Walked forth to ease my pain
> Along the shore of silver streaming Thames
> Whose rutty bank, the which his river hems
> Was painted all with variable flowers,
> And all the meads adorned with dainty gems …
>   Sweet Thames run softly till I end my song …[3]

Michael Drayton wrote a song to Beta – can this possibly be his dread sovereign lady Queen Elizabeth? – which begins:

> O Thou fair silver Thames, O clearest crystal flood! …[4]

All very lovely, if that's your taste; but was the river really like that?

The Thames rises near Kemble in Gloucestershire, and flows for 215 miles through the English countryside until it spreads into a wide estuary and reaches the sea at Gravesend. The distance from Chelsea to Greenwich is 16 miles, and from Greenwich to Gravesend 20 miles. The river flows at 3½ knots an hour. On its way it gathers silt, which makes its water an opaque grey, very far from a 'clearest crystal flood'. It is tidal as far as Teddington, with high tides twice every 24 hours. The difference in water level between low and high tide can be as much as 25 feet.[5]

The Lord Mayor had jurisdiction over the whole stretch from Staines to the Medway, dating back to a deal with Richard I, in 1197. The King transferred to the City his authority over this part of the Thames, in return for cash, which he badly needed, having overspent on the Crusades.[6] This enabled the City to impose a unified traffic policy on the main approach to the capital. The river was the most convenient route to the markets and bright lights of London, for traders, farmers from Kent and the home counties, and foreign visitors from the continent. As John Stow put it, 'this river opens indifferently [impartially] upon France and Flanders, our mightiest neighbours, to whose doings we ought to have a bent eye and special regard'.[7]

The long ferry from Gravesend

A visitor from the continent had first to survive the Channel crossing. The plight of Frederick Duke of Würtemburg, in 1592, will be all too familiar to passengers on a Channel ferry on a bad day. 'Not being used to the sea we were seized with horrible vomitings and most of our party … thought they were dying.'[8] He completed his journey, wan and shaken, by land. He could have landed at Gravesend and gone up to London by the 'long ferry'.[9] This regular public service had the possible disadvantage of carrying livestock as well as passengers, such as lambs (20 for 8d), calves (2d each) and boars (alive 8d, dead 4d). In view of the boars, it might be pleasanter, if you could afford it, to hire a barge for 4s, including four rowers and a steersman.

River traffic was – in theory at least – tightly controlled. Yet in 1598 a tilt-boat (a large rowing-boat with an awning or canopy over it) carrying ten passengers over the legal limit was run down by a hoy at Greenwich, with the loss of nearly everyone on board, and wherries were still plying which were so 'shallow and tickle [*sic*]' that they were under the legal requirements of at least 22½ ft long and 4½ ft wide, 'thereby great peril and danger of drowning hath ensued'.[10]

Apart from the other river traffic there was not much to look at between Gravesend and London, unless you were as lucky as the Duke of Würtemburg. Despite his rough Channel crossing, on his way home he must have felt stronger, or had a short memory, so he decided to take the long ferry down to Gravesend. 'The waves were very high and boisterous, and we saw a great many large black fishes called sea-hogs which are from 8 to 10 feet long.'[11] Another German visitor, Thomas Platter, who took the long ferry up to London in 1592, merely noted that 'the banks of this river ... are wooded and gay with pleasant hamlets and homesteads'.[12] He did not notice the shipbuilding yards at Blackwall and Woolwich, but he could not miss the tall lead-roofed turrets of the Tudor palace of Placentia at Greenwich, twenty miles from Gravesend on the south bank, with its stairway down to the river, and a massive water gate to admit the royal barge.[13]

Henry VIII had been born at Greenwich, his brother Arthur had married Katherine of Aragon there, and Henry's son Edward VI was sent there to profit from the fresh country air, but he died of tuberculosis three months later. Elizabeth had been born there, and loved the place. Apart from going on progresses to stay with lucky nobles – whether or not they could afford it – she mostly lived in Greenwich in the summer. When Martin Frobisher arrived at Greenwich with his fleet in 1576 on his way down the river to Canada and, he hoped, China, 'her Majesty, beholding the same, commended it, and bade them farewell with shaking her hand out of the window'.[14]

After Greenwich the tiny hamlet of Rotherhithe on the south bank had only a church and a few houses to attract the tourist's attention.[15] From time to time an alehouse could be seen, near enough to the bank to be used by ships waiting for a berth upriver.[16]

On the north bank, the gallows at Wapping in the Woze was usually occupied. For pirates a special death was waiting for them there: they were hanged down at the low water-mark, 'there to remain till three tides had overflowed them'.[17] A few more bends in the river, and the ancient stone walls of the Tower of London rose on the right (north) bank.

Opposite the Tower the visitor could probably see among the trees Bermondsey House, built after the dissolution of the ancient Benedictine abbey of Bermondsey, recycling the stones from its demolition. The abbey orchards and gardens, pastures and pools still survived on the twenty-acre site. From 1567 the Earl of Sussex lived here, and Queen Elizabeth visited him, even coming to his death-bed in 1583. (In Hofnagel's painting of a wedding at Bermondsey, there is what looks like a church tower on the right, through the trees; this must have been the new house, as the abbey had been demolished in 1541.) After Bermondsey House there were three corn-grinding windmills on the south bank of the river. The City had spent £2,600 on those mills, but it ran into trouble with the Privy Council and building was held up until the dispute – whatever it was – had been resolved.[18]

The legal quays, and up-river

The long ferry ended at the legal quays, just before London Bridge, where cargo had to be loaded and landed and assessed for customs and other duties.[19] Another German visitor was impressed:

> Ocean-craft are accustomed to run in here in great numbers as into a safe harbour, and I myself beheld one large galley next the other the whole city's length from St Catherine's suburb [just east of the Tower] to the bridge, some hundred vessels in all, nor did I ever behold so many large ships in one port in my life.[20]

There were ingenious cranes, which caught the eye of Alessandro Magno from Venice.[21] The sketch in his notebook shows a boat discharging its cargo of barrels at a wharf. Alongside the boat is a small cabin raised on poles, containing a large skeleton wheel, big enough for a man to sit *inside* it. From the wheel a rope goes up, out of the cabin, over a pulley, along a jib, over another pulley and down to the boat, where a barrel is attached to it with hooks. By pedalling in his wheel, the man can raise the barrel without undue strain. Someone at ground level then turns the cabin round, and the man takes up position on the other side of the wheel – still inside it – and gently lowers the barrel down to the waiting cart.[22]

To go on, up-river, from the legal quays you would take another boat. Most people who wanted to continue their journey past the Bridge landed on one side of it and walked round to the other side of it to take another boat. It was possible to 'shoot the Bridge', but only if the tide was exactly right. When Queen Mary sent her sister Elizabeth to the Tower under suspicion of plotting against her, in 1554, the barge she was in

> could not shoot the arch, and lay hovering upon the water for a time, the danger was too great for the bargemen to plunge into it as they were ordered. Their unwillingness gave way to peremptory command, but in trying it again the stern of the boat struck the ground, the fall was so big and the water was so shallow; the boat paused a while under the bridge and at last cleared it, and she was landed at Traitor's Gate.

Where, according to tradition, Elizabeth sat down on a stone – she must have needed to after that ordeal – and said, 'Here landeth as true a subject as ever landed at these stairs.'

After the Tower, the narrow streets of the City crowded down to the river's edge, until they gave way to the beautiful mansions along the Strand, and finally the royal palaces of Whitehall and Westminster. On the south side[23] the land was marshy, and had not been built over except for Southwark, but it provided ideal sites for the animal-baiting rings and the playhouses, easily reached by water, but away from interference by the City.[24] After them there were only rather soggy fields, until the village of Lambeth and the Archbishop of Canterbury's London palace there, conveniently opposite the seat of secular government at Westminster.

The river's moods

The river could be temperamental, from glassy to choppy, 'weltering up and surging' to almost dry. Without Bazalgette's Victorian embankments it was shallower than now, and much wider, though a contemporary statement that it was 1,000 feet wide at Westminster is surprising.[25] The winter high tides often brought floods, which made the water so muddy that 'you shall take haddock with your hand beneath the bridge as they float aloft upon the water, whose eyes are so blinded with the thickness of that element that they cannot see where to become'.[26] (More modern thought suggests that the lack of oxygen in the mud had driven the poor fishes up to the surface, to breathe.) In January 1564 'the river Thames was so agitated that the tide recoiled twice, five hours before its time'. In 1579 there was a heavy snowfall; when the thaw came 'the water rose so high in Westminster Hall that fishes were found there after the waters had subsided',[27] which must have smelt appalling, although someone had the sense to sweep them up and leave them in the palace yard outside 'for who so list, to gather up'.[28] Yet just the year before a freak low tide had meant that 'men might stand in the middle of the Thames'.[29]

The river sometimes froze solid. In 1537 Henry VIII and his then queen, Jane Seymour, and the whole cavalcade of courtiers had crossed the river on horseback, to Greenwich Palace. There was a famous Frost Fair on the river in the winter of 1564, with archery contests and dancing, and football played 'as boldly as if it had been dry land', and 'all sorts of carriages and diversions', and 'the people went on the Thames in greater numbers than in any street in the City of London'.[30] But it took less than a complete freeze to put the watermen out of business, and force them to beg until the river was clear again.

Fog must have been a constant river hazard. One evening in 1575, Elizabeth took her barge down-river to see her friend the Countess of Pembroke at Baynards Castle, and stayed later than she meant. By ten o'clock 'being so great a mist as there were divers of the barges and boats that waited of [for] her lost their ways and landed in wrong places but thanks be to God Her Majesty came well home without cold or fear'.[31]

The poets liked to dwell on the 'crystal stream' of the Thames. Far from being translucent, it was, and is, a uniform opaque grey because of the silt it carries, but it must have been fairly unpolluted, judging from all the fish in it. Down in the narrow streets by the Bridge, in Pudding Lane, 'the butchers of Eastcheap have their scalding house for hogs there, and their puddings [intestines] with other filth of beasts are voided down that way to their dung boats in the Thames';[32] and at the other end of London, the Queen's slaughter-house at her palace of Westminster gave directly on to the river. Although industrial waste and effluent was not supposed to be dumped in the river, it was difficult to stop it, espcially on a dark night with no watchmen about.

Great occasions

The river provided a superb processional route between the royal palaces of Westminster, Whitehall and the Tower. After Mary's death Elizabeth came to London and stayed for a week in the Tower before she 'went in procession by water, to Somerset place [*sic*], trumpets sounding much melody accompanying'.[33] In 1559 she went from Westminster to the Tower 'attended by the Lord Mayor and aldermen in their barges, and all the citizens in their barges, decked and trimmed with targets [shields] and banners of their mysteries [livery companies] … shooting off lustily as they went, with great and pleasant melody of instruments which played in most sweet and heavenly manner'.[34] All this shooting off lustily could be risky. In 1568, 'on the occasion of Her Majesty proceeding in her barge on the river, one Thomas Appletree discharging his piece [gun] the bullet ran through both the arms of one of her watermen, but the Queen understanding that the shot was by casualty [accident] pardoned the offender', not before he had had some very nasty moments.[35]

The Queen seems to have enjoyed river trips, quite apart from state occasions. On another visit to the Pembrokes, but in better weather, 'after supper the Queen's Grace rowed up and down the Thames, and a hundred boats about her Grace, with trumpets and drums and flutes and guns and squibs, hurling on high to and fro till ten at night … all the waterside with a million people looking on'.[36] One hot June night in 1559, 'about eight of the clock at night the Queen's Grace took her barge at Whitehall, and many more barges, and rowed along by the bankside by my Lord of Winchester's palace [on the south bank, just west of the Bridge] … and so crossed over to London side with drums and trumpets playing … and so to Whitehall again to her palace'.[37]

Queen Elizabeth's personal barge had glass windows and two splendid cabins, beautifully ornamented with painting and gilding.[38] For a royal trip one summer's day it was made even more beautiful 'with garlands of artificial flowers and covered with a canopy of

green sarcenet [thin silk], wrought [embroidered] with branches of
eglantine, on embroidery, powdered [scattered] with blossoms of
gold'.[39] Can William Shakespeare have had this lovely sight in his
mind when he described Cleopatra's barge on the Nile?

> The barge she sat in, like a burnished throne,
> Burned on the water. The poop was beaten gold,
> Purple the sails ... the oars were silver ... [40]

Elizabeth's barge fell a little short of that, and the hard sweaty work
of rowing was done with strong wooden oars from another boat in
front 'so that it might glide more smoothly', which intrigued a visitor
from Basle who may not have seen this arrangement before.[41]

Did Elizabeth ever wish she could just go for a quiet boat trip
without all that noise? The parish church at Lambeth, across the
river from the Queen's palace of Westminster, must have wished she
could: but every time she was spotted coming down her private stairs
or jetty to go down to Greenwich or up-river to Richmond, the
church bellringers had to turn out to salute her with a peal. Their
usual charge, carefully noted in the churchwardens' accounts, was 3s
4d – not so much, only 2s 6d, when they were merely celebrating her
birthday or the anniversary of her accession, presumably because
these calls could be predicted and arrangements made, without
calling the bellringers away from their work at a moment's notice.
The ringers would need sustenance – 'to the ringers to drink 3d'.
They had a strong bargaining position, in negotiating with the
churchwardens. By 1596 a new rate had been agreed: 'The ringers
for Her Majesty's remove shall have every time of her passage
[passing] here 3s, and for Her Majesty's birthday 3s 6d, and for the
coronation [anniversary] day 6s 8d.' No wonder, with all this wear
and tear, that the bells needed constant repairs and even renewal:
'paid to Mr Mote for the new bell £14 11s 8d' in 1599, a considerable
inroad into the church's finances.[42]

Every year since 1422 the Lord Mayor had gone by water to
Westminster on his election, to swear fealty to the monarch. By the
sixteenth century this was a magnificent regatta. 'On the 29th day
of October [the Lord Mayor's Show used to be on 29 October,
before the eighteenth-century rectification of the calendar, which is
why it is now in November] the new Mayor took his barge towards
Westminster ... with the aldermen in their scarlet robes and all the
crafts of London in their livery and their barges with their banners

and streamers, of every occupations' [coats of] arms: and there was
... great shooting of guns, and trumpets.'[43] In fact not all the livery
companies could, or would, afford this lavish expenditure, and not
all of them had their own barges. The Carpenters' Company hired
their barge out, for 10s 4d, 'when the Mayor goeth to Westminster'.[44]
The Butchers' Company had to hire a barge, for 20s, to attend the
Queen's coronation parade.[45]

As well as the livery companies, private citizens who enjoyed conspicuous consumption kept their own barges. Sir Francis Drake was
able to live in style, in 1574, in a mansion called The Herber, 'where
he kept his barge in which he was frequently rowed on the river',[46]
a pleasant memory while he was circumnavigating the world three
years later.

Tilt-boats, wherries and watermen

Alessandro Magno found that a tilt-boat with a canopy could be
hired

> at various points that are used by groups of people to travel to various
> towns [up-river] or to cross the river, or to enjoy themselves in the
> evenings. It is just as pleasant as it is to go in summertime along the
> grand canal in Venice ... [giving] a very fine view of beautiful palaces
> and gardens, and many boats go there for pleasure

– like hiring a minibus for an office outing.[47] And although I have
found no reference to this, surely these happy trippers sang and
played music as they went? Music, as Samuel Pepys and George II
both found, sounds so much better on a river. Elizabeth's river trips
were accompanied by trumpets and flutes; surely the citizen out for
an evening took his lute with him, or a trumpet or two?

> While a very fine long bridge is built across this strait [narrow water],
> it is more customary to cross the water or travel up and down the
> town, as at Lyons and elsewhere, by attractive pleasure craft, for a
> number of tiny streets lead to the Thames from both ends of the
> town; the boatmen wait there in great crowds, each one eager to
> catch one, for all are free to choose the ship [sic] they find most
> attractive and pleasing, while every boatman has the privilege on
> arrival of placing his ship to best advantage for people to step into.[48]

In other words, it was like trying to catch an Italian bus, there being no queuing system.

At least once you were safely aboard you knew how much to pay. An Act of Philip and Mary,[49] which applied to the river between Windsor and Gravesend, had recognised the need for some sort of control:

> Heretofore for lack of good government and due order amongst wherrymen and watermen ... many mischances [have] happened ... to a great number of the King and Queen's subjects, as well to the nobility as to the common people ... by reason of the rude, ignorant and unskilful number of watermen, which for the most part been masterless men, and single men of all kinds of occupations ... which do work at their own hands [self-employed], and many boys, being of small age and of little skill [who] do for the most part of their time use dicing and carding and other unlawful games ...

Now the watermen were to be controlled by eight rulers or overseers, 'the most wise, discreet and best sort of watermen', appointed by the Lord Mayor. Watermen were to serve an apprenticeship of two years, and then be certified as competent by the rulers. On two-men wherries at least one of them had to have such a certificate *and* one of them must have been rowing on the Thames for at least two years. Single oarsmen on the river had to show they were in employment or apprenticed. The Lord Mayor and aldermen were to set controlled fares, to be 'written and set up in the Guildhall in the city of London, Westminster Hall and elsewhere', and the dimensions of river boats were to be controlled. It took the Lord Mayor some years to get round to this, but by 1559 the new rates were published.[50] A two-oared wherry between London and Greenwich would cost you '8d with the tide, and against the tide 12d'. You could cross the river in a wherry for 1d, or a smaller 'sculler' for a halfpenny. You could go all the way up to Windsor in a tilt-boat, with four oarsmen and a steersman, for 10s, or just as far as Barne Elms in a wherry for 10d. Business trips between Blackfriars and Westminster cost 3d, and between the Temple and Westminster only 2d.

> The watermen of London and Westminster found considerable employment in ferrying persons to and fro the playhouses etc. at Bankside: several attempts were made to introduce similar places of amusement into the city of London, but they were strenuously opposed, not only by the Lord Mayor, who disapproved of them, but also by the watermen and their friends, as being against their interests.[51]

(Why is it surprising to find lobbying so flourishing, so long ago?) The Lambeth churchwardens were always having to go down to the city on legal business, or to see about their bells. The item was neatly entered as 'botehier' (try saying it aloud: boat hire). They paid 2d for 'botehier over the water and back again' on one trip in 1588.

The German tourist who described the waiting ships was also impressed by the rowing boats, called wherries. He found 'charmingly upholstered and embroidered cushions laid across the seats, very comfortable to sit on or lean against, and generally speaking the benches only seat two people next to one another. Many of them are covered in, particularly in rainy weather or fierce sunshine. They are extremely pleasant to travel in and carry one or a couple of boatmen.'[52] It says something for the Elizabethan wherries, that a Venetian tourist, too, found them very comfortable.[53]

The 2,000 wherries and small boats on the river provided employment for 3,000 watermen, not counting the oarsmen and steersmen in grandees' barges, who did well at 6d a day 'without meat or drink'.[54] The watermen relied on the fares paid by their passengers, their only expenses being repairs and replacements, and their quarterly dues to their company. But it was a chancy, sometimes dangerous trade, dependent on the weather and popular demand, and their skills made them subject to 'pressing' or impressment – compulsory service with the Navy in times of national emergency. This had been going on since 1355, and stopped only in 1814. If a waterman tried to evade the press-gang, he risked two weeks' imprisonment and 'banishment' from the Thames for a year and a day.[55] At the time of the Armada, in 1588, most watermen joined up voluntarily, which must have made it difficult to travel about London.[56] A more peaceful and potentially rewarding occasion came in 1601, when five ships sailed for the East Indies. 'Many of the watermen entered the service ... it being a favourite service for apprentices to make one or two voyages during their apprenticeship.'[57]

Although it is a little after our period, I cannot resist the picture of a waterman in Sir Thomas Overbury's *Characters* published in 1614–16:

A waterman is one that hath learned to speak well of himself ... He is evermore telling strange news, most commonly lies ... His daily labour teaches him the art of dissembling, for like a fellow that rides to the pillory he goes not that way he looks. He keeps such a bawling at Westminster that if the lawyers [who practised in the courts there] were not acquainted with it an order [to keep the peace] would be taken with him. When he is upon the water he is fare-company [*sic*]: when he comes ashore he mutinies and contrary to all other trades is most surly to gentlemen when they tender payment. The playhouses only [i.e. alone] keep him sober, and as it doth many other gallants, make him an afternoon's man [when the playhouses were open]. London Bridge is the most terrible eye-sore to him that can be. And to conclude, nothing but a great press makes him fly from the river; nor anything but a great frost can teach him any good manners.

Flood control

The Statute of Sewers had been passed in 1531. 'Sewers' meant primarily storm and surface-water drains. The preamble to the Act refers to 'the outrageous Flowings, Surges and Course of the Sea ... as also ... land-waters and other outrageous springs'. Commissioners of Sewers were to be appointed for all the districts within the Lord Mayor's Thames jurisdiction. They could make and enforce orders on the owners of riparian land, raise money by precepts, and impose fines.

The Court Minutes of the Surrey and Kent Sewer Commissioners show how they stood no nonsense.[58] The Archbishop of Canterbury was ordered to '[re]new the sluice at the wall against his Grace's ground leading towards Lambeth'. The Masters of St Thomas's Hospital were told to unblock their part of the comon sewer, and the Bishop of Winchester was ordered to 'cleanse a rod [5½ yards] of length going into the park in the parish of St Saviour'. At a lower social level William Bestern, brewer, was told to 'turn his water-course of the filth of his yard and house from the street into the ditch of his backside as it hath been for it is noisome to the Queen's people and infective ... and doth fill up with the said filth one ditch or pisser to the common sewer', which throws a murky if obscure light on general environmental habits. The usual order was on the lines of – 'to cope and make higher the said banks and walls, substantial and strong and four feet broad in the top at least' or to 'cut up the bank and scour and grave the river', or to 'scour his sewer'. Even overhanging branches were noted and the owner told to cut them back.

The precept was set at a fairly high level. The Bishop of Winchester was assessed at £5 in 1571, for his 60 acres on the south bank. If the assessment, or any subsequent fine for default, was not paid, the Commissioners' officers could forcibly enter the offender's premises and take and sell his property. It looks as if the Commissioners deliberately set the rates high, allowing for mitigation in deserving cases. The widow Manning was due to pay 33s 4d, but she was allowed to settle for only 2s 6d.

Fishing

Magna Carta had ordered that 'all weirs ... out of the Thames' were to be removed. Weirs were a profitable method of fishing, by setting stakes across a river to make a trap. Somehow, despite Magna Carta, they survived. In 1580 the Lord High Admiral got the Privy Council to complain to the Lord Mayor that weirs choked the river from London Bridge to Windsor, making it almost unnavigable: 'please deal', as a modern civil servant would say. The Lord Mayor replied tartly that it was the Lord High Admiral's own fault, for interfering with the Lord Mayor s jurisdiction, and anyway

> the river, eastwards from London Bridge, had become so decayed that ships or vessels which, within twenty or forty years past might have come up to the pool against St Katherine [just east of the Tower of London] could not pass at low water without danger between London and Greenwich. The channel being choked, the lands adjoining were overflowed to the danger and destruction of the fry [young fish] and brood of fish, whereby the City lacked the good store of fish which used to be taken from the river ...

– and the Privy Council and the Lord High Admiral should take appropriate action.

Whoever won that round, in 1598 a foreign visitor noticed how 'everywhere [was still] spread with nets, for the taking of salmon and shad'.[59] There was another rousing correspondence about these nets, between the fishermen, called trinkermen, and the Lord Mayor. The trinkermen said that their nets, which had a 1½-inch mesh, had been allowed since 1423 or earlier. The Lord Mayor said the trinkermen had not only destroyed the fry but fed it to pigs. Because of their offences, 'the passage of the river [was] made very dangerous, so much that ships which formerly came to St Katherine's could not now come to Blackwall [much further downstream]. Tiltboats and wherries were scarcely able to pass from London to Greenwich at low water', so please confirm the Lord Mayor's right to sort this out.[60] (I do not know the end of this story. It was still going strong as late as 1611. Interesting, though, to see the mesh size of fishing nets being a source of grievance, so long ago.)

As the Lord Mayor said, London depended on fish. A sturgeon was caught in the Thames in 1583, 'which, according to usage, had been sent by the hands of the Waterbailiff to be presented to Her Majesty'.[61] 'Fat and sweet salmon' and all kinds of other fish abounded: trout, perch, bream, dace, flounders, shrimps and eels, according to Harrison. 'Only in carps it seems to be scant', but they were gradually appearing 'from the floods breaking gentlemen's fishponds', so that the carp in private ownership found their way to the river.[62] A pod of eleven whales had been beached, in 1240. One of them 'was pursued by the fishers and could scarcely pass through the arches of London Bridge'. It was finally killed at Mortlake.[63] There were 'several whales in the river, and a sword fish, and a fish called Mors Marina' (Marine Death) in 1457, but I have found no record of whales in Elizabeth's time.

The swans

Going back to the poem by Turberville with which I began, what is the 'needful meat' of swans? If the poet meant fish, the swans were well catered for; but I think they prefer vegetation. They were said to be so tame that 'they take food from men's hands'.[64] A foreign visitor who arrived in 1584 took a boat thirty miles up-river to Oatlands (near Walton on Thames), where the Court was, and back to the City, and 'all the time the river was full of tame swans, who have nests and breed on small islands formed by the river'.[65] Another visitor commented on them in 1598: 'The sight of them swimming in flocks ... is vastly agreeable.'[66] (The reader puzzled by this eighteenth-century phrase is right – it occurs in Horace Walpole's 1757 translation.) Harrison also referred to their 'infinite number'.[67]

The correct collective noun for swans is a 'game'. The Dyers and the Vintners had licensed games of swans. The owner of each bird could be identified by the nicks on its beak, one nick for the Dyers, two for the Vintners, at an annual ceremony called swan-upping (which is still done, but now the birds are ringed, not nicked). All unmarked swans, or swans with five nicks, belonged to the Queen 'when at large in a public river'.[68] Hence the number of taverns at the 'sign of the Swan with Two Necks', their necks having been transmogrified from nicks.[69] Anyone who altered these marks risked a year's imprisonment, under the Order of Swans of 1570.

Thomas Platter 'encountered many tame swans on the water, which the Queen has plucked annually for repairing the down in the royal household, and no harm may be done to them on pain of punishment'.[70] Plucking a large protesting bird reputed to be able to break a man's arm with one blow of its wing when angry, must have been a hazardous operation. I have found no confirmation of Platter's statement, but while it may have been just one more piece of tourist misinformation it does make some sense, and provides another reason for keeping these beautiful birds other than to eat them at feasts, which they often were.

CHAPTER 2

The Main Streets,
Water Supply and Sewerage

This chapter does not fill in the details, such as the side streets and alleys, houses, markets, theatres and gardens. It points out the more obvious routes, so that you can follow them in your mind's eye. Some surviving buildings can serve as landmarks, and many street names can still be found on a modern map. In the City, the Guildhall and the Tower of London, and St Paul's Cathedral (rebuilt after the Great Fire of 1666, but on the same site) have not moved. The present London Bridge was built in 1967, on much the same site as its predecessors. In Westminster, the medieval Great Hall is still there, beside the grandiloquent nineteenth-century Palace of Westminster. The Abbey and St James's Palace (much restored) still remain. Lawyers still work in the Temple, although nowadays they have only to cross the road to get to court, instead of taking a boat up to Westminster Hall. The red brick and grey stone of Lambeth Palace are still there, across the river. (See the map, plate 7.)

For this quick survey I shall suppose us to be walking about London on a summer's day in 1598, when John Stow's *Survey of London* was published.[1]

Southwark

The City bought the 'liberties of Southwark' from the crown in 1550 after many years of bickering. Sixteenth-century maps of London tend to show only the City, the Bridge and a fringe of buildings on

Bankside, but Southwark stretched south for a mile from the river, including the former abbey at Bermondsey, and the built-up area along the river was a mile long, east and west of London Bridge. It had long been a favourite place for foreigners – 'strangers' – to settle. By 1510, for example, there were 400 continental craftsmen in the furniture trades in London, such as carvers, stool-makers, joiners and upholsterers, and most of them had settled in Southwark.[2]

Unless they decided to take the long ferry, all travellers from Kent and the continent reached the City via Southwark – farmers with their flocks of sheep and loads of cherries, statesmen with their entourages, grandees returning from a foreign tour and foreigners 'doing' England, visitors up from the country, and spies and Catholic priests hoping their disguises were impenetrable. Traffic came to a standstill during the great Southwark Fair every September, but even at ordinary times the road was clogged with traffic. All this made a pause for refreshment along the way irresistible. The street was lined by pleasant houses and tree-shaded inns.[3] On the left there used to be an ornate mansion belonging to the Duke of Suffolk, but it had been redeveloped into 'many small cottages of great rents' by the 1590s.[4] By now, over all the other usual smells, the traveller could smell the unmistakable reek of the river at low tide. The bridge was near.

London Bridge

London Bridge was the only way to cross the river with carts or flocks. The wooden bridge that the Romans had built was prone to destruction by fire or enemy action. Its future improved in 1176 when it was rebuilt in stone. It was a marvel of medieval construction. No wonder Londoners were proud of it. It had twenty arches of squared stone, thirty feet wide and twenty feet apart.[5] The piers were protected by small islands of stone and brushwood called starlings. They certainly fulfilled their designed function of protecting the piers from impact and tidal erosion – the Bridge lasted until 1830 – but they gradually accumulated debris and silt, narrowing the channel between them until every tide produced a dangerous mill-race. In the 1580s this hydraulic power was tapped, at both ends of the Bridge. In 1581 Peter Moritz was allowed to put a massive waterwheel into the northernmost arch, with another in the next one a year later, and in 1588 the two most southerly arches were occupied by corn-grinding mills. All this only increased the turbulence through the remaining arches.

Peter, chaplain of St Mary Colechurch, who designed the bridge, put a substantial chapel in the middle of it, dedicated to Thomas à Becket, the Archbishop of Canterbury who had opposed the royal power and died for it six years earlier. Thomas was later sanctified, and a popular cult grew up round his memory, which Henry VIII was determined to eradicate, not viewing Thomas's politics with favour. The chapel was hastily re-dedicated to another St Thomas, the Apostle, but by 1553 it had been largely destroyed.[6] Peter's bones were discovered in its foundations, years later.

There was a drawbridge about a third of the way across, which could be raised to let shipping through to the markets beyond the Bridge, but it had not functioned since 1500 when Henry VII decided, to the consternation of the Bridge overseers, to sail his royal barques under the Bridge. By 1576 its tower had been 'taken down ... being in great decay, and soon after made a pleasant and beautiful dwelling house'.[7] The drawbridge tower had been useful for displaying the heads of traitors – a nasty habit that had begun in 1305 with the head of the Scottish rebel William Wallace and continued until 1746. When the drawbridge tower was demolished, the heads were moved to the Great Stone Gateway, the first gateway to the Bridge on the Southwark side, to give approaching visitors a welcoming grin. In 1599 a visitor from Basle, Thomas Platter, saw

> stuck on tall stakes more than thirty skulls of noble men who had been executed and beheaded for treason and for other reasons. And their descendants are accustomed to boast of this, themselves even pointing out one of their ancestors' heads on this same bridge, believing that they will be esteemed the more because their antecedents were of such high descent that they could even covet the crown ... thus they make an honour for themselves of what was set up to be a disgrace and an example. Just as only recently here in Basel the young earl of Suffolk, grandson to the duke of Norfolk, in order to raise the honour of his family, showed that he was so well connected that his forefathers' heads too were on the tower of London Bridge for having coveted the English crown.[8]

This demonstration of English snobbery must have seemed strange to the good citizens of Basle.

The most eye-catching building on the Bridge was without doubt Nonsuch House, perhaps inspired by Henry VIII's palace of Nonsuch down at Merton. It was a Renaissance extravaganza made entirely of wood, even down to wooden pegs instead of nails, with turrets and gilded columns and carved galleries, projecting over the river on both sides. It was prefabricated in Holland, and put together on site, which must have held up the traffic over the Bridge for quite a long time.

The Bridge was treated as a prime building site for more than five hundred years, 1200–1758. By Stow's time it was 'replenished on both the sides with large, fair and beautiful buildings, inhabitants for the most part rich merchants and other wealthy citizens, mercers and haberdashers', who kept their shops on the ground floors. Long after, when the old houses were being cleared from the Bridge in 1746, the workmen found 'three pots of money, silver and gold, of the coin of Queen Elizabeth', presumably the cash hoard of an Elizabethan merchant.[9] Some of the houses were four storeys high. At least they had a unique advantage. Their privies, not relying on cess-pools, drained straight down to the river. Or one could always empty pots out of the windows, having first checked the wind direction.

Stow recounts a charming story of a little girl, dating from 1536:

> Sir William Hewet was a merchant, possessed of a great estate of six thousand pounds per annum, having three sons and one daughter, Anne. The maid, playing with her out of a window over the river Thames, by chance dropped her in, almost beyond expectation of her being saved. A young gentleman named Osborne, then apprentice to Sir William Hewet, at this calamitous accident, leaped in and saved the child. In memory of which deliverance, and in gratitude, her father afterward bestowed her on the said Mr Osborne, with a very grand dowry.

And it is pleasant to relate that both Sir William and Edward Osborne became Lord Mayors, in 1559 and 1583 respectively.[10] But no doubt other casualties were not so lucky.

The traffic problems were intractable, as the prosperous merchants struggled to get to their own front doors through herds and flocks and itinerant street sellers and sightseers, and their customers despaired of reaching the shops. There was even a 'man child Christopher, ¾ [nine months old]' who was abandoned there and had to be taken to Christ's Hospital.[11]

There were three gaps between the houses, where you could enjoy the view of the Tower of London and the majestic Gothic pile of St Paul's, or count the merchant ships waiting to unload at the Custom House or the hundreds of wherries darting about on the other side, or watch young men playing water sports in holiday time.

The City gates

Although the gates are long gone – they were all demolished in the eighteenth century – they were such a fact of Elizabethan life that we need to look at them in detail. Forget any idea you may have of a gate in a farmyard wall. Imagine substantial buildings with spacious rooms that could be used for all kinds of purposes, straddling the roadway. Three of them, Aldgate, Aldersgate and Ludgate, had been part of the Roman plan a thousand years earlier, according to Stow. Beginning, as he did, at the Tower of London, there was a narrow gate, or postern, just past the moat. Then came Aldgate, which still had a working portcullis. Through it lay the main road to the east. So far the wall ran nearly due north. After Aldgate it turned north-west to Bishops Gate, guarding the route to Norfolk, Suffolk and Cambridgeshire. The identity of the eponymous bishop was unknown to Stow, who knew most things about the London of his day. By 1479 the duty to repair it had fallen on the Hanseatic merchants, who wielded a strong commercial power at the time, and they rebuilt the gate 'beautifully', according to Stow. Next there was Moorgate, another postern, which gave access to the open space of Moorfields.

The next gate was Cripplegate, rebuilt in 1491. Stow states, but carefully does not confirm, the derivation of the name from the cripples who used to beg there. When the body of Edmund the Martyr came through the gate in about 978 they were miraculously cured. This was the gate through which Elizabeth first rode into the City in state, in 1558. Soon after Cripplegate the wall made a right-angle bend south, and then straightened out again to almost due west. Soon after that bend came Aldersgate. There was a tall timber-framed building on its inner side with 'divers large rooms and lodgings'. Then there was a postern made in the time of Edward VI, to connect his foundation of Christ's Hospital, just inside the wall, with his father's refounded Hospital of St Bartholomew in Smithfield.

Then followed New Gate, 'new' being a comparative term – it

was built 'about the reign of Henry I or King Stephen' (1100–54), and had been refurbished by the executors of Dick Whittington's will, in 1423. We may have problems with our prisons, but we never accommodate prisoners in gates, so the use of both Newgate and the next one, Ludgate, for this purpose seems odd until you remember that the 'gates' were multi-storey blocks, pierced by archways. Newgate had been used as a royal gaol since at least 1218. The City seems to have taken it over by 1382, since when it was used for freemen of the City who had committed serious crimes.

The last gate in the circuit was Lud Gate. According to Stow it may have been built by an ancient Briton, King Lud, in 66 BC (but he was not sure about it, 'wherefore I overpass it, as not to my purpose', an admirable habit). It had certainly been one of the Roman gates, leading to the west. Since 1378 it had been the prison used for freemen of the City who were imprisoned for minor offences such as debt. It was rebuilt by the City in 1586, at the huge cost of £1,500, but you cannot put statues of 'Lud and others' on the east side, and Her Majesty Queen Elizabeth on the west side, for nothing. On its lead roof was an open area where the prisoners might have 'fresh air and ease' more peacefully than in the prison's 'large walking place' at ground level.[12]

Originally the wall went straight on down to the river, but the Dominicans ('black friars') whose friary occupied a large area there persuaded Edward I (1272–1307) to bend the wall to enclose their territory, so that it met the Thames at the mouth of the Fleet river. The Romans had also fortified the bank of the Thames, but commercial and residential use and land reclamation had long destroyed their works.

One macabre feature of all the gates: they were useful for displaying the bodies of criminals, especially those convicted of treason: for example, 'John Story ... who before had been condemned of high treason, was drawn from the Tower of London to Tyburn, and there hanged, bowelled and quartered, his head set on London Bridge and his quarters on the gates of the City'.[13]

To the north

By Stow's time the main south–north artery ran from the Bridge by Fish Street and then due north across the City by Gracechurch

Street, out through Bishopsgate and on towards Hackney. (Gracechurch Street is still there. Its name tended to vary between Grace Church Street, Gracious Street and Grass Street, in Stow's time, as well as the version eventually adopted, by which I shall refer to it.) As far as its junction with Cornhill, the road was slightly uphill. There was an elaborate conduit or fountain half way up Gracechurch Street. Stow never mentions whether animals as well as humans benefited from these conduits, but surely a cart driver would manage to give his horse a drink after the hectic passage across the Bridge and the pull up Fish Street.

Bishopsgate Street, north of Cornhill, was not so tightly packed as the area near the river. There were some sumptuous houses there, such as Crosby Hall and Sir John Gresham's house, lately made into a college. You could probably see on your right a particularly interesting conversion of former monastic property, at St Helens' Priory. At the gate, there might be a bottleneck which gave you time to contemplate the heads and bits of bodies stuck on long stakes on the top of the building. Once through the gate, you soon passed Bethlehem Hospital ('Bedlam') on your left. You set out along Bishopsgate Street Without (i.e. outside the walls), with gardens and ribbon development on both sides. About 120 yards from the gate, you passed on your right the former Priory of St Mary Spital (later known as Spitalfields: now mostly under Liverpool Street station). You were about a mile and a quarter from the north end of the bridge, and outside the City's bounds. That was why two playhouses were built there, the Theatre in 1576 and the Curtain in 1577, where the Lord Mayor could not close them down.

The east/west route via Cheapside

The most fashionable, most impressive thoroughfare in the City was Cheapside, or more correctly Poultry and West Cheap. (Cheap means market place, regardless of the price or quality of the goods.) Three streets converge at the east end of Cheapside: Three Needle Street (now Threadneedle Street), Cornhill and Lombard Street. This trivium is easy to spot on any modern map. Where they met was a space occupied by the Stocks Market, which is now the site of the Mansion House. It had nothing to do with stocks and shares, which had not yet been invented: there was a permanent stocks there. On

Three Needle Street the most prominent buildings were the hall of the Merchant Taylors' livery company, and the Royal Exchange opened by Queen Elizabeth in 1570, a few houses from the junction of Three Needle Street and Cornhill. The centre branch, Cornhill, led almost due east, to Aldgate, for Whitechapel and the eastern counties. The third branch was Lombard Street, leading on to Fenchurch Street, which curves north-east again, to Aldgate. There were two impressive mansions in Lombard Street, one built recently by a goldsmith and the other going back to the time of Edward III.

Cheapside had everything. It had always been spacious. In 1331 King Edward III held a tournament there, 'the stone pavement being covered with sand [so] that the horses might not slide when they strongly set their feet to the ground'. There were three monuments in the middle of this space: the Great Conduit near the east end, the Standard half way down and Cheap Cross at the west end. Bucklersbury (still there) to the left of the Great Conduit was where the apothecaries and grocers sold herbs and spices, making a welcome change from the normal London stinks. Falstaff derided fops who 'smell like Bucklersbury in simple-time', simples in this context being herbs for medicines.[14] Some of the houses along Cheapside were five storeys high and ornately decorated, especially Goldsmiths' Row opposite the Cross. Sixty-three properties here were owned and occupied by goldsmiths, including the delightfully named Affabel Partridge, one of the Queen's mint-masters, who was prominent in the reorganisation of the coinage. Some were just shops, some combined residential and shop premises, and some incorporated workshops and furnaces as well. The signs on their frontages creaked and swung, such as the Black Bear, the Acorn, the Three Wells, the Broad Arrow, the Holy Ghost, the Black Boy, the Leg, the Bottle, the Crown and the Red Cross.[15] The names belonged to the sites, or the buildings, and did not, as that list makes clear, denote the trade carried on there.

The west end of Cheapside leads into Newgate Street. There was an interesting district to your right, known as the Liberty of St Martins le Grand. The foreign craftsmen who settled there were notorious for the counterfeit jewellery they made, to the annoyance of the Goldsmiths' Company. The area still had an ill-defined exemption from the Lord Mayor's jurisdiction.[16] If you took a detour in that direction, you would hear more Flemish, Italian and French being spoken than English.

Once through Newgate, the road dipped sharply down to the bridge over the Fleet river, via Snow Hill. (Snow Hill is still a steep slope. The Victorians flattened out so much of London, in this instance by routing traffic over Holborn Viaduct, that one forgets the gradients, unless bicycling. Look over the edge of Holborn Viaduct and you will see what I mean.) The Fleet river was a mixed blessing. Butchers and leather-tanners saw it as a useful means of getting rid of their trade refuse. Residents objected to the resultant stink. (The dispute was not settled to everyone's satisfaction until the Fleet was culverted. It still flows, underground.) Once up the other bank and along Holborn, life became much quieter, unless the students in the Inns of Court happened to be rioting. At Staple Inn you passed the Bar (both Staple Inn and Holborn Bar are still there, but in Victorian guise), which marked the boundary of the Lord Mayor's jurisdiction to the west. If you kept going long enough along this road, you should get to Oxford. A few miles from the centre of the City, you would pass on your right Tyburn Gallows (roughly on the site of Marble Arch), which was even more isolated when it was first built in 1388.

Thames Street

Thames Street ran along the back of two huge riverside houses built by medieval barons. Going east from Blackfriars, the first is Baynards Castle, where Elizabeth's friends the Pembrokes lived. The next was Bygot House, no longer inhabited by Stow's time. Then further east Thames Street gave access to a network of narrow streets leading down to the river, none longer than 150 yards, some only the width of one house apart. At the stairs (jetties) at the ends of the streets, you could shout 'oars' or 'westward ho!' or 'eastward ho!' for a boat, if there was not one already waiting.

Queenhithe, about half way to the Bridge, used to be the main landing place for goods until the river became too silted up, the drawbridge fell into disuse and the boats got bigger; but it still handled river traffic from the countryside up-river. Billingsgate, just to the east of the Bridge, had become the main depot. Almost at the Tower of London was the Custom House, built in the first year of Elizabeth's reign. (Its successor is slightly west of the old site.)

St Paul's / Ludgate / Fleet Street

When Sir Christopher Wren was contemplating the ruins of the City after the Great Fire in 1666, he planned a magnificent setting for his masterpiece, the new cathedral. Architects have been trying to achieve this ever since. But St Paul's still sits obdurately at the western end of the City, with no splendid vista to enhance it. Absurdly, it looks like an afterthought plonked clumsily among the existing streets, if you try to make sense of it on a map. It is, of course, oriented due east, whereas the street layout follows the river, which does not flow exactly west/east here. There never was a vista framing the City's main place of worship. (The best view today is from across the river, from Tate Modern.)

In Stow's time, standing at the west porch of the enormous Norman cathedral, you looked down Bowyers Row towards Ludgate. Once through the usual traffic jam at the gate, and down Ludgate Hill, you came to a bridge over the Fleet river. (From now until Temple Bar the street is called Fleet Street.) The Fleet prison was 100 yards north of the Fleet bridge, and the former royal palace of Bridewell, converted to use as a workhouse, lay to the south, where the Fleet river flowed into the Thames. After the Temple on your left, and other Inns of Court to your right, you passed Temple Bar (shown on modern maps but, of course, not on the Elizabethan version), and once again you had left the Lord Mayor's jurisdiction.

The City to Westminster

The stately procession of mansions along the river proclaimed the lineage of their owners. After the Temple came Essex House, then Arundel House, Somerset House, the Savoy, Bedford House, Durham House and York House, until the river bent south past the royal palace at Whitehall. Since the natural traffic route between the nobles and the Court was by water, the most elaborate frontages of their houses faced the river, and elegant stairways and landing stages awaited the barges and private boats used by the grandees and their visitors.

Gates on the Strand were needed when bad weather made the river impossible, and for wheeled traffic and the crowds of supporters and serving men who often accompanied their masters. The other (north) side of the Strand was fringed by modest development only one house deep. The Strand lay parallel to the river until the sharp southerly bend in the river, where a side street headed north (now Cockspur Street) and the main road continued, following the river, to the palaces of Whitehall and Westminster. At the junction of the two roads, in the village of Charing, was the last of the crosses erected by Edward I in 1290 to commemorate his wife Eleanor, whose coffin rested there on its way from Nottinghamshire to Westminster Abbey in 1290. (The present Charing Cross in the station forecourt is a Victorian pastiche not even in the right place, which is now occupied by the statue of Charles I looking down Whitehall.) On the other side of the junction lay the royal mews (the site of Trafalgar Square). The public road went straight through Whitehall Palace to Westminster Abbey, Westminster Hall and the old Palace of Westminster, where the kings of England had lived, from William I to Henry VIII. (This is the line of the present Whitehall.)

It seems extraordinary for a palace to be built across a public highway. Access was to some extent controlled by a series of gates across the road. It is fair to say that Whitehall was not just one palace building, but a complex more like a small village. It was designed for Cardinal Wolsey, but Henry VIII liked it so much that he allowed Wolsey to give it to him in 1530.

Road surfaces

Some of the principal streets were paved. A Venetian tourist in 1562 described them as 'spacious and well paved with limestone and flint'.[17] But there were not many paved streets in his native city, so perhaps he was easily impressed. Some streets were cobbled. Before the Reformation, road repairs had been a fitting object for charitable bequests, but that source had dried up. It is hard to tell how many streets in Elizabethan London were paved, or how well. By an Act of 1543 the residents in some 'suburbs' – that is, outside the City walls – had been obliged to pay for the street outside their houses to be paved. This included the Strand. Cheapside was mostly paved by the 1550s.[18] In 1572 the Lord Mayor and the city surveyors were considering paving the road *outside* Aldgate, which surely implies that the road inside the gate was already paved.[19]

Bishopsgate Street was paved as far as the hospital of St Mary Spital outside the gate.

Where roads were not paved, what was the road surface? Perhaps it was just gravel, or beaten earth turning to mud in wet weather. Here is the Venetian ambassador, describing Elizabeth's coronation procession in January 1559: 'Owing to the deep mud caused by the foul weather and by the multitude of people and of horses, everyone had made preparation by placing sand and gravel in front of their houses.'[20] In July 1561 the route east out of London, which the Queen would take to go on one of her annual progresses, 'was new gravelled with sand, from the Charterhouse through Smithfield and through St Nicholas' shambles, Cheapside, and Cornhill, to Aldgate and Whitechapel'.[21] Were the City roads particularly dirty that summer? Or was it done regularly, or at least every time the Queen was going to use that road?

Machyn, from whose *Diary* the description comes, did not record any other such preparation, so we are left wondering. Perhaps the answer is in an entry in the records of Gray's Inn in 1559: 'upon the petition of many [of] the inhabitants of Gray's Inn Lane for the paving of that part of the lane leading into the fields', the Inn agreed to bear part of the cost if the tenants bore the rest.[22] Chancery Lane was paved in 1597, the cost shared between Lincoln's Inn and the residents on the other side of the road.[23] So perhaps road surfacing was a piecemeal affair, done as and when residents demanded it and were prepared to pay, or when the City authorities decided that the expense would be balanced by commercial advantage.

Transport

Most people walked. After all, the whole of London including Westminster and the river frontage of Southwark was only three miles long and two miles wide, according to William Smith, Rouge Dragon Poursuivant, in 1588. If you had a heavy load, you could hire a porter or use a pack animal. If you had the means, you could save your clothes from the muck of the streets, by riding horseback. The horse harness could be magnificent. The inventory of the household goods of Sir Thomas Ramsey, Lord Mayor, who died in 1577, included 'two velvet bridles with the two furniture [*sic*] of black velvet trappings, studded', valued at £4.[24] Lord North spent £7 10s on a velvet-trimmed saddle and harness, in 1578.[25] Women rode sidesaddle, or sat pillion behind the driver. These pillion saddles could be roomy and comfortable, with leather bags as well for light luggage.[26] Horses were usually geldings. They could be security-marked, by a brand or a cut on their ears, but the notorious traders in stolen horses merely obliterated the marks, moved the horse well away from its home, added a few more marks and sold it at a nice profit, despite all the laws passed to stop them.[27]

Queen Elizabeth when she wanted maximum public exposure, and elderly ladies who preferred privacy, sometimes used litters, the curtains of which could be opened or closed.[28] But as Stow said, 'the world runs on wheels with many whose parents were glad to go on foot'. William Boonen, a Dutchman, had started the rot by introducing Queen Elizabeth to his newfangled coaches, in 1564. They cannot have been very comfortable. The Queen's, covered with brass-studded red leather, had a maximum capacity of two, twelve wheels but no springs.[29] Within twenty years anyone who was any-one had some sort of wheeled transport. The Earl of Bedford's 'two coaches and two coach horses' were valued together at £10, in 1585.[30] The Earl of Essex's 'two old coaches', one covered with leather, were perhaps more elaborate; they were valued at £10 and £8.[31] Some women no doubt justified a coach, to their husbands, as cost saving:

> If their mistress is to ride abroad she must have six or eight serving men to attend her, she must have one to carry her cloak and hood lest it rain, another her fan if she use it not herself, another her box with ruffs and other necessaries, another behind whom her maid or Gentlewoman must ride, and some must be loose [available] to open gates and supply other services ... There is a new invention, that is, she must have a coach, wherein she with her gentlewoman, maid and children and what necessaries as they ... are to use, may be carried with smaller charge [expense] less cost and more credit ... for one or two men at the most, besides the coachman, are sufficient for a Gentlewoman or Lady of worthy parentage.[32]

By 1600 the Lord Mayor banned theatrical performances in private houses, 'in which there is daily so great a resort of people and so great a multitude of coaches whereof many are Hackney coaches ... that sometimes all the streets cannot contain them'.[33] This is the first mention I have seen of the ancestors of London's black cabs or, to give them their proper name, Hackney carriages, Hackney simply meaning 'for hire'.

The booming foreign trade meant that the weighhouse in Cornhill was in constant demand. 'A strong cart and four great horses' attended by a team of eight porters were needed 'to draw and carry the wares from the merchants' houses and back again'.[34] From the 1560s 'long wagons' began to roll up to London along the country roads, destroying the already pot-holed surface, from provincial centres such as Canterbury, Norwich, Ipswich, Gloucester and Oxford. By 1575 there was a regular service to Oxford, leaving London on Wednesdays and due back on Saturdays,[35] or so the schedule said; it seems a bit optimistic to me.

Traffic

Stow bemoaned the current state of traffic:

> The number of cars, drays, carts and coaches, more than hath been accustomed, the streets and lanes being straitened [that is, narrowed, because of encroachments on them], must needs be dangerous, as daily experience shows. The coach man rides behind the horses' tails, lashes them, and looks not behind him. The Drayman sits and sleeps on his dray, and lets his horse lead him home ... the fore horse of every carriage should be led by hand, but these good orders are not observed ...

A Venetian tourist noticed that 'they often use carts pulled by two, four, six or more horses ... the carters go whistling behind to urge them along. They use a certain whip which is very long ... and makes cracking noises. The carts for carrying people are lighter and are protected with waterproof covering.'[36] These carts and coaches were hard to stop, even if the driver was alert. Bridget Serten, aged twelve, was 'killed by chance with a cart near Aldgate going in to London'. She got caught between the portcullis and the gate, and was, hideously, crushed to death.[37] A Frenchman killed a carter one dark night in 1562 because the carter 'could not give him room, for press of carts'.[38] There were recognised 'standings' for carts, but whenever the drivers ignored the rules there was 'great disorder in the City'.[39]

There was, of course, no Highway Code – no rules about giving priority to oncoming traffic through narrow lanes, or giving way to

traffic coming from the right, let alone driving on one predeter-
mined side of the road. It must have been like driving in a Chinese
city: you see an empty piece of road and make for it, cutting across
anything and anyone to get there. But who could have enforced
rules, if there had been any, when, say, a flock of geese that had
walked from Norfolk met a flock of sheep being driven up from
Kent? Add in the normal traffic, and then something extra, such as
a royal occasion, and the traffic comes to a standstill. In 1564,

> on the 30 day of August it was enacted that all such as would sell
> their wares, plate or household stuff to their most advantage ...
> should bring the same wares etc. to Leadenhall [market] on Monday
> and Friday, there to be sold to them that would give most for it.
>
> In this year was brought to the city great plenty of fruit, for there
> came in one market [on a single market day, presumably] ...in to
> Gracechurch Street 14 carts, besides a great quantity that was
> brought on horseback, in paniers and dossars [huge baskets carried
> on men's backs]: this continued the most part of the summer.[40]

This additional pressure must have caused unimaginable chaos.

When Queen Elizabeth chose to go on her summer progresses,
she did not travel light. The procession of courtiers, gentlewomen
and servants was followed through the streets by 300 carts carrying
the royal luggage.[41] As if wheeled traffic did not make enough
trouble, every now and then a noise ahead told you to get out of the
way fast, as the Earl of Shrewsbury came into town 'with a hundred
men riding', or young Lord Talbot went to visit him 'with sixty
horse'.[42] There could be minor stoppages that cleared themselves,
for instance when a master's horse paused to urinate, and all the
servitors following him waited politely, caps in hand, until the horse
had finished.[43]

Oncoming traffic might be more sinister. Richard Stoneley
happened to be riding along Cheapside one December morning in
1581, after his morning prayers, when 'there came one Edmund
Campion [the most celebrated of the outlawed Jesuit priests] drawn
upon hurdles [there were confederates with him] to Tyburn and
there suffered execution'.[44] Stoneley noted it in his diary, but without
any expression of shock. Elizabethan justice could be brutal in its
execution. You might equally meet men or women being whipped
through the city, their backs raw and bloody, or a criminal being
'carted', or you might see a petty criminal in the stocks or the pillory,

withstanding a rain of mud and missiles. And you might decide to take another route altogether if you found that your intended way passed under a gateway with part of a rotting human body on it.

After the church bells had rung the curfew every evening there was comparative quiet until the gates reopened at six, or sunrise, the next morning. Curfew was rung every night, from St Mary-le-Bow and other churches. After that time – nine in the summer, dusk in the winter – the City gates forbade entry, no citizen should be out in the streets, the taverns were shut and the shopkeepers' shutters were closed, until six the next morning – earlier, at dawn, in the summer – when the City gates were reopened and the pulse of life quickened again. The word curfew is derived from the Norman-French *couvre-feu*, i.e. covering the fire. According to Stow, William the Conqueror had imposed a total ban after eight at night, when 'all people should then put out their fire and candle, and take their rest'. But William's rules had been progressively eroded until by Elizabeth's time one suspects that respectable citizens going on their lawful occasions could feel fairly confident of getting home unchallenged, although the lawless minority might well fall foul of the Watch, just as they might nowadays under the police power to stop and search.

Water supply

We take piped water for granted. When the water company cuts the supply, we panic and queue up at the standpipes. The situation was not nearly so bad as I had at first imagined, for the Elizabethan Londoner. You could go and get it for yourself – you never had to go far, there was a free supply within a few minutes' walk, for most people. Or you could pay someone else to carry it to your house for you. There was also a small proportion of London residents who had water piped to their houses.

'Conduit' seems to have been used both for the fountain where the water flowed out, and for the pipe leading to the fountain. It can be difficult to sort out which, in the records. I will use 'conduit' or 'water fountain' for the taps etc. dispensing the water, and 'pipe' for how the water got there, and I hope I get it right. 'Bosses' were small conduits, sometimes built into the wall, particularly a church wall, rather like small Victorian drinking fountains.

As long ago as the thirteenth century, London's natural springs and wells were failing to provide for the modest increase in its population. Various expedients were tried to defray the cost of watering London. In 1237 the Picardy merchants gave £100 – a very substantial amount in those days – towards the cost of bringing water from the springs at Tyburn, in return for trading privileges. Bringing water in from distant springs became a frequent charitable legacy by any pious Londoner. Richard Whittington, that admirable Lord Mayor, endowed two conduits, one at Billingsgate and the other at St Giles Cripplegate. He also paid to have water laid on to the prisons at Newgate and Ludgate, in 1432. Sir William Eastfield brought water from Tyburn to Fleet Street, and Highbury to Cripplegate, in 1438. After the Reformation, charitable bequests, which had required prayers for the donor's soul, dried up, but private citizens went on sharing the burden with the City authorities. William Lambe rebuilt Holborn Conduit in 1564, for £1,500, a Carnegie-scale amount (Lambs Conduit Street is named after him, but his conduit has gone).[45] In 1583 Barnard Randulph, common sergeant (a high office) of the City, gave £900 'to the water conduits'.

A statute of 1543 had given the City power to bring water from Hampstead Heath, Hackney, Muswell Hill, Marylebone and other places within five miles of the City, though it is not clear how far this was put into effect. Another would have let them bring in water from the river Lea, but they never quite got round to it. (Hugh Middleton's 'New River' did not leave the drawing-board until 1609.) But the municipal responsibility for these distant supplies provided a splendid excuse for municipal jollifications. The conduit-head at Marylebone had to be so carefully inspected every year that a banqueting house was built for the purpose. In September 1562 the Lord Mayor, the aldermen, the masters and wardens of the twelve livery companies, and friends

> rode to the conduit heads for to see them, after the old custom. Before dinner they hunted the hare, and killed, and so to dinner to the head of the conduit … and after dinner to the hunting of the fox and there was a goodly cry for a mile and after the hounds killed the fox at the end of St Giles and there was a great cry at the death, and blowing of horns. And so rode through London, the Lord Mayor with all his company to his own place in Lombard Street.[46]

And all this after a long hard day's work on City business.

Water pipes were sometimes tree-trunks with a central hole bored out, but more usually were made of lead, which possibly added to Londoners' diseases but never seems to have done much harm to the Romans, who also used it for water pipes.[47] Since lead had a value on the open market, the pipes were occasionally stolen, as in 1560 when two thieves cut off almost the whole water supply, for which they were whipped.[48]

Conduits could be elaborate. The Cross in Cheapside was one of those memorials to his queen erected by Edward I wherever her coffin rested on its way to burial in Westminster, in 1290. It had been rebuilt in 1486, and regilded as late as 1554, but when Mary's devout Catholicism had gone, it clearly irritated some people because it incorporated a statue of the Virgin Mary with the infant Jesus in her arms. They were vandalised in 1581 and again in 1596. This time the restorers added a classical touch in the form of an alabaster image of Diana, 'and water [was] conveyed from the Thames, prilling [sic] from her naked breast', but she was vandalised in her turn.[49]

The Great Conduit in the middle of Cheapside used water from both Tyburn and Paddington. It had been the first, and remained the most important, of London's public water fountains.[50] The third monument in Cheapside, known as the Standard, also included a conduit. There was another elaborate conduit in Fleet Street, fed with water piped from Paddington via Tyburn and Marylebone. It was 'a fair tower of stone garnished with images of St Christopher on the top, and angels round about lower down, with sweet sounding bells before them, whereupon by an engine placed in the tower they at divers times of the day and night chimed such a hymn as was appointed'. It was rebuilt, with a larger capacity, in 1582.

Stow observed sourly that the public good achieved by all these conduits was 'for the poor to drink and the rich to dress their meat'. Washing was not in his mind. But a small household's needs could be supplied without too much difficulty by a waterbearer. The Waterbearers' Company had been incorporated in 1496. Its members walked the streets of London with tall conical containers on their backs holding about three gallons – exactly the shape of an old-fashioned coke hod, for anyone who remembers coke-burning domestic stoves, and a very practical shape for a heavy commodity. I don't know what they charged, but I suspect it varied depending on whether they had simply filled their water-vessels from the river or taken the purer water dispensed by a conduit. In an account of a schoolboy's preparations for school, written in 1573, the boy is trying to make up for lost time, having got out of bed late. He tells the household page to bring him some water 'to wash my hands and my face. I will have no river water for it is troubled [muddy]. Give me well or fountain water.'[51]

Engineers and quills

The huge water-wheels under London Bridge were built by a Dutch hydraulics engineer whose name was anglicised as Peter Morice. In 1574 he had convinced the Lord Mayor of his expertise, by pumping a jet of water as high as the steeple of St Magnus Church beside the river – the first well-documented sales pitch. The Lord Mayor was so impressed that he granted Morice a lease of the northernmost arch of the bridge for 500 years, at 10s a year: a bargain the Lord Mayor's successors regretted for several centuries. After various financial crises Morice's pipes first gushed water in Leadenhall on Christmas Eve 1582. Encouraged, he installed a supply in Old Fish Street, and asked for another arch of the bridge, to extend his operation. It was 'a great commodity to that part of the city and would be far greater if the said water were maintained to run continually, or at the least at every tide, some reasonable quantity as at the first it did, but since [by 1592, when this was written] is much or almost altogether slaked [dried up]'.[52]

Meanwhile a competitor had entered the market, one Bevis Bulmer, 'gentleman', according to Stow. He had been granted by the City part of Bygot House on the river bank, and built there 'one large house of great height called an engine ... for the conveying and forcing [pumping] of Thames water to serve in the middle and west parts of the city'. Morice's system had the disadvantage of relying on tidal power, and his supply could be intermittent. Bulmer's engines seem to have worked better, using a chain pump powered by wind and horses.[53]

It was perhaps no wonder that the waterbearers viewed Morice and Bulmer with less than favour. In the early days of Morice's development their position had been carefully considered by the Lord Mayor and the Lord Chancellor, who had decided that they would 'still have as much work as they were able to perform so far

as the water of the conduits would satisfy'.[54] But Frederick Duke of
Würtemburg's secretary noted solemnly that waterbearers were
'said to be unruly' in 1592.

Since most domestic consumers could help themselves from the
conduits free of charge, and the new pipes were under City control,
it is not easy to see how Morice and Bulmer covered their expenses,
let alone made profits. But private residents could bypass the
waterbearers by having water piped into their houses, and this must
be where the water undertakers' profits came from. The supply pipe
was very narrow gauge – the thickness of a swan's quill – and the
agreement allowing you to connect to the main water pipe was
called a 'quill'. In 1559 one of the officers of St Bartholomew's
Hospital, who lived in the hospital, was allotted 'a tenement [here
just meaning a house], a yard, and a quill of water'.[55]

St Bart's had its own water supply, as we shall see, but I include it
here to show how such agreements worked. They were much prized.
In 1594 Lord Burghley wrote to the Lord Mayor, 'please supply Lord
Cobham with a small Quill', and Lady Essex asked the Lord Mayor
to 'please continue the pipe of water formerly granted to the Earl of
Essex for the use of Essex House' in 1601. Seven years later, strictly
speaking after our period, Essex House was cut off again. The Lord
Mayor wrote to the Lord Chancellor – how had he got into the act?
– that the Essex House quill had been stopped because the water in
the conduits was very low and the poor were 'clamorous'. Their
only source of water was disappearing, so it had been necessary to
cut off several quills, and anyway there had been complaints about
the 'extraordinary waste of water in Essex House, it being taken not
only for dressing meat [cooking] but for the laundry, the stable, and
other offices, which might be otherwise served'. When you remember
that Essex House was on the banks of the Thames, you see his
point: like washing your Rolls-Royce during a hose-pipe ban, in full
view.

You may not be familiar with the amount of water that would
come through a swan's quill. The following may help, although
again it is strictly outside our period and it seems to have been a
fairly hefty quill. 'Alice, Countess of Derby, allowed a quill of
water from the City's main pipe, to yield three gallons an hour, at
her dwelling-place in St Martin's Lane, 2 June 1618.' At least she
asked. There was a reprehensible amount of water extracted by
unauthorised means, making it necessary for the Lord Mayor's men

to search the courses of the main pipes from time to time, and cut off all unauthorised branches.[56] By the 1580s most conduits were supervised by paid Keepers, so they would notice when the water levels were sinking inexplicably.

   Some properties had their own water supply. These could be wells in the yard or garden, sometimes shared, like the cess-pit, with the neighbour. But sometimes landowners had made elaborate arrangements to bring water from the same aquifers as the City used, in the hills round London. Both the Charterhouse and nearby St Bartholomew's Hospital had such private arrangements. The Charterhouse, a Carthusian priory, had been founded in 1371 to commemorate more than 50,000 people who – according to Stow – had died of a plague epidemic two years earlier. They had been buried in thirteen acres of unconsecrated ground outside the City boundaries, since the parish churchyards were full. The burial ground was retroactively blessed, being known as the Pardon Churchyard, and a Carthusian priory was built there. By 1431 the monks were ready to construct a system of pipes with occasional ventilation shafts, from Barnsbury in Islington across land owned by other monasteries, via a series of springs and wells, to a cistern in a conduit house in the monks' great cloister. From there various branches supplied the communal offices of the priory, such as the buttery and the kitchen, and the 'lavatory' (which was where the monks washed), before ending in the gardens. It was both a sophisticated piece of engineering and an example of co-operation between landowners. The pipes lasted more than three hundred years.[57] The supply to St Bartholomew's Hospital (founded in 1123), and Christ's Hospital next to it, ran along the same lines.

Refuse disposal

It is not easy to see what happened to refuse. There was much less of it than we generate with our unending packaging, and bottles and cans and newspapers. In a brilliant recycling scheme, the butchers' offal from Eastcheap and Newgate shambles was supposed to be taken to two 'barrow houses' on the river front, thence to Bankside to feed the bears,[58] but in that case why did Falstaff say, 'Have I lived to be carried in a basket, like a barrow of butcher's offal, and to be thrown into the Thames?'[59] Kitchen refuse might be bought by a woman who toured the streets calling out, 'Any kitchen stuff, maids?' The muck from London streets, which would include a fair propor- tion of ash from the cooking fires, was already being bought for the market gardens outside London.

Residents were supposed to deal with their own domestic refuse responsibly – but how? And where? Each ward in the City had officers called scavengers to see that people observed their duty. They may have paid labourers to do the actual work of sweeping up the mess. Lincoln's Inn paid 5s 'to the scavengers for cleansing the street before the gate of the Inn [in Chancery Lane] for a year'.[60] In the end it probably came down to the kites and pigs that haunted London streets – the best scavengers of all.

Public toilets

There were a few. Never where you wanted them, of course, but mostly near running water. There was one at the bridge over the Fleet river just outside Ludgate. The bridge was a substantial stone building 'on the which towards the south, be also certain lanterns of stone for lights to be placed in the winter evenings, for commodity of travellers', as Stow described it, but he was too reticent to include the further 'commodity' that travellers and passers-by must have welcomed – a lavatory. We know of it only because Christ's Hospital took in a child 'born in the jacques [pronounced jakes: lavatory] at the Fleet Bridge'. Another child admitted to the Hospital had been found 'in the common privy at the Queenhithe', another site over or near running water, beside the Thames.[61] There were three privies in Tower Street in 1579,[62] which may not have been over any water. They probably stank in hot weather: just the kind of place Andrew Boorde warned prospective house-buyers about. 'Permit no common pissing place [to] be about the house or mansion.'[63] Richard Whittington had died in 1423, but his famous Long House on the riverside between Billinsgate and Queenhithe, accommodating 64 users at a time, equally divided between men and women, was still in use.[64]

CHAPTER 3

The Buildings

At the beginning of Elizabeth's reign, 'fair houses in London were plenteous, and very easy to be had at low and small rents, and by reason of the late dissolution of religious houses many houses in London stood vacant, and not any man desirous to take them'.[1] Henry VIII's takeover of all papal property in England had perhaps stunned Londoners. It took time for the penny to drop because this had never happened before. Henry disposed of most properties to his friends, for cash or their continued support. Nevertheless such a huge and sudden availability overwhelmed the market, while developers – a new breed – worked out what to do next.

As late as Mary's reign, the Venetian Ambassador was regretting that 'the city is much disfigured by the ruins of a multitude of churches and monasteries belonging heretofore to friars and nuns'.[2] But by the time her sister Elizabeth had made clear her intention to rule with the agreement of her loving subjects but without the Pope, and waves of foreigners were finding this climate preferable to the religious persecution in their native lands, demand had quickened. All over the City, new and refurbished buildings began to emerge from clouds of dust and shouting, in the back gardens of established houses and the ruins of former monastic properties, in the suburbs on green-field sites and in holes and corners in the built-up area.

Timber-frame construction[3]

The 'black and white houses' in Ludlow are the last word in touristic picture-postcard style, but they have survived because medieval builders were skilled and the materials they used were appropriate.[4] Timber frames filled in with local materials could go up quickly – and if need be could come down again as quickly, and be moved to another site, if the authorities looked like catching up with an illegally built development. The playhouse in Shoreditch had to close because of a dispute with the ground landlord. Undeterred, the players themselves took the structure to pieces after Christmas 1598, moved the timbers across the river to a new site on Bankside, and got it up and running again by 20 January 1599.[5]

Every timber-framed building in London was supervised by a master carpenter, and built by his apprentices, journeymen and labourers. The Worshipful Company of Carpenters operated a tightly closed shop, in the City and suburbs. They controlled the market in, and the use of, timber.[6] They were 'preferred before those of like science among all other nations' – but the Carpenters' records regularly note applications to employ 'foreigners', not members of the Company, who might get on with the job cheaper and faster, since London builders were prone to 'covetousness [overcharging] joined with a lingering humour [delaying]'.[7] Young men flocked from all over England and even the highlands of Scotland, to qualify in this lucrative trade.[8] In those days when the only supplement to manpower was a pulley and a horse, the sheer physical strength of a young man was a useful asset. There was no formal education. Apprentices learned from their masters. They might begin as young as 8, or as old as 27, but in no case could they hope to earn their own living until at least seven years of apprenticeship were over and they were at least 26.

The way to put a house together from lengths of wood had not changed much over the centuries.[9] Mortise-and-tenon and dovetailing joints had been refined, but not altered, since 1300.[10] The elegancies of lap and scarf joints were commonplace to carpenters, gouging accurate holes in hard wood and leaving vital bits sticking out, with only hand tools, guided by eye and practice.

What is the difference between a frame and a house? John Stow constantly refers to frames.[11] Goldsmiths' Row was 'the most beautiful frame of fair houses and shops that be within the walls of London ... it containeth ten fair dwellings and fourteen shops, all within one frame'. A frame was like the girders of a modern building. It could be divided internally according to the wishes of the client or the builder's assessment of the market. Whether intended as one house or for multi-occupancy, each main frame was divided into 'bays' at intervals varying between 5 and 20 feet, by skeleton walls (also called 'frames') which kept it rigid and marked the internal divisions.

The first consideration was timber. The best was oak, being hard and weather-resistant. It could be used within a year or two of felling. Sweet chestnut and elm were alternatives. Trees do not grow obligingly straight, nor are their trunks tidily square in section. Beams of up to twenty feet long could be sawn from a good tree. The first step was to dig a pit, so that one man could pull and push the saw from below, and another, the 'top-sawyer', could reciprocate, and see what they were doing, from on top. When the church-wardens of the parish church of Lambeth decided to pull down and rebuild a church property, their first expense was 16 pence for 'felling a tree and making a sawpit'.[12]

If the site was uneven or damp – as it usually was in flood-prone London – the frame was insulated from the ground by a low plinth of brick or stone, on which the sill beams rested horizontally. There were slots in the sill beams, to take the upright members of each frame.

The winding narrow streets and constricted working space could make it difficult to manoeuvre long beams. Off-site prefabrication had long been the answer. Westminster Hall had been magnificently re-roofed at the end of the fourteenth century. The roof that you can still see weighs 660 tons, and covers nearly half an acre.[13] It was prefabricated in Farnham, more than 30 miles from Westminster as the crow flies and even further as the wagon and the barge move, and carried overland to Ham, and then down the Thames. Nonsuch House on London Bridge was wholly prefabricated in Holland.

Each frame was first laid out flat on the 'framing-ground', whether on- or off-site, and fitted together. The necessary joints were cut at this stage. The joint fixing a main horizontal beam ('bressumer') to the top of a vertical beam, in particular, was beautifully designed, especially if it was to support a storey projecting from the storey below. Depending on space and the size of the finished building, whole frames, especially internal frames, might be assembled ready for 'rearing'. (Anyone who has watched a film of the raising of an American barn will by now have the idea.) If it was necessary to take the frame apart for rearing elsewhere, each timber was marked so that its sequence in the on-site construction was clear.

Construction was done in stages, floor by floor (see plate 14). Rearing a whole frame took the combined strength of the labour force, but most beams could be lifted by one or two men. The churchwardens of Lambeth Church, anxiously watching every penny, paid out 6d for 'bestowing on the workmen at the pulling down of the [old] house in bread and beer' and 4d 'in bread and beer at the rearing of the [new] house'.[14] Bressumers had to be lowered down on to the prepared sockets in the tops of the vertical beams. This delicate operation, for which pulleys or a simple crane might be used, called for both strength and accuracy. The finished building might be as high as five storeys. Work must have gone slowly in the winter, with no artificial light. There is a reference to working by candlelight, but that was a refurbishing job,[15] so it may have been limited to internal walls.

Often a building was extended beyond its foot-print – to use a modern term – by extensions jutting out ('jutties' or 'jetties') from successive storeys. There seems to have been some control of these 'encroachments'. According to the Carpenters' records, anyone who put up a 'counting house, study, jutties, perprestures or penthouses in the City or the suburbs without special licence from the Master [of the Company] shall pay six shillings and eight pence' – and in some cases the record adds that the offender was ordered to 'pluk and take down' the structure. Why counting houses and studies, let alone perprestures, whatever they were, and penthouses, should have been tarred with the same brush as jetties I have been unable to find out. But jetties were a status symbol, so perhaps fines, and even bribes to persuade the authorities to turn a blind eye, were not so important as these visible signs of wealth projecting from the walls.

In 1369 the authorities had objected to a 'gette' 19 feet long, 4 feet to nearly 5 feet wide, and over 7 feet high. It was still there in 1526.[16] A house in Soper Lane had a jetty the whole length of the building, 20 feet long and more than 3 feet wide, which overhung the neighbour's sawpit in the next property and must have been a confounded nuisance to him.[17] The floor area of a house could grow by as much as 3½ feet[18] in each jetty, on each storey, so by the time you got to the top of a tall jettied house in Cheapside, roofed with lead and tiles, no wonder it 'shook in any great wind'.[19] In 1596 the owner of a house in Soper Lane was licensed by the City to set up three columns in front of his house, one foot forward from his 'plate or groundsill', on payment of 1s 4d per annum.[20] Perhaps the columns were propping up a sagging jetty.

Once the frame was up, the plasterers moved in. Internal walls were filled by reeds or small branches (wattle) or thin timber strips (lathes) pushed into slots in the timbers, to support a mixture of clay and whatever else was handy, such as horsehair, to strengthen it. This 'daub' or plaster would not be the shining white favoured by restorers, but the gentle colours of the local earth. The same technique was used for the outer walls. Again, the result was a pleasing earth colour, interspersed with the pale greys and browns of the oak or other timber – not a stark black and white. Usually the panels of exterior walls were both decorated and strengthened by added cross-members. Here is where any short curved branches came in handy. They were split, not sawn, so that two mirror-image curves could oppose each other in a pleasing pattern.

Both wattle and daub, and lathe and plaster, tended to spring gaps, which let in the draught until they were patched up. Brick infilling was used in prosperous houses. It certainly stopped the draughts, but it had the disadvantage of rigidity – when the frame moved, as timber was bound to do, the bricks cracked. Not all spaces were filled up. Obviously there had to be doors. Windows were often separately jettied, like miniature bow windows, and fitted into sockets in the frame. Brick chimneys were increasingly common, and space had to be left for them. There might be a privy ('house of office') with its shute to the cess-pit below the house, on each floor, or only on the top storey or the ground floor of a five-storey building, which surely was far from convenient.[21]

The glazier's work completed the building. The Lambeth church-wardens paid the large sum of 21s 6d 'for glazing of windows', out of a total expenditure of £29 12s. In most houses, glazed windows were a fairly new luxury that had quickly become a necessity. In some, such as Bess of Hardwick's prodigy house in Derbyshire, the whole elevation glittered with glass. Although they were necessarily smaller, some houses in London emulated her extravagance. A mansion in Crutched Friars produced the same effect of being made mostly of glass, by filling every panel with it, leaving only the bressumers to be decorated with riotous gargoyles and heraldic shields. Whether or not it was unique is impossible to tell. It survived until 1792, altered only by the replacement of some of the diamond window panes with Georgian sash windows and rectangular panes.

New stone and brick houses

New stone houses could depend on a useful source of material – the worked stones of the old monasteries, some dating from the original construction in the twelfth century.[22] (Here is the origin of the grand addresses that so impressed young Catherine Morland in Jane Austen's *Northanger Abbey*.) The Cluniac monastery at Bermondsey had been founded in 1089, the second monastic foundation after the abbey of Westminster. It lasted for four and a half centuries. 'The abbey church was then pulled down by Sir Thomas Pope, Knight, and in place thereof a goodly house of stone and timber built.'[23] Lord North, one of Henry VIII's privy councillors, got his hands on the ancient foundation of the Carthusians out at Clerkenwell. Uninhibited by any reverence for the past, he wrenched the monks' quarters into a modern-day mansion, complete with great hall and library, fit for a king – or a queen, for it was here that he entertained Henry's daughter Elizabeth on her way to her accession in 1558.[24] Another Henrician man on the make, Thomas Audley, took a different line with the Augustinian priory of Christchurch near Aldgate, founded by Queen Matilda in 1107. He contrived a series of poky little houses out of the chapels at the east end of the medieval church, where Elizabethan men and women went about their daily lives unperturbed by any monkish ghosts.[25]

Stone building was the province of the Master Masons, as timber framing was the sphere of the Master Carpenters.[26] But not many new stone buildings were erected in the Elizabethan era; indeed, it was sometimes hard, as Audley found, to unload stone on to the market, 'for all the buildings then made about the City were of brick and timber', according to Stow.

The Romans had used brick, Christopher Wren used brick. The Tudors loved its warmth and adaptability. It had, in addition, the practical merit of convenience. London has no local stone, but its clay makes excellent bricks on-site, with no transport costs. The best-known public building in London was the Royal Exchange, opened by the Queen in 1571. Sir Thomas Gresham, merchant extraordinary in the Netherlands, saw the massive potential of a Bourse or commercial exchange in London which should replace the Bourse in Amsterdam, attracting not only English merchants but traders from the continent and as far away as Russia. The City after careful consideration agreed. It even bent its rules and allowed him to use a Flemish architect and Flemish masons and labourers.

A site on Cornhill was compulsorily acquired, and the City donated 100,000 bricks. Stone for facings was imported. By May 1566 the site had been cleared, Sir Thomas laid the foundation stone, and construction began. The Flemings must have worked hard (perhaps the gold pieces left by every alderman, 'which the workmen took up', helped), for it was useable by December 1568.[27] It was a handsome building in the Renaissance taste, with an arcaded court-yard big enough for 4,000 merchants at a time, a tower where free concerts were given during the summer, and a gallery with 150 small shops where milliners and haberdashers sold essentials such as mousetraps, bird-cages, shoehorns and lanterns, armourers sold new and second-hand armour – always useful – and apothecaries, booksellers, goldsmiths and glass sellers catered for impulse buying.[28]

Survivals

Despite all this tumult of building and rebuilding, many old buildings survived. Detailed study of five parishes straddling the east end of Cheapside has traced the titles of many small houses, insignificant to anyone but a devoted researcher, back to the early thirteenth century.[29] The most noticeable survivals were the parish churches. London's 107 parishes can nearly all be traced back to 1200, some even to before the Norman Conquest.[30] The church of St Mary-le-Bow was founded in 1091.[31] Each parish had its church. Since some of the parishes were tiny – All Hallows Honey Lane covered only one acre – the churches were often within spitting distance of each other. Some of the more exotic names, such as St Lawrence Pountney and St Martin Outwich, commemorate the pious founders of those distant days, who provided not only a church but a priest to pray for their souls in it.[32]

Another category of ancient buildings was the halls of the Livery Companies, sometimes dating from the days of the twelfth-century craft guilds. They were scattered through the City, and were well known to, and used by, their members.

Then there were mansions that had escaped the rapacious de-velopers' eyes and slumbered on quietly. There was a house called the Heber or Eber (arbour?) in Dowgate, one of the narrow streets between Thames Street and the river, with two gardens, a vine and its own mooring for a private barge. Stow traced it back to Edward III's time. In 1584 it was rebuilt, and Sir Francis Drake lived there from 1588 to 1593.

Crosby Hall[33] had been built 'of stone and timber, very large and beautiful, and the highest at that time [1466] in London ... Richard Duke of Gloucester, and lord protector, afterward king by the name of Richard III was lodged in this house; since the which time Anthonie Bonvice, a rich merchant of Italy, dwelt there ... Divers ambassadors have been lodged there ... Sir John Spencer, alderman, lately [when Stow was writing, in 1598] purchased this house.'[34] He was one of the richest men in London.[35]

Goldsmiths' Row, which we looked at in the context of timber-frame construction, had been built in 1491 by Thomas Wood, a goldsmith. It was 'beautified towards the street with the Goldsmiths' arms and the likeness of woodmen, in memory of his name, riding on monstrous beasts, all which is cast in lead, richly painted over and gilt...this said front was again new painted and gilt over in the year 1594'.[36] It must have been a dazzling sight.

The Guildhall was begun in 1411. This was where the Lord Mayor and the aldermen settled the affairs of the City. Successive donors embellished its fittings and exterior, but for once Stow lets us down and does not describe its appearance. (Even now, after being burned and rebuilt twice and refurbished several times, it retains the general outline of a medieval building.)

There is still a market at Leadenhall, but the present buildings date from 1881. The original building was a fourteenth-century mansion with a lead roof – hence the name – built round a court-yard, which had been used to store and sell provisions for many years before the City acquired it in 1411 and formally established it as a market.

Baynards Castle, so called because it had been built near the site of a castle built by Baynard, who came over with William the Conqueror, had been rebuilt by Henry VII in 1428, by when, as Stow said, a house could be 'not ... strongly fortified and castle-like but far more beautiful and commodious'. It had been Henry VII's favourite London palace. Henry VIII gave it to Katherine of Aragon. By Elizabeth's time, the Earl of Pembroke lived there. Its walls rose forbiddingly – whatever Stow said – out of the river, unlike the mansions further upstream, which mostly had gardens sloping down to the bank.

The very names of these mansions are like an incantation of Tudor power – Leicester House, Arundel House, Somerset House, Russell House, Durham House. In the middle of them was the Savoy, another house with its feet in the river. In 1268 it had been given to a monastery in Savoy, which kept it for two years – just long enough to imprint the name still borne by the site – before Queen Eleanor bought it back. It suffered various indignities, such as being blown up by drunken pillagers by mistake, until Henry VII sensibly ordered that it should be rebuilt as a poorhouse, but it never seems to have functioned properly. Instead, the noble occupants of the surrounding mansions had to put up with constant disruption from the petty criminals and vagrants who squatted there.

To identify the river palaces can be confusing, since they tended to change their name depending on who was living there at the time. York House became part of Whitehall Palace, largely rebuilt by Henry VIII. It was handy for hunting in his new deer park round his country palace out at St James's. Probably for that reason, since they were both obsessed with hunting, both Henry and his daughter Elizabeth preferred it to the old palace of Westminster further up the river, first built by Edward the Confessor before the Conquest and mainly used by Henry VIII and his successors for administrative purposes.

Out in the country, Henry VIII had evicted the nuns caring for lepers in a hospital dedicated to St James, and built himself a red-brick hunting lodge on the site.

A last detail: none of the houses had street numbers. It was no good coming up from the country and looking for no. 100 the High Street. You would have to ask around, for the Rose or the Maidenhead, the Bull on the Hoop (not to be confused with the Black or any other kind of Bull), the White Leg, the Three Legs, the Unicorn, the Naked Boy, the Angel and Bartholomew or the Cow Face.[37] It would certainly help if you knew the right parish, where someone would be bound to recognise a description of your friends if it were catty enough. The name belonged to the site; it was not related to the trade, if any, carried on there.

CHAPTER 4

Interiors and Furniture

House moving

Did ordinary Londoners move house often? We move when our jobs are relocated or we go up or down in the world, or the cosy bachelor flat cannot accommodate a wife let alone a toddler. I suspect that the average Elizabethan Londoner with a tolerable living space did not move as often. Simon Forman moved from the inner city to the fresh air of Lambeth, in 1601 when his medical and astrological practice was prospering; 'for carriage of two loads of stuff 3s 4d'.[1]

A bride moving into her husband's family home on the death of his father was as likely then, as now, to want to imprint her own taste on her surroundings, but I suspect that her leverage was not as effective then, and she would have to live with his father's outmoded taste until she could find a reason for whitewashing it over and starting again. She may have moved into a new house. A newly-wed husband was likely to be a young man recently out of apprenticeship, earning a wage for the first time, as a journeyman. Stow was always complaining about the number of small houses going up all over London, so perhaps there was a steady market in what estate agents nowadays call 'first homes', where the décor could be new but basic.

Interior walls and wall coverings

The plaster used to fill in lathes or wattles was made of lime, sand and animal hair. It did not have the brilliant whiteness of modern plaster using gypsum. Over the intervening centuries some restorers have favoured the stark contrast between 'age-darkened' oak and pure white infilling, for both the interiors and the outsides of timber-frame houses. Such a pity. Oak left to itself ages gracefully to a pale silvery brown. Tudor plaster, uncoloured, was a light creamy beige.

But why stop at plain plaster, when with little cost you could transform your walls? Local earths could add shades of ochre or a warm pink, vegetable dyes a soft blue. If you were sure you would spend nothing more on the décor, this would be worth doing. But the next step up in the interior decorator's portfolio – to use modern terms – was wall paintings. Dismiss from your mind any unfortunate scrawls your children may lately have made on the immaculate magnolia. These could be elaborate, spectacular – and expensive. And, of course, they were there for good.

Wall paintings often had improving messages, either explicit or implied from the symbols so dear to the Elizabethans. There was a room in the Garter Inn in Windsor 'painted about with the story of the Prodigal, fresh and new'.[2] The story of the prodigal son was a favourite, maybe because it gave splendid opportunities for depicting luxury as well as poverty, and made a pleasant series of episodic panels. An all-over pattern of geometric shapes or imitation panelling might be relieved with horizontal texts or proverbs in black-letter script. These were not always so improving. Lord Clinton had a room in his London house painted with customs and costumes of the world, and one of Elizabeth's Secretaries of State, Sir Thomas Smith, had a room in his house in Essex all painted with mythological scenes in lovely soft colours of orange and turquoise on a grey background, which must have been stunning.[3]

Another permanent wall covering was patterned paper. Unsurprisingly, not much of this has survived, so it is difficult to say how much of it was used.[4] The few samples in the Victoria and Albert Museum are wood-block printed sheets with designs outlined in strapwork and enclosing heraldic or floral motifs, in one or at most two colours. About 15 inches by 9 inches was a normal size for each sheet. They could be butted together to make a complete design repeat. The paper was fairly thick, so that it could be stuck straight on to the plaster, with a paste of flour and water or a skim of plaster. To my eye the patterns look too bold and busy to be congenial in large expanses, but how can one judge the taste of four and a half centuries ago?

If the money would not run to wallpaper, how about the ballads and broadsheets that were for sale everywhere for practically nothing? An alehouse keeper could probably pick them up – literally – for nothing when his customers left them behind. Pasted on to the walls, they would not only cover the bare plaster but provide hours of free entertainment for customers, and give the literate ones a chance to show off to the others. At a higher social level, coloured prints of improving subjects could be bought for 4d for a set of six, and nailed or stuck to the wall.[5]

Painted cloths were a further possibility. It is tempting to think of them as cheap alternatives to tapestry, but this was not always the case. Bess of Hardwick, to whom money was no object, commissioned an astonishing set of painted cloths from her master painter John Balehouse, depicting biblical scenes in colourful detail. Sir Nicholas Bacon was a prominent figure in government. Of the nine main upstairs rooms in his London house, one was decorated with painted cloths.[6] The two ground-floor rooms of Simon Forman's house in the City were hung with 72 yards of painted cloth valued at 4d a yard. Alice Allen, who died in 1594, carefully distinguished in her will between 'a painted cloth', 'a new painted cloth' and 'three old painted cloths'. Even the old ones were worth leaving to a daughter, although they needed sweetening with 'a medley gown' as well.

Biblical subjects were popular, especially from the Old Testament, since the New Testament could cause raised eyebrows if the subject offended whatever religious tendencies were prevalent at the time. The prodigal son was always a popular subject,[7] as well as Susanna and the elders. (I cannot myself see much moral value in this tale of dirty old men, but I am looking at it with years of women's liberation behind me, and it did give an opportunity for tasteful scenes of female nudity which were permissible because they were in the Bible.) Most artists, with the exception of John Balehouse, painted their characters in the height of contemporary fashions, including ruffs, which cheers up some of the gloomier biblical stories no end. The detail in painted cloths could be astonishingly fine. It was used for dress fabrics as well; one of Queen Elizabeth's skirts was made of a rich textile covered with symbolic animals and fishes, all painted in minute detail. There must have been some technique for preventing the pigment from running, but I don't know what it was. If such elaboration was not to the taste of the customer, he could find simpler versions stencilled with small all-over designs, or painted to resemble expensive wood panelling.

One advantage of a painting on cloth rather than on the wall was that it could be taken away, bequeathed or sold, as long as it was clearly not permanently fixed to the wall, when it became a landlord's fixture.[8] The usual method of hanging was to hook the top of the cloth at short intervals on to a rail or possibly on to nails in the wall, which would just pass the 'tenant's fixture' test unless the landlord chose to be awkward. Another advantage was that if some character in it fell out of favour, he could always be scraped out.[9] In 1572 the Drapers' Company thought it politic to 'new-stain' the hangings in its parlour to delete 'divers blasphemies' – the pictures of the Blessed Virgin Mary, who had been the Company's patron saint before the Reformation. Ideas had changed, and hangings had to change too.

I have so far assumed that the cloth used was white, or undyed. Dyed fabric could also be patterned with a painted design, which could be done with a stencil. The Earl of Essex had 'a piece of hangings [*sic*] of red linsey wolsey, with borders and pillars painted'.[10] These hangings must have looked wonderfully warm, and stopped at least some of the draughts.

Gilt leather and embroidery

The peak of popularity for gilt leather came in the seventeenth century. In Elizabeth's London it was just entering the fashionable world. The Earl of Leicester had seven sets at his country mansion at Kenilworth in 1588, 'paned [in panels] gilt and blew' or 'gilt and black', telling the stories of Saul and the ubiquitous Susanna. The technique originated in Moorish Spain, and was brought to their Netherland possessions by the Spaniards. They used gold leaf to colour and shade swirling floriate designs, which still gleam from the walls of rich merchants' houses in Antwerp. By the time English decorators began to use it, the gold had given way to a varnish that gave the intaglio pattern embossed on each sheet of leather a convincing golden glow.[11] Leather was useful for rooms where food would be served because it does not retain smells as textiles do.

It would daunt most modern embroiderers to undertake the hangings for a whole bed, let alone a room, but the well-to-do

Elizabethan lady prided herself on her skill with the needle, and in any event she probably left the biggest pieces to be professionally embroidered. There was a fashion for embroidery called 'turkey-work', using the knotted technique of the Turkish and Persian carpets that were beginning to infiltrate the London market. The Countess of Bedford embroidered 'two window turkey carpets ... the one of them being wrought with roses and marigolds'. These were either draught excluders or cushions for window seats, or both.[12]

A convenient way of embroidering was to do separate small designs such as one flower or a heraldic device, and then appliqué them on to a hanging. Bess of Hardwick carried appliqué-work to its extreme. She was well placed to get her hands on the rich vestments of the outlawed Catholic Church. Although many of them were of unimaginable splendour, their shapes did not, maddeningly, lend themselves to interior decorating, so Bess had them cut up and incorporated in a series of hangings for Hardwick Hall. These are so magnificent that they pacify the incipient shudder at the thought of using such sumptuous textiles as a kind of domestic rag-bag.[13]

Tapestry

You may share my lack of enthusiasm for tapestries. It springs from the dreary shades of sludge which in general are all that are left from centuries of dust and ultraviolet light. Blue is a particularly fugitive dye, fading to grey. Red goes a pale shadow of pinky beige, green turns dirty olive, yellow has disappeared. There is in the British Galleries in the V. & A. a cushion cover that is mounted, by a stroke of genius, so that one can see the unfaded back, as well as the elegant, faded right side. The touches of red sing, blue is as bright as a gentian, yellow smiles like sunshine. And no matter how brilliant the museum display technique, one is seeing a tapestry motionless. In life, there was a space between the tapestry and the wall (creating an ideal hiding place for spies, lovers, etc.) and the hangings probably stirred in the draught, while the colours flickered in fire light and candle light. The most costly pieces glinted with gold and silver thread, pearls and precious stones.

William Sheldon, seeing the potential of the market monopolised by Flemish producers, opened his tapestry works in Barcheston, Warwickshire, in 1561, staffed by English weavers but still using continental designs. He did not, however, manage to break into the competition; the Mortlake factory was more successful, in the next century.

The restoring and renovating of tapestries is a highly skilled task. Even when they were newer, and needed cleaning, the cost was high. The Company of Merchant Taylors decided to have their arras (tapestry from Arras in Flanders) cleaned, in 1587. It cost them 7s a square Flemish 'olne' or ell, and there were 408 'olnes'. The cleaning cost more than £144, so the arras must have been worth it.[14]

There was a small second-hand market. Sir Christopher Hatton had nearly bankrupted himself hoping to attract Elizabeth to his great house at Holdenby. She never came. After his death his heir was glad to realise £321 6s for a set of huge tapestries that Bess of Hardwick bought for her New Hall. The asking price had been £5 9s 9d more, but Bess balked at Sir Christopher's arms incorporated in them, so she got the price reduced by the cost of having the arms rewoven – and then covered the offending arms with her own arms, painted on pieces of wool cloth.[15] Sir Christopher's heir can't have been alone in needing to find purchasers for valuable objects, but I have so far found no recognised middleman like Christie's or Sotheby's of our day. At the other end of the scale was that notice we saw in Chapter 3. Anyone who wanted to sell 'household stuff' could come to Leadenhall Market and try their luck.

Wood panelling

If a tenant did not plan to stay long in the house, he would not embark on 'wainscoting', because by the Custom of the City, which had the force of law, wood panelling became part of the wall, to which, necessarily, it was fixed, so the tenant's expense in installing it benefited the landlord. This was a fruitful subject of litigation, and prudent landlords might well include a provision in the lease expressly forbidding the tenant to remove the wainscot.[16] The previous taste had been for carved panels that showed off the craftsman's skill, such as the 'linen-fold' arrangement that looked like a neatly folded pile of cloth, and no doubt many such panels remained, in old houses. But new walls were more likely to be wainscoted with plain, framed, oblong or square panels, often from floor to ceiling. Seasoned oak was best, since it was less likely to shrink. Although its silvery grey was attractive, it was usually painted. The framework of the panels could be red, and the infilling painted with brilliant colours, silver and gold.

This was a splendid place to show off your armorial bearings, if you had any: failing that, the royal arms were decorative and demonstrated loyalty, or grotesques and nymphs proved your classical education. Sometimes the craftsman got a bit above himself and, working from prints of classical scenes, managed to produce only eight, or – worse – ten of the well-known Nine Worthies. The framework need not be rectangular. Fluted or carved pilasters and arcades could be bought ready-made, for pinning to the framework with wooden pegs. Rather sturdy caryatids could purport to hold up the ceiling, and strapwork could adorn every possible surface. The effect as a whole was certainly lively.[17]

Ceilings and floors

Here, colour gave way to white, but the surface could be just as eloquent of the plasterer's skill as anything a member of the Painter Stainers' Company could achieve on the walls. The surface to be covered was divided by ribs that interlaced and curved over the ceiling. Each rib was decorated, and every enclosed space contained a repeated pattern, or the portrait in relief of a biblical or mythical person, a flower or a heraldic motif. At intervals, where the ribs converged, a hanging pendant masked the junction and added to the visual confusion. These ceilings were demanding, especially in the long galleries typical of Elizabethan houses. One could not take in all their allegorical references in one quick look. A glance upwards should suffice to inspire classical or religious thought as one paced along, until the next glance. Better still, the immediate effect should impress the neighbours.

Sometimes this exuberant skill was extended to cover the top part of the wall, in a frieze. Again, this could look to the Bible or the classics. The position lent itself to charming processions of animals, with rather portly 'oliphants' and giraffes, ending in Noah's ark over the doorway.

Sometimes a builder could re-use the floor tiles of former monastic houses, glowing gently in ochres and reds. But the usual floor,

especially on the upper storeys, was wood, often covered with rushes
and sweet-smelling herbs. Woven matting was replacing loose rushes
by the end of the century. If you have visited an Elizabethan
National Trust house early in the season, you will have noticed two
pleasant aspects of the rush matting faithfully reproduced by the
Trust. New rushes have a lovely smell, and they are quiet and
comfortable to walk on.

At a grand christening in the summer of 1561, the floor of the
church was 'strewed with green rushes and ... herbs', which must
have scented the whole church and perhaps reminded some people
of the old days, when the smell would have come from incense. At
a very grand occasion indeed, the 1562 procession of the Garter
Knights at Windsor, the Queen's chapel was 'strewed with green
rushes'.[18] The hall of Gray's Inn was floored with rushes in readiness
for a particular feast in 1570: cost, 1s 2d.[19] The floor of Lord North's
great chamber was covered with 'twelve score [240] yards of matts'
in 1575.[20] It is surprising to find them still on the floor when it is to
be used for dancing – 'let wantons tickle the senseless rushes with
their heels'[21] – but I suppose you got used to bits of rush in your
dancing shoes.

Thomas Tusser advised:

> While wormwood hath seed, get a handful or twain
> To save against March, to make flea to refrain.
> Where chamber is sweeped, and wormwood is strewn
> No flea for his life dare abide to be known.[22]

A little earlier, Erasmus had been very rude about the horrors,
including fleas, that lurked in unchanged rushes, but as far as one
can tell fresh rushes were as much part of good housekeeping for an
Elizabethan woman as vacuuming the carpet is for us.

Furniture

Perhaps the most surprising thing about Elizabethan furniture is
how little there was of it then. The next surprise is how much there
is of it now. English oak was the usual wood, although imported
'walnut tree' and other exotics were coming in. The trade in
antiques has long recognised that 'Tudor Oak' is a valuable cachet
on a price tag, so it is not uncommon, even in museums (with the

notable exception of the V. & A.), to find a piece looking every inch Elizabethan, contrived out of a later piece, possibly with genuine sixteenth-century bits where they showed, especially if the later piece was too massive to be easily saleable as it stood.[23]

But to revert to the first surprise; it is easier to understand this if you remember that serious amounts could be spent on textiles and wall coverings to give rooms a comfortable or even a luxurious atmosphere, in which the furniture played a minor role. Bess of Hardwick spent between £5,000 and £6,000 on building Hardwick Hall, and considerably more on the textiles with which she adorned it.[24] Her expenditure on furniture was minor, in comparison. Of course, she was not typical – she was too rich, and too determined. But it is a justifiable conclusion, I think, that the upwardly mobile house-owner was more likely to think first in terms of wall coverings, bed curtains and other textiles than of hard furniture. Anyway, he may have inherited some pieces from his family and they lasted for many years.

For the rich, inventories of their possessions when they died listed everything of any value. These can be fascinating, not least because so many rich Elizabethans seem to have been unable to throw anything away. Robert Dudley, Earl of Leicester, Queen Elizabeth's beloved, died in 1588. His goods were valued at about £8,000, including his magnificent clothes, and armour worth £436. But on their rounds of his magnificent mansions the assessors so often noted things that were 'very old' or 'past service'.[25]

Rooms were gradually acquiring specific uses. The medieval great hall was superseded by a dining chamber for the owner and his family and friends. It was furnished with a table, probably having leaves that pulled out to extend it ('a draw table'), replacing the medieval board on trestles. Exotic woods such as imported timber were coming into the top end of the trade towards the end of the century. In 1581 Richard Stoneley, a comfortably off civil servant, spent 60s on a 'fine table of walnut tree with gymotts' (sic: the nearest I can find to gymotts is 'guilloche', that familiar decoration resembling two twisted cords).[26]

There would be at least one chair with arms and a back, stools and benches. The stools were stored under the table, on its stretchers, their seats facing outwards.[27] In the inventory of the Earl of Leicester's belongings is a poignant entry: 'a little chair for a child, of carnation [red] and green cloth and tinsel, and a cradle'.[28]

In 1589 the youngest Warden of the Carpenters' Company donated – possibly nagged by his wife, fed up with sitting uncomfortably at company feasts – 'a little chair of wainscot [wood panelled] with a back for a woman to sit thereon, with letters for his wife's name'.[29] But mainly chairs were upright, hard and uncomfortable, softened with separate cushions.

In a grand house there would be a separate room for servants and visitors who did not rank high enough to eat with the master. The tables in those rooms would look much like the table in the master's dining chamber, but the seating was only benches or stools.

Cupboards were important pieces of furniture, but the word has radically changed its meaning. A cup board (originally two words) was a board or wooden shelf, or set of shelves, on which to display the household's collection of silver cups and other valuables. If the household did not run to much silver, pewter was equally well displayed on it. There were two, three or more shelves, and sometimes doors enclosing part of them for greater security. The cupboard took a prominent position in any room – so much so that when a member of Gray's Inn misbehaved himself, he was summoned to 'come and appear at the cupboard in the hall' to hear what punishment the Benchers had inflicted on him.[30] The hall was where the Inn's corporate life was carried on, and the cupboard displaying the Inn's impressive collection of silver symbolised its power over its members. It was not the kind of hidey-hole for mops and pails that one first thinks of. In 1559 'my Lord of Arundel gave to the Queen's grace a cupboard of plate',[31] and he would not have given her anything that was not splendid.

A well-furnished dining chamber would contain a buffet, similar to the cupboard, but with a different purpose. The drinking habits of the time involved the guest calling for a drink every time he felt dry. He was brought wine or beer in a clean – at least, rinsed – glass or drinking vessel, from this buffet. When he had swallowed his drink the glass went back to the buffet. In the best households there was a big copper tub of cold water, to cool the wine in, and another wooden tub of water – also cold, presumably, at least by the end of the meal – for rinsing the glasses etc. At least the washing-up was done as the dinner went along, but this does not sound a good way to get the glasses clean, especially if the women guests were wearing the equivalent of lipstick.

There were other cupboards in various living rooms, known as 'presses', 'court cupboards', 'livery cupboards' or 'aumbries', all terms dear to the antique trade. Obviously one had to have somewhere to hang one's clothes, and a 'press'[32] would accommodate them. Sometimes it would include a drawer. A court (from the French *court* = short) cupboard was not as tall as a press. A Iivery cupboard began life as a medieval store cupboard for your 'livery': that is, the food part of the wages in kind which your master or employer paid you, consisting of food and clothes – hence the modern meaning of the word, which has dropped the food side altogether. By the sixteenth century it was still a food cupboard, but had lost its function as an individual's store cupboard in which to keep enough food to keep him going during the night.[33] Its distinguishing mark was the ventilation holes in its doors, incorporated in the design, and – one supposes – too small for mice to get in. An aumbry seems to have been a general name for cupboards.[34] Hall and parlour cupboards often had three tiers, like the display shelves, but with part enclosed by doors, and a drawer in the frieze. In addition, chests of varying degrees of elaboration were scattered through the house, providing something to sit on as well as somewhere to store things.

One item of furniture is remarkable for its absence from museums and antique shops – the counting board or counter. This was not the surface on which a merchant displayed his cloth etc., which was called a ware-bench. It was a table on which he did his counting or reckoning. Anyone who was likely to have to deal with figures would have one, and the more prosperous he was, the more counters he was likely to have around the house and trading premises. The surface was usually marked with parallel lines on which 'jettons' (small disks) were laid, representing the sums the operator was dealing with. Once the function of such counting boards was over, it would be easy to plane away the lines. A delightful, small, convenient 'Tudor table' emerged.[35]

Beds were substantial. The Great Bed of Ware, now resplendent in the British Galleries in the V. & A. Museum, is not a typical example. Its vast size was celebrated even in Shakespeare's day.[36] But it will serve as an exemplar of how normal beds were constructed. The framework was, of course, oak. The four corner posts were joined together at the base and the top. There was a head board at the pillow end, carved or covered with textile. The corner posts of the Great Bed of Ware were carved with rather massive figures, and each of them incorporated a natty little bedside table – there was plenty of room for them in the grand scheme. The posts of more normal beds were not quite so hefty, their lines often softened with a baluster curve.

The floor of the base was criss-crossed with rope threaded through holes in the timbers, interlaced from side to side and end to end. That would give a slight degree of spring, and could be easily mended if it succumbed to the weight of however many occupants the Great Bed of Ware held – seven? eight? On top of the rope, a mat woven of rushes, to keep the dust from rising (or falling?), and perhaps help to spread the load of the mattresses and occupants. Then there were at least two mattresses (called, confusingly, 'beds') of canvas stuffed with wool or straw. Then you get to the sleeping surface, another mattress, perhaps stuffed with feathers or down. When Mary Queen of Scots was being moved to Tutbury in 1585, she requested three or four *hundredweight* of feathers, 'to amend old and thin beds and bolsters, etc.'[37] The sheets were linen, the blankets wool; the coverlet could be elaborate.

Round the top of the framework were beams to which were attached rails carrying floor-length curtains. The beams themselves, like the sides of the base, were covered by valances. All the visible wood could be carved, and all the hangings could be elaborate, either made of rich materials, or covered with embroidery, or both. The roof of the top framework, the 'tester', was covered with fabric. There were opportunities for display at every visible stage.

The Earl of Bedford had 'a large bedstead carved and gilded' with a 'quilt of crimson damask laid lozenge wise with gold twist embroidered with a border wrought with cloth of gold and fringed with gold'. The tester was embroidered with Henry VIII's arms, matching valances fringed with gold or red silk, and three long curtains of red damask edged with gold fringe. The whole lot was valued in 1585, when the Earl died, at over £36. It had belonged to Henry VIII, as had the Earl's 'best bed of cloth of gold and silver with King Henry VIII's arms in it'.[38] It is amazing how objects have this power of migrating, and lasting. The Earl's second wife left her two grandsons various travelling beds called sparvers – perhaps she thought they would enjoy being able to pack and leave fast when it suited them – and a 'trusse bedstead' (another kind of travelling bed) 'carved and gilt, a testern [canopy] of cloth of gold paned with white and yellow silk, with curtains of white and yellow sarcenet [a light silk]'. And this was travelling light ...

Once all surfaces had been decorated, the tester could be crowned with feathers. Elizabeth's household accounts for 1595 include an entry 'for dyeing and washing of seven plumes of fine feathers containing three score feathers with twelve fine feathers and three dozen and six tops of egrets feathers to perform the said seven plumes for one bedstead'.[39]

The curtains round a bed meant that the occupants could be sheltered from draughts, and curious eyes, but it was not regarded as normal to sleep alone in a room, even if the only other occupant was your servant in the 'trundle' or 'truckle' bed pulled out from under the great bed. Bed curtains were so taken for granted that even the beds for some of the poor patients of St Bartholomew's Hospital had curtains.[40]

A useful item of bedroom furniture was a close stool, the fore-runner of commodes and chaises perçées and thunder-boxes, only more comfortable, as long as you were not unduly worried about hygiene. In 1565 Elizabeth commissioned 'four close stools covered with black velvet embroidered upon and garnished with ribbon and gilt nails, the seats and laythes [?] covered with scarlet [a fine wool cloth, not necessarily red] fringed with silk and gold, and four pans of pewter'. They had 'cases of leather lined with canvas to put them in', so they may have been for use on her famous progresses.[41] On a humbler level, Richard Stoneley spent 4s on having one mended, and buying a new pan for it.[42] A close stool did not, apparently, do away with a chamber pot: an anxious housekeeper, supervising the maidservant's preparation for her mistress's 'going to bed', says, 'See that the chamber-pot be under the bed, is the close-stoole's bason clean? Put clean water in it.'[43]

A young courtier, John Harington, invented the forerunner of the flushing water closet in 1596, and described it in his *New Discourse of a Stale Subject, called the Metamorphosis of Ajax.* (This was a witty title at the time, since stale meant urine, and privies were known as jakes.)

> It doth avoid at once all the annoyances that can be imagined: the sight, the savour, the cold, which last, to weak bodies, is oft more hurtful than both the other, where the house [of easement: outside privy] stand over brooks ... if it be ... rinsed with water as oft as occasion serves ... you will keep your privy as sweet as your parlour, and perhaps sweeter ...

His book included detailed instruction on how to make one, with diagrams that make clear where the water is to be stored, because there are fishes swimming in it. But he was ahead of his time, and although Elizabeth, his godmother, had one installed in her palace at Richmond, the idea lapsed, and people stayed with what they knew: that is, close stools for the delicate, and privies or a pot emptied out of the window for the others.

Cradles were made with rockers underneath, two knobs at the end for the nurse to maintain the rocking motion, and some sort of canopy to keep the draughts away. Day beds were a fashionable innovation brought to England by the Italian craftsmen who were fitting out Henry VIII's palaces.[44] I found them twice in Shakespeare, once where Richard III is commendably not 'lolling on a lewd day-bed', and again where Olivia is sleeping on one.[45] They don't look particularly comfortable: a flat, hard surface with two sloping ends, but they would be well padded with cushions, and were more graceful to recline on for a short nap than the cumbersome beds.

A bedchamber was the place for a mirror. Confusingly, they were called 'glasses' but were usually made of polished steel, not glass. The magnificent furnishings of Leicester House included, in 1588, 'three great glasses', of which one was steel, the other two crystal.

The hard seats of chairs and stools may have been ameliorated slightly by Elizabethan clothes, but in practice their flat surfaces were softened with cushions, which were an art form in themselves. They could be as big as bean-bags, or small and exquisite. They could be soft enough for indolent lounging, or rigid enough to be laid along the window frame to stop the draughts. They were, either way, just the right size for embroidery, sometimes so alarmingly scattered with precious metals and jewellery that one lowered oneself on to them with trepidation. In the picture of Queen Elizabeth receiving ambassadors, she is standing, but three of her ladies are – surprisingly, in the presence of their monarch – reclining on the floor, apparently on big, puffy cushions. When Elizabeth felt the approach of death but refused to go to bed, she lay on such cushions, on the floor. The accounts of the livery companies often show purchases of cushions. The Cutlers' Company bought many 'quishons with oliphants', elephants being part of its coat of arms.[46]

William Harrison took cupboards, and what was on them, as one indication of the owner's status:

Noblemen's houses [have] abundance of arras, rich hangings of tapestry, silver vessel [*sic*] and so much other plate as may furnish sundry cupboards – one thousand or two thousand pounds at least. Knights, gentlemen, merchants and other wealthy citizens [have] great provision of tapestries, turkey work, pewter, brass, fine linen and costly cupboards ... of plate worth five to six hundred or a thousand pounds ... Inferior artificers ... have learned also to garnish their cupboards with plate, their ... beds with tapestry and silk hangings and their tables with carpets and fine napery ...[47]

Carpets were still treated as decorative coverings for tables or the shelves of cupboards. The size of the tables, however, made these carpets rather larger than the average modern tablecloth. The Cutlers' Company had a 'carpet for the high table [patterned] with flowers, seven yards long and one and a half yards broad'.[48] Some fashionables were putting the carpet on the floor. Lord Leicester's goods included 'a long foot turquoy [turkey] carpet', and there was another 'foot carpet' in the chapel closet.

Table linen was another new way of spending money, especially for livery companies. The Carpenters lashed out on 'table cloths for the High Table and the parlour and two dozen wrought [embroidered] napkins and three coarse table cloths for the Hall', in 1564, and then made a great fuss six years later about buying 'four dozen napkins, to be issued to any liveryman [the higher-ranking members] eating, and then collected, washed and kept'.[49]

Sir Thomas Ramsay had 26 dozen damask napkins, when he was Lord Mayor in 1577. He had to do a lot of entertaining, so 312 napkins were only just enough. The Earl of Bedford's table linen, listed after his death in 1585, included 'two long damask tablecloths ... in length 8¾ yards, in breadth 3 yards', which throws light on the size of the tables in use in his household. Three yards seems to have been an average width for tablecloths in grand houses. If you reckon that the table top cannot have been more than three feet, at most, from the floor, and if the tablecloth came down to the floor on both sides, that still leaves a yard of linen to go across the top. In the Bedford establishment there were also damask 'towels' seven yards long and three-quarters of a yard wide, which presumably were used by the guests as they washed their hands before and after the meal.

Silver

Staying in the Bedford establishment for the moment, there were two silver basins and two silver ewers with covers, in the 'ewery' – where the diners washed their hands – valued at over £60. Most of the silver was in the dining room. This was the kind of collection that would grace a cupboard, in normal circumstances, and it must have made a magnificent show. I can pause at only a fraction of the list, just enough to give you, I hope, an impression of the whole. There were 30 silver dishes, 24 gilt plates and 28 silver plates. Bowls came in 'nests' or sets of six, one nest being valued at £86. There were five 'great plates' and two 'chargers' – large flat dishes, weighing 117 ounces each – five 'cups for sack with covers' valued at over £49, and seventeen knives. There were forks – but only two, silver and parcel gilt (with a pattern of gold), for serving food – the use of forks generally, for eating, was just dawning. There were eighteen candlesticks, silver and parcel gilt. There were three silver gilt 'salts', six silver ones, and 'one gilt trencher salt with a cover.' (These elaborate salt cellars were placed on the table to mark the boundary between people whose status entitled them to sit 'above the salt', nearer to the host, and the lowlier people who sat 'below the salt'.) Imagine the light of candles flickering on the gorgeous dresses and jewels, and the display of silver on the table and on the cupboard, at a formal dinner.

Seeing these glorious displays in one's mind's eye, the thought comes – how did they clean all that silver?[50] I have been unable to find a definitive answer. One authority I consulted was Isabella Beeton's *Book of Household Management*, first published in 1861, some three hundred years after the period I was looking for. Her book states that it was part of the footman's duties to wash in clean hot water 'all plate and plated articles which are greasy, wiping them before cleaning with the brush'. If, astonishingly, you have no footman, the duty devolves on the housemaid. She has to

> wash the plate well to remove all grease, in a strong lather of common yellow soap and boiling water, and wipe it quite dry; then mix as much hartshorn powder as will be required, into a thick paste, with cold water or spirits of wine [methylated spirit]. Smear this lightly over the plate with a piece of soft rag [she recommends the tops of old cotton stockings] and leave it for some little time to dry.

When perfectly dry, brush it off quite clean with a soft plate-brush, and polish the plate with a dry leather.

Hartshorn was used as a household remedy in the sixteenth century (the powder from a stag's antlers was a source of ammonia), so it could presumably be bought at the apothecary's. Perhaps the Elizabethans, too, used something on these lines.

CHAPTER 5

Gardens and Open Spaces

There are no Elizabethan gardens left to see. There are well-researched modern reconstructions, such as the one at Hatfield House. There are maps and plans that happen to include gardens, and pictures that show glimpses of the kind of garden the painter, or the sitter, thought suitable to fill in the background. Writers of the time described their actual or ideal gardens, but they often had a particular hobbyhorse such as medicinal plants, or grand designs suitable for a more extensive property than the average London plot. Take Francis Bacon, for instance. He wrote an essay on gardens, which begins well: 'God Almighty first planted a garden. And indeed it is the purest of human pleasures. It is the greatest refreshment to the spirits of man; without which, buildings and palaces are but gross handyworks.' But he thought in terms of 'princely' gardens of thirty acres or more, so his advice is not always useful.

Garden design

The archetypal Elizabethan garden is usually imagined as a knot garden. Bacon did not think much of them: 'As for the making of knots and figures with divers-coloured earths, that they may lie under the windows of the house on that side which the garden stands, they be but toys: you may see as good sights many times in tarts.' But there was a lot to be said for knot gardens. They were equally pleasing – or dull – summer and winter, rain or drought. Their elaborate design could pay graceful compliments to the owner's pedigree, in that age of symbols. And once 'set', which could be expensive, they only needed a tidy-up from time to time, to trim and replace where needed, and pick out dead leaves in the autumn. As usual, pictures show them in pristine condition, but have you seen the mess a couple of blackbirds can make, scattering sand while they look for worms? The 'divers-coloured earths' might be replaced by low-growing foliage plants, which could have aromatic leaves. Box was often used for the outlines of the knot, but it does tend to die back in patches. The silvery leaves of sea lavender or artemisia might be better, either instead, or combined with the dark box to imitate an intricate interlaced pattern of two differently coloured cords. Bacon may have thought them vulgar, but they were popular if you had the space and the money. They could still be seen in a view of Arundell House, as late as 1658.[1]

The alternative to knots, and perhaps more popular, was to have rectangular beds, usually arranged in a garden plot symmetrically divided by paths. One expects these beds to be symmetrical too, but they were often fitted into a square by some of them being L-shaped and some shorter, or longer; a muddled layout to us, but it pleased the makers. No bed was more than three feet wide, so that a weeder could comfortably reach across it without stepping on the earth. The beds were usually raised, the soil being held by boards or low mini-fences of woven osiers or twigs. These needed periodic renewal, hence the charges in gardening accounts for 'great osiers at 13d the 100'.[2] There were sometimes low railings as well. A contemporary picture of a garden design shows a rail at about knee level, dividing rectangular beds from a broad walk, with fruit trees trained on the brick walls of the garden.

Where the paths met in the middle of the garden would be the obvious place for a fountain. They could be a cake-stand shape or a nymph-clutching-a-vase type, but either way they imply that not only water but also enough water pressure, or some kind of power – a small boy behind the scenes, when needed? – was available. Bacon strongly advised against still pools; they 'mar all, and make the garden unwholesome and full of flies and frogs', and he was probably right.

You can appreciate a formally planned garden, especially a knot garden, best from a high viewpoint. This could be the parlour window, if the garden did 'lie under the windows of the house'. Or you could build your own viewing platform, on a 'mount'. Bacon was very keen on mounts 'with three ascents, and alleys, enough for four to walk abreast ... and the whole mount to be thirty foot high; and some fine banqueting house, with some chimneys neatly cast, and without too much glass'. It is fair to Bacon to explain that in his day a 'banqueting house' could be just a place to enjoy sweetmeats and a glass of wine in the garden after dinner, although it could be grander, like the temporary banqueting house 'made with fir poles and decked with birch and all manner of flowers' which was put up in Greenwich Park for a tournament, in 1559.[3] His 30-foot high mount was definitely for country mansions with extensive gardens, but the idea could be used in London, and indeed Bacon installed a mount in the garden of Gray's Inn, and Lincoln's Inn built one in 1593.[4]

If you were, or pretended to be, a classical scholar, you could design your mount as an allegorical ascent of man from birth towards heaven, and so on. But if you just wanted to show off your garden to your friends, it need not be so elaborate, and a seat or two at the top would do, with a table for your glasses. If you could not face the earth-moving involved in building a mount, you could have some sort of building in the garden itself – a long raised gallery, like the galleries in country houses of the time, open on the garden side but otherwise roofed and walled, and sometimes even having its own fireplace – but by now we are nearly into Bacon's 'princely' gardens.[5]

Several more features remain to be crammed into our ideal garden if possible, before we can begin to plant it. There should be paths 'finely gravelled and no grass, because of going wet'.[6] 'Callis' (Calais) sea sand was best, or river sand. If you did opt for grass, it had to be scythed, which could rarely produce the billiard-table smoothness of nowadays. There should be shaded walks, which 'the wealthy make like galleries, being all open towards the garden and covered with the vine spreading over'. Vines were much less labour-intensive than roses, so most people planted them 'for the lesser travail'. As well, or instead, the owner might have arbours made of willow or ash poles, willow needing renewal every three years but ash only every ten.[7]

In a contemporary illustration, two men are carefully tying in climbing roses, over an arbour with a table in the middle and seats round the sides. Whether the owner opted for a round arbour or a straight walk, he could go there to check the progress of his plants, and 'for the delight and comfort of his wearied mind', by himself or with his friends.[8] When he had bored his friends long enough – garden enthusiasm does not change – they could move to the bowling alley.

Another contemporary illustration seems to show a bowling place in the corner of the garden. This time the labour costs of the rosy arbour have been heeded, and vines cover the top, and the end and the side set against the garden walls, leaving open the other end and one long side facing the garden. There is a board, like the gravel board at the foot of a fence, round the enclosure, perhaps six inches high, with a lower section in the middle of the garden side, and on the ground, carefully drawn – shading and all – four round balls.[9] The whole thing is only slightly longer than it is wide, so that it looks more like somewhere you would play pétanque or boules than a bowling alley the shape of a modern skittle alley, which can often be found in Treswell's *Surveys*.[10] The same book shows another corner of the garden set aside for beehives, and enormous bees are zooming in like helicopter gunships. There are also large pots of flowering plants supported by bent hoops of wood or osier, just like the ones for sale in garden shops nowadays (see plate 25).

A maze was another fashionable feature, rather like a knot garden in its elaboration – and dullness.

There were some surprisingly large gardens, even in the middle of the city. They could be tucked away behind the frontage of small houses that gave little hint of their existence to the passer-by. A prime example was Sir Edward Darcy's house off Billiter Lane.[11] He had a plot 70 feet by 101 feet planted with trees, with a tall fountain in the middle of it, and another plot marked 'garden' in the plan, nearly as big, with its own brick-built tower or viewing platform, with, no doubt, room for some chairs and a table at the top. Quite often access to the garden was complicated, topographically or even legally. A man who died in 1558 left his house and garden to his son, but his widow could use the garden during her lifetime: a potentially irritating situation, especially if the son was married.[12] Another man who died in 1583 directed in his will that his widow could use the garden of another property he owned some way away, to dry her washing.[13] Imagine trailing through the streets with a basketful of wet washing, and then arriving in someone else's garden, without warning, to hang it out.

But sometimes it was pleasant to leave inner London for a garden in the suburbs outside the walls, rather like the little dacha plots outside Moscow. The invaluable Stubbes disapproved of them:

> In the fields and suburbs of the cities they have gardens either paled
> [fenced] or walled about very high ... and lest they might be espied
> in these open places they have their Banqueting houses with galleries
> [and] turrets ... wherein they may, and doubtless do, many of them
> play the filthy persons ... their gardens are locked and some of them
> have three or four keys a piece whereof one they keep for themselves,
> the others their Paramours have ... then to these gardens they repair
> with a basket and a boy, where they, meeting their sweethearts,
> receive their wished desires.[14]

Well, you could not expect the lady to carry her own picnic basket,
could you?[15] But one wonders how Stubbes managed to see all that
over the high brick walls.

A contemporary map (see plate 17) shows an intriguing property
between Moorfields and Bishopsgate Street, called *Giardin* [*sic*] *di
Pietro*. You went in by a secluded gate in a lane between the street and
the open space of Moor Fields. There was a tree-shaded bank at one
end, bordered by a stream, and more trees on another side, and those
familiar rectangular plots of flowers. Who was Pietro? His is the only
name on the map. Could he have opened the first Italian *ristorante*,
with tables outside under the trees for hot summer evenings? Not far
away, there was just the kind of area that so maddened Stubbes,
along Goswell Street: 'small tenements, cottages, alleys, *gardens,
banqueting houses* and bowling places', where no doubt some of the
citizenry got up to no good.[16]

Further out of London there were 'many fair and comely
buildings especially of the merchants of London who have planted
their houses of recreation ... environed with orchards [and] gardens
with delectable walks, alleys and great variety of pleasing dainties':
the first appearance of the two-home syndrome?[17]

Water is always a problem in gardens. In the ideal world, there
would be just the right amount of rain, falling during the night, or
an obliging spring that could be trained to flow in neat irrigation
ditches through your garden, as Thomas Hill showed in his *Gardener's
Labyrinth*. In the real world of sixteenth-century London, those
developers who had managed to get their hands on former monastic
properties were probably in the best position because the monks had
usually had piped water laid on. The Carthusian monks at the
Charterhouse had cultivated their garden until 1538, when it fell

S. Paules Church

THAMESIS

The Beare Gardne   The Globe

1. (ABOVE) Part of *View of the River Thames* by Jan Visscher, 1616. The spire of St Paul's Cathedral was destroyed by lightning in 1561, and had not been rebuilt by the time of the Great Fire in 1666. The multi-storey building on the left of the picture, on the river bank, was Baynard's Castle. The sailing barges with square sails carried produce to London from the counties upriver. The small passenger boats, or wherries, were rowed by one man, sometimes two (see page 14).

2. (RIGHT) Detail of the south bank: there is a queue waiting to get into the Globe playhouse.

The Globe

3. Detail from *The Feast at Bermondsey* by Hoefnagel, c. 1570. Bermondsey was a semi-rural village on the south bank of the river, opposite the Tower of London. There is a small boat-building yard on the river bank, to the right of the central tree.

4. Another detail from *The Feast at Bermondsey*: a woman in a pink skirt is riding pillion, in front of her a woman in a long black skirt is riding side-saddle. In front of her the man in pink trunk hose looks more comfortable, astride. The foremost rider has a hawk on his arm. In the foreground are two children, dressed as miniature adults. Beside them, a serving man carries his shield on his back, slung from the sword over his shoulder.

5. A sketch by a foreign visitor, 1614, of London Bridge, with three passengers being rowed across the river by two oarsmen in a wherry. The woman looks very uncomfortable, in her stiff clothes. At the south end of the bridge, on the left of the picture, you can just make out (over the second arch) a number of posts on top of the building, with blobs on the ends; these were the heads of traitors (see page 22).

6. Another sketch by a foreign visitor – a rare record of the clothes worn by ordinary working men such as carters and porters.

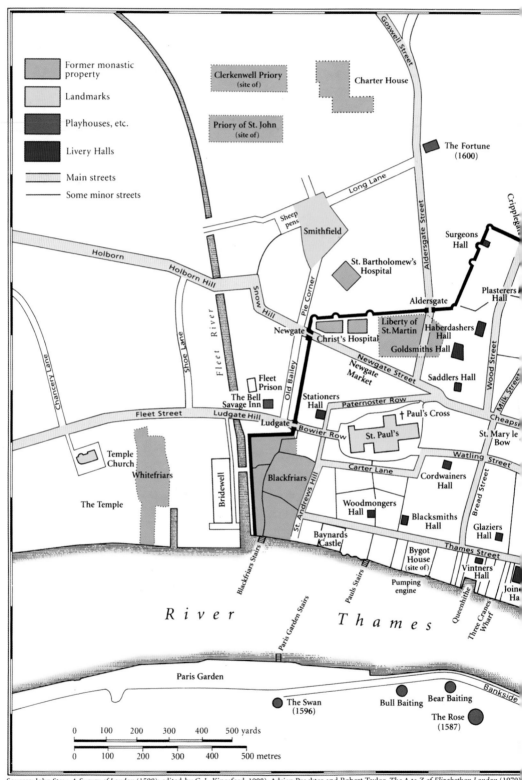

Former monastic property

Landmarks

Playhouses, etc.

Livery Halls

Main streets

Some minor streets

Goswell Street

Clerkenwell Priory (site of)

Charter House

Priory of St. John (site of)

The Fortune (1600)

Long Lane

Cripplega

Sheep pens

Smithfield

Aldersgate Street

Surgeons Hall

Holborn

Holborn Hill

St. Bartholomew's Hospital

Plasterers Hall

Pie Corner

Aldersgate

Snow Hill

Newgate

Christ's Hospital

Liberty of St. Martin

Haberdashers Hall

Shoe Lane

Fleet River

Newgate Street

Goldsmiths Hall

Wood Street

Milk Street

Chancery Lane

Old Bailey

Newgate Market

Saddlers Hall

Fleet Prison

The Bell Savage Inn

Stationers Hall

Paternoster Row

Paul's Cross

Cheapside

Fleet Street

Ludgate Hill

Ludgate

Bowier Row

St. Paul's

St. Mary le Bow

Temple Church

Whitefriars

Bridewell

Blackfriars

Carter Lane

Watling Street

Cordwainers Hall

Bread Street

The Temple

St. Andrews Hill

Woodmongers Hall

Blacksmiths Hall

Glaziers Hall

Baynards Castle

Bygot House (site of)

Thames Street

Vintners Hall

Pumping engine

Queenhithe

Three Cranes Wharf

Joine Ha

Blackfriars Stairs

Paris Garden Stairs

Pauls Stairs

River

Thames

Paris Garden

Bankside

The Swan (1596)

Bull Baiting

Bear Baiting

The Rose (1587)

0   100   200   300   400   500 yards

0   100   200   300   400   500 metres

Sources: John Stow, *A Survey of London* (1598); edited by C. L. Kingsford, 1908), Adrian Prockter and Robert Taylor, *The A to Z of Elizabethan London* (1979) and Andrew Gurr, *The Shakespearian Stage, 1574-1642* (1980). John Gilkes delineavit 2003.

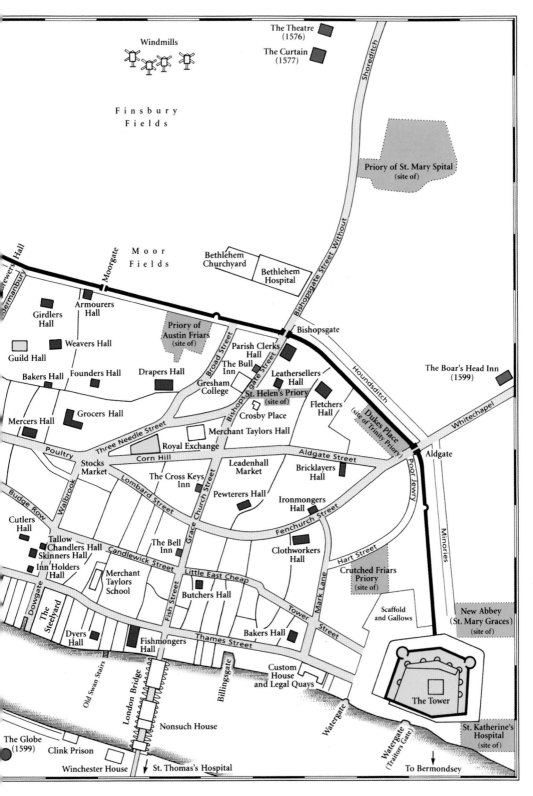

7. Map showing the playhouses and the inns where plays were performed, the animal-baiting rings, most of the livery companies' halls and the sites of the medieval monasteries.

8. (ABOVE) The Lord Mayor, wearing his gold chain of office and preceded by his Sword Bearer. No Londoner could fail to notice this all-powerful pair.

9. (LEFT) This house in Crutched Friars was built some time in the 1560s, and lasted unchanged for nearly two centuries save for some ground-floor replacement windows.

10. Lord Burghley presiding over the Court of Wards and Liveries, a department of the Exchequer. The wardship of rich minors, which belonged to the Crown, could be bought from this Court. Burghley is said to have made over £3,000 out of applications for wardships. Note the spectacles held by the man on Burghley's left, and the miscellaneous headgear.

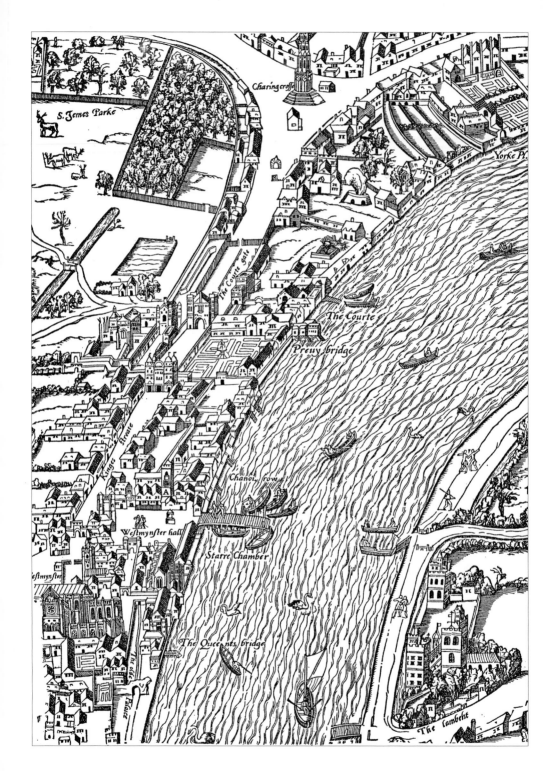

11. Part of a map of London in 1562 by Ralph Agas, showing Westminster. The Abbey is at the bottom left corner, facing Lambeth across the river. Westminster Hall, which still survives, is the long block along the river bank. The 'Preuy bridge' (private landing-stage) gave onto the newer Palace of Whitehall. To the left of the Court Gate is an elongated S-shaped wall; this is the tilting ground used for tournaments. Beyond is St James's Park, well stocked with deer.

into Henry VIII's hands. Ninety-one trees were uprooted and taken away, let alone shrubs.[18] It had drawn its own water supply from the hills of Islington since 1430, and the monks surely arranged an adequate supply for their garden, but I do not know whether the pressure would have been strong enough for a fountain when Lord North took it over.

The Inns of Court

Gray's Inn was fortunate in having Francis Bacon on its governing body as a Bencher. Before he replanned them in 1598–1600, the gardens, known as the Walks, were laid out in long straight beds,[19] with nearly 100 elm trees.[20] So they must have been transformed by the £60 6s 8d spent on a mount and 71 more elms – which must have been very crowded unless some of them had died since they were counted in 1583 – 8 birch trees and 16 cherry trees, let alone 1,600 woodbines and 3,000 eglantines and quantities of pinks and violets and vines. The banqueting house on the top of the mount was topped by a griffin, which the Inn had recently adopted as its emblem.[21] The Temple famously had white and red roses in its garden, chosen, according to tradition, by each side as its logo in the Wars of the Roses.[22] In 1601 there were wide paths and banks there, with knots and beds of fragrant flowers.

The green space surrounding Lincoln's Inn Hall was planted with elm trees,[23] with 'fair walks' under them.[24] The Master of the Walks had a mount built in 1593, five years ahead of Gray's Inn. Apart from the elm trees being planted, cut down and chopped up for firewood or to heat the brick kiln in the grounds, I could find no horticultural detail in the Inn's records so far as they have been transcribed.[25] According to a plan of the walks as they were in 1568, compiled in the last century, the whole of the western area of the Inn site was called the Coney Garth, dating from the twelfth century. Coneys were rabbits reared for eating, so maybe it is not surprising that no gardener thought it worthwhile trying to grow flowers if the rabbits were still around. In 1572 the Inn decided that 'it shall be lawful from henceforth for any man to destroy the conies' in the far end of the garden, so perhaps the problem eased from then.

Livery companies and churchyards

You could not walk far in central London without seeing a hall belonging to a livery company, with its garden for the members' enjoyment. The Drapers spent £76 on their garden in 1569–70, rather more than Gray's Inn – the Drapers were doing very well.[26] They already had an old mulberry tree, and they bought new flowering trees such as apples, pears, plums and cherries, as well as filberts, privet for a new maze, 100 damask roses and a fountain that cost £20. The gardener was told to exclude anyone not in the upper ranks of the company. The bowling alley, a very common amenity, was refurbished at the same time, and proved so popular that members had to be reminded that playing bowls on Sundays was forbidden.[27]

The Carpenters spent a modest 46s 4d, in 1560, on (for once I'll use the original spelling) 'dyggyng and downgyng [dunging: manuring] and setting and sowying of erbys [herbs: plants] and makyng the bowlyng alee', and some more on a bench under the pear tree.[28] Eight years later they decided they could afford to enlarge their garden, by taking in a plot that had brought in 15s a year.[29]

The Clothworkers' garden had a vine which needed regular pruning, and beds stocked with double primroses, daisies, angelica and rosemary.[30] The Merchant Taylors, clearly realistic men, decided in 1598 that

> by reason of the great multitude of company which resort unto this Hall at Quarter days [to pay their rents] … it is thought if the Company should be at the charges of making any curious knot … upon their garden the same would be spoiled and defaced. It is therefore thought convenient that the same be converted into a grass plot and alleys.

It was bad enough having to spend money every year on pruning and tying up the vine.[31]

The Grocers replanned their garden in 1598, spending £44 2s 9d on new brick-edged beds and borders filled with well-manured compost (106 loads of dung), bay trees and box hedging, new herbs and plants.[32] The Goldsmiths even had two gardens, one beside their hall in Cheapside and another outside Cripplegate, with a banqueting house and a bowling alley.[33]

Some parish churchyards were too overcrowded by the dead to

have space for the living. Sometimes the Parish Council decided to make money by allowing building on God's Acre.[34] The parishioners of St Mary Woolchurch, in the very centre of the City, decided to improve their finances by building a row of lettable properties on part of the churchyard. The rest was made into a garden, with elm trees and an arbour, and bay trees – but it was surrounded by a high brick wall, and I do not know who had a key.[35]

Yet every now and then there was a glimpse of a quiet spot. The petty canons of St Paul's had at least got a garden out of the Duke of Somerset's demolition of the cathedral cloister and library in 1549 to use the materials for his new Somerset House.[36] Occasionally, when the site of a church that had belonged to one of the dissolved orders was redeveloped, its churchyard was left as 'a garden plot', although it is not clear from Stow's account whether such gardens were private property or open. Still, at least the sight of them would refresh the eye.[37] St Helen's Church, contrived out of the majestic priory near Bishopsgate, retained a churchyard shaded by several large sycamore trees, and a willow, and fruit trees, and areas of grass that the sexton was paid to mow.[38]

Gardening techniques

Thomas Tusser's *A Hundred Goode Pointes of Husbandry* was published in 1557. Most of it is about farming, but some gives gardening advice. I will inflict on you only a short sample:

> At spring, (for the sommer) sow garden ye shall,
> At harvest (for winter) or sowe not at all.
> Oft digging, remooving and weeding (ye see),
> Makes herbe more holesome and greater to bee ...

> Now [*sic*] set doo aske watering with pot or with dish
> New sone doo not so, if ye doo as I wish.
> Through cunning with dible, rake, mattock and spade,
> By line and by leavell, trim garden is made.

And so on, and on ... I thought it would make it more interesting if you saw the original spelling. 'Remooving' surely means transplanting. 'Now set' must mean newly set, or transplanted, seedlings, which do need a lot of water, whereas 'new sone' must mean newly sown seeds, which you should not water because you will drown them – better to sow in already damp earth. He had, in other words, a lot of sense. He was no worse than his contemporaries in advising you to sow when the moon was waxing:

> Cut all things or gather, the Moone in the wane,
> But sowe in encreasing, or give it his bane [don't do it].

Perhaps inspired by Tusser's commercial success, Thomas Hill launched his *Moste Briefe and Pleasaunte treatise, teachynge howe to Dress, Sowe and Set a Garden* in 1563, re-issued as *The Profitable Art of Gardening* in 1568, with a revised and expanded version in 1577 which he called *The Gardener's Labyrinth*. Labyrinth was another name for that fashionable garden feature, a maze. Not wishing to flood the market, he used a pseudonym, Didymus Mountaine, but it was surely not too difficult to guess who 'Mountaine' was. All three versions are at least in prose, but not much easier to read than Tusser.

The *Labyrinth* had a huge success. It begins: 'The worthy Pliny (in his XIX Book) reporteth …' and goes on quoting Pliny, Dioscorides, Cicero et al., ad nauseam. This was the style of the time. All writers had to quote the ancients, to gain any credibility, no matter how irrelevant their readers might find them. Ignoring Pliny, you can find a great deal of sound advice. Hill shares with all gardeners a preoccupation with fertiliser and compost: that is, 'dung'. Undiluted 'dung which men make' is not a good idea; asses' dung is better because an ass 'for his leisurely eating digesteth easier, and causes the better dung'. He also emphasises the importance of preparing the ground properly, laying out the beds carefully and installing drainage.

You may be surprised to find in the *Labyrinth* directions for growing oranges, lemons, pomegranates and *dates*, planting them in chests 'which at will may be rolled hither and thither' – out of strong sun, or into shelter from cold. Pomegranates had been growing in sheltered parts of England for the last two hundred years, but dates? (There may be a confusion here: 'dates' may have been a kind of plum.)[39] By 1599 Sir Francis Carew was managing to grow Seville oranges, protecting them in winter in a heated 'tabernacle', as John Evelyn described it a century later. Carew is also noteworthy for manipulating the time schedule of a cherry, by keeping a tree dark and cold for two months, so that when Elizabeth arrived to see him in the late summer of 1599 he could offer her some out-of-season fresh cherries.[40] Melons too could flourish, if treated right.

Hill has some remarkable suggestions for pest control, derived, of course, from Pliny and his mates. How about burying the skeleton head of a mare in the garden, or dragging a speckled toad round the garden on a piece of string, at night, and then putting it in a pot and burying it? But you have to remember to dig the toad up again and throw it 'a great distance off', otherwise the plants growing where it was buried will be 'unpleasant of smell'. To be fair, that was one of Apuleius's, for which Hill makes no personal recommendation. He suggests olive oil or soot for snails (Oxford snails would come for miles for a nice extra-virgin oil) and for that other pest, moles, put a live mole in a pot – first catch your mole – and after a while 'he will cry and [all the other moles in the neighbourhood] will hastily draw near unto him and minding to help him forth will fall into the pot'. But what do you do with a potful of crying moles?

Hill also comes up with some practical advice that you might find in any modern gardening book, about companion planting, for example – the theory that strong-smelling flowers like tagetes and garlic will deter pests from carrots and roses. I have not tried his advice on salads, but here it is: plant in a ball of sheep's dung, two or three lettuce seeds, the same of basil, endive, leek and parsley – or if the sheep's dung is too small, use a ball of horse dung, which in London was all too easy to get. Then you will get just one all-purpose salad plant. On the other hand, his advice on growing parsley, a notoriously difficult seed to persuade to germinate, may not be so useful: 'if you will have the leaves of the parsley grow crisped then ... stuff a tennis ball with the seeds and beat them well against the ground' before you sow them.

An ancient Greek gives a helpful precaution against damage by hail, involving the skin of a crocodile or a hyena. If you are nervous of lightning damage, a hippopotamus skin is the thing to use. By now, the gentle sixteenth-century reader may be regretting that she spent good money on Hill's – or Mountaine's – book.

Hill was probably right in recommending careful hand weeding rather than using 'an Iron instrument', but I doubt if watering with lukewarm water, as he suggests, would bring roses into flower any earlier. He held out the prospect of making red roses white, and vice versa, or 'party-coloured' (striped), but only if you bought his 'little treatise' on the subject, which I have not done. Perforated clay watering pots had been in use since the previous century, but Hill describes, laboriously and opaquely, a copper one 'much used in the

chiefest gardens about London', which may well have been constructed on the same lines as a modern watering can, except that it
had holes in its long spout instead of a rose.

Planting plans

The range of available plants had been enormously increased by
Spanish, Portugese and English explorers. 'How many strange
[foreign] herbs, plants and annual fruits are daily brought unto us
from the Indies, Americas, Taprobane [Sri Lanka], Canary Isles
and all parts of the world' – an achievement in itself, to conserve
plant material alive in the conditions of sixteenth-century voyages.

I wish Hill had said what had arrived from Taprobane. It certainly
was not tea. But nasturtiums had come from Peru, with the flower
we mistakenly call African marigold, which started in Mexico.
'Spanish bayonet' was the name given to the spiky plant we know as
yucca, also from Mexico and central America. Marvel of Peru (the
Four O'Clock flower) and the passion flower so satisfying to religious
gardeners had arrived,[41] as had canna lilies. The French marigold
Tagetes patula arrived fifty years after its African cousin, but stank just
the same. Sunflowers were cheerfully sprouting over the fences –
John Gerard had one fourteen feet high, in his garden. In 1596 Chile
and Peru gave us potatoes, not to be confused with sweet potatoes,
which arrived a year later from tropical America, perhaps in the
same ship as tomatoes. China sent day lilies (*Hemerocallis*) and
the white mulberry, which survived but did not thrive – one of the
familiar purple-fruited kind had been growing in the Drapers'
Company's garden since 1364, and lasted nearly into this century.

The new London gardeners seem to have been more optimistic
than their predecessors about introducing plants and trees that grew
in central Europe and round the Mediterranean, and might be
induced to grow in England. Probably some failed and dropped out
of history, or were not worth persisting with, like the white
mulberry. But the range of fruit trees was extended by peaches and
apricots, flower beds were enriched by rock roses (*Cistus salvifolia*)
and a wider range of pinks, the small-flowered clematis (*C. viticella*
and *C. cirrhosa*) climbed everywhere, larkspur came in from the
Mediterranean and its cousin *Delphinium elatum* made the journey
from Siberia, with yellow foxgloves. *Primula auricula* from the Alps

was warming up for its theatrical performances in the next century. Crown imperial, that splendid plant with the unfortunate foxy smell, had arrived from southern Turkey. There were already lilacs and laburnum, but another laburnum and the Judas tree with pink flowers on its trunk had come from the same region.

The French and Italians, too, were developing new plants. The Earl of Essex wrote to his agent in Paris for the best possible seeds 'among the Italians, as well for herbs and salads as for all kind of rare flowers besides, seeds for melons and such like, asparagus and all kinds of radish'.[42] Lord Burghley told his son Thomas, who was in Paris to improve his education, to send him 'anything meet [suitable]' for the garden he was creating for his Norfolk mansion, and also 'a man apt for his garden', but Thomas never found a French gardener prepared to brave the English climate. A little later, Burghley asked Thomas's tutor to send him a lemon tree, a pomegranate tree and a myrtle tree, 'with directions for culture'. The tutor sent by return a lemon tree and two myrtles – no pomegranate – plus directions. They had cost a crown each, which the tutor said was 'very cheap'.[43]

So all in all, the choice was much wider than it had ever been. The Elizabethans were not to know that the pace of change would double and treble in the next few hundred years, when serious plant-hunters scoured the world solely with the aim of finding new plants.

In any picture of an Elizabethan garden, the planting looks sparse. No cramming them together so that in theory the flowers crowd out the weeds. Each plant was given its own space, and looks all the better for it. Then, often only one kind of flower was planted in each bed, not the tasteful medley that we go in for. And although there was a great variety available, each plant's flowering season was short, so a garden was never a profusion of blooms.

William Harrison endearingly describes his own London garden, in 1577.[44] 'Let me boast a little of my garden' – as all gardeners do. It was only 300 feet square, but he grew nearly 300 'simples' (medicinal herbs) in it, 'no one of them being common or usually to be had'. It probably smelled lovely, but it did not necessarily look a picture, herbs being often rather straggly. William Turner wrote about an astonishing variety of medicinal plants, which he lists with their useful qualities, such as that leopard's bane (*Doronicum*) 'laid to a scorpion makes her utterly amazed'. But forgetting for a while their medicinal potential, here are some of his plants:

flowers – alchemilla, aquilegia, comfrey, daisies, foxgloves, golden rod, hyssop that bees love, lavender, marigolds, poppies, scabious, tansy

vegetables – artichokes, asparagus, cabbages ('coleworts'), *cannabis* [my italics], lettuce, radishes, turnips and many kinds of herbs.

To us, many of the flowers in an Elizabethan garden would look more like wild flowers than our carefully hybridised varieties, since modern varieties have been bred to maximise flower size and length of season, often at the expense of perfume. An Elizabethan gardener laid great emphasis on perfume. Arbours had fragrant climbers round them and sweet-smelling flowers and shrubs near them, such as wallflowers, pinks, rosemary and lavender. Spring bulbs included 'daffadowndillies' and tulips. Roses were red, white or striped. I have seen a recipe for pouring various potions on to a lily bulb, to change its blooms from white to red, but I somehow do not think it would work. A high proportion of plants in a small garden would not be grown for their flowers at all, but to supply basic medicines for the household, such as any housewife would know how to prepare. She would have a plot near the kitchen for culinary herbs as well, and if there was room she might grow her own fragrant 'strewing herbs' for her floors, and other sweet-smelling herbs 'planted in gardens for the flowers sake, to the decking up of houses'.[45]

John Gerard brought out his famous *Herbal or the General History of Plants* in 1597. It was impressive and sold well, being filled with information and plant portraits. He listed some interesting plants such as 'turkey corn' (maize), plane trees, which he said were not found in England, and the kind of moss 'found upon the skull or bare scalp of men and women lying long in charnel houses' – that potent ingredient of sixteenth- and seventeenth-century medicine. This has an appropriately macabre illustration. He also described various exotic trees and plants, such as pomegranates, which he said grew in Granada but not in England.

Two years later he published a list of all the trees, plants and fruits growing in his London garden, and one beings faintly to doubt his veracity. We do not know the size of his garden, and it is difficult to plot its exact location. It was probably where Furnival Street is now, halfway between Fetter Lane and Shoe Lane, on land that had been owned by the Abbot of Malmesbury up to Henry's dissolution of the monasteries and then became the property of Lord Burghley. Gerard had been supervising Burghley's gardens in the Strand and out at Theobalds since about 1577,[46] so Burghley gave Gerard the use of this third garden, which Gerard always referred to as 'his' garden.[47] There he planted – so he said, in his famous *Catalogue* – trees such as a fir, two kinds of pine, a 'great maple', a sweet chestnut (the horse chestnut came later), fourteen cherry trees, a 'nettle', ten different kinds of peach, an orange tree, three different kinds of mulberry tree, an apricot, a walnut tree, a white poplar, an elder, a yew tree, a service tree, a pomegranate and a plane tree, not to speak of numerous herbaceous plants and shrubs. At the end of this impressive list is an 'attestation' signed by Gerard's friend Matthias de l'Obel, testifying that he really had seen all the entries on the list, in Gerard's garden. But in his own copy of the *Catalogue* de l'Obel crossed out the 'attestation' and wrote on it 'Haec esse falsissima [This is completely untrue]'.[48] So perhaps the *Catalogue* is not altogether reliable. But Gerard must be credited with a 'bombast tree', very useful for stuffing breeches; 'bastard and Spanish potatoes'; 19 kinds of 'flowerdeluce' (iris), including the Florentine species from which fragrant orris-root powder was made; 17 kinds of 'iacint' and 13 kinds of daffodil, including the 'checkered daffodil' (fritillary).

Costs

The Earl of Essex's Parisian seeds were not going to come cheap. Lord Burghley tapped his commercial contacts in Flanders, for seeds and expertise.[49] The nobility 'made their provision yearly for new seeds out of strange countries'.[50] The Flemish and Huguenot refugees may have brought some favourite seeds with them as a reminder of home. Most people probably managed to exchange seeds with neighbours, as they still do. But the monasteries' horticultural skills had gone, and the day of the professional seedsman had not yet arrived.

The design of garden tools remains much the same, although now we make them of different materials and sometimes power them otherwise than by human muscle. Tusser's 'dibble, rake, mattock and spade, line and level' still do necessary jobs. The costs of tools listed in livery companies' accounts does not look exorbitant. The Carpenters paid 14d for a rake and a trowel, with another 6d for two watering pots, plus 18d for 'mowing the grass, cutting the roses and gooseberries' in 1575. (Gooseberries were often used as decorative standards.) From such accounts it looks as if any task needing skill beyond that of a labourer would be done by a jobbing gardener, who could charge about 1s 5d a day,[51] a surprising amount when a journeyman's annual wage was only £2 10s.

Open spaces

Going north through the wall at Moor Gate led you straight into Moor Fields. The first half of the Fields seems to have been reserved for laundresses, to dry their washing, and you would not be popular if you – or your dog – trod on the linen spread out on the grass. Staying on the path, you got to Finsbury Fields on your left, with its windmills creaking round on a windy day. If you had left the City by Bishops Gate, you could soon take Hog Lane and reach the open space known as the Spitel. This had been the grounds of a priory, St Mary Spital, but was open to the citizenry by the time the map (see plate 17) was made. (It is more familiar as Spitalfields, now mostly under Liverpool Street Station.) John Stow, writing in 1598, could look back to when Hog Lane 'within these forty years had on both sides fair hedgerows of elm trees, with bridges [over streams] and easy stiles to pass over into the pleasant fields, very commodious for citizens to walk, shoot and otherwise to recreate and refresh their dulled spirits in the sweet and wholesome air' – but by 1598 it was all garden houses and small cottages. The developers were catching up.

The same thing was happening to the road out of Aldgate to the east, where Stow remembered a 'common field which ought to be open and free for all men', but was by the end of the century a mess of 'filthy cottages' and illegal refuse tips, let alone traffic and cattle, so that there was no longer any 'fair, pleasant or wholesome way for people to walk on foot', as there used to be. But there was a pleasant walk along the south bank, from Lambeth to Paris Garden,[52] where you could stop for a drink and a game of bowls or a hand of cards, before you got to the Bankside amusements, bull baiting, bear baiting and theatres. It would be noisy and crowded at the Southwark end of the Bridge, but after that you got to Bermondsey, and an inviting beerhouse in a wood at Horsley Down.

To the west there were more drying-grounds for laundresses beside St Martin's Lane, and along the Hay Market, and open fields on both sides of Drury Lane and Gray's Inn Lane (now, Gray's Inn Road), once you had passed Gray's Inn. In fact there were open fields within easy walking distance of anywhere in London.

The roof of St Paul's Cathedral provided a surprising open space, once you had, like Thomas Platter, 'climbed three hundred steps to the Church roof, which was broad and covered with lead, so that one may walk there, indeed every Sunday many men and women stroll together on this roof. Up there I had a splendid view of the entire city of London, of how long and narrow it is.'[53]

One other kind of open space needs explaining: the tenter grounds, identifiable on maps by their long strips with posts at each end and along their length. These were where cloth finishers dried and stretched their textiles by fixing the selvedges to hooks on rails, top and bottom, to keep the cloth taut while it dried. (Hence, to be 'on tenterhooks' means being under nervous tension. The stretched canvas of a tent comes from the same idea.) There were some on either side of Moor Fields, and more along the outside of the wall east of Bishops Gate. One would not be able to walk there, but at least those areas were not being built on, and when a dyer had finished a batch of crimson, or popinjay blue, they must have been a colourful sight.

Part Two

THE PEOPLE

The stage is set. Where is the cast? There is no heroine here, nor villain, and hardly any plot. There are thousands of people milling about, living and dying and shouting and quarrelling and writing poetry, and quietly going to church. But where are the older people, about whom our present age is so worried? Why are there so many foreigners? That sumptuously dressed woman riding through the crowd – is she a typical Londoner? Or is the market woman with her basket a better example? Some of the men are dressed in amazing clothes, but why are so many of the young men dressed alike, in blue? And why are there so many beggars?

The next chapter will consider life, death and the illnesses in between. Next, foreigners will make their bow. Then ordinary Londoners will take the stage, managing their ruffs, and eating and drinking, and getting married and buried and educated, and making good, or breaking the law and falling to the bottom of the pile. Religion is important to them; no one can ever read the inside of someone's mind, but at least the outer observances can be noted.

CHAPTER 6

Health, Illness and Medicine

Expectation of life

We do not have reliable contemporary figures from which to calculate the expectation of life at birth, in London, in the Elizabethan era. For men it has been estimated at 20–25 years in the poorer parishes, and 30–35 in the wealthier parts of London, with many prosperous men surviving into their fifties.[1] More than half the population of England was under 25,[2] and this figure needs adjusting for London to take into account the crowds of young people in their teens who made for the capital to find jobs and apprenticeships. At the other end of life, Thomas Paynel wrote in 1541: 'nowadays, alas, if a man may approach to forty or sixty years men repute him happy and fortunate.'[3] A diarist born in 1528 recorded sadly that he was 'growing towards the age of forty, at the which year begins the first part of the old man's age'.[4]

How long a new-born baby will probably live is a notoriously tricky problem. As she gently rocks the cradle, the godmother foresees the perils of childbirth, for a girl; the dangers of possible war, for a boy; and the endemic and epidemic illnesses lying in wait for every child. But once a baby girl survived weaning on to dubious foods, and the fearsome diseases for which no preventive or effective treatment was available, there was with any luck a quiet period for her until marriage and child bearing. If she survived that, the odds lengthened again. If she reached the menopause, there was no youth-prolonging, bone-strengthening hormone replacement therapy. She could succumb to some respiratory germ, or a hip fracture, or cancer, or the lowered resistance of old age, just as we can, but without modern medicine

to help. In general terms, an Elizabethan woman would be contemplating old age at 40, whereas now she can plan for the half of
her life still before her. The pervasive significance of this different
perspective is difficult to realise. Take one example: the words in the
marriage service, 'till death us do part', implied a much shorter
married life then, than now.

The Bills of Mortality

We pride ourselves on the accuracy of our computer-based records,
yet in 2001 a bunch of scientists spent months researching into a
disease of sheep, never noticing that they were looking at the wrong
brains – cows', not sheep's. With this in mind, the record keeping of
the Elizabethans, without computers, was astounding. One instance
was the count of the number of deaths in London, called the Bills
(lists) of Mortality.

The Bills had begun in 1532, with weekly totals of deaths from
plague.[5] This was probably a temporary exercise, during a particularly bad epidemic. By 1555 a regular system was in place, operated
by the parish clerks. For 1563, another bad plague year, Stow could
consult records (now lost) showing total deaths of 23,660, of which
20,136 were plague cases.[6] By 1582 the Company of Stationers was
able to send Lord Burghley a 'simple book' or annual summary of
the deaths in the whole of London, from 1577 onwards.[7] In 1593,
another bad plague year, a diarist was able to make 'a note of the
whole year from the 21 of December 1592 to 20 December 1593 – Died
of all diseases 16,844, whereof of the plague 10,662. Christened this
year 4,021. Parishes clear of the plague – none.'[8]

The figures were collated from returns made by the 'Viewers' or
'Searchers' of the dead: two old women who might otherwise be on
parish relief, employed to go to any house where a death had been
notified to the parish clerk via the Cryer, and certify the cause of
death. Their diagnosis was based on experience – they would
certainly recognise a plague death.[9] They must have been walking
foci of infection themselves, which was why they had to put their
reports in a box at the foot of the stairs in the Stationers' Company's
hall, without going near anyone there.[10] They were paid by the
parish, 2d a body. The Lambeth churchwardens gave its Searchers
4s 8d in 1579 – only 28 bodies, Lambeth had a good year that year.[11]

The Plague

The Black Death, in which around a quarter of Europe's population in 1347–51 died, was probably an epidemic of plague.[12] The people who survived perhaps acquired some immunity to the bacillus, but it became endemic in England, particularly in crowded London. It must have been terrifying to see a plague death and wonder whether this was just the usual summer risk, or the harbinger of a raging epidemic.

The Great Plague of 1665, in which according to the Bills 68,596 people died, was the last, and the most famous, of its periodic outbreaks. But there were several virulent epidemics in Elizabeth's time, which are less known simply because they lacked a Pepys or a Defoe to chronicle them. The year of her coronation, 1558, was a bad plague year. In 1563, nearly a quarter of London's population died. From then the bacillus *Yersinia pestis* attacked roughly every four years until 1582, then ten years went by until the next epidemic. It recurred in 1597 and again in the year of Elizabeth's death,[13] which complicated the arrival of her successor James I and VI from Scotland. In St Botolph's parish, nearly a quarter of the deaths notified between 1583 and 1600 were plague cases.[14]

From *In Time of Plague* (1600) by Thomas Nash:

> … Rich men, trust not in wealth,
> Gold cannot buy you health;
> Physic himself must fade;
> All things to end are made;
> The plague full swift goes by;
> I am sick, I must die.
> Lord have mercy on us …

'What disease is there in the world so venomous in infecting, so full of pain in suffering, so hasty in devouring, and so difficult in curing, as the plague is?'[15] In case this leaves you in any doubt, a modern view:

> Bubonic plague is basically a rodent disease. It strikes humans when infected fleas, failing to find a living rat once a rat host has been killed, pick a human instead. When the flea bites its new host, the bacillus enters the bloodstream. Filtered through the nearest lymph node, it leads to the characteristic swelling (bubo) in the neck, groin

or armpit. Bubonic plague rapidly kills about two-thirds of those infected. There are two other even more fatal forms: septiceamic and, deadliest of all, pneumonic plague, which doesn't even need an insect vector, spreading from person to person directly via the breath.[16]

Plague affected more men than women, perhaps because the granaries, docks and warehouses where rats proliferated were male precincts.[17] What could be done? Probably the only sensible measure, for those days, was to isolate the sufferers. By regulations of 1568 any house where a plague patient lived had to be shut up for at least twenty days,[18] with the sufferer and his family inside, and a 'paper' saying 'Lord have mercy upon us' nailed to the door. The Lord Mayor assured the Privy Council that some of his own officers would check on the parish clerks to make sure that this was being done.[19] It was not quite so heartless as it sounds. The parish paid some 'honest discrete person' whom the parish constable was told to 'have at all times in readiness – they must have been getting fairly thin on the ground by then – to go to each house, every day, and buy food for the occupants, and no doubt to report when the Searchers and the dead cart were needed there. If this involuntary unemployment, or pre-existing poverty, meant that the occupants could not pay for food, the City would provide.

In 1580 the Privy Council warned the Lord Mayor that a ship had arrived in the Thames from Lisbon, where plague was known to be raging: the ship and its crew must be quarantined. The Lord Mayor blamed God, who was understandably angry with Londoners for not observing the building regulations, and not going to church, but on the contrary 'haunting plays', of which both God and the Lord Mayor disapproved. All bedding and clothes used by an infected person were to be burned – again, very sensible, but hard for poor households who normally looked to wear a dead man's clothes for years after his death. When anyone was allowed out of the infected house they had to carry a white stick a yard long, to warn passers-by to give them a wide berth.[20] All the dogs 'that run from house to house dispersing the plague' were to be killed, and no swine were to be kept in the City. If only the authorities had taken just one more step, and decreed that cats, which would catch the true criminals, were to be preserved at all costs ...

The Lord Mayor also undertook to see that the 'streets and other places about the City [were] cleaned every other day', surely an extreme measure. The governors of St Bartholomew's Hospital thought seriously, in 1594, about building a 'plague house' at St Giles in the Fields out in the country beyond Cripplegate, but their good intentions were overtaken, or adopted, by the City.[21] The isolation hospitals built long ago for lepers, and standing empty since leprosy had almost gone, were pressed into service. But anyone who could, got out of London as soon as the prominently displayed Bills showed an increase in the normal plague figures. London in 1563 'was now so sorely visited with the plague of pestilence' that even a poor schoolmaster 'doubted to tarry there any longer'.[22]

Smallpox and other diseases

Like the plague, smallpox was endemic in London, peaking into epidemics from time to time. Queen Elizabeth went down with it in October 1562.[23] On 10 October she felt unwell and went for a bracing walk, but soon she had a high fever. Yet she had no rash. A German physician, Burcot, correctly diagnosed smallpox, which Elizabeth refused to believe, as long as she could. But by 16 October she was unconscious and Burcot was recalled. He advised that she should be wrapped in red flannel and laid beside the fire to keep warm, and she should take some of his potion. Sure enough, in two hours she came to, furious that spots had appeared on her beautiful hands. A vivid picture of a bedside manner: Burcot exploded, 'God's pestilence! Which is better? To have a pox on the hand or in the face, or in the heart and kill the whole body?' Elizabeth's astonishing constitution got her out of bed in six days, but her friend Lady Sidney, who had nursed her, caught the disease and was so hideously scarred that she never appeared publicly at Court again.

This wide variation was probably typical of smallpox. Elizabeth took to thick white make-up, and her pockmarks faded. Lacking her resistance, many died, and many more were left blind or disfigured. Pockmarked faces must have been a common sight. The best way to deal with smallpox, if they had only known, was to have a mild attack in childhood, conferring – just as vaccination was to do later – a lifelong immunity, but smallpox was usually fatal to small children.

Apart from rapid killers such as plague and typhus ('the bloody flux'), a large proportion of the populace must have felt chronically below par for years, before they died and were included in the Bills. 'Consumption' (tuberculosis) was endemic in London. It accounted for nearly a quarter of the deaths in St Botolph's between 1583 and 1600 – the same proportion as the plague, in a period that included the particularly bad plague epidemic of 1593.

Syphilis, then called the foul or French pox or the Neapolitan bone-ache (blame the foreigners), was increasing. Whether syphilis had afflicted the ancient Greeks is a moot point. The usual view is that it came back in Columbus's ships from his conquest of the New World. We exchanged European measles for American syphilis. In their native territories, both organisms had been living quietly and comfortably, but as soon as they moved they became virulent, aggressive and lethal.

Scurvy is a debilitating, potentially fatal illness caused by a lack of vitamin C in the diet. It so weakened the crews on long voyages that they often could hardly work their ships back to their home anchorage. The survivors of the gallant sailors whose victory over the Spanish Armada had been celebrated by the nation in August 1588 tottered off their ships in September, incapacitated by scurvy and other diseases caused by the inadequate provisioning of the fleet.[24] Children also suffered from it. William Clowes met it both in the Navy and in Christ's Hospital, 'where I had twenty or thirty [children] infected with the scurvy at a time'. His treatment included the usual purgations and blood-letting, which were unlikely to have done any good, but he did cure even advanced cases with ale, 'in which has been steeped a quantity of freshly picked scurvy grass'.[25] One of the duties of the apothecary on the staff of St Bartholomew's Hospital was to ensure a supply of scurvy grass for the patients, throughout the year.[26] Scurvy grass – which grows on coastal salt-marshes, dunes and sea cliffs around Britain – is rich in vitamin C,[27] and it was cheaper than citrus fruit,[28] but if you could get it, Simon Forman advised four spoonfuls of lemon juice twice a day.[29]

Malaria flourished, under the names of agues and fevers. The marshes on the south bank of the Thames must have provided an ideal breeding-ground for mosquitoes. The link between mosquitoes and malaria was not discovered for another two centuries; meanwhile people endured agues, 'tertian fever' (recurring every three days) and 'quartian fever' (recurring every four days) and even 'quotidian fever' (recurring every day) as part of normal life. Malaria has a further, unseen, knock-on effect, in lowering the body's resistance to other ailments. There was no cure. Everyone had their pet ague remedies, but none really worked.

And childhood was an obstacle course of disease. In 1560 Thomas Phaire wrote a whole book on 'the things necessary as to remove sicknesses whereby the tender babes are oftentimes affected, and desolate of remedy', a phrase that goes to the heart, still, of anyone who has heard a sick baby crying.[30] He listed epilepsy, palsy, quinsy (a painful complication of tonsillitis), stomach ache, diarrhoea, worms, kidney and bladder stones, measles, smallpox, shingles, indigestion, bad dreams – a litany of anxious nights and grieving parents, now for most people in the developed world merely a hideous chapter of history.

Diseases such as multiple sclerosis, motor neurone disease, meningitis and a host of others that have been identified and publicised in recent times were not known of in the sixteenth century, but they are not new, and people died of them then, not knowing why. Sometimes there is a hint of diseases known all too well to us: for instance, a stroke. Struck by what, or whom? The sixteenth-century answer would be the moon, or a planet.[31] Or you could die 'of a thought', as Margaret Russell did in 1593, 'who before had been tempted with an evil spirit and now died of a thought, as by the crowner's quest [coroner's inquest] was supposed'.[32]

Care of the sick

Those who could afford it came to London to be near the foremost medical authorities. In 1582 the Earl of Sussex came to stay with his friend Sir John Peter, in Aldersgate, 'for the recovery of his health … which god give him good success therein'.[33] The sick poor were, if they were lucky, taken into the two great medieval hospitals that had survived the depredations of Henry VIII, St Bartholomew's and St Thomas's. Since the first condition for admission was poverty, we will look at them in Chapter 15, dealing with the poor.

Mental illness

Andrew Boorde recommended that the patient be 'kept in safeguard in some close house or chamber where there is little light, and that he have a keeper the which the madman do fear'.[34] His head should be shaved once a month, to keep it cool, and he should not be stimulated by visual images, not even on the painted cloths then commonly used in interior decoration. At least the pranksters in *Twelfth Night* did not shave Malvolio's head, but they got him shut up in a dark room as a madman.[35] In a case of depression, 'he that is become mad with sadness ... to him ought fair be spoken ... many things should be promised him and *some* be given [my italics: surely the disappointment would make him even sadder?] ... if it is a woman [she] ought to be refreshed with men and to their company admitted; the same bringeth them to their right mind again'.[36]

The Hospital of St Mary of Bethlehem ('Bedlam') had specialised in the care of mental illness since 1403, and by the sixteenth century could be described as the only specialised fee-paying hospital in London.[37] Henry VIII at least preserved it, by transferring its management to the City, which in turn handed it over to the Governors of Bridewell, who unfortunately were more interested in the sane criminals in Bridewell than in the mad patients in Bedlam. Some information about the hospital buildings comes indirectly from the Elizabethan underworld. One of the well-known cat-egories of beggars was an 'Abraham man' who 'feigneth himself mad'.[38] The name came from the main ward in Bedlam, called the Abraham ward. It was probably about 200 feet long and 51 feet wide, with cells on each side of it for the patients, one to a cell.[39]

The running of Bedlam was left to a series of Keepers, who made what they could out of it. At last, in 1598, the Bridewell Governors were shamed into inspecting the place, and were appalled by what they found. Nothing had been spent on the upkeep of the buildings, the 'great vault' (cess-pit) badly needed emptying, and the kitchen sink and drains needed replacing. 'We do find divers other defaults in the said house in such sort that it is not fit for any man to dwell in, which was left by the Keeper, for that it is so loathsomely and filthy kept not fit for any man to come into the said house.' But there were 21 patients there, to whom the Bridewell governors referred, by a slip of the pen no doubt, as 'prisoners'. One had been there 25 years. He had been sent in by Bridewell, so the Governors should have known about him. They had dispatched five others to Bedlam over the past ten years. Every patient was paid for, by his or her parish, a relation or a livery company. The charges varied from 12d to 20d a week, presumably at the discretion of the Keeper, who charged what he thought the market would bear – and extracted what he thought he could get away with.

The patients were a mixed bunch. Not all were poor. In 1551 'William Brady, merchant, being frantic ... [was] committed to Bedlam there to be closely kept and chained [so] that no man speak with him.' I have no other information about their treatment, if any. It seems to have consisted in just keeping them alive. Some of them came from outside London, which disposes of the cosy idea that Bedlam offered a safe haven for mentally ill Londoners, let alone poverty-stricken ones. Antony Green, Fellow of Pembroke Hall in Cambridge, had come in about six months earlier. The Dutch Church paid for one of their congregation, the Lord Admiral paid for John Dalton, and Lady Stafford had been paying for a widow to stay there for the last eight or nine years.

The most intriguing story I found was John Summerscales or Somerskall, sent in by the Treasurer of Gray's Inn 'at the request of the Benchers about three years past and is allowed for [paid for] by them'. He had been appointed fourth butler of the Inn in 1590, but he went sick in 1593 and was put on paid sick leave, at a generous 5s a week. By 1594 a new butler had to be appointed, who 'shall have ... such fees as were due ... to the said Summerscales and thereof shall pay to [Summerscales] yearly during his lunacy £3 6s 8d'. We do not know what was wrong with him, but the Inn promised that he should have his job back 'if it shall please God to restore [him] to his perfect sense and memory again'. Thereafter the Inn paid the cost – 11s a quarter, just over 10d a week – direct to Bedlam. He was still there in 1602, but seems to have been discharged some time in 1611 when 'it pleased the bench [of Gray's Inn] to bestow on John Somerscales one of the butlers of this house the sum of twenty marks [about £7] in commiseration of his poverty and in recompense of his place and full satisfaction of all pretence [claim] to be restored to the said office.' He will not have had any treatment during the whole time he was there – about sixteen years. All he did was to survive. Still, it is a pleasant story of employment relations.

Diagnosis and treatment

A fluttering or slow pulse could be felt by the physician, though he lacked an accurate second hand to his watch.[40] The patient's general appearance was a diagnostic help. But urine was the best indicator of health. Neatly packaged in a glass vessel ('urinal'), it could be rushed through the streets by special mounted messenger – it was best to be fresh – from patient to physician, who could diagnose without ever seeing the patient, just by holding the urinal to the light. Falstaff asked, 'What says the doctor to my water?'[41] When Malvolio was thought to be mad, the best thing to do was to 'carry his water to the wisewoman' for her diagnosis.[42] Simon Forman preferred to see the patient with the urinal; cases had been known of the messenger spilling it on the way, and substituting his own.[43] Some physicians even claimed to be able to tell by uroscopy whether a patient was suffering from a venereal disease.[44]

Even if an accurate diagnosis had been possible – then what?[45] Your beloved is ill: surely something can be done? Patients provide the physician's income: to earn his fee he should be seen to act energetically, the patient may well recover and he can claim the credit. If the case goes the other way, it was the fault of the patient, or his stars.

The first – and sometimes the last – useful thing for the patient to do was to invoke divine assistance. Richard Stoneley had been enjoying life, in his quiet way; but in 1582 'this day after prayer I kept home all the day being sick of an ague with sore cough and ended that day at my books with prayer to God, whatsoever he sendeth, either health or sickness before death, shall [be] to me *valde bonum* [equally good]'.[46] The next thing to do, of course, was to 'put away sin'. No more 'haunting of lechery', a well-known cause of pestilence.[47] But Stoneley felt more cheerful, or less pious, the next day, and bought a 'purgation' from a doctor. He then coughed all night, but surely one cannot blame a cough on a laxative?

Purgations were not always convenient. Imagine phoning your office to say you wouldn't be coming in because you were waiting for a laxative to work. There was a problem about patients' records: not the usual one, that they had been lost, but that they had been made at all, for which the College of Physicians strongly reprimanded Simon Forman. He countered that he had to keep a careful note of each patient, since he might see up to twenty a day; and if, for instance, he advised one to take a purge, but the patient had to put it off 'because of necessary business', Forman would need to turn up his notes when the patient came back.[48] Perhaps the College was just jealous of his thriving practice. Purgations were part of a normal physician's pharmacopoeia. So were clysters (enemas), suppositories, ointments and complicated pills, which were thought to slip down more easily, and do more good, if they were coated in gold.[49]

Some of the advice makes one's hair stand on end. Here are just a few of Thomas Phaire's suggestions for children.[50] A careful dose of 'Syrup of poppy' might help a wakeful child, but what about the brains of a hare rubbed on to teething gums, or a powdered burnt swallow, feathers and all, for quinsy, or some of the patient's own 'dung', also burnt, with a little honey? A teething baby would be glad to chew on 'the first cast tooth of a colt, set in silver and horn, or red coral in like manner'. 'The stones [testicles] of a hedgehog [if you can find them] powdered' should stop 'pissing in the bed'. Earthworms and pigeons' dung came in handy for shingles. The 'skin of a mouse clapped all hot' on a chilblain should help. Epilepsy would be easier to cure in a child over the age of seven, but you could try mistletoe 'taken in the month of March and the moon decreasing', or 'the stone that is found in the belly of a young swallow'. Who had found, let alone tried, that one?

Intestinal worms, of which Phaire gives a detailed description, could be expelled by a drink containing 'the herb that is found growing on oysters by the sea side'. A swelling of the navel should be treated with 'cow's dung seethed [boiled] in the milk of the same cow'. As to stones, 'there is few [diseases] so violent or more to be feared ... in all kinds of ages', but he could only advise dried peony roots in honey, or oil of scorpions – 'you may have it at the apothecaries' – or powdered medlar stones, which are 'wonderful good for to break the stone without danger, both in young and old'. Richard Stoneley relied on a preparation of white wine and salad oil, powdered crabs' eyes and the bone in a carp's head.[51]

With all these imaginative measures, it is surprising to find Phaire's advice on smallpox and measles, both caused, he thought, by diet, contagion, or conception during menstruation. (Intercourse during menstruation was long held to produce monstrous births, which were, of course, the fault of the woman. But conception during menstruation is not possible.) 'The best and most sure help in this case is not to meddle with any kind of medicine but to let nature work her operation.' The sores could be bathed gently in a herbal lotion, and anointed with hot bull's blood, or the dripping from a roast swan.

A few more handy hints for adults. In case you happen to be

poisoned, have a potion of rue, figs and walnuts always handy, and when the need arises add a whole unicorn's horn. If unavailable, a powdered one will do. But surely a whole one was unnecessary. A young Swiss tourist was shown a unicorn's horn, in Hampton Court Palace, which he visited in 1599.[52] It had been 'filed down to heal the sick'. In a case of plague, 'above all other things let him not despair', despite the well-known fact that 'in this sickness the worst is ever to be feared'. Meanwhile 'take a cock and pull the feathers off about his fundament and put a little salt in it and set his fundament upon the said botch [bubo] keeping him on a good while ... if the cock die ... take another young cock and split it quick [alive] asunder and lay it on the botch'.

'Travail of the mind' needs tranquillity and rest, 'and chiefly one ought after dinner to keep him from all things that trouble the memory, as studying, reading, writing and other like.' Old people over forty should 'comfort their bodies with some natural heat and meat of good nourishing ... wheat bread and good wine'.

William Clowes wrote his *De Morbo Gallico* (Concerning the French Pox) in English, despite its title, in 1585. This 'pestilent infection of filthy lust', which 'increaseth daily', could be cured by (1) perfect amendment of life, (2) punishment, and then (3) submitting to Clowes's cure. As Hippocrates said, extreme remedies are to be used against extreme diseases, so weigh in with the mercury, which although generally poisonous could be modified, for instance by the spittle of a fasting man, to make it comparatively innocuous. The Muslim physicians' treatment of skin lesions with mercury had been known in the West for many centuries, so the obvious step when confronted by a syphilitic chancre was to apply as much mercury as possible. Little else was available until the discovery of Salvarsan in 1910, and it did have some success in the early stages of the disease. Clowes claimed that he and his surgeon colleagues at St Bart's had cured more than a thousand patients in five years, but syphilis can recur decades later, when Clowes and his colleagues had long gone.[53]

John Hollybushe's snappily titled *A Most Excellent and Perfect Homish Apothecary or Homely Physic Book for All the Griefs and Diseases of the Body* was published in 1561.[54] Hollybushe was a methodical man. He dealt with each region of the body, and its diseases, in logical progression. In 'Concerning the head and his parts', he started with 'falling of the hair' (doves' dung, burnt; if unobtainable, try the ashes of little frogs), and touched on lice and nits (comb with an ointment of mercury and swines' grease, which might work quite well, as nits would lose their grip on greasy hair). Only then did he lift, as it were, the scalp, and get down to colds (shove a bit of turnip up your nose) and 'pains in the head'. For the latter, a 'wonderful experience ... set a dish or platter of tin upon the bare head, filled with water. Put an ounce and a half, or two ounces, of molten lead therein [*don't* spill it] while he hath it upon the head. Or else make a garland of vervain and wear it day and night.' 'All men that have feeble brains ought to beware of beans and lentils ...' 'Whirling in the head so sore that he thinks that the earth turns upside down', which was treatable with herbs, should not be confused with drunkenness, which undeservedly 'cometh oft by superfluous and undigested vapour' and was treatable with salt foot-baths. If you met a hopping man, he probably had tinnitus, and had put some oil of hempseed in his ears and 'after it let him leap upon his one leg upon that side where the disease is'. For retention of urine, he recommends the 'loppet' [?] of an onion, put into the penis, 'but if you have not that then take two or three lice, so great as you can get, and put them into the yard [penis] into the innermost hole that goeth into the body and put a little cloth therein that they may creep in, and he shall make water very well'. The lesson, if any, to be drawn from this is that lice were easier to find than onions.

Moving down to the lungs, he surveyed asthma (treat with 'the lungs of a fox washed in wine, herbs and liquorice') and 'pthisick' (tuberculosis). Phaire recognised this disease as incurable, but 'so that their life should be prolonged' suggested asses' milk and snails in their shells. 'You must live merry, and play at some pass time for pleasure, without labouring.' To which many patients would no doubt mutter that chance would be a fine thing.

The last psychological insight I will quote from Phaire is his treatment of that mysterious ailment called 'rising of the mother', when the uterus 'mounts up toward the midriff and the stomach, with intolerable pains'. (In the next century Sydenham made medical history by putting his mind to this curious aspect of femininity, and noticing that it could affect men too. Nevertheless it was still called hysteria, from the Greek word for womb.) One possible cause was 'too much abstinence of Venus', which unless it was a printer's error meant too little sex.

There was one therapy which would not have been generally

available: being touched by the Queen. There was a strongly held belief that the English monarch had a divine power to cure what was called the King's Evil – no matter that the monarch was a queen at the time. The illness, also known as scrofula, was a tubercular infection of the lymph glands at the neck. The cure had started with holy Edward the Confessor, the last English king (1042–66), and had gone on ever since.[55] Elizabeth duly 'touched', though she must have hated putting those long elegant hands on the sores. Clowes referred to this 'grievous malady, known to be miraculously cured and healed by the sacred hands of the Queen's most royal majesty ... through her Princely clemency a mighty number of her Majesty's most loyal subjects, and also many strangers born [foreigners] are daily cured and healed, who otherwise would most miserably have perished'.[56] The ceremony included the gift of a gold coin to be worn round the neck. (Samuel Johnson, one of the last people to be 'touched', wore his on a ribbon round his neck, all his life.)

Medical theories

What possible relevance to sixteenth-century Londoners could Hippocrates have, or Aristotle – even brought up to date by Galen (died c.216) and the two Muslim scientists known in the West as Avicenna (d.1037) and Averroes (d.1198)?[57] The answer has to be that no one had made much progress in medical knowledge, since their day.

The mainstay of medical thought was still the theory of humours. Put very briefly, it ran thus. Human life depends on a proper balance of the four elements, fire, air, water and earth, represented in human terms by four 'humours': blood, phlegm, choler and black bile. Before treating a patient, the physician must decide what kind of man he is. According to one authority a sanguine man would be 'liberal, amiable, inventive, bold, lecherous' and red-faced, and a phlegmatic man would be 'dull of understanding ... full of colour'. A choleric man would be 'envious, covetous, subtle, cruel, a watcher, prodigal, lean and of yellow colour'. A melancholic would be 'solitary, soft-spirited, fearful ... envious, covetous, black [dark] of colour',[58] which, if you were a woman looking for a congenial mate, did not leave much option. But even an amiable, sanguine man might veer into melancholy when he met old age at 40. The physician had also to know which of these humours related to the symptoms he observed in his patient. Then putting the two together he would be able to prescribe an appropriate remedy, which again had to be assessed for its humoral qualities. This was the reason for the blood-letting they were so fond of – balancing the patient's sanguine humour, blood, like balancing a central heating system. The extraordinary thing about all this is how long it lasted – for many centuries, until gradually physicians began to question the increasingly complex doctrines that had grown from the simple Greek theory, and were prepared to trust the evidence of their own eyes, which showed that the theory did not work.

Christian thought had meanwhile adopted another idea, easier to take on board, if just as far-fetched. God created nothing without a use. Although man came top in God's 'Great Chain of Being', he was not always very bright. God knew we might not always find the right use for some of the greenery He had scattered over the earth, so He kindly left signposts for us – 'signatures'. Therefore an orchid, which if you really try can look like a testicle, although I don't see it myself, is obviously good for venereal problems.[59] William Turner in his *Herbal* (1568), having paid the obligatory tribute to Galen et al., goes methodically round the plants in his own garden describing their signatures and uses, until he gets to his raspberries, where he is stuck. All he can suggest is raspberry wine, 'which doubtless should be good for many purposes'. And if only you find the right clue, 'there is no sickness ... but there is medicine for it', as observed in 1561 by Moulton Thomas, doctor of divinity and member of the order of friar preachers, which sounded impressive even though the order had been abolished in England 25 years earlier.[60] Friar Lawrence had the same idea, in Shakespeare's *Romeo and Juliet*:

> O mickle is the powerful grace that lies
> In herbs, plants, stones, and their true qualities,
> For nought so vile that on the earth doth live
> But to the earth some special good doth give[61]

Astrology too played a huge part in medical care. An average Londoner might lay out a penny for an almanac to see what lay in store for him, or rather more for Moulton Thomas's month-by-month advice. In April, he would find, 'it is evil to take purgation. It is not good to wed a maid for she shall be barren, but it is good to wed a widow ...' Or he might decide to consult the magician/astrologer/

medical expert Simon Forman, who was loathed by the medical establishment of the time but assiduously consulted by the great and the good, and many lesser people. By 1597 Forman's practice was booming. He was doubly useful because he could often use his magical powers to find missing objects and desirable marriage partners, as well as throwing in a medical consultation.[62] His colleague or competitor John Dee, whose practice included the Queen herself, held firmly to astrology. 'We also may daily perceive that man's body, and all other elemental bodies, are altered, disposed, ordered, pleasured and displeasured by the influential working of the sun, moon and other stars and planets.'[63]

The medical establishment

Physicians were at the top of the professional pecking order. The College of Physicians had enjoyed chartered status since 1518, and they were recognised to be gentlemen, with university degrees from the only two English universities, Oxford and Cambridge.[64] Foreign degrees were also accepted, from universities such as Padua and Leiden, where the medical training was far better. Of the nine physicians known to have been living in London in 1568, three at least were of foreign origin, and presumably had foreign qualifications.[65] Roderigo Lopez, the first physician appointed to St Bartholomew's Hospital, and the Queen's physician, was a Spaniard. (His nationality may have caused the accusation in 1594 that he had plotted to poison the Queen. He was arrested and executed, on flimsy evidence.) There were two Venetians, Carolus and his son Julius Borgarutius. The origin of 'Nonnez, doctor in physic', who lived in Tower ward, is not known. The Return of Strangers compiled in 1593 included a Fleming, and a French physician who had been in England since 1571.[66]

The College spent more time and energy on fighting its corner with the other branches of the profession than on applying any developments in medical knowledge. It achieved theoretical control over the apothecaries and the surgeons in 1540 – but the rules were impossible to enforce. Many unregistered practitioners carried on as they always had. Despite their apparent aloofness from practical medicine, the College was granted in 1565 the very useful gift of four cadavers a year from the gallows, on which to base public lectures on anatomy. These became one of the enjoyable sights of London.

Only physicians could prescribe or administer 'inward' medicines, even enemas. If a surgeon thought his patient needed an enema or a drug, he had to get a physician in to prescribe it. Surgeons were not gentlemen, or ladies. The Surgeons' Guild had amalgamated with the Barbers' Guild in 1520. Surgeons were tradespeople, like barbers, and like barbers they served a practical seven-year apprenticeship, after which they had a licence to practise – 'limited', in theory, but it was enough for most members. Their Guild, like the College of Physicians, was entitled to four executed criminals' corpses a year, for demonstration purposes. In 1567 they appointed Julius Borgarutius, one of the two Venetian physicians, to lecture their members on anatomy. There were probably about 70–100 surgeons in London by the end of the century, of whom at least five came from abroad.[67] Very few men went on to the next step, which was a master's degree in anatomy and surgery, and a full licence to practise, granted by the Bishop of London.

Some London surgeons had qualified abroad. Epover Fredericke had arrived from Holland in 1569, and Godfrey Masone had come from Cleves in 1575, the same year that William Chamberlen arrived from Rouen.[68] Chamberlen brought with him his obstetrical forceps, but he kept its design a family secret which was passed down through three generations of Chamberlens, until the death of William's great-grandson in 1720, when according to legend one was found in a box under the floorboards in their house. It had been possible to hide it from curious eyes during its use, because for all that time modesty demanded that the woman in labour must be covered with a sheet, so no one saw the Chamberlen forceps in operation. Elinor Sneshell, surgeon, a widow from Valenciennes, had been in England for 26 years in 1593, although she may not, of course, have been practising all that time. Another woman surgeon, Elizabeth Moulthorne of Antwerp, had just arrived.

The most famous Elizabethan surgeon was William Clowes, who transformed the surgical practice of his day.[69] He served in the Army in 1563, and was then transferred to the Navy. He held staff appointments at St Bartholomew's Hospital and Christ's Hospital. So he had an unrivalled clinical experience of the damage caused by guns, swords, syphilis and scurvy. Clowes got his Bishop's Licence in 1590, after his appointment as Surgeon to the Fleet. He wrote numerous textbooks, in a downright English far removed from the high-flown Latin prose of physicians. He was much given to aphorisms. 'Fingers are the best instruments, and scabbards make good splints', and a surgeon should have 'a lion's heart, a lady's hand and a hawk's eye'.

If you have a strong stomach, here is Clowes's advice on amputating a leg:

> Prepare the patient two hours before, with 'some comfortable caudel'. (Can one hope that this contained a hefty slug of opium or alcohol? Simon Forman recommended a preparation of hemlock to make the patient 'sleep soundly, while you cut him or burn him … to make him awake, rub the palms of his hands and soles of his feet with wine vinegar'.[70] Possibly Clowes is being careful here, bearing in mind the rule that surgeons could not prescribe 'inward medicines'.)
>
> Then get in a preacher to 'exhort him to patience in adversity', and warn his friends that he may die.
>
> Position the patient at the end of a strong bench, with one strong man behind him holding both his arms and another 'to bestride the leg that is to be cut off and he must hold the member very fast about the place where the incision is to be made … he shall have a large strong hand and a good fast grip', because it is up to him to minimise the bleeding. Sometimes 'by the skillfulness of the holder only four ounces of blood are lost', which even with present-day resources would be commendable. The 'good fast grip' acted as a tourniquet.
>
> Then another man holds the leg lower down.
>
> 'Be sure to have a sharp saw … then boldly, with a steady and quick hand …' I won't go on.
>
> After dressing the ends of the blood vessels with Clowes's particular styptic – he had discovered that the conventional practice of dipping the stump in boiling oil did more harm than good – cover the stump with a wet ox bladder, which would contract as it dried, exerting uniform pressure to stop bleeding.
>
> 'Then you shall as easily as possibly may be carry the patient to his bed … let him lie with as much quietness as you can.'

In one morning's list as St Bartholomew's Hospital, Clowes successfully amputated seven legs and arms, 'where, with the assistance of Almighty God, we stayed all their fluxes of blood [haemorrhages]'.

Limbs could be amputated, 'visible griefs' excised, but not even Clowes could open up a living human body. There was a single exception to this. Stones in the kidney or bladder can cause acute pain. Although there were plenty of allegedly infallible pills and potions to disperse them, none worked. As far back as Hippocrates there had been 'practitioners of the craft of cutting for the stone', to whom he recommended physicians to leave such matters. By the early sixteenth century, lithotomy procedures were sophisticated enough to leave only the occasional patient incontinent, but they were carried out by specialist lithotomists, not by surgeons.

Apothecaries belonged to the powerful Grocers' company. By the end of the century there were probably about a hundred of them in London, many of them clustering in one street just off Cheapside, Bucklersbury. In their shops, at least according to Shakespeare,

> A tortoise hung,
> An alligator stuff'd, and other skins
> Of ill-shaped fishes ...[71]

But they were very useful to Londoners. They could be relied on to produce that invaluable unicorn's horn in a crisis, and quicksilver (mercury) if the Foul Pox had touched the household, and all kinds of distillations that would be complicated if not impossible to make at home. An apothecary's shop, alligators and all, must have been a pleasant place to stand and chat with your neighbours while you waited for his attention, and even his advice. And because so many herbs were used in medicines, the shops smelled wonderful, which must have made a nice change.

Herbalists and wise women were specifically allowed to practise, by Acts of Parliament in 1542–3. Unlike physicians, they charged fees that ordinary people could afford. They often accepted payment in kind, such as food or service. One estimate of their numbers in the last two decades of the century is a surprising 250.

Midwives were licensed by the Church, since they might have to baptise a very sick baby before it could be brought to a properly qualified (and paid) parson. They had to swear that they would prevent abortion, exclude magic – difficult, in those days when a good luck charm would be almost universal – and try to get an unmarried mother to disclose the father's identity so that he could be forced to maintain his child, thus saving its costs to the parish. It seems to me unlikely that these women would bother a girl *in extremis* with such considerations. No test was made of a midwife's technical competence. But many babies were delivered by women whose only qualifications were their personal experience of childbirth, and the commonsense of their own mothers.

And at the bottom of the pile come the pettifoggers and charlatans and quacks, omnipresent no matter how rigidly the medical profession tried to eradicate them. Pettifoggers 'do hunt after hurt and wounded men' to whom they offer the services of a really good surgeon, with whom the pettifogger splits the fee. As to charlatans and quacks, people will always buy an elixir that promises eternal life/beauty/health/ all three, if the price is right. And on a grey and hopeless day, a few pennies invested in a guaranteed beauty cure may well be worth the cost, until disillusion catches up. Still, it was fun while it lasted.

The next century was the golden age of quacks, but one 'cure' popular in the seventeenth century is just visible in the sixteenth: the remarkable 'weapon salve'.[72] Suppose you are wounded by a sword. *If you can*, get the sword and anoint it with this amazing ointment – to you, a special price. Don't bother with your wound, except to keep it clean. For only the cost of the salve, you can be sure that your wound will heal. The trickiest part is getting hold of the sword, which belonged, presumably, to some villain who wished you harm, and he is unlikely to be standing about waiting to give it to you. Clowes was scathing: '[A quack] said also that his skill was such that if a man were wounded at York, bring him the weapon that hurt the patient and he would cure him, forsooth, by only dressing of the weapon and though he never see the patient. As certain as the sea burns!'[73]

Another Clowes broadside on quacks:

> Then rises out of his chair, fleering and jeering, this miraculous surgeon, floriously glittering like the man in the moon, with his bracelets about his arms, therein many jewels and stones of St Vincent's rocks [?], his fingers full of rings, a silver case with instruments hanging at his girdle and a gilt spatula sticking in his hat … he said he had attained unto the deep knowledge of the makings of a certain quintessence which he had learned beyond the seas of his master, … a great magician … this shameless Beast [said] that if a man did drink of his Quintessence continually every day a certain quantity … a man should not die before the day of the Great

Judgement ... and it would preserve him in that state he was in at thirty years of age ... although a man were 100 or 6 score years of age.

What a sales pitch.

Accidents and emergencies

This is where Clowes shone. One day out at Mile End a man was peacefully watching the archery practice, when a barbed arrow went into his leg. The inevitable officious bystander 'which professed surgery' tried to pull it out, but of course left the arrowhead in. Clowes was there, providentially, and excised it.

There was a multiple accident at the Bear Garden, when 'all the gallery there did fall down and killed and hurt many patients'. One of them had a fractured skull, which Clowes probed with his fingers till he found where the bone had been pushed down into the brain. While 'a strong man stedfastly [held the patient's] head with his hands', Clowes drilled holes in the man's skull with a trepan, to relieve pressure, 'then with an instrument called a Levator I raised up the depressed bone, which being done immediately his speech [which had been 'hindered'] amended' and in time the patient made a full recovery.

Another case, a fractured thigh. Clowes reduced the fracture by getting the (usual) two strong men to pull on the leg above and below the break, while he got the bones into the right places, 'and caused the two men which extended the member by little and little to release their hands, whereby the patient found himself greatly eased'.[74] 'Eased' he may have been, but grateful he was not. 'Both he and his friends seemed to be discontented with me for that the fractured member was somewhat shorter than his other leg.'

Foreigners

Blackamoors and lascars

John Hawkins is better known for introducing tobacco to England, and fighting the Armada, than for setting up the English slave trade. There is in the State Papers Domestic a proposal by him dated 16 September 1567 to 'lade negroes in Guinea and sell them in the West Indies in truck of [in exchange for] gold, pearls and emeralds', the diabolical threeway traffic.[1] Men and women captured or bought on the west coast of Africa were packed into ships and transported over the Atlantic, to be sold in the Spanish West Indies, which were short of labour, the native Caribs having disobligingly died out. Once the English sailors were home, they could invest some of their profits in paltry trade goods, and start again. Sometimes a few slaves were brough to the English market. By the end of the century, the long-lasting fashion for black servants to attend gentlewomen had begun. Paul Baning, alderman, had three 'blackamoor' maids.[2] 'A negar whose name was supposed to be Frauncis ... servant to Mr Peter Miler a beer brewer' appears in the burial records of Aldgate parish in 1596.[3] It looks as if they were employees, not slaves, which they would have been in the West Indies. Queen Elizabeth herself had a negro servant, but that did not stop her from issuing a proclamation that 'there are of late divers blackamoors brought into this realm, of which kind there are already too man considering how God has blessed this land with great increase of people of our nation ... those kind of people should be sent forth out of the land'. A Lubeck merchant offered to help by shipping them back to spain and Portugal, where he was sure of a good market, but his overtures came to nothing, and the proclamation was never strictly enforced.[4]

The Elizabethans seem to have distinguished between 'Moors' from Morocco and the Barbary coast of north Africa, 'Ethiops' from some fabled interior of Africa where Prester John ruled, and 'blackamoors' from west Africa. They do not seem to have had any specific antipathy to a dark African skin. It was certainly fashionable to be fair, and the trendy London woman went to some lengths to preserve her peaches-and-cream complexion, but Shakespeare made no particular point of Othello's colour. He is 'a noble Moor in the service of Venice'. Roderigo refers to him as 'thick-lipped', and Desdemona's father, still shocked by the news of his daugher's elopement, refers to Othello's 'sooty bosom', but that was in the heat of the moment before he realises that they are properly married. Othello wonders why – as he mistakenly thinks – Desdemona no longer loves him: 'haply [perhaps], for I am black', but it is just as likely that it is because of the age gap. If there was a popular prejudice to be exploited, surely Shakespeare would have done so in *Othello*?[5] There was no political correctness to be observed in those days.

I have included lascars here, although I have no direct evidence for them. Elizabethan ships were by now competing with the Dutch in the trade to the Spice Islands in the Far East. Their crews were often so ravaged by scurvy and tropical diseases that the captains must have enlisted local men accustomed to the sea, to get their ships back to London. Then what? At least by the time they arrived – if they survived – these unfortunates could speak English. They probably made their way to the seamen's quarter of London, down the Thames bank past the Tower, and merged into the background until the next ship.

Foreign tourists

'They [the English] care little for foreigners, but scoff and laugh at them ... one dare not oppose them, else the street-boys and apprentices collect together ... and because they are the strongest, one is obliged to put up with the insult as well as the injury' – so found the Duke of Würtemburg, no less, when he, or rather his tutor, wrote up the journal of his educational tour to England in 1592.[6] Perhaps the young German duke was lucky. In 1558 a French law student had found that 'the people of this nation have a mortal hatred of the French'.[7] Certainly the French were blamed for the French Pox, when it was not the Italians (the 'Neapolitan bone-ache').[8]

Thomas Platter was a young Swiss who came to London in 1599. Although he may have been treated no differently from other visitors to the Tower of London, one cannot help suspecting that the guards/guides saw this foreign tourist coming, and took him for a ride.[9] He methodically and stoically listed every tip he and his friends had to fork out: 'three English shillings' in the first room of the Armoury, another tip in the next room, and in the next 'we gave largesse for the third time'; in the last Armoury room a fourth gratuity; then up and down, here and there, seeing an ancient tapestry – 'the fifth gratuity' – and the roof of Julius Caesar's tower (?), which netted the guide 'the sixth gratuity'. The seventh was after seeing the Mint, and 'having now for the eighth time also made a gratuity to the soldiers we returned to our hostel', surely devoid of cash and energy. He does not seem to have been so unlucky anywhere else.

All tourists need a phrase-book.[10] Caxton printed *Dialogues in French and English* in 1483. It was still selling in 1600. The 1589 edition, giving translations from English into Flemish, German, Latin, Italian, Spanish and French, would be a great help to a tourist in an inn.

On arrival:

'My she [female] friend, is my bed made? Is it good?'
'Yes Sir, it is a good feather bed, the sheets be very clean.'
'Pull off my hose and warm my bed, draw the [bed] curtains, and pin them with a pin. My she friend, kiss me once and I shall sleep the better. I thank you fair maiden …'

And when leaving:

'Where is the maid? Hold, my she friend, there is [a tip] for thy pains.'

Immigrants

Is Europe a good thing? If you close your eyes, will it go away? Why do these foreigners want to come here anyway? And should we let them in or throw them out?

We have never been really sure of the answers. In Elizabeth's day England was becoming known as the only country where someone who protested against the Pope's authority over this world and the next could be tolerably safe. There were economic migrants as well, as English prosperity increased. During a long and heated debate in the Commons, Lord Burghley summed up the problem. It had 'brought honour to our kingdom to be accounted a refuge for distressed nations' – a splendid sentiment foreshadowing the Statue of Liberty – *but* 'our charity must not hinder or injure ourselves'; in modern terms, 'not in my back yard'.

Foreigners had their uses. In 1599 a Dutchman who had lived in London all his life wrote that 'the most toilsome, difficult and skilful works are chiefly performed by foreigners'.[11] As to 'toilsome', this sounds like the gast-arbeiters invited to sweep the streets of Switzerland. Inevitably, they left no record of their lives.

But many were prosperous. Jacob Verselyn had left his native Murano to set up a glassworks in Crutched Friars some time before 1568, and had revolutionised glass production by using soda-ash from seaweed, the supply of which presented no problems.[12] Diricke Anthony from Cologne was 'chief graver of the mint and seals' to Edward VI, Philip and Mary, and now, Elizabeth. He had twenty grandchildren, all in London. The Queen's grocer was a Spaniard. At the apex of the pile was Sir Horatio Pallavicino, a Genoese merchant and one of the richest men in London in 1568. He stepped into Sir Thomas Gresham's shoes in 1579, as Elizabeth's chief financial and diplomatic agent abroad.

The main tide of immigrants came from the territories we know as Holland, Belgium, northern France and the northern part of Germany. They tended to settle in Southwark, St Martin le Grand and Blackfriars, and in small packed enclaves in the suburbs and the City, but not in the inner parishes. (Note, to clear up a possible muddle: 'Dutch' is in some contexts the inaccurate translation of 'Deutsch'. A 'Dutch' man may come from the German-speaking or Flemish-speaking parts of the Low Countries, or the German states. The most that could definitely be said of him was that his native language, whether German, Walloon or other, was unlikely to be French, Italian or English.)

The ties of family, religion and commerce attracted a steady stream of immigrants, which turned into a flood whenever things became particularly nasty for Protestants in Europe. As soon as official hostility relaxed in their native country, the French, in particular, set off home again. The Protestants from the Low Countries were more apt to settle permanently here. A few dates to bear in mind:

1560: Aachen expelled Protestants.
1562: 1,200 Huguenots were massacred in France.
1566: Dutch revolt against Spain began; mass exodus of Protestants.
1567: 2,000 Protestants were massacred in the Netherlands.
1572: the Massacre of St Bartholomew's Day in Paris caused an exodus of the surviving Huguenots, many to England.

The City, although sympathetic in theory, found the foreigners hard to take. In 1571 the Citizens of London put in an official complaint about foreign merchants and craftsmen. Although only freemen were allowed to own property in London, and subdivision of existing houses was prohibited, foreign merchants were breaking the law. They not only 'took up the fairest houses in the city', they then subdivided them, or took in illegal lodgers. They 'feed the markets at their pleasure' by holding imported goods for longer than the statutory limit of six weeks. They traded between themselves, and 'sent to everyman's house' – the original doorstep salesmen – instead of going to the open market like everyone else, and then they remitted their profits to their country of origin instead of increasing English wealth. They 'keep themselves severed from us in church, in government, in trade, in language and marriage'. The craftsmen broke the apprenticeship rules, and illegally imported manufactured goods from abroad.[13] In a word, they were foreign.

The Privy Council was torn two ways. It was anxious to harness foreigners' ability to do 'difficult and skilful work', and persuade them to teach Londoners, who were lagging behind in new marketing opportunities. Lord Burghley even had two Flemish tapestry weavers appointed to Christ's Hospital, to teach the boys their skills. On the other hand, the Council had to keep the City's support. To assess the whole problem, the Council ordered counts of foreigners, at increasingly frequent intervals, to see whether they were really such a threat as the City thought.[14] A census made in 1573, after the Massacre of St Bartholomew's Day, found over 7,000 'strangers', of whom 2,561 'confess[ed] themselves that their coming hither was only to seek work for their living'. The arrival of these energetic economic migrants was probably a greater threat to Londoner craftsmen, and more resented, than the plight of those driven to emigrate for religious reasons.

By 1579, in yet another survey, the census-takers found just over five and a half thousand aliens, which was consistent with the probable average figure throughout Elizabeth's reign. In an estimated population of 150,000–200,000 they were not, one would have thought, a significant problem – but they felt like it to native Londoners, xenophobic as ever. Londoners' animosity simmered on. In 1580 the Lord Mayor issued a precept 'for the well treating of strangers', but you do not change people's attitudes by orders.[15] Anti-foreigner handbills appeared in the streets. The Privy Council authorised the City to use torture, if necessary, to discover where they were coming from, but without result.

The 1593 Return of Strangers[16]

By now the technique of census taking was sophisticated. As he went from parish to parish in his ward, the alderman – or more probably his deputy – would have with him the parish constable and 'one or more of the most sad [respectable] and discrete persons' of his ward, *and* – it must have been quite a crowd – the minister of the relevant foreign church, or some other trustworthy foreigner who could interpret if necessary. The foreigners could be put on oath.[17] For the census ordered in 1593 the aldermen of each ward were, as usual, to make

> with as great secrecy as may be ... diligent search ... within all parts in your ward what and how many foreigners are residing ... of what nation, profession, trade or occupation ... how many servants ... how long they ... have been in the realm, to what Church every of them resort, whether they keep [employ] any English-born people in their house or otherwise set them to work, or whether any of them sell any [prohibited] wares ... whereby the prices of things be enhanced or Her Majesty ... decreased in her customs.[18]

So once again the aldermen and their entourage set off round every ward in the metropolitan area, quill pens and inkpots at the ready, combining as best they might secrecy and diligence, rapping on the door of anyone who might be foreign, and grappling with these pestilential foreign names. Whom did they find?

Some strangers had been in England, most probably in London, for decades, and must have been all too accustomed to these constant questions. Agustyn Bassano, musician to the Queen, had been here 32 years, and his colleague Innocent Coemes had come here from Venice 50 years ago, presumably as a baby. Michael Aret, a Dutch shoemaker, had lived here 28 years, and ran a considerable enterprise, employing nine strangers and nine Englishmen. There were 24 foreign shoemakers in all, including the Widow Drewett, who had been here 22 years and employed eight people, and Robert la Houle, who had been here 18 years and had enough trade for four English apprentices. Most strangers seem to have been well aware of the rule that they must employ as many Englishmen as they did fellow-strangers – unless the truth was that they heard the census-takers coming and hid their young foreign apprentices in the coal cellars.

Jacob Verselyn/Verzelini/Vasselin from Murano still 'keeps the glasshouse' with eight compatriots, making up his quota of English with a journeyman, two serving men and six women. Surely he was a son or grandson of the Jacob Verselyn recorded at the glasshouse in 1568? Many foreigners made themselves opportunities in the luxury trades where native-born Londoners could not or would not compete. Over 500 strangers were employed in the cloth-making trade. There were two French button-makers living in St Martins le Grand, employing between them nine strangers and nine Englishmen. There were three feather-dressers, Sebastian Bonefey who had been in England for more than 40 years and had accumulated eight children aged between thirteen and two – what wonderful playthings his stock-in-trade must have been – and Katherine Dollme who had been here 30 years, and there was still room for John Hascard. The Italian Peter Fauvell, who had been here 40 years, made undoubtedly fashionable hats. There were three diamond cutters from Antwerp, including Antony Cuthance who had been here 19 years. They seem, understandably, to have worked alone. Goldsmiths too had small households in general. Mme Bennet, a French widow, was a gold-smith, and so were Blommars who had been here 18 years, Peter Clownes who had been here two years longer, and Garrett Vanderbuss who had been here 40 years. Señor Bystoe from Genoa, perfumer of gloves, had an English wife and had been here 34 years.

In the medical profession, Peter Chamberlen, surgeon (surely related to William Chamberlen, who arrived from Rouen in 1575), and his wife, both from Rouen, had been here since 1567. They had three children, a journeyman and an English maid. Another surgeon, this time from Holland, Epover Frederick, had been here 24 years and had two English apprentices, and Godfrey Masone of Cleves, surgeon, had been here 18 years. One wonders what they thought of their female colleagues Elizabeth Moulthorne, surgeon, of Antwerp, a newcomer of six years' standing, and the widow Elinor Sneshell, surgeon, who had been here 26 years. Gideon de Laune, apothecary, had been here 18 years, and had only one stranger apprentice with his two English ones. The senior branch of the profession was represented by William de Lawne (related to the apothecary?) from France, who had one English apprentice, Raphael Thorris from Flanders, and Godfrey Mefine, an Italian described as a 'doctor' – but he may have been a doctor of law, not a physician. And there were five midwives, including a French widow, Phyllis de Port, and another midwife from Ghent. It must have been comforting for stranger women to know that they would be attended in childbirth by someone speaking their own language.

There were sixteen schoolteachers, including Sebastian Arryatt, a Frenchman born in 'the Halpes' and here already 20 years, Philip Columbe from Arras, and Debone from Lille, here for 22 years. Katheren Gaste 'taught children', perhaps at dame-school level, and supplemented her income by sewing. Christopher Haris 'of Normandy' had one son of eight years 'who works' and two little girls who did not, yet. John Jewe, widower, from Dieppe, had eight scholars boarding with him: three Miffant brothers and five other boys aged between eight and thirteen, all except one born in Dieppe. Was he running a language school for French boys?

The most intriguing households of all were run by the foreign starchers. Starch, which sounds so innocuous, was a red-hot subject for reformers, who deplored it as the invention of the Devil. But without it those 'monstrous ruffs' would flop like old rags. Here are two stalwart ladies: Dionis Welfes, born in Antwerp, who had been in England since starched ruffs became fashionable, in 1568 – one longs to know how old she was in 1593 – who 'has one stranger woman … and keeps 4 English women servants and sets 4 Englishwomen to work', and the widow Stedon, a Dutch lady who had come ten years later, and whose establishment rivalled Dionis Welfes's in size. Beside them Richard Garrett, 'starcher, English' and his Dutch wife, who had no apprentices or other employees, were trying to go it alone.

Then there were oddities like the two widows, both spinsters –
they earned their living by spinning – who had been here over
twenty years, and a mason from Bruges – was he helping with some
of the more elaborate stonework going up in London? Derik
Derickson had been here fifty years but was still only a 'botcher or
mender of old garments': hardly an economic threat. There was a
'French playing-card maker' and another described only as a
'card-maker'; and a 'tomb maker' who had a flourishing trade,
employing four journeymen and two apprentices – did he ever
employ widow Vanderporne, 'carver in stone'? If you were looking
for hawk-hoods and lures, you would go to William Marten, a
Dutchman who had an overseas trade in hawks. He probably knew
Arthur Seland, falconer. A keen tennis player would find his way
to Peter Ringer, racket maker. M. Beauvais' business of making
crossbows could support three journeymen and three apprentices,
all English. Antony Martine, pilot to the Earl of Cumberland, had
come to England three years ago from Tenerife; his knowledge of
the waters round his native island might be very useful in a quick
raid on the Spanish fleet.

At the bottom of the pile, the census-takers found John Danhaye
from Antwerp, 'a poor man' with a wife and two children; Valentin
Blee, John Denne and James Fever, all 'bad men'; Barbara
Erwrappers, a 'labouring woman' from Antwerp; and Mouea, a
'blackamoor' aged twenty – nothing more is known, not even
his/her sex. Perhaps Mouea's face caught the eyes of the three
maids in Alderman Baning's house – they too were 'blackamoors'.

And apart from everyone, a French family perhaps wondering
whether they were safe to go home soon, after six years of exile:
Antony Mallnarte, 'gentleman', and his wife, from Orléans, with
two boys born in Orléans and four little girls born in England. He
was the only gentleman in the long detailed list.

The grand total of the 1593 Return was 7,013: 4,570 strangers
born abroad, plus 2,443 born in England, many of them children.
Not much of a rise after all, since 1568, when there had been 6,704,
and marginally down on the 1573 total of 7,143. No comparably
exact figure of London's total population is available, but it has been
estimated at 200,000.[19] The strangers were more of a perceived than
a real threat.

Naturalisation

Foreigners could acquire English nationality, if they thought it was worth the cost involved. There were two ways. You could buy a Patent of Denization from the Crown, or for even more money you could get Parliament – if it was in session, which it mostly was not – to grant an Act of Naturalisation. In the whole of Elizabeth's reign 1,762 patents were granted, and only twelve Acts passed. Probably most foreigners did not bother. Sir Horace Pallavicino became a denizen in 1585, and so Elizabeth could knight him in 1587, but his was an unusual case.[20] There are denizens scattered through the 1593 Return of Strangers, but they still came under 'aliens'. The main advantage of denizen status was that the holder could acquire real property, and bequeath it to his children as long as they were born in England after the grant of denizenship. In theory a denizen could also join a livery company, which for a Londoner was an essential step to success; but it seems that few did.

Tax and other penalties

Even if a foreigner became a denizen, it did not change his status for tax purposes. He sometimes had to pay twice the amount assessed on a native Londoner, as well as all kinds of other petty taxes and duties payable only by aliens, which must have been irritating. So it is not surprising that many aliens felt they were just as well off in their existing status.

The Hanseatic merchants had had no need to consider denization. They had been allowed to live in their self-contained community, with special trading concessions, ever since the twelfth century, much as Britain enjoyed extra-territorial concessions in Shanghai and Hong Kong in the nineteenth century. By the sixteenth century their main trade to London was timber, cordage and grain from north Germany and the Baltic, and they were not popular for cashing in on the periodic crises in wheat production caused by poor English harvests. In 1551 the understandable objections of the native merchants had brought most of their privileges to an end. They continued to occupy their hall at the Steelyard[21] on the river, and other property, and to enjoy their exemption from taxes, until 1578.[22] They finally had to leave the country in 1598. At least their presence had the indirect result of the standardisation of weights. The Hanse merchants complained bitterly about having to use the London merchants' measures – which they did not trust – after 1578. A proper system of standard weights, with regular official inspections, was imposed on everyone in 1582.

Aliens, whether denizens or not, were not allowed to have 'open shops' which enticed passers-by to come in and buy the goods being made and sold there. If an alien had a shop that gave on to a street or lane, he had to obscure his windows by a lattice. This was gradually recognised as ludicrous, in those days when daylight was the only source of light except candlelight, and by 1587 aliens were allowed to arrange things – quite how? – so that passers-by could not see them, but they could see to work. Nor were they supposed to take apprentices: but this seems to have been allowed in practice. In general, the moral seems to have been to keep away from the limelight and cause no trouble, and with luck the authorities would turn a blind eye unless one of the periodic down-with-foreigners campaigns was running.

Social organisation

The authorities were always interested to know which church, if any, a stranger attended, in case they needed to apply pressure, through its minister. Most foreigners living in London belonged to one of two churches. Edward VI had given the nave of the friars' church in the dissolved Augustinian monastery in Broad Street to the Dutch church. Mary had cancelled the grant, but it was restored by Elizabeth. These good Protestants must have surely been distracted, sometimes, to find themselves praying in an enormous church built so magnificently, so long ago, by pious Catholics, even though its tombs and ornaments had been despoiled. But at least the building was sound and in good repair when they got it back, and responded to their congregational singing as it had done to the monks' plainsong. The community increased rapidly under Elizabeth, from 700 communicants two years after the church reopened, in 1561, to nearly 2,000 in 1568.[23]

The French community took over St Anthony's Church round the corner in Threadneedle Street. There were fewer members than of the Dutch church, numbering only 1,800 in 1568. Both churches were organised along similar lines, while they differed in membership. The French church could muster more men likely to be accepted in English Court and political circles where they could lobby for its members, but the Dutch church had more economic clout; by 1592 the Flemish silk twisters were employing between them more than 1,000 English workers, and when the Dutch church complained to the authorities of harassment, they had to be listened to.

Native Londoners attended their parish churches scattered through London, as a matter of course, and the sight of hundreds of identifiable foreigners streaming into just two neighbouring churches every Sunday may have fostered an idea that they were more numerous than they were. In the 1570s, the Privy Council insisted that the existing voluntary arrangements for immigrant communities to settle elsewhere than London – for instance, the communities of Flemish weavers in Norwich and Maidstone – be made compulsory, to try to defuse this animosity.

It was true (see the Londoners' Complaint of 1571 on page 114) that the foreign churches in London had an admirable 'government'. Anyone applying to join either church had to prove that he had led a sober life abroad, as well as satisfying the examiners that he was sincere in his faith. From 1573 anyone set down as 'of no church' in a Return of Strangers ran the risk of banishment, so it was as well to adopt a public allegiance to one or other. Both churches were run by councils of eight elders (twelve after 1571), who kept their members under tight control. There was no rushing into matrimony, for example. A young couple intending to marry had to go through a formal betrothal in front of the minister or an elder, which should ensure, if all went well, that neither party had left a spouse back in France. They had to produce evidence that their parents consented, even if this meant sending someone to their home town to see the parents, and no doubt check on any existing liaisons, and the elders might warn an innocent young man that he had made a notoriously bad choice. The English marriage rules were less stringent, so some couples opted for marriage in their parish church instead, but this meant that they could never go back to the French church.

Once a couple was duly married, adultery was not taken so seriously in the strangers' churches. Spouses could be reconciled by counselling, and wife-beaters were told to mend their ways. Martin le Picquart had that bad habit of working late – or so he said – and his wife was told not to nag him when he came home tired. One optimistic courting couple arranged to meet secretly in a tavern, but nothing could be hidden in that community; Susanne Roger could say that they both went in, and neither had come out during the hour she spent watching. Perhaps they were discussing the price of fish, but church members were expected to avoid even the appearance of naughtiness. An elder's wife had danced at a wedding: shocking. Her husband was told to bring her in for a reprimand. And that reprimand would be public, in church, during the main service, when everyone would hear; which again caused a small trickle of resentful members, into English parish churches.

On the other hand, the foreign churches did look after their own. If any member was not seen at Communion, or was thought to be ill, the elder responsible for that district went to see him. Two members could help him with advice about his will, which had to be translated from Dutch to Latin to satisfy English rules. He was no doubt encouraged to follow the example of many fellow members and leave a legacy to the church, but he could be sure his property would be disposed of honestly after his death, particularly because an elder, or the notary, often witnessed the will or acted as an executor. If he needed financial help, perhaps to bring his wife over to join him, or to start a new business, loans were available. A commercial dispute with a fellow-member – and there was much trade within the foreign community, although deplored by the citizens of London – could be referred to arbitrators appointed by the church: probably merchants themselves, who would understand the case far better than any English judge.

In a sudden crisis, a member could apply for a payment from the poor box, and each church had a poorhouse. If he was ill, medical care could be arranged. In the dreadful plague of 1563 the Dutch church appointed a paid surgeon to look after their sick. Both churches ran energetic fund-raising campaigns, but many contributions came from sympathetic English people; the Bishop of London gave the huge sum of £320 to the French church after the St Bartholomew's Day massacre of Huguenots. And when the Queen was on one of her periodic financial drives, the foreign churches were prepared to stand up to her. She asked for £800 to defray the cost of the futile Netherlands campaign, in 1585, but they said they had already given £1,072, and that was that.

It would be rewarding to find a picture of these resourceful men and women. We can surely say that they were unlikely to favour the extremes in cut and colour flaunted by fashionable Londoners, but more than that we have nothing, except a tiny glimpse of a poor Dutch tailor who complained of being harassed, although he worked only for fellow-strangers, 'which do wear apparel but [only] after Dutch fashion'.

CHAPTER 8

Clothes and Beauty

Ruffs[1]

These extraordinary contraptions set off the sitter's head in portraits of the time like the head of John the Baptist on a charger garnished with a pie-frill. Everyone wore them, women and men, working people and courtiers. They were rarely becoming, they cost a fortune to buy and maintain, and they were unspeakably uncomfortable, especially to those with short necks or beards or both. I have only once seen them commended in contemporary prose, by a young Venetian tourist in 1562, when they were not yet so 'monstrous'. In an uncharacteristic burst of imagination, he described them as having 'the shape of water-lilies and violets'.[2]

They began as the narrow frill that happens when you gather the billowing fullness of an Elizabethan shirt into a band at the neck, leaving perhaps an inch of the shirt to stick up from the top of the band in a frill. It stands upright because of the high collar of the doublet.[3] If you stiffen the frill slightly by edging it with a fine cord, it can be persuaded to make a wavy pattern. Then the doublet collar gets higher, and so does the frill. By about 1570 – remarkable how long this extraordinary fashion lasted – the neck band and the frill part company with the shirt altogether, and become a band as long as the wearer's neck size, buttoned or tied with tape at the ends to fit the neck closely, plus a strip of material anything from two to nine inches wide and sometimes as much as *six yards* long, sewn on to the band in minute regular cartridge pleats.[4] It may possibly help the non-dressmaker to imagine a ruff lying flat on the table, next to a large mushroom which is stalk side up. Each gill of the mushroom, radiating from the stalk, is a pleat at the neck edge of the ruff. (Or then again it may not.)

There may be as many as 600 of these pleats in an elaborate ruff. If the material of the frill is not extremely fine, it would make an unwearably bulky mass at the neck edge, so the first essential is to use a lawn or cambric as fine as possible. Some ultra-fashionables wore two or three ruffs, one on top of the other in tiers: 'three falling one upon another, for that's the new edition now'.[5] A working man's or woman's ruff still has the neck band and the pleats, but the fabric is coarser, and the strip shorter and narrower, so that it stands up on its own. An apprentice's ruff was not supposed to be more than 1½ yards long, which would make a very modest ruff.[6] A maidservant's clothes, listed on her admission to St Bartholomew's Hospital in 1569 and returned to her on her discharge, included 'three pair of ruffs'.[7]

Now to make the figures-of-eight or 'sets'. You start at the outer edge of the circle of pleated fabric. You have a 'poking stick' about 18 inches long, with a rounded end like a finger, and you carefully push it in, towards the neck edge, pulling and smoothing the fullness round the poking stick with your other hand as you go, to make a wide curve.[8] Then you make the next set, but the other way up. You slowly work your way round the circle, producing a series of curves alternately facing upwards or downwards. Poking sticks varied in size, and produced differently sized curves. At first they were made of bone, ivory or wood, but by 1573 someone had realised that heated steel would work much better.

'Setting' a ruff needs astonishing patience, let alone the skill to end up with the same size of sets as you began with, and to avoid making holes in the fine fabric as you go. No wonder that the ruffs that have survived sometimes have exquisitely done darns in them. The customer can tell the laundress to set her ruff in big, wide curves, or more, smaller curves, depending on the day's fashion and the wearer's whim. As each set leaves the laundress's hand, it jostles its neighbour and – with luck – stands up in a regular figure-of-eight pattern. The 600 tiny pleats at the neck edge have turned into 250 sets.

The ruff was a splendid vehicle for conspicuous consumption. It could be decorated with valuable lace, tiny jewels, embroidery, or all three at once. It could be no wider than a modest frill under the ears, or it could be 9 inches wide, overlapping the shoulders. The colour was usually white, but not the brilliant fluorescent white beloved by modern advertisers; rather, a gentle ivory. Cuffs were made in the same way.

So far, so good. But even if you pin the edge of each set to its neighbour at the outer edge, or fix them together with a tiny dab of wax, this ruff would not be wearable for longer than a few minutes without collapsing like a ruined soufflé, and if you went out in the rain it would 'go flip flap in the wind like rags'.[9] The answer was starch, 'the Devil's potion' according to Phillip Stubbes, 'which when they [ruffs] be dry will then stand stiff and inflexible about their necks', which he obviously regarded as sinful. The Flemish ladies had long used it to keep their linen neat, and they brought starch with them when they emigrated to England. English women admired its effect, and when Dingen van der Passe came to London in 1564 she could charge £4 or £5 for lessons in starching.[10] But this difficult art was better done by specialists; hence the two Dutch women whose thriving businesses were included in the 1593 Return of Strangers (see page 117 above).

The ruff was first washed, and allowed to dry. Then the thick starch paste – rather like wallpaper paste – was brushed into every fold, and it was dried again. Then it was damped, and the difficult process of setting began. Ruffs were often coloured at the starching stage with soft vegetable dyes, producing pink, yellow or mauve tints; much more flattering than white, but rarely visible now in portraits because of later restorers' conviction that all ruffs were white and therefore the neckwear of any portrait subject should be 'cleaned' until it was. They could also be a pale blue, using smalt,[11] but for some reason Elizabeth took against blue ruffs, in 1595.[12] In a magnificent exercise of the royal prerogative she told the Lord Mayor to tell the aldermen to tell the parish beadles to tell the occupants of every house in their parish that 'Her Majesty's pleasure is that no blue starch shall be used or worn by any of her Majesty's subjects',[13] so the said loyal subjects had better hastily get some cochineal and dye the offender mauve.

Even when a ruff had been starched, it still needed an anchor to keep it up at the back and down in front. This was a 'supportasse' of wire covered in silk, pinned on to the neckline of the dress or doublet, so that the ruff could in turn be pinned to it. No wonder pins featured so largely in Elizabethan clothes. The Queen's wardrobe staff ordered them by the thousand – 19,000 'small head pins' for six months in 1565, at 1s 8d a thousand.[14]

Once this delicate object had been starched and set, it had to be carefully treated. A gentlewoman would tell one of her servants to carry her 'box with ruffs' to a party, and her maid could pin it on when they got there, as long as they got there in plenty of time – the whole process could take hours.[15]

Men's dress[16]

'Except it were a dog in a doublet you shall not see any so disguised as are my countrymen of England', wrote Harrison in 1577.[17] There has never been a time in which male clothes bore so little resemblance to male bodies. A man does have a penis, but not in constant erection as flaunted by a codpiece. Men do sometimes run to paunches, but never on the same lines as a peasecod belly. The various fantasies of their breeches would make a modern designer swoon, but those upholstered knickers bore no resemblance to the male pelvis.[18]

Only their legs were left undistorted. The merciless effect of displaying a less than perfect leg is very apparent in a joint portrait of Mary Tudor and her husband, the year before her death, in which poor Philip's legs are shown in all their weediness. Elizabeth's favourite, Robert Devereux, Earl of Essex, had legs any model nowadays would be proud of, if Nicholas Hilliard's miniature of him is anything to go by. And legs mattered. Juliet's nurse comments on Romeo 'though his face be better than any man's, yet his leg excels all men's'.[19] 'With a good leg and a good foot … and money enough in his purse, such a man would win any woman in the world.'[20] Dekker's Honest Whore sighs for a 'kind gentleman … indifferent handsome [but] meeyly limbed and thighed'.[21]

Back to clothes, and beginning at the top, after the ruff: the doublet went on over the shirt, and buttoned down the front with a row of small buttons, which could vary in value from jewels to wood. The nobility sometimes preferred hooks and eyes, tucked away so as to be invisible – even then, they could be made of silver. The doublet had a short stiffened skirt from the waist, varying in length from time to time, but long enough to cover the row of holes or laces at the waist on to which the breeches were tied. Later in the century these 'points' were replaced by sturdy hooks and eyes.

The peasecod belly effect had a long innings, 1575–1600, but it is difficult now to see any charm in it. In the Hilliard miniature of Essex, the beauty of his legs eclipses the ugly pointed belly above them. We rarely see peasecods (pods) in these days of frozen peas, but if you have not seen a pea in its pod lately, imagine that the doublet follows the line of the chest down to about diaphragm level. It then parts company with the chest, and curves outwards and then back again to a point somewhere below the waist. To keep that line, it had to be carefully stiffened and padded ('bombasted'). It wouldn't accommodate a beer belly so it wasn't dreamed up by the Fat Men's lobby if any. Luckily for us, Phillip Stubbes disapproved of them and gave a clear description of the objects of his disapproval:

> Being so hard-quilted, and stuffed, bombasted and sewed, as they can verily hardly either stoop down, or decline themselves to the ground, so stiff and sturdy they stand about them ... there was never any kind of apparel ever invented that could more disproportion the body of man than these doublets with great bellies, hanging down beneath their pudenda, and stuffed with four, five or six pound of bombast at the least.[22]

The sleeves of the doublet were also padded. By 1575 they too had left behind any correspondence with a human body, and were stiffened and bombasted into 'trunk sleeves', the shape of a leg of mutton (or the hugely puffed sleeves of Edwardian ladies, known as leg-of-mutton sleeves) or 'full' sleeves, which were so full that they had to be bombasted and stiffened with wire, reeds or whalebone. Still, they had their uses. In a case of theft heard in Essex in 1594, the defendant 'took half a pound of bacon out of his sleeve, and two hens and a cock which the [witness] did suspect he had stolen': a not unreasonable suspicion. In contrast, the fashion of opening the sleeve all the way down the front and then fastening it at intervals with ties or clasps, and pulling the white shirt sleeve through the gaps in puffs, seems quite modest. Often the more elaborate sleeves were detachable, tied on to the doublet at the shoulder.[23] These ties, or the shoulder seams, were hidden, and the shoulders given added masculine breadth by 'wings' made of the doublet material.

The waist was marked by a girdle. Quite how it negotiated the peasecod belly is not clear. The girdle was usually – and for the poor, always – made of leather, but of course you could if you felt underdressed adorn it with gold and silver, pearls, gems and embroidery. The plain man's girdle was more likely to carry his purse and the smaller of the tools of his trade, such as a pen-case and ink-horn. In the story of *Arden of Faversham*, based on a long-running murder trial, one of the villains happened to be carrying a 4-lb pressing iron at his belt.

Armour was becoming obsolete for serious purposes, but was still worn for the tournaments and jousts that Elizabeth enjoyed watching.[24] The Earl of Essex owned two complete sets, one engraved and gilt, the other 'plain white part gilt'.[25] Sometimes nobles who might take part in such events chose to have their portraits painted wearing just the gorget, the piece that protected their neck and upper chest, to show how brave and soldierly they were. Whether they wore gorgets in normal life I doubt.

Over the doublet a man would wear a jerkin. Working men wore leather jerkins, their betters went in for cloth of silver, fine Spanish leather: anything decorative. The jerkin was lined, but not padded or stiffened, and it was long enough to cover the doublet and part of the legs. The working man's jerkin could be of tough leather such as oxhide, which was handy as protection.

On top of the jerkin came a gown. It is so difficult to imagine all these layers of clothing, when most young men go about in jeans and a T-shirt. Surely some of them were optional extras. But there was much more propriety in dress in those days, and a gown meant respectability. A student of Lincoln's Inn had to wear one not only in the Inn, but 'in London or Westminster', or he would be fined. At least his gown was only knee-length. Older men wore them to the ankle, with open sleeves hanging to nearly the hem. The front edges could be furred or decorated with braid, or the whole thing lined with a rich fabric that would show as the wearer moved. A loose gown for wearing at home was called a 'nightgown'.

As an alternative to the gown, the cloak. Only social inferiors went out without a cloak. It could be ankle length (from the 1570s) or more usually crotch or waist length. It could be cut as a complete circle, known as a 'compass', or as a half circle, known as a 'half-compass'. It could be embroidered, lined, furred or braided. It was a useless but decorative garment, needing constant twitching to keep it on. The usual way was to tie it on with cords from the neck edge, taken round to the back and tied behind, or if worn over one shoulder only, as for most of Elizabeth's reign, to take the cord under the opposite arm and tie it behind, or round the arm. Try it, next time you have a compass of fabric; but not if you are in a hurry. The most magnificent of Elizabeth's courtiers, the Earl of Essex, had among his 26 cloaks in 1588 'a Dutch cloak of black velvet richly embroidered, lined with striped cloth of gold' worth £20.[26]

One of the dottier versions of a cloak was a mandillion, fashionable from the 1580s. It was basically a loose hip-length jacket, with sleeves – only the whole thing was worn sideways so that the neck lay on the shoulder, the front came down one side and the sleeves flapped uselessly.

For rainy weather you might find handy a felt cloak called a gabardine, which must have weighed a ton if it did get soaked. In really foul weather the cloak could be belted at the waist:

> Now happy he whose cloak and cincture can
> Hold out the tempest …[27]

Going back to Stubbes, surely breeches were more 'disproportioning' garments than doublets, in some of their wilder forms. The basic garment, worn by all working men, was a pair of baggy breeches, fastened to the doublet at the waist and ending above or below the knee. But that was only the starting point. If you were a fashionable man, and you had such good legs that you wanted to display their whole length, the style for you was the round hose like two canteloupe melons at the tops of your legs, as short as the shortest mini in the days of mini-skirts. If you felt that was going a bit far, or not far enough, you could pick almost any length, from crotch to below the knee. Whatever shape you chose would need padding and stiffening to keep it so. Breeches could be so voluminous that a visitor admiring five small pictures (miniatures?) absentmindedly tucked them away in his breeches 'and forgetting went away with them' – that at least was his story when he returned them later, explaining that it had been 'only a jest'.[28]

A further complication was 'paning' (from the same root as 'panels'). This involved making the breeches in two layers, a very full lining that could be of sumptuous fabric, and an outer layer of stronger – but still rich – fabric cut into strips ('panes') joined to the lining at the waist and lower hem, swinging loose between those anchorages and flopping from side to side as the wearer walked. Then you could pull the lining through the panes, into puffs. There were, of course, several layers under the puffs, of more functional linings, interlinings, padding and canvasing, to keep the breeches in shape. It may come as a relief to know that a short stretch of the outer fabric, unpaned, was used for the seat. Pockets were usually let into the side seams of the breeches.

There was a feeling in high places that these exaggerated garments should be discouraged. They were all very well for a courtier with good legs, but for the average working man – surely not. Almost annually, Elizabeth forbade them, by proclamation, but fashion is not ruled by legislation. In 1562 she, or rather her Privy Council, tried another expedient. Nine tailors in St Martin le Grand and fifty in Westminster had to undertake not to put more than 1¾ yards of kersey into any pair of hose, and to cut them. 'to lie close to the legs, and not loose or bolstered as in ancient times'.[29] What success, and what effect on their competitors, these bonds had I do not know.

Codpieces gradually detumesced during Elizabeth's reign, and had given way to a buttoned or lace-up front fastening by the end of it. But they were a curious expression of male dominance while they lasted.[30] They were hollow, stiffly padded appendages, varying in shape between a banana and an avocado pear, sewn to the front of the breeches at their lower end so that they stuck up and out, and tied to the breeches a bit further up with a lace or 'point' that could easily be untied. If a banana fails to convey the right image, think of a padded and slightly shorter version of a primitive man's penis-guard. The more I think of them, the more I suspect that they were just decoration, as non-functional as a ruff, decoratively covering the front edges of the breeches but leaving the penis in peace behind them.[31] But why leave them plain, when they too could have their own panes and puffs, bows and bombast? And they had other unexpected uses, such as a safe place for your purse and/or your handkerchief, and perhaps a refreshing orange or two. They also made a handy pincushion (remember they were heavily padded) in case your ruff needed repinning:

> A round hose, madam, now's not worth a pin
> Unless you have a codpiece to stick pins on.[32]

On the other hand, as a young man remarked with feeling if obscurely, 'he that wooeth a widow must not carry live eels in his codpiece'.[33]

Sometimes breeches had sewn-on extensions of the same fabric, called canions, fitting the thigh down to just above the knee. To get these reasonably tight, but still allow the wearer to walk, careful tailoring was needed.

When short round hose and long 'netherstocks' (stockings) display the male leg in portraits, there are of course no wrinkles in the netherstocks, let alone ladders and holes (it is difficult to remember that these are long silk stockings, not nylon tights), and they are immaculately clean, an artistic licence when you think of walking through the filthy London streets. Hand-knitted netherstocks had been available since about 1550. Knitting was done in the round, on several needles, just as hand-knitted socks are, still.[34] A frame to knit them by machine had been invented in 1589, but Elizabeth disapproved of its potential effect on the labour force, so it never swept the market. The most desirable netherstocks were of knitted silk, which would have a certain elasticity. The knitters incorporated into the design, elaborate clocks (patterns rising from where the foot and the leg have to be fitted together at the ankle: visible if you look closely at woollen socks now, but not in the kind that has no shaping at the ankle). By the 1580s, the fashionable wearer would have clocks further decorated with embroidery in gold and silver, plus spangles (like sequins – one would have thought they would snag and ladder the netherstock). They were tricky to put on because 'then must the long seams of our hose be set with a plumb-line', a difficult feat.[35]

Knitted wool or linen netherstocks were cheaper and harder wearing than silk. But as anyone will remember who wore woollen stockings before the advent of nylon, they bagged horribly at the knee. The London citizen going about his daily life must surely have paused often to hike up his netherstocks through his knitted garters.[36] Cross-gartering might hold them up better, by putting the garter round the leg twice, above and below the knee, looping over itself at the back and tying in a bow at the front. They had been fashionable in the 1560s, but by the time Malvolio thought himself irresistible in his yellow cross-gartering the general view of cross-garters was that they were fuddy-duddy – 'like a pedant that keeps a school in the church'.[37] When Hamlet was looking like a madman, 'his stockings [were] fouled, ungartered and down-gyved to his ankle'.[38] But for the fashionable man, garters could provide yet another site for decoration.

Women's dress

Elizabeth herself wore increasingly elaborate garments as her iconic image grew to depend more on the visual impact of her clothes and less on her personal beauty – which did fade, as it does, whatever her courtiers said. So her clothes are not necessarily a guide to the clothes worn by lesser mortals. But since we can refer to a detailed list of them, it is tempting to use them as a guideline for more normal wear.[39] The accounts of foreign tourists, too, are useful here.

The basic elements of a woman's dress were a bodice and a separate skirt. The bodice was flat-fronted. What full-bosomed women did, other than a general spreading of the masses, is unclear; after all, pictures of 1920s clothes would have you believe that women had suddenly given up breasts, which is improbable. The working woman's bodice showed a modest décolletage covered by a 'partlet', or smock, at the neck, or rather more if the wearer was unmarried. The bodice came to a point in front, below the waist, which even for working women was stiffened by a wooden or whalebone busk down the front of the bodice lining. Her skirt might follow the fashionable lines of an overskirt divided down the front to show a 'forepart' or underskirt, or it might simply be gathered on to a waist band. Since she would normally wear an apron over it, it is hard to tell, from the few pictures of working women.[40]

Elizabeth's amazing garments were constructed on the same basic lines, except that her pointed bodice came well below her waist, giving her upper body that curious look of an ice-cream cone. It was kept flat by rigid busks down the inside of the bodice or in a separate boned bodice. Because she was an unmarried virgin, she sometimes wore a disconcertingly low neckline. Exactly how low is difficult to say. In 1597, when Elizabeth was 64, the French ambassador was startled to 'see the whole of her bosom ['toute sa gorge'], and passing low ... her bosom is somewhat wrinkled, but *lower down* her flesh is exceeding white and delicate'.[41] It may be that *la gorge* just meant upper chest then – the area covered in the male version by a gorget.[42] But reformers deplored the fashion, seeing everywhere 'these naked paps, the devil's gins [traps]' and 'breasts [which women] embuske up on high, and their round roseate buds immodestly lay forth'.[43] It is never easy, with a reformer, to know exactly what he sees and what he thinks he sees.

The bodice had separate sleeves, fixed on with laces or pins. This meant that although Elizabeth never seemed to wear the same dress twice, in fact she could put a different pair of sleeves to each bodice, and a different skirt to it too, and look quite different. It also makes sense of the habit of giving ladies' sleeves to their favourites at tournaments, to wear on their helmets as favours, which always seems a bit impractical until you realise that they could just take a spare sleeve along with them to the tilt ground and give it to someone they fancied. The wardrobe of the poor maidservant we met earlier on her discharge from St Bart's contained one 'cassock' (a loose gown, the only one she had) of black cloth and two pairs of white sleeves.

The shape of the skirt depended on what was worn underneath it to distend it. Farthingales were stiffened with rows of reeds or willow twigs or rope.[44] They had made their appearance with Katherine of Aragon. Mary Queen of Scots had taken to whalebone for farthingales as early as 1562, but it took the English Queen nearly twenty years to catch her up. (Mary no doubt had the advantage of fashion advice direct from France. Elizabeth tried her best to get a French tailor, but none would come.) A pyramid shape was fairly easy to make, by rows of stiffening increasing in diameter, and it would be a rare woman who did not manage to contrive one somehow.

The drum-shaped or 'wheel' farthingale, which became fashionable in Court circles, was more complicated. It was achieved either by a wheel-shaped structure of wire or whalebone, or an underskirt with the top row of stiffening immediately below the waist, and further rows at intervals down to hem level, all of the same diameter.[45] The skirt stuck out at right angles from the body, and could be up to 48 inches from side to side. It had to be draped over the ungainly framework of the farthingale, first taking up a deep fold in it all round, to lie on top of the horizontal surface of the farthingale in soft pleats that were carefully pinned in place at its outer edge, and then allowing the pleats to drop to the hem. This could take some hours, on a bad day. When Desdemona wants to go to bed, she summons her waiting woman to 'unpin' her.[46] Elizabeth's wardrobe staff ordered 14,000 'great farthingale pins' for just six months, in 1565, at 6s a thousand, plus 20,000 middle farthingale pins (4s a thousand), 25,000 great velvet pins (2s 8d) and 39,000 small velvet pins (1s 8d).

The fashionable Elizabethan woman was a walking pincushion, liable to come unstuck, showering pins, at any sudden movement.[47] And, of course, safety pins had not yet been invented. The working woman who wanted to emulate a Court lady could create nearly the same effect by a 'bum-roll' tied round her waist, lifting the skirt up at the back and sides but leaving it flat in front, which took much less time.

Children

Until they were five years old or more, boys and girls were dressed alike, which makes macabre sense when the toll of mortality in those early years was so heavy. Little boys in family portraits were shown to be boys by having a sword or a hobbyhorse, and little girls had dolls. By the time he was about seven, a little boy had been 'breeched' and was proudly wearing a small version of his father's clothes. For underwear, there is an astonishing survival from the sixteenth century in the Museum of London: a child's vest, socks and mittens, all knitted in what had once been soft white wool.[48]

Colours, fabrics and decoration

You might choose a particular gown because it suited you, or because its colour would send a signal that you may not have wanted to put into words. The messages conveyed by goose-turd green or puke brown seem clear.[49] Popinjay blue or lusty-gallant red sound more cheerful. Yellow and orange were always popular. 'Tawny', an orange/brown, was used for mourning, surprisingly, because it sounds so pretty. 'Sad' colours were dark. 'Scarlet' did not mean red, but a particular kind of very fine worsted cloth. Queen Elizabeth was fond of wearing black with white, which suited her fair complexion and auburn hair admirably. They had the added advantage, in 1564, of symbolising eternal virginity, a message that the Spanish ambassador cannot have missed when she chose it for his audience to press his master's marriage proposal on her.

Elizabeth was rarely out in the rain like lesser mortals. Few textile dyes were colour-fast, another fact that does not appear in portraits.

> Your mistresses dare never come in rain
> For fear their colours should be washed away.[50]

Both Queen Elizabeth and Phillip Stubbes, and no doubt many other people, thought they should be able to tell a person's status from his or her clothes. This had been usual in medieval times, but the distinctions were becoming disgracefully blurred by the sixteenth century, and there was not much that could be done about it, except to disapprove. Here is Stubbes, on the sin of Pride of Apparel and the lack of a 'comely order' in dress:

... by wearing an apparel more gorgeous, sumptuous and precious than our state, calling or condition of life requireth ... No people in the world is so curious in new fangles as they of England be ... [we should] wear attire every one in his degree ... it is very hard to know who is noble, who is worshipful, who is a gentleman and who is not

– which any reasonable person should be able to do at sight.

Queen Elizabeth was able to attack the problem from a different standpoint. Her father Henry VIII, her brother Edward VI and her sister Mary had all passed 'Acts of Apparel', but they were all disregarded. Elizabeth's efforts were not much more successful. One of her very first decrees was about apparel, in 1559, and equally unregarded orders were issued at intervals throughout her reign. In 1562 she forbade 'great ruffs and great breeches'. Sword blades were to be no longer than 1¼ yards, dagger blades no longer than 12 inches, and buckles were not to have long pricks – the latter three provisions to try to discourage the London habit of fatal brawls. But her citizens refused to observe the rules.[51]

In 1580 she ordered that 'no person shall use or wear ... excessive long cloaks ... nor great and excessive ruffs ... upon pain of her high indignation'. That year there was a resounding row in high circles, all about ruffs. The Lord Mayor had taken it upon himself to give a 'friendly admonition' to a young man for 'wearing excess of ruffs in the open street' before he realised that the young man was the son of the Lord Chief Baron, a senior judge. The young man replied 'in a very contemptuous speech' and his father was 'very offended' . Please, wrote the poor Lord Mayor, could the Lord Treasurer sort it all out?[52]

In 1584 even the threat to tax a citizen on his apparent wealth, as evidenced by the way his wife dressed, did not work. Here are some of the elaborate provisions of a decree issued in 1597, which illustrate how Elizabeth saw the proper way for other people to dress, and incidentally give a superb picture of the textiles available to the well-dressed Elizabethan:

For men's apparel, Her Majesty doth straightly charge and command

That none shall wear in his apparel,
  Cloth of gold or silver tissued
  Silk of colour purple
under the degree of an Earl, except Knights of the Garter in their purple robes only.

[None shall wear] Cloth of gold or silver
  Tinselled satin
  Silk or cloth mixed or embroidered with gold or silver
  Woollen cloth made out of the realm [i.e. imported]
under the degree of a baron, except Knights of the Garter, Privy
Counsellors to the Queen's Majesty

and so on, down the dizzy ranks of nobility and gentry, forbidding
velvet in gowns, cloaks, coats 'or any uppermost garments', and
'netherstocks of silk' to anyone under the degree of a knight, except
'gentlemen ... attending on her Majesty in her house or chamber',
and a knight's eldest son, and 'such as have been employed in
embassies to foreign princes', and anyone who had a disposable
income of at least £200 a year. Anyone of or above the rank of a
knight's eldest son – but not his brothers – and anyone else with a
mere £100 a year could wear velvet hose and doublets as well, and
satin cloaks. And, with the usual exemptions, no one under the
degree of a baron's son could have velvet or 'damasking with gold
or silver' on their horses. Meanwhile the Inns of Court were doing
their best to uphold the law. In 1574 the Benchers of Gray's Inn
ruled that 'none of the society of this House shall wear any gown,
doublet, hose or any outward garment of any light colour'.[53] The
other Inns passed similar orders.

'For women's apparel, her Majesty doth ... command that' only
countesses could wear cloth of gold or silver tissued, or purple silk,
except viscountesses who could go so far as cloth of gold or silver
tissued 'in their kirtles only'. When the Queen got to baronesses,
we see the spread that lowlier ladies were forbidden: cloth of gold
and of silver – as you would expect – plus tinselled satin, 'satins
branched with silver or gold, satins striped with silver or gold,
taffetas branched with silver and gold, taffetas with silver or gold
grounds' and 'any other silk or cloth mixed or embroidered with
pearl, gold or silver'. Unless you were a baron's eldest son's wife or
a Lady of the Privy Chamber or a Maiden of Honour you could not
even wear gold or silver lace or 'garnishings for the head trimmed
with pearl'. At least knights' wives could wear velvet outer garments,
and silk netherstocks. The list goes right down to 'a gentleman's wife
bearing arms' (having a coat of arms: armigerous), who could wear
damask and grosgrain gowns but *not* embroidered taffeta.

And the Act goes on – and on and on. Every rank and office had

12. Wallpaper: a black and white wood-block print (see page 52).

Rusticæ Anglicanæ   *Modus vendendi Lupos pisces apud Anglos.*

13. Two country women bringing their produce to market. They wear cloths over the lower part of their faces, to protect them from the dust of the roads. Two women are selling pike. A water-bearer shows how those ungainly vessels were carried.

14. Building a timber-frame house (see page 43).

15. A lady out shopping in Eastcheap meat market, with her maid to carry her purchases. The meat for sale is displayed on spits. The two women appear unperturbed by the flock of sheep and two bulls close behind them.

16. Ordinary people going to market. One woman carries a basket, the other rides a horse laden with panniers. Both women, and the man, wear ruffs.

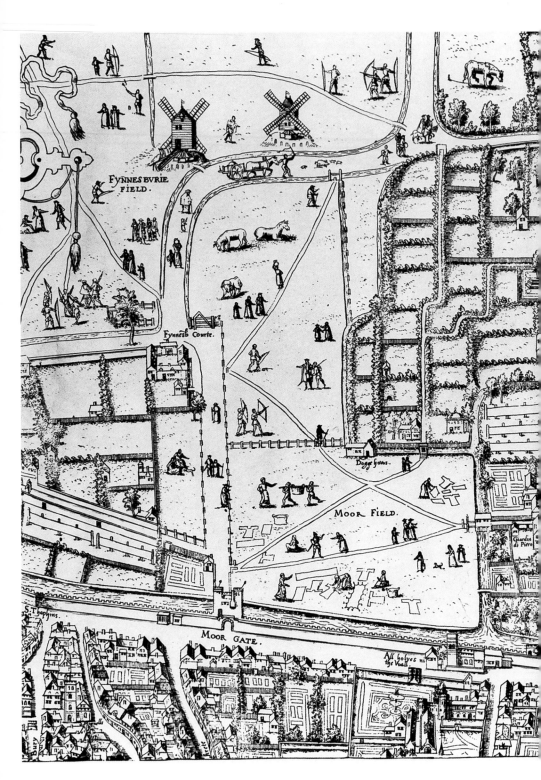

FYNNESBVRIE FIELD.

FYNNESB COVRTE.

Dogge howns.

MOOR FIELD.

Giardin di Pietro.

S.T. hophins.

MOOR GATE.

All golyes ni the Voods.

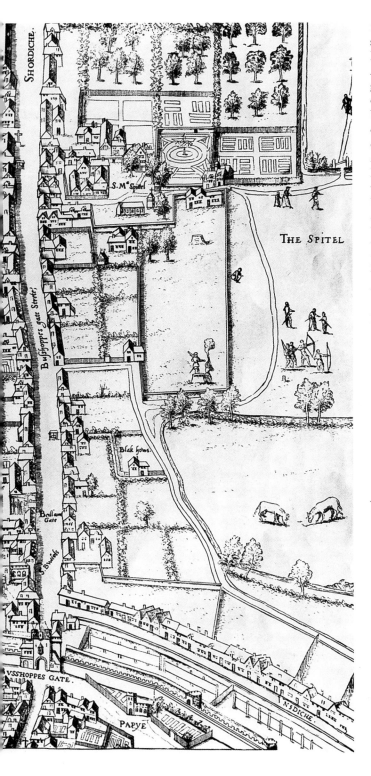

17. Part of the oldest surviving map of London, made by Ralph Agas around 1559. Many gardens are shown, most of them laid out in long beds (see page 69). Poles carrying the heads of criminals can just be seen above Bishopsgate and Moorgate. One washerwoman has brought her washing to dry in Moor Field, in a basket carried by two boys – like the basket Falstaff famously hid in. While the washerwomen wait for the shirts and smocks and household linen to dry, they sit and spin. Beyond the fence, men are practising archery, apparently shooting at random, unlike the man firing his musket at a butt in a walled enclosure, on the other side of Bishopsgate Street. Several tenter grounds are shown (see page 83), including one just outside Bishops Gate at 'Unsdiche' – Houndsditch. 'Bedlame' is on the left of the road, after Bishopsgate.

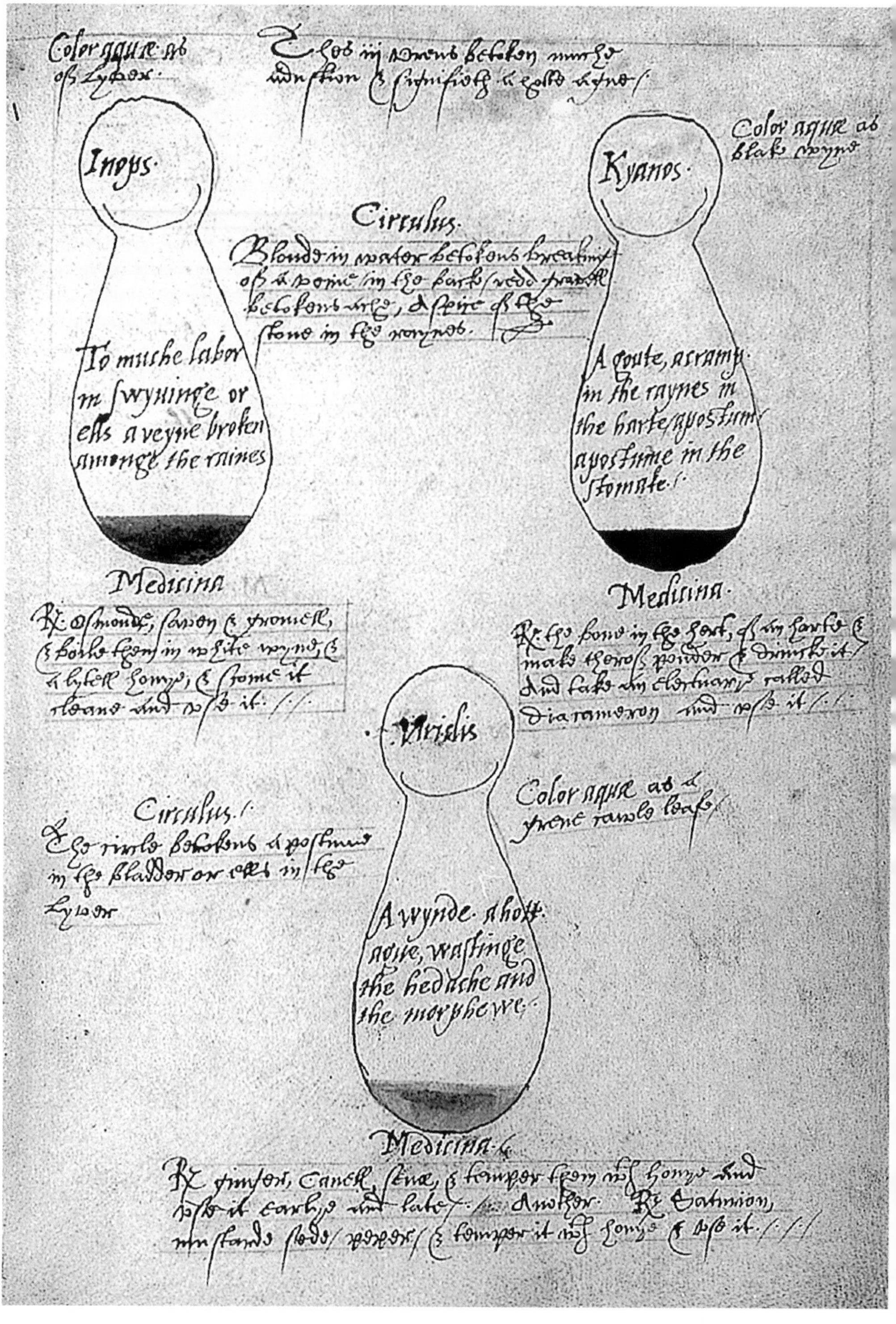

18. Diagram of urine flasks from a Medical Compendium, c. 1575. Urinoscopy was a widely used diagnostic tool (see page 98). This chart shows various colours of urine, the possible causes of the ailment – 'too much labor in swyuinge [sexual intercourse] or else a vein broken amongst the raines [kidneys]' – and the appropriate prescription.

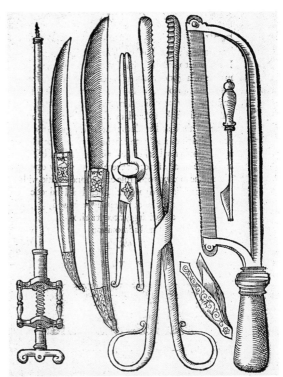

19. Surgical instruments for use in 'curing gunshot', from a book by William Clowes (see page 105).

20. An illustration from another book by William Clowes, on the 'cure of the disease called morbus gallicus' (the French pox, i.e. syphilis). The elderly man at the top left is resisting the sales pitch of the charlatan's assistant, and saying – naturally, in Latin, here freely translated – 'happy the man who has learnt caution from other men's dangers.' The salesman seems to be holding up two sheets of testimonials from satisfied customers, but they are all lies – 'mendax'. The man with the natty garters has his arm in a sling. Then – the Charlatan himself, in all his meretricious glory (see page 108). On the table, inevitably, a flask of urine, with a pair of scissors, a box of drugs, and other things. The dog under the table is inexplicable. The third assistant has a wooden leg, and a crutch. I have no explanation for the man in bondage gear.

21. A drawing of the tobacco plant, with a pipe smoker,
from a book published in London in 1570.

its appointed livery, and if you did not know what yours was, it was up to you to find out. 'All which articles ... her Majesty straightly commandeth to be exactly and duly observed in all points ... and the parties offending to be further [?] punished as violaters ... of her royal ... commandment' – she did not exactly say how.

As well as embroidering these beautiful textiles, they could be mangled in various ways: 'here's snip and nip and cut and slish and slash', as Shakespeare said.[54] Pinking made decorative patterns in the garment by small cuts with a special knife. If the cuts were big enough, the fabric of the lining could be pulled through in puffs. Even longer cuts, from nearly top to bottom of a bodice for instance, could give some degree of elasticity to these inelastic garments. A boy's leather doublet in the Museum of London has a pattern of small cuts all over it, which might make it easier for an active lad to move in. The most outlandish treatment was 'razing': with a very sharp little knife, cut the weft only, in a pattern. (The weft is the horizontal threads woven/weaved/weft across the long warp threads. It is occasionally called the woof, but weft is safer. Surface decoration came mainly from the weft. The warp, which went the whole length of the roll of fabric, had to be strong enough to support the fabric, but did not usually show.) To raze an already sumptuous fabric without making a hole right through it by cutting the warp threads as well must have taken a steady hand and a good light.

The only textile fibres then were silk, linen, cotton, wool and hemp. Silk could be spun into thread of varying thickness, and woven into fabric of different weights and appearance, from the finest gauze ('cyprus', 'sarcenet', which was much used for linings, and 'tiffany', used for puffs) to taffeta, which was not quite so fine, velvet,[55] plush (a deeper pile than velvet) and satin, particularly the satin woven in Bruges ('satin of Bridges'). 'Tissue' was woven from silk thread twisted round a gold or silver core. Linen could span the gamut from the finest gossamer-weight holland and lawn for ruffs, to heavy-weight dowlas and lockram for working men's shirts. A blend of linen and wool made linsey-woolsey and fustian, much used for hard-wearing breeches.

The poor wore, no doubt, what they could get, but they could usually manage wadmol, a coarse woollen, or rug, a warm tough shaggy fabric, even if the garment had been worn by many previous wearers. The life of garments could be prolonged by judicious patching, and even by turning them inside out and remaking them. In Shakespeare's *Henry VI Part II* a character is talking about Jack Cade's rebellion in 1450: 'I tell thee, Jack Cade the clothier means to dress the commonwealth, and turn it, and set a new nap on it.'[56]

Underwear and nightwear

Men made do with their shirt tails as underpants. Women, as we have seen, might wear a farthingale from the waist, and a linen smock next to their skin, but knickers had not been invented. Elizabeth had 'a pair of bodies [a bodice] of Spanish leather spotted all over with flowers' in 1594, possibly because by then she relied on some support for her ageing bones. Most women wore stiffened bodices of some sort. The words 'stays' and 'corsets' had not yet come in. Few outer garments could be washed, but body odour may not have been quite as bad as you might think, because the garment next to the skin – a smock or shirt – was linen, which was certainly washed frequently, and bodices were often lined with linen, which was taken out and washed.

Both sexes took to waistcoats under their doublets or bodices in cold weather – the Earl of Essex wore a red one for his execution, and so did Mary Queen of Scots – and both sexes wore nightcaps in bed, with a longer variant of the daytime smock or shirt, or an old daytime one. In 1581 Richard Stoneley bought himself a velvet nightcap for 12s 6d – quite a lot of money then – but he may have worn it around the house, especially if his hair was getting thin, rather than in bed.[57] Women's stockings ended above or below the knee, kept up by knitted garters. Poor Mary Queen of Scots carefully planned her execution *ensemble*, including pale blue worsted stockings 'clocked with silver, and edged on the top with silver, and next her leg a pair of jersey hose, white'. Under-socks or stockings were often worn, to protect the silk ones from wear and sweat.

Shoes and headgear

Queen Elizabeth had 40 pairs of velvet shoes, until about 1575 when she went over to Spanish leather. Needless to say, the velvet shoes were 'pinked, cut and ravelled', lined with scarlet satin and embroidered in gold. When her favourite shoes wore out, she had them 'translated' – taken apart and remade, with new bits where needed. She cannot have been the only one who could not bear to part with comfortable old shoes. Men posing for their portraits also wore this flimsy footwear, but whether they wore them outside the studio is another matter. Soft-soled pumps were popular for dancing. Pantofles seem to have been soft shoes for indoors.

For any kind of walking both sexes wore leather shoes, or ankle-boots called 'start-ups'. Men might wear thigh-length boots, especially if their legs were less than perfect. 'Boot-hose' were worn under boots, folded over at the top of the boot to show the embroidery on the boot-hose. By the end of the century, fashionable ladies were wearing shoes with heels made of wood, and cork inner soles.[58] Pattens with thick leather or wooden soles, strapped to the shoe, could keep you out of the worst of the mud. Alessandro Magno from Venice was impressed by our 'excellent boots for the rain', which the poor man needed during his summer visit in 1562.[59] There were various kinds of overshoe, from the thick-soled leather ones worn over boots in the country, to the elegant Spanish leather kind with the upper reduced to a toecap, probably not long enough to keep them on. Phillip Stubbes inevitably disapproved of them: 'Shall he not be fain to knock and spurn at every wall, stone or post to keep them on his feet … with their flipping and flapping up and down in the dirt they … gather a heap of clay and baggage together, loading the wearer with importable burden.'

Hats made an important fashion statement. Stubbes – who else? – disapproved of their various shapes, high and pointed or flat and broad 'like the battlements of a house', worn with 'a great bunch of feathers of diverse and sundry colours … feathered flags of defiance to virtue'. Some people just wore them to keep their heads warm. They were made of all the textiles available, mounted on an inner canvas or felt block to keep their shape. Beaver, from the New World, was an alternative. Stoneley bought a beaver hat in Southwark, untrimmed, for 26s 8d, and took it to a haberdasher to have it trimmed for another 10d.[60] The Earl of Essex had ten velvet caps, five old taffeta hats and six beaver hats, in 1588.[61] Elizabeth had one of hers trimmed with 'two plumes of feathers, one white and black the other red and yellow, with two tops of egrets feathers on them trimmed with silver and spangles of silver'.[62] Elderly men over forty, and some women, wore coifs, close-fitting linen caps with earpieces, tied under the chin, and a flat square woollen cap on top for outer wear.

Stiffened hoods shaped like the eaves of a house, covering the hair, continued to be worn, although they gradually lost their fashionable status. The front edge was a good place on which to display a jewelled or embroidered border ('billament'). Young married women and virgins could go about bareheaded. Cauls (nets) of gold thread with pearls, covering the hair under a hat or cap, or by themselves, were popular and becoming, no matter what the rules said.

Accessories

Elizabeth is often shown holding a feather fan, the feathers fixed upright in the handle. Folding ones came in towards the end of the century, sometimes made of perfumed leather.

Women wore silk or velvet masks or 'vizards' outdoors, covering the whole face to protect their complexion. They look rather frightening to us because, I suppose, of their terrorist overtones. They had holes for the eyes, and were sometimes kept on by clenching an internal button between the teeth.

When Elizabeth rode through the cheering crowds welcoming her on that cold November day in 1558, she was wearing a 'scarf'. Very sensible, you may think; but a scarf was not a nice warm woolly muffler but a glorious vehicle of ostentation. The invaluably disapproving Stubbes describes it 'fluttering in the wind with great tassels at every end, either of gold, silver or both'.

Gloves had elaborate gauntlets, often embroidered. Leather gloves were imported from France or Spain. The leather was often perfumed. The few surviving pairs of gloves said to have belonged to Queen Elizabeth look too elongated even for her long fingers. They may never have been worn; it was the done thing to carry them rather than wear them – a sure way to lose one.

Handkerchiefs used for blowing your nose could be stowed in a man's pocket or his sleeve. Did women have pockets? Perhaps their noses never ran. The decorative kind that Othello made such a fuss about would be wafted about in the hand, not used.

The long end of a woman's girdle was useful for hanging things from, such as a fan, a small mirror, a pomander or a muff.

In a book written at the end of the century by a French teacher for the benefit of his pupils, their need for a wide vocabulary inspires him to write a scene about 'the Rising in the Morning' of which I will give you a small sample. I have kept the sixteenth-century spelling, which should not be too opaque. The mistress has got up in a foul temper and is giving her maid hell:

Will you kepe me heere all day? Where be all my things? Goe fetch my petti-coate bodyes; I mean my damask quilt bodies with whale bones ... when shall I have my under-coate? Give me my peticoate of wrought crimson velvet with silver fringe ... where be my stockings? Give me some clean socks, I will have no worsted hosen, showe me my carnation silk stockings: where laid you last night my garters? Take away these slippers, give me my velvet pantofles ... give me rather my Spanish leather shoes, for I will walk today ... [After the desperate maid has tried a little flattery, as she dresses her mistress's hair] give me my whood, for methinketh it is somewhat cold, and I have a rewme which is falne on the left side of my head ... [She's got as far as her ruff and cuffs –] Is there no small pins for my cuffes? Look in the pin-cushion ... give me my girdle and see that all the furniture be at it: look if my Cizers, the pincers, the pen-knife, the knife to close letters, with the bodkin, the ear-picker and my seal be in the case: where is my purse to wear on my gown? And see that my silver comfet box be full of comfets ...[63]

Fairly soon after that, she is ready to go.

Furs and jewels

There is nothing like fur to keep you warm, as polar bears know well. Leicester, who as an earl could wear anything he wanted, had a velvet cloak 'furred with sables', a 'long gown of wrought velvet laid about with a gold lace, faced with sables', another 'faced with silver bear', and a 'robe of crimson velvet furred throughout with miniver'.[64] Elizabeth got her sables from an unexpected source, the mad Ivan the Terrible, Tsar of Russia, who for a short time in 1587 thought she might make him a wife, supplanting various others he already had. To this end he gave her 'four pieces of Persian cloth of gold and two whole pieces of cloth of silver ... a fair large Turkey carpet, four black very rich timbers [one timber = 40 skins] of sables, six white well grown luzerance [lynx] skins, [and] two ... gowns of white ermine'.[65] He got nowhere, but she kept his presents.

Elizabeth dripped with pearls. After the execution of Mary Queen of Scots, Elizabeth bought the six long ropes of pearls and the 25 nutmeg-sized ones that Marie de Medici had given her daughter-in-law on her marriage to the French Dauphin in 1558.[66] She added to these, various offerings from her hopeful courtiers, and occasionally she even bought some herself. The New World was proving to be rich in pearls, as well as gold and silver. The Spaniards had established a pearl fishery on the coast of South America, the 'Spanish Main(land)', which Sir John Hawkins saw in 1568. The next year, he and Sir Francis Drake came home with – according to the infuriated Spanish ambassador – 'a small trunk of pearls', as well as vast amounts of gold. In 1580 Drake's voyages netted so much Spanish treasure that no one exactly knew how much there was of it, especially when various hands, including Drake's own, had taken their shares before it could be counted. Most of it eventually found its way to the Tower of London, but no proper inventory was ever made. It was mainly in gold, but there was 'a huge quantity of pearls, some of great value', according to the Spanish ambassador, who had not been fooled by the thin pretence that Drake had come home empty-handed – see his inventory, which listed 'nil'.[67] Few of her subjects could compete with their queen in jewels, but Bess of Hardwick did her best with four pearl ropes to below her waist, and the Duchess of Somerset could rise to a rope of more than 1,000 seed pearls, and two others each more than two metres long.

By 1590 diamond cutters had developed new skills, transforming a dull medieval gleam into a glittering coruscation. Settings changed appropriately, to focus light and attention on the stone. As well as demonstrating the wealth of the wearer, or her husband, in an instantly recognisable way, gemstones often had another significance. Jewels were useful prophylactics. Thomas Phaire advised his readers to 'bear about you precious stones (if you have them) specially a jacinth [a kind of red zircon], a ruby, a garnet, an emerald or a sapphire, which has a special virtue against the pestilence, and they be the stronger if they be borne upon your naked skin, chiefly upon the fourth finger of the left hand, for that hath great affinity with the heart'.[68] If you had the common sixteenth-century neurosis about being poisoned, you should wear a toadstone: the palatal tooth of a fossil fish, which looked no more attractive – it was a mottled brownish colour – than it sounds. But a bezoar was if anything worse: the best kind came from the intestines of Persian goats. A 'turkey stone' (turquoise,) changed colour near poison. Queen Elizabeth had two pieces of that invaluable unicorn horn, mounted as jewels. Simon Forman had a gold and coral ring containing magic signs, which he wore on 'the little finger of the left hand, and it prevails against witchcraft, devil's possession ... thunder, lightening, storm and tempest, and ... to make one famous in his profession and to overcome enemies'.[69]

The new classical taste inspired cameos exquisitely cut from onyx and sardoyx. Huge irregular pearls the size of broad beans could resemble dragons or sea monsters, in the right setting. Symbolic meaning could be conveyed to a suitor by your choice from your jewellery chest: a ruby heart meant 'compassionate care'.

How did you wear all these jewels? On your fingers, or your ears – a single ear-ring was fashionable for both men and women, tied on or fastened through pierced ears – or round your neck. Heavy 'carcanets' filled the space between neck and upper chest. A woman's gold chain, which was handy for carrying a miniature of her beloved or a minute looking-glass or even a tiny devotional book, was lighter than the massive chains men wore to show how rich and important they were. Sir Thomas Ramsey, Lord Mayor in 1577, had a 'great chain of gold' worth more than £110. Every Lord Mayor as he walked about his City could easily be recognised by his heavy gold chain and his furred gown, even if you did not notice the City sword-bearer walking in front carrying an upright sword.

Clothes could literally cost a fortune. Many young men coming to Court mortgaged their estates to buy themselves a wardrobe that might catch the Queen's eye. Pearls, gems and precious metal embroidery decorated them in such profusion that some garments must have weighed a ton. A skirt could be bordered, or ' guarded', at the hem or on each side of the front opening with a strip of gem-encrusted embroidery, sewn on but removable for use on another skirt. A lady went to the theatre one day, with her page carrying a torch to light her up the dark stairs to the theatre gallery. A pair of villains, seeing her valuable borders ('estimated at 1,000 crowns'), blew out the torch. The page had to leave her alone while he went to get it relit. One of the villains lunged at her in the darkness, groping her private parts and expecting her to clutch at them in modest self-defence, so that his confederate could rip off the borders. But the intrepid lady was more concerned with her valuables than her virtue, and clutched her borders instead. Exit thieves, frustrated.[70]

Hats could be adorned with valuable brooches as well as feathers. Elizabeth was given a white beaver hat, in 1600, 'the jewel ... above £100 price, beside the pendant pearl which cost me £30 more'.[71] Such jewels could be pinned on sleeves or bodices, as well.

Washing etc.

Elizabeth took her own close stools (portable lavatories) with her on her progresses through the countryside. Her transport included a 'close carriage' where they were probably kept. After all, she could hardly nip behind a bush. In 1565 she ordered 'four close stools covered with black velvet embroidered upon and garnished with ribbon and gilt nails, the seats and lathes covered with scarlet fringed with silk and gold and four pans of pewter with cases of leather lined with canvas to put them in'.[72] One may as well be comfortable. Sir Thomas Ramsey's huge house in Lombard Streeet contained three 'lead pots for privies', but nothing recognisable as a close stool or a wash-hand basin. The Earl of Essex's mansion on the river had an 'old close stool' in a small room off a lady's chamber, and a 'close stool with a pan' in his own room. Otherwise, there were public privies scattered about, mostly beside the Thames. Houses, or pairs of houses, had their own cess-pits, filled by shutes from the 'house of easement' or 'house of office' – rarely more than one – in each house, and emptied very occasionally.[73] Many small houses lacked even that amenity. The streets were filthy; no one would notice an added contribution from the household chamber pot, especially after dark.

It is always a vexed question to decide how much previous ages washed and/or smelt. Certainly we use far more water than the Elizabethans. There is little evidence of what they did in the privacy of their own homes, but however they abluted, it was not in a comfortable bathroom with hot and cold running water. An advice book published in 1547 described the getting-up process: 'When you be out of your bed stretch forth your legs and arms and your body, cough and spit, and then go to your stool ... after you have evacuated your body and trussed your points comb your head ... and wash your hands and wrists, your face and eyes and your teeth with cold water' – and that's it.[74]

There are recipes for soap in household books, and entries for 'washing balls' at 2d each, in diaries. These would be finer than the soap sold for 3½d a pound.[75] The wonderful evocation of Elizabethan boyhood in the textbook written by a French school-teacher, Claudius Hollyband, has the boy telling a manservant to 'bring me some water to wash my hands and my face. I will have no river water [from the Thames] for it is troubled [muddy]. Give me well or fountain water. Take the ewer and pour upon my hands.' The maid protests 'can you not wash in the bason?' and he replies, 'Wilt thou that I wash my mouth and my face where I have washed my hands …?', the thought of which apparently horrifies him.[76] And that, so far as ablutions go, is that. Still, it's more than the irritable lady whom we've already met does. She seems to have got pretty fully dressed before she tells her page to 'Go to, give me some water to wash, where's my musk ball? Give me rather my paste of almonds [sounds like a facial scrub] for it scoureth better: where is my piece of scarlet to wipe my face?'[77]

They certainly washed their hands before and after meals, but the full early-morning ablution does not seem to have existed. As to deodorants, the roots of fleur de lys, more usually called orris root, 'taketh away the strong savour coming from the arm holes'.[78] 'Artochoke' did the same, according to Thomas Hill, but I'm not clear how.[79] 'Of the rank savour of the armholes, this vice in many persons is very tedious and loathsome.' The first essential was to rebalance the offender's humours, then 'wash the armholes often-times with the water wherein wormwood hath been sodden, together with camomile and a little quantity of alum'.[80] (Alum probably worked. It's an ingredient in modern deodorants.)

Cosmetics

Cosmetics were simple. Dekker's Honest Whore relies on a phial with white colour in it, and two boxes, one with white, the other with red paint: but her page comments that 'it makes her face glister [shine] most damnably'. The white was probably ceruse, containing lead, which produced the desirable smooth white complexion, masking some of the ravages of smallpox. It could be enlivened by a touch of vermilion on the cheeks.[81] The snag was, it was toxic. Also, it tended to discolour in wear, to a menacing grey. Simon

Forman swore by a potion made by boiling snakes in alcohol: 'after I drank of that water … it made me look fresh and took away all my grey hairs when I was 56 years old and many took me not to be above 40 or 42'.[82]

Hair – or 'hairs', as the Elizabethans said – could be coloured black with elderberries or yellow with marigolds, kept in order by combing – no brushing, yet – and adorned with jewelled pins.[83] A woman's hair was elaborately dressed, if that was her lifestyle. Periwigs were fashionable, even before Elizabeth's lovely auburn hair turned grey and sparse and she took to fantastic full wigs. Of all the many herbal remedies I have read, one stands out as the most improbable: broth made from *alchemilla mollis* (lady's mantle) 'is good also to lay on women's breasts that are too loose and hanging down'.[84]

Ben Jonson said it all:

> Which lady sleeps with her own face a' nights?
> Which puts her teeth off, with her clothes, in court?
> Or which her hair? Which her complexion?
> And in which box she puts it?[85]

It is unlikely that men shaved themselves. Richard Stoneley's annual expenses included £1 for the barber, who cut his hair as well. The baby's-bottom smoothness aimed for nowadays was more likely to resemble designer stubble by the end of the week if the barber was on a weekly contract. In 1559 the Benchers of Lincoln's Inn were trying, as usual, to reform the young men who were members of the Inn. Among other rules, they ordered that 'no fellow of this house shall wear any beard above a fortnight's growth', which might mean just missing one weekly barber's appointment.[86] Men are, of course, always shown in portraits as immaculately clean-shaven, their hair and beards neatly trimmed.

Teeth

There is a well-known story of how Elizabeth, whose teeth in her old age were few, yellow and probably severely carious, refused to have any of them out. The Bishop of London even volunteered to have one of his extracted, just to show her how little it hurt, but she was not persuaded, and spent much of her last days with one finger in her mouth, not like a baby but like someone with bad toothache. If only she had used burned rosemary wood, powdered and tied in a linen bag, to rub her teeth with, it 'doth both make the teeth white and flee [drive out] the worms in them', which as everyone knew made the holes, if you did not 'flee' them first.[87] 'To make a tooth to fall out' when the worms have beaten you, try touching it with little green frogs, boiled, being careful not to touch the next tooth as well. 'Likewise doth the tooth of a dead man.' But for mere toothache try 'the grey worms breathing under wood or stones having many feet and when they be touched do they cluster together like porkenpickes ... pierced together with a bodkin ... and then put into the tooth that aches, alays the pain'.[88]

If finally you decide to have the tooth out, the best expertise available was that of the 'juggling, tooth-drawing, prating mountebank' in the local market-place.[89]

CHAPTER 9

Food and Drink

The markets

We are so used to deepfreezers and refrigerators that it is hard to imagine having to shop for food almost every day. Some staples like salt and flour and spices could be laid in, but the English diet of meat and fish had to be bought as fresh as possible. Provisioning London needed complex organisation. Cattle walked into Smithfield market from Essex, Suffolk, Kent and Bedfordshire. Fruit was carried up from Kent, or shipped down the river from the shires, in the summer. On some days as many as twenty fishing boats jostled for position at the wharves. Particular foodstuffs were sold in particular markets, where the right to sell depended on whether you were a member of the relevant livery company and a freeman of London, or a countryman from outside London – a 'stranger'. Naturally the rules favoured the Londoners.

The main markets were:

Leadenhall, on the east corner of Gracechurch Street and Cornhill, a general market strong on meat and poultry, with limited access for country vendors. (It is still there, and still sells food.) It was a stone building with arcades round a courtyard with a well, and a tower at each corner. As well as a granary to provide for the poor in hard times, it was the place where the City stored the material for the pageants and processions that were such a part of City life. In theory, 'foreigners' could sell meat there on Wednesdays and Saturdays only, morning and afternoon, but this rule was subject to negotiation, and the Wednesday concession was cancelled in 1564.[1] London butchers had permanent, privately owned stalls there. These stalls could be valuable properties. In 1595 two of Her Majesty's ladies-in-waiting took up the cause of Agnes Bartlett and her father, complaining to the Lord Mayor about fourteen butchers' stalls that had been bequeathed to them but not transferred.[2] A young Venetian visitor was astounded by all this meat: 'It is extraordinary to see the great quantity and quality of the meat – beef and mutton – that comes every day from the slaughter-houses in this city, let alone the meat that is sold at a special market [which must have been Leadenhall] every Wednesday [he seems to have missed Saturdays] for meat brought in from outside the city.'[3] There were 89 butcher retailers in the City in 1550, rising to 113 in 1599.

The *Stocks Market*, where 25 fishmongers and 18 butchers, all Londoners, had their stalls. (The Mansion House now occupies its site.) One explanation – there are other versions – of its name is from the stocks there, which were the only fixed stocks in the city in the thirteenth century, when it received its royal charter.

Along *Cornhill and Cheapside* for flowers and vegetables, poultry and dairy products, with part of Cheapside reserved for country sellers, and along *Newgate Street* for meat. The flower-sellers had pitches on the south side. No 'root-seller' was to have more than three baskets of produce to sell, and no vegetables were to be washed in the street. (But I bet the flower-sellers took advantage of the Great Conduit to scatter their flowers with water to keep them fresh and pretty, as did the flower-sellers who sat round the fountain in the base of Eros in Piccadilly before the Second World War.) The Newgate end was a market for corn and meal, with its own market house. *St Nicholas Shambles* at the west end of Newgate Street was, as its name shows, occupied by butchers. They had no slaughterhouses, so they used to kill their animals in the street until it was forbidden, in 1516. One wonders how they managed after that.

Eastcheap, a street market for London butchers, with slaughter-houses. A contemporary picture of it in *Hugh Alley's Complaint: a Caveat for the City of London* shows joints and whole carcasses displayed as if on spits, in front of each house, and a flock of sheep and some rather fierce-looking oxen being driven to the slaughterhouses by two men with pointed sticks and a large dog. A lady and her maid are walking in front of them, unaware and unperturbed. They are probably quite accustomed to such sights.[4]

Gracechurch Street, available to country vendors, for dairy products, pork and veal, fruit and vegetables. In the same series of pictures, women are selling sausages and pigs' heads neatly set out on stalls, other women have fruit for sale in baskets, and two men are brandishing large knives over – rabbits? piglets?[5]

Fish Street, for Londoner fishmongers. The drawings in *Hugh Alley's Complaint* show some very large fishes, but perhaps he was just making it clear that it was a fish market.

Queenhithe, on the river, for fruit and grain arriving from the area upstream from the Bridge. A new market house was built in 1564.

Billingsgate, near it, another general market, selling fish, fruit and grain, and salt from France. Billingsgate did not begin to specialise in fish for another hundred years, but there were already tensions between the Yarmouth fishermen who supplied the market, and the London dealers. Some gentlemen in Sussex and Surrey made a business out of their fishponds: 'the fishmongers of London do use to buy these fish by the score or hundred ... and bring them to London in cask, 20, 30, 40, 50 miles, and vend them by retail'.[6]

Southwark, a general market open four times a week, along the approach road to the Bridge, supplied by Londoners and country vendors.

Smithfield, where live animals were sold on Wednesdays and Fridays.

All markets were under the control of the Lord Mayor and his counsellors, and all prices were fixed by them. The ideal but un-realistic picture of a market trader was someone who personally sold the goods he had produced, for instance a country vegetable grower, or who interposed himself only minimally between producer and customer, for instance a butcher who bought his beef on the hoof at Smithfield market, butchered it himself and sold it on his stall.

The Elizabethans were obsessive about three offences connected with markets: forestalling (intercepting goods before they even got to the market, of which 'lewd women' were thought to be often guilty), engrossing (buying up the whole supply of something, to resell at an inflated price) and regrating (buying in one market to sell in another).[7] People who did these things were not only criminal but immoral as well, and deserved all the punishment they got. Robert Wood was fined 6s 8d in 1580, for forestalling sheep at Paddington, 'being within fifteen miles [of the City]'.[8] As usual, it was the small offenders who were caught; there was a strong popular suspicion that the large-scale operators escaped.

The markets were supposed to open six days a week, from 6 to 11 a.m., and 1 to 5 p.m. But in 1592 the residents of Cheapside, a prestigious address after all, were complaining that the market in front of their doors was operating seven days a week, and staying open till nine o'clock at night, by candlelight if necessary. You could buy milk, fruit and vegetables on Sundays, but only before 7 a.m., 8 a.m. in winter. This is another rule that one suspects was optimistic. But the scandals grew so clamorous that there were riots in 1595. When the tumult had died the Lord Mayor and his Common Council passed a new set of regulations, and required, for the first time, accurate, officially checked scales to be used in all markets, using the new weights introduced in 1587, standards for which were kept at the Guildhall.[9]

One of the chores of food shopping is getting it all home. The young Venetian Alessandro Magno was struck by this: 'The English-women have great freedom to go out of the home without menfolk; the husbands do not spent their time in household jobs but the women themselves carry the goods if they are poor ... or make their maids do so if they have them.'[10]

There were 127 master bakers in London in 1559, seventeen of them in Southwark.[11] Every loaf they made had to be 'sealed' – marked so that the maker could be identified. This was because for centuries the weight of a loaf had been controlled to fit the price fixed by the Lord Mayor. There was a complicated formula for this, theoretically allowing the baker a reasonable profit after deducting his expenses, such as the cost of materials and the maintenance of his family, even down to two children, one dog and one cat. Although it had worked well enough in the thirteenth century, it had become increasingly out of kilter, and after much agitation by the Bakers' company it was reformed, in 1597, after a run of three hundred years.

Most bakeries were small concerns, with only one oven, employing two or three journeymen and two apprentices. Only a very few bakers had up to five ovens. The bread was sold either direct to customers' houses or in the market; street vending was forbidden. A different company made coarse brown bread for sale to innkeepers for their customers' horses. There was constant bickering between the 'white bakers' and the 'brown bakers'. Queen Elizabeth knocked their heads together and gave them a combined royal charter in 1569, but they separated again in 1580. Perhaps the white bakers resented the fact that the royal charter had cost them £183 in bribes and inducements, to which the brown bakers had not contributed.

Other food shops

The records of the Grocers' Company show that between 1550 and 1599 the number of grocers in London rose steadily from 280 to 377. There were grocers and pepperers in Bucklersbury and Poultry. If you did not see a cheese you wanted in Gracechurch Street market, you could try the cheese shops in Bread Street. When the sugar loaf in the kitchen store room was almost finished, you might try a place that sold sugar loaves in the spacious old rooms of the Bishop of Hereford's former London home in Fish Street. You could always pick up a pie or a fruit tart from the cookshops in Thames Street, and buy in some stockfish (dried salted fish) there too.[12]

Shops could be tiny. On prosperous Cheapside there were three which were each just 25 feet wide and 12 feet deep, with a 'solar' (upper storey) above. Round the corner in Soper Lane, a less prestigious address, the shops had narrower frontages. One was 11 feet 3 inches wide by 17 feet deep, another 6 feet wide by 12 feet 9 inches deep, and a third was just over 1 yard wide.[13]

Before leaving these shops, a word about street signs. There is a misconception that before the Great Fire of 1666 London shops hung signs over their premises showing what was sold inside. This was not so. Any building could have a sign outside it, whether it was a shop or a private house. The name on the sign belonged to the site, or the building on it, not the owner or his occupation.[14] If it was a shop, the sign would not necessarily be connected to the trade. All the grocers in Bucklersbury must have had different signs swinging overhead. Two have been identified in a list of London signs: one was a harp and the other a harrow. Two of the goldsmiths in Cheapside traded under the Angel and the Black Boy, respectively.[15] When you think of the only signs that have survived to this day, pub signs, you realise that the White Swan does not deal in swans, and so on.

Street sellers

Alessandro Magno was very impressed with London oysters, which were still being 'cried in all parts of the streets' thirty years later when Frederick Duke of Würtemburg arrived to look round.[16] Fishwives were allowed to sell fish in the streets from their baskets or panniers – they were among the few street sellers who had their own transport in the shape of a donkey or a horse. 'Timely fruit' such as cherries and strawberries in season – which were more like alpine strawberries, small and fragrant, not the bloated red tasteless monsters of nowadays – could be sold from baskets as long as the vendor kept moving.[17] Radishes and young lettuces were sold the same way, sausages came in lengths and onions came in ropes, not yet sold by beret-wearing bicyclists. Hot codlings (baked apples) and pies advertised by their smell.[18] These are only a few of the street vendors who for one reason or another have survived in records. There were many more who did not earn this immortality, but whose existence was a part of Elizabethan housewives' daily shopping.

Fish days

Only a few years earlier, the good citizen had abstained from beef and eaten fish on certain days, for the sake of his soul. When Elizabeth came to the throne, he still had to eat fish, but for the sake of the Navy. At first the rules were issued by proclamation. No one, not even the butchers themselves, could eat 'flesh' during the forty days of Lent, or on other forbidden days, and no butcher could slaughter animals at those times. The punishment was a fine or six hours in the pillory or ten days' imprisonment. This was taken seriously enough for a butcher who killed four oxen at the beginning of Lent in 1561 to be fined £20 for each ox, and a tavern landlady to be pilloried in 1563 for eating flesh, while for the same offence 'four women were set in the stocks all night till their husbands did fetch them home'.[19] An Act of 1563 'for the better maintenance and increase of the Navy' added Wednesday to the traditional days of Friday and Saturday, having carefully explained that eating fish 'is purposely meant ... for the increase of fishermen and mariners and repairing of port towns and navigation, and not for any superstition ... [nor] for the saving of the soul of man'.

This made 156 days, almost a third of your life, when flesh was forbidden. But it was not quite as bad as it seemed. On Wednesdays it was lawful to have one dish of meat as long as there were three dishes of fish; and exemptions could be bought, the cost depending on who you were. 'Lords of Parliament and their wives' had to pay 26s 8d to the poor-box for an annual flesh-eating licence, knights and their wives 13s 4d, 'persons of lower degree' 6s 8d, and anyone who had 'to eat flesh for their health' could get a temporary licence from their bishop or parson. These fines could be a useful part of a parish church's income. The accounts of the churchwardens of the parish of St Michael, Cornhill, record a receipt in 1599 of 6s 8d 'of Mr Crook for his licence to eat flesh in Lent', which would have covered the cost of paying 'to the poor woman that was brought abed in the alley, 3s, and paid to Nicholas Payne for keeping of the said poor woman in his house, 3s 4d'.[20]

If you gave a dinner party, you might purposely invite someone known to have a flesh-eating licence so that you could justifiably put at least one meat dish on the table for him – and anyone whom he might discreetly share it with. The accounts of a visitor from Wiltshire show him duly eating fish on most Fridays, but by no means always. One Friday in May his appetite got the better of him, and he sat down to a leg of mutton, a loin of veal and a pheasant, with veal, chickens and rabbits for supper. It is fair to add that the visitor was probably feeding his 'family' of serving men as well as himself, which would account for these quantities.[21] Also, 'fish' and 'flesh' were not so clearly defined as one would expect. 'White meat' such as veal, game and poultry counted as fish in that it was not beef. But I think mutton counted as meat.

The butchers providing flesh to the licence-holders had themselves, of course, to be licensed, hence they were called 'Lenten butchers'.[22] Considering the devotion of Englishmen to meat, it is not surprising that all this produced friction between the Lord Mayor, who had to enforce the rules, dignitaries who wanted him to bend them, and the Privy Council which had passed them.

25 February 1579: Lord Mayor to Bishop of London: re his request that his own butcher be allowed to kill flesh – no, the Bishop would be supplied by a licensed butcher. (The *Bishop*, of all people.)

9 March 1581: Privy Council to Lord Mayor: re fishmongers' complaint that 40 butchers were licensed, and 'sundry tabling houses' (eating houses) were selling meat in Lent – action please.

11 March 1581: Lord Mayor to Privy Council: re the above – the number of licensed butchers was 4, not 40. As to the table-keepers, many had already been dealt with; the rest would be dealt with as soon as possible.

24 January 1582: Lord Howard of Effingham to Lord Mayor: re licence to kill – please license David Newholt of Little Eastbury. (Reply: no.)

24 January 1587: Lord Mayor to Walsingham: 'great disorder had yearly been committed by the butchers of the City, who being of a rude and uncivil kind could hardly be kept from killing flesh in Lent. A number of honourable persons usually made request to have certain persons licensed, who were dissatisfied upon refusal': Privy Council to deal, please.

12 March 1590: Lord Mayor to Privy Council: re licensed butchers, again – Privy Council to deal, please.

(By 1591 there were still, no matter what the fishmongers said, only six licensed butchers.)

8 February 1591: Lord Mayor to Privy Council: re Privy Council's order that unlicensed meat should be impounded and sold to hospitals and prisons – the watchmen were careless. Why not pay them with half the meat impounded?

And there this spirited correspondence, extracted from the City's records, ceases.[23] As to the 'sundry tabling houses', Falstaff warned the hostess of one of them that 'there is an indictment upon thee, for suffering [allowing] flesh to be eaten in thy house contrary to the law', but she insouciantly replied, 'All victuallers do so. What's a joint of mutton or two in a whole Lent?'[24]

Cooking and recipes

There was a fashionable trend towards French cooking. The Earl of Leicester wrote to his agent in France asking him to look out for 'a good young Protestant cook'; he had already sent 'a young man brought up in my kitchen' to spend a year 'with some good principal cook in Paris'.[25] A well-trained London housekeeper could 'wash, wring, brew, bake, scour, dress meat and drink, and make the beds'.[26] The kitchen implements at her disposal would be knives and spoons and big cooking forks, skimmers and colanders, ladles for basting, frying pans, cauldrons and pipkins (small saucepans) for boiling or stewing, small 'chafing-dishes' for cooking delicate recipes over a small brazier, and spits for roasting. Meat and birds would be roasted on a spit or 'broache' in front of the open fire. Spits could be big enough for a swan or a huge joint of beef or a whole pig, or fine enough for little birds such as blackbirds and larks.[27] They were turned by a 'spitjack' involving weight-driven ratcheted wheels, or by a small boy/scullion called a 'turn-broche', or a dog, a 'turnspit cur'.[28]

Not everyone had ovens. A pie could be sent to the neighbourhood baker to be baked in his oven, which put it at the mercy of his
apprentices, as described in a contemporary dialogue:

> *Father:* me thinketh that it [the pie] is too much baked.
> *Wife:* no forsooth, it is but well; but it is a great pity that the liquor
> [gravy] is so run out.
> *Father:* it is the fault of the baker ...

And from the same source:

> *Father:* ... will you have some cake? Truly it is but dough, I would the
> baker had been baked when he did heat the oven.[29]

The housewife would know when to take her cake or pie round to
the baker when she heard the baker's apprentice shouting in the
street, 'Come to the bakehouse.'[30]

We take such care to slaughter animals in peace and quiet, partly
because we think that if the animal is stressed its meat will be tough.
It is the more extraordinary that Elizabethan butchers could be
fined by their livery company, under an ordinance of 1423 and still
enforced, for 'killing a bull unbeayted [*sic*]': that is, a bull that had
not been hunted or baited in the ring.[31]

In general, their recipes call for more spices than we use, and sugar
and honey and fruit such as oranges, prunes and dates were added
to meat dishes. The result was more like Moroccan or Lebanese
food than English 'meat and two veg'.

The recipes are unnerving in their use of the personal pronoun.
A coney (a rabbit reared for eating) was feminine. When you had
stuffed one with pepper and currants, 'prick her head between her
hinder legs and break her not. Put her into a fair earthen pot with
mutton broth'. A hare was feminine too; 'take the hare and flay
[skin] her'. On the other hand, capons (de-sexed cocks) were still
masculine. 'Take a good capon and scald him and when he is fair
washed put him in your pot ...' This recipe adds sugar, herbs,
nutmeg and ground almonds, with other things, and you serve it
garnished with prunes and barberries. Another capon recipe boiled
'him' until half-cooked, then added six or eight oranges and some
sugar, cloves, mace and cinnamon, with two ground nutmegs.

Some of the raw material has fallen out of favour in our kitchens.
It is a long time since I heard of anyone cooking a sheep's head, and
I have never met, nor want to meet, a calf's lungs on the table. Nor

do I see myself making a 'blamemangle' (blancmange) with 'all the brain of a capon', or using 'the brains of two or three cock sparrows', even though the end result was 'a tart that is a courage to a man or woman'.[32] Gingerbread nowadays is unlikely to be gilded with gold leaf.

To cook in the oven, we use foil, or a baking dish. The Elizabethan cook used a 'coffin' of hard plain pastry, enclosing the meat and keeping the juices in. The coffin was not for eating. 'Take your kid and parboil him, and wash it in verjuice [a very sour fruit juice] and saffron, and season it with pepper, salt and a little mace. Then lay it in your coffin with sweet butter and the liquor it was seasoned in. And so bake it.' A pie was different:

> To make a pie of humbles [more usually, 'umbles': deer's entrails; hence, 'to eat humble pie'. It was a perfectly respectable dish, then]. Take your humbles being parboiled, and chop them very small with a good quantity of mutton suet and half a handful of herbs following: thyme, marjoram, borage, parsley, and a little rosemary, and season the same, being chopped, with pepper, cloves and mace. And so close your pie and bake him.

Fish was poached, or fried – in butter if the household could afford it.[33] Dried salted cod called haberdine or poor Jack was cheap enough to feed even the poor, but 'which is lamentablest of all, that without mustard'.[34] Mustard seems to have been a popular condiment. There is a hint of something horrific in: 'To boil a carp: take out the gall, cast it away, and so scald not your carp nor yet wash him. *When you do kill him* [my italics] let his blood fall into a platter, and split your carp into the same blood ...' What tame lives we live. Salmon, turbot and conger eel could all be poached in strong ale, which would surely take away any taste they had; but if they were a bit high, perhaps it was just as well.

Vegetables were boiled. Cabbage was often stuffed with minced spiced meat. Salads combined a surprising variety of raw ingredients, which could have even more surprising hidden meanings.

> Here followeth the salatte of love, concerning the posies [poetic meanings] of things that are commonly put in a salad:
> Asparagus – renewing of love
> Borage – you make me glad
> Bugloss – I am pleased with you

Scallion [like spring onions] – I love you not
Cabbage lettuce – your love feedeth me
Bitter lettuce – I love you not
Olives – your love annoyeth me
Rosemary flowers – I accept your love
Winter savory – I offer you my love

And lastly and most poignantly, 'radish – pardon me'.[35] Which made the presentation of a carefully composed salad a minefield for the guest who knew, and potential disaster for the guest who did not. What if he confused a lettuce leaf? Or had never really thought of his hostess affectionately, but had a passion for rosemary flowers? If he lasted until the fruit course, he was still unwise to relax. Strawberries meant 'I am altogether yours', raspberries were an invitation to come again, figs indicated that he pleased his hostess much, and if by any chance there were lilies of the valley about, they meant 'kiss me'.[36]

Sweet puddings and tarts were predictably highly seasoned. Strawberries in red wine with sugar, cinnamon and ginger, or cherries with mustard, cinnamon and ginger could be tasty. They would go well with 'trifle': 'take a pint of thick cream, and season it with sugar and ginger and rose water … make it luke warm in a dish on a chafing dish and coals. And after, put it into a silver piece or a bowl, and so serve it …'[37]

You might like a shortcake with your strawberries. The following recipe illustrates just how laborious cooking could be.

Take wheat flour of the fairest you can get, and put it in an earthen pot, and stop [stopper] it close [tightly] and set it in an oven and bake it, and when it is baked it will be full of clods, and therefore you must searce [sieve] it through a searce. And the flour will have as long baking as a pastie of venison. When you have done this, take clotted cream, or else sweet butter, but cream is better, then take sugar, cloves, mace and saffron, and the yolk of an egg, for one dozen cakes one yolk is enough; then put these aforesaid things together into the cream, and themer [blend] them altogether, then put them to your flour and so make your cakes … you must bake them on papers, after the drawing [withdrawal: taking out of the oven] of a batch of bread.

No quantities, no timing device, no thermostat, all dependent on common sense and experience. And something else was needed – muscle power.

To make fine bisket bread: take a pound of fine flour and a pound of sugar, and mingle it together, a quarter of a pound of anniseeds, four eggs, two or three spoonfuls of rosewater, put all these into an earthenware pan. And with a slice of wood beat it *the space of two hours* ...[38]

Meals

The situation of our region, lying near unto the north, doth cause the heat of our stomachs to be of somewhat greater force: therefore our bodies do crave a little more ample nourishment than the inhabitants of the hotter regions.[39]

Breakfast was probably some weak beer to drink, with a piece of bread. 'Butter is good to eat in the morning before other meats [food] ... a little portion is good for every man in the morning if it be new made' – which it mostly wasn't.[40] 'Butter and sage and bread and beer' was an adequate breakfast in 1589.[41] If you were one of those fortunate people who feel strong in the morning, you might try 'a piece of brawn and a Christmas Pie'.[42]

There were two cooked meals to provide every day. According to Harrison, nobles, gentlemen and merchants sat down to dinner between eleven o'clock and noon, and supped about six in the evening. Working people dined about noon, and supped about seven or eight in the evening. 'As for the poor, they generally dine and sup where they may' – if at all.[43]

Gentlemen and merchants who were entertaining guests might have four to six dishes on the table at once, but only half that amount when it was just the family.[44] On more formal occasions, several meat or fish dishes arrived on the table at the same time, as the 'first course', all with their proper 'appurtenances' or sauces. When people had had enough of them, they were taken away and another collection of meat or fish dishes was brought. Then those were removed in their turn, to make way for the sweet pies and fruit. But there was no clear division between 'meat' and 'sweet'. Each course might include something we would definitely regard as a sweet to be served last and separately.

Thomas Nashe was almost as good at disapproving of things as his contemporary Stubbes. His views on English meals:

We ... eat more meat at one meal than the Spaniard or Italian do in a month ... they draw out a dinner with salletts ... we must have our tables furnished like poulter[er]s' stalls ... strange birds, China mustard and odd patterns to make custard by. Lord, what a coyle have we, with this course and that course, removing this dish higher, setting another lower, and taking away the third.[45]

The main meal was midday dinner. While you waited for the meal to be served, you might toy with slices of radish dipped in salt 'the better to procure an appetite to meat'.[46] Or you might take a few oysters, raw with brown (barley) bread[47] or a little salt beef with mustard.[48]

'Here followeth', in a cookery book published in 1596, 'the order of meats, how they must be served at the table with their sauces for flesh days at dinner.'[49] The first course was

potage or stewed broth. Boiled meat or stewed meat. Chickens and bacon. Powdered [salted] beef. Pies. Goose. Pig. Roast beef. Roast veal. Custard.

The author is naturally considering the kind of formal dinners that would make his book essential reading for the cook and the hostess, and boost his sales. He does not list any vegetables, but they were certainly on the table, and merited a special section in his own book. An Act was passed in 1559 prohibiting the import of cabbages and 'turnops', as unncessary imports, along with dolls and tennis balls.[50] The vegetables could, after all, be grown at home.

The second course was

Roasted lamb. Roasted capons. Roasted conies [rabbits]. Chickens. Baked venison. Tart.

And in case the company was still hungry,

the service at dinner: A dozen quails. A dish of larks. Two pasties of red deer in a dish. Tart. Gingerbread. Fritters.

The fruit tarts and pies might be brought on as a last course, without a meat dish, and they might be followed by cheese and fruit. 'Scraped' cheese with sage and sugar seems to have been popular.

But the place to go for good eating was your livery company. Harrison described the huge spreads of exotic food, and 'jellies of all colours ... in the representation of sundry flowers, herbs, trees, beasts, fishes and fruits', let alone marchpane, tarts and so on. The Drapers' feast in 1564 cost a total of £82 9s 4d, entertaining 89 guests over three days to a sturgeon and miscellaneous birds, from swans and herons to larks (8d a dozen). Members and friends provided 40 bucks (male deer), which were made into 168 pasties that mostly went to the wardens' wives, to make up for not inviting them to the feast, which was for members only. The 'musician and his whole noise' (combo) cost 13s 4d, and 5s 11d went on perfumery and flowers.[51] The Merchant Taylors got through 30 bucks 'besides other meats' at their annual feast in 1559, so did the Grocers, with 'great cheer' two years later.[52] Harrison makes the point that on 'Quarter Days' in a livery company, when all its members gathered to pay their dues and – in modern terms – to network, 'they do nothing inferior to the nobility'.

Bucks and swans seem to have been used almost as currency. The Carpenters had at least two tenants who paid their rent part in cash, part in a promise of a buck to be delivered 'on the next dinner day', and another who paid £2 a year rent, plus a swan. They spent 12s on a swan 'to give the Lord Mayor for a present', in 1558, no doubt for good reasons.[53] They had another tenant, a brewer, who paid his rent in beer.

Sometimes the invitation was for a 'banquet' after dinner, such as the top people in the Skinners enjoyed in the summer of 1560: 'Master Clarenceux [one of the heralds] made a great banquet for the Master and his company, first spice-bread, cherries, strawberries, pippins [a kind of apple] and marmalade, and suckets [sweets], comfets [ditto] and portingales [oranges] and divers other dishes, hippocras, Rhenish wine, claret wine, and beer and ale great plenty; and all was welcome.'[54] The Drapers went round to the tavern – the Flying Horse in Maiden Lane – for 'a banquet of pears, plums, quodlings [another kind of apple] and apples with one piece of sturgeon ... and wine and sugar, the price whereof was 24s' after a tiring August day checking the cloth measures at St Bartholomew's fair.[55] But 'a last year's pippin of my own grafting with a dish of carraways [seeds]' would be just as refreshing at the end of a meal.[56]

Table manners

What were you supposed to do with this stupefying amount of food?

The first thing to remember was the proper vocabulary. Any gentleman knew that carving was an art, best left to the carver, who would know Wynkyn de Worde's *The Book of Kervinge* backwards, even though the first edition had come out in 1508. (The last was printed in 1613.) There were 38 special terms for carving. You did not just cut a joint into bits, you would

> break that deer
> rear that goose
> list that swan
> trush that chicken
> disfigure that peacock
> splat that pike
> culpon that trout
> alay that pheasant
> wing that partridge or quail
> thigh all manner of small birds
> undertranch that porpoise
> tame that crab, and
> barb that lobster.

The carver was not finished yet. He had to see that the appropriate sauce was added to each dish. For a crab, for example, it was up to the carver to 'break him asunder in a dish, make the shell clean and put in the stuff again, temper it with vinegar and powders, then cover it with bread and send it to the kitchen to heat, then … break the great claws and lay them in a dish'.[57] Not surprisingly, the livery companies hired carvers for their great occcasions. The Carpenters paid a carver 6s 8d for their feast, in 1558, while the minstrels got only 5s 6d, and the 'preacher for his sermon' a mere 3s 4d.

In less exalted homes, where there was a butler but no carver, the wife let the side down in front of guests by saying to her husband, 'I pray you, pull in pieces that capon, and help your neighbour' and the husband, who was as usual rather cross, said 'cut that turkey cock in pieces … Sir, shall I be your carver? Will you have this hen's wing?'[58]

Forks were still rare. In Ben Jonson's *Volpone*, a man who wanted to be taken for a Venetian 'must … learn the use and handling of your silver fork at meals'.[59] For most people, 'fingers came before forks', and it was the more important that your fingers – and your neighbours' fingers – should be clean.[60] The first step was to wash your hands, in public, with the other guests and household. Most inventories of household goods included ewers or jugs, and basins, and towels, which were somewhere near the hall or dining chamber, not equipment for the bedroom. The Earl of Essex had three plain silver basins and ewers,[61] the Earl of Bedford had two silver basins and two ewers, with covers, worth £60, and three other basins and ewers, in the 'ewery' in his house.[62]

In the contemporary dialogue quoted above, the master of the house comes in hungry, with friends, on a Sunday morning, and expects his meal to be served immediately. 'Let us go to dinner; let us go sit … [then, remembering himself] go to, let us wash hands', at which one guest says, 'As for me, I have washed', and the other – probably hoping to stave off more bad temper from his host – says, 'And I have handled nothing since that I have washed.'[63]

In a slightly more elegant household, a lady brings some friends home for dinner. She too seems to be bad-tempered with hunger, or over-eager to impress her friends. Having thoroughly berated the servant for negligence, she says, 'Go to, let us wash hands, but let us have our oysters first, for we should be forced to wash again' – but no one wants any, and she agrees that eating oysters in the dog-days (or according to our rule, when there's no 'r' in the month, i.e. summer) is not a good idea. So, 'give us therefore to wash'. Three guests are invited to wash their hands in the same basin as their hostess – 'come, wash with my lady and me, we may wash well four in a basin' – but they politely hang back: 'Pardon me Madame, we will wash after you.' The hostess presses them not to be so 'mannerly'. 'As for [a young male guest] I will give him leave to wash with the maidens, for he is not yet married.' This last bit is intriguing. There was clearly some camaraderie, even a sexual overtone, in all these preliminaries: reminiscent of the business of offering and lighting cigarettes, which broke the ice at the beginning of an acquaintance, in the days when cigarette smoking was a socially accepted habit.

Hands clean, you can sit down. But be careful where you sit. The master takes the top of the table, of course. The children and the servants sit at the foot of the table, or at another table, even in another room. It is the spaces in between that are tricky. Thomas Wythorne took a job as tutor, in 1557.[64] He was understandably status-conscious, after a searing experience of being treated as a toy-boy by a previous employer. This time, he stipulated that he should be 'used as a friend and not as a servant. Upon this, they not only allowed me to sit at their table but also at their own mess [sharing the dishes served to them], so long as there were not any to occupy the ... place that was a great deal my [social] better.' If there was only one table in the room, you could check where the ornate 'salt' was, and decide whether you should sit above it, or below.

In front of you, on the tablecloth, are a plate and a spoon. You have your own knife with you – clean, of course – but a knife may be provided too, and just possibly a fork. The bossy lady we have already met nags her butler: 'Why have you not covered [i.e. set the table] with the table cloth and napkins of damask? ... Set at every trencher plate a knife, a spoon and a silver fork ...' There is no glass beside your plate. This for once is not the fault of the butler; glasses and silver drinking cups stand ready on the cupboard, with all the other silver.

Grace is said. You can start. The general idea is that you help yourself, if you can, with the end of your knife or your (rare) fork, to whatever you can reach. But take it gently:

> If the fish be pleasant, either flesh or fish
> Ten hands at once swarm in the dish:
> And if it be flesh, ten knives shall thou see
> Mangling the flesh, and in the platter flee:
> To put there thy hands is peril without fail
> Without a gauntlet or a glove of mail.[65]

Some knives have a prong at the end, for convenient spearing of choice bits. If you fancy something definitely out of reach, you can hope your host will notice, and send the dish down to your part of the table, or you can simply ask whoever is nearest. You should look after your neighbours in the hope that they will look after you. It sounds chaotic. And in all this to-ing and fro-ing the food gets totally cold. If you feel strongly about having hot food, it can be warmed in a chafing dish.[66] But few people seem to have thought this important until very recently.

A schoolboy is being taught table manners:

> ... wipe not thy mouth with thy hand, nor sleeve, but with a napkin, for, for that cause it is laid before thee. Touch not any part of the meat, saving that which thou wilt cut off, for thyself. Perceivest thou not how thou [de]filest thy sleeve with fat? If they [the sleeves] be open, cast them on thy shoulders. If they be not open, turn them up to thine elbow. If they fall down, pin them up with a pin [a use for those ubiquitous pins stored in codpieces].[67]

When the meal eventually comes to an end, grace is said, the company washes their hands again, and they totter away replete.

Drink

Alessandro Magno, usually a reliable witness, recorded with a straight face that 'at the numerous banquets [I think the translator uses this in the modern, not the Elizabethan sense] when they are seated together, it is the custom to slap men on the shoulders and cry out "frolic!", which means "enjoy yourself" and to pat women on the belly. Each one slaps the man or woman near to him.'[68] (Where *had* he been?) But the custom of 'pledging' is confirmed by another foreign commentator:

> The English are great drunkards: for if an Englishman would treat you, he will say in his language ... 'will you drink a quart of Gascoigne wine, another of Spanish, and another [of] Malmsey?' In eating and drinking they will say to you above a hundred times ... 'I am going to drink to you'; and you should answer ... 'I pledge you.' If you would thank them ... you must say ... 'I thank you with all my heart'.[69]

It is still the custom on ceremonial occasions in Gray's Inn for a massive silver loving cup full of hippocras, or spiced wine, to be passed round the members of the Inn dining in Hall, each standing in turn to drink to the memory of Good Queen Bess, and taking a sip or slurp – but with extreme care: tilt it too much and the wine goes into your ears and down your front. As the person drinking is concentrating, his neighbours stand too, traditionally so that they can defend the drinker from any enemy taking advantage of this momentary preoccupation to stab him in the ribs. (The words of the toast make me wonder whether this is not, like so many old traditions, of Victorian origin, but I daresay many ancient institutions have similar, and authentic, customs.)

At dinner, bottles of wine were set to cool in a metal cistern of cold water under the buffet. The wine will have been decanted into the bottles from the barrel; it was not sold in bottles. As you ploughed your way through what looks like a gargantuan meal, or if you could see a pledge coming, you needed a drink, so you asked the servitor to fill you a glass, you drank, and you gave the glass back to be washed. The servitor rinsed it in a wooden tub beside the wine cooler (wooden because delicate Venetian glass was less liable to break against wood than in a metal basin) and put it back on the buffet, thus avoiding 'much idle tippling', according to Harrison; I suppose it might. Drinking glasses from Murano were more prized than gold or silver cups, astonishing as it seems to us.

The wines on sale included malmsey, Greek and Corsican wines, Romaniske, Romney, secke, aligaunte, bastard, tint and others.[70] (Translated, malmsey = madeira, romney = Romani Conte, secke = sack = dry white Spanish, aligaunte = aligote, a white burgundy, bastard = another burgundy, tint = Spanish red, but my kind informants were stumped by Romaniske. Romanian? Italian?)[71] Vintners had to be licensed, and wine was subject to a fixed rate of duty, which was notoriously evaded by smugglers, until the Act against Smuggling of 1559 imposed severe penalties on anyone landing goods other than at licensed quays, where ships were liable to be searched, and on any port employee conniving at evasion.

'Moderately drunk, [wine] doth ... quicken a man's wits ... The better the wine is, the better humours it doth engender. And because wine is full of fumositie it is good therefore to allay it with water. Wine ... doth comfort old men and women, but there is no wine good for children and maidens ... old men may drink high wines at their pleasure.'[72] So, I have presumed for several years, may old women. It was quite usual to dilute wine with water, at meals.[73] Wine was not always sweet enough for the English taste. An anecdote about confidence tricksters gives a glimpse of drinking habits in taverns. The villain persuades two innocent victims to have a drink with him. They all go into a tavern, where he orders a pint of white wine and a pint of claret. The wine arrives, with two cups, one for each kind of wine. They all taste one kind, out of one of the cups, then the villain 'takes the other [cup] up and tastes the other pint of wine', which he said was 'somewhat hard', so off he goes with the cup, ostensibly to get the landlord to add some sugar and rosewater to improve it, but actually to make a quick exit, plus cup.[74]

'The general drink is ale, which is prepared from barley and is excellently well tasted, but strong and intoxicating.'[75] Beer is ale flavoured with hops, which made it keep better as well as taste different. Another difference may be that ale 'for an Englishman ... makes him strong', but beer 'doth make a man fat and inflate the belly'.[76] The beer in noblemen's houses was one or two years old, but for ordinary households it was likely to be recently brewed.

Harrison's wife and her maids brewed once a month, as a matter of course. It was a complicated and labour-intensive process, beginning with grinding 8 bushels of malted grain – imagine hand-grinding 64 pint mugs filled with grain – 'upon our quern, whereby the toll is saved' and, surely, Mrs Harrison and her maids were exhausted. But evading tax ('toll') has always spurred people to action. It then had to be brewed three times over in their 'furnace', and barrelled up, resulting in 24 gallons of beer 'meet for poor men such as I am' – but he was not all that poor, he was on £40 a year.

Beer did not meet with Magno's approval: 'healthy but sickening to taste. It is cloudy like horse's urine and has husks on top.'[77] It is fair to add that brewers had the reputation of retailing filthy Thames water.[78] In 1574 there were still 58 ale brewers to 33 beer brewers in the City,[79] but beer gradually replaced ale as the national drink over the course of the century. The cost of a barrel of beer was fixed at 4s.[80] One foreign visitor noticed that beer was drunk 'out of earthen pots with silver handles and covers', for people of 'middling fortune', the poor managing with pewter. 'With their beer they have a custom of eating very soft saffron cakes, which give an excellent relish to the beer' – like soggy potato chips in modern pubs.[81]

Queen Elizabeth was fond of metheglin, distilled from honey and herbs. Mead was metheglin without the herbs. Both were good for you.[82] Hippocras was sweetened spiced wine. As well as home-brewed distilled liquors, acqua vitae (brandy) was being made commercially, on a small scale, by Jane Garrett, the wife of a foreign leather dresser and merchant, in 1593.[83]

'Water is not wholesome food by itself.' If you must, drink rain-water, or spring water from the conduits, which should be filtered and allowed to stand for two or three hours if it is to be used for brewing or cooking. If you propose to add it to wine, boil it first.[84]

Mineral water from a well near Coventry was 'sent daily all over England', which sounds so commercially familiar that one imagines carts laden with barrels of it plodding their way along the country roads to every pub. But it may have been for external use only, since its merits were discovered, in 1579, by 'a wounded man [finding] it healed his wound'.[85]

Cows' milk and ewes' milk were 'nutritive' and very good for melancholy men and old men, and children, especially boiled with a little sugar. But they were 'not good for them that have gurgulations in the belly'.[86]

Eating out

Alessandro Magno put up at an inn kept by an Italian compatriot in London. He was favourably impressed by the meals, 'a choice of two or three different kinds of roast meat at a meal, or meat pies, savories, fruit tarts, and excellent wine'. The livery companies quite often patronised their local inns. The Cutlers even held their annual feasts in taverns, including the Swan in Gray's Inn Lane, the Mermaid, and the Bell in Holborn.[87] If you were drinking in a tavern, 'it is the custom ... to erect partitions between the tables so that one table cannot overlook the next',[88] and the wine was supposed to be served in 'sealed quarts', not open in 'stone jugs'.[89]

According to Magno, '[The English] are not ashamed ... to eat in inns, or to drink either: if anyone wants to give a feast he orders the meal at the inn, giving the number of those invited, and they go there to eat. The inns are very clean and they treat well any who go there.' Nashe, as usual, saw the dark side:

> is it not a pitiful thing that a fellow that eats not a good meal's meat in a week ... now and then (once or twice in a term) comes to the eighteen-penny ordinary [table d'hôte at an inn], because he would be seen amongst cavaliers and brave courtiers, living otherwise all the year long with salt butter and Holland cheese in his chamber?[90]

Taverns could be insalubrious, as the Dean of St Paul's found out, according to the record of a 1590 lawsuit: 'The said Farrington converted ... a part of the said tenement next joining to the said Dean of [St] Paul's house by one common wall ... into a tavern at the which Dean's back gate the resorters to the said tavern do usually unload themselves of all their drink taken in the said tavern', which the poor Dean very reasonably objected to.[91]

Sex, Marriage, Family Life and Death

Sex outside marriage

Is sex necessary? It is only recently that women have claimed that they are entitled to a satisfying sex life. And in our days, every sense is assaulted, all the time, from pre-puberty to old age, by sexual references. It is more complicated than it may seem at first, to think oneself back to the sixteenth century, and correlate our interest in this absorbing subject with the place it had in Elizabethan lives.

Sex was certainly less public. But for whom was certain gardening advice given, if not for lovers? Young men fresh from their Italian tour 'be the greatest makers of love … with bargains of wearing colours, flowers and herbs to breed occasion of often meeting of him or her and boldly talking of this and that'.[1] A quick reference to Turner's *Herbal* or some similar work should produce helpful hints on furthering a flirtation. Artichokes, for instance, could be useful in some circumstances: 'as this herb provoketh lust in women so it abateth the same in men'. Saffron boiled in wine was not only a moth repellent and 'keeps a man from drunkenness, but also encourageth unto procreation of life' – every man should have it handy.[2] Even viagra doesn't keep the moths out. Coriander seeds in sweet wine were an effective aphrodisiac in moderation, but too much 'bringeth man unto a frenziness'.[3] Leeks and onions were also said to be aphrodisiac, but had different disadvantages, surely. If the young man succeeded in getting his girl into bed, 'a branch of Southernwood [known even now as Lad's Love] laid under the bolster doth move the desire to the Venereal act'.[4]

Rue might be useful at the bedside too, as a contraceptive: this advice was not openly given – it had to be deduced from the warning that 'young married wives may [i.e. should] seldom eat of this herb for fear of hindering conception'.[5] In many societies abortion is practised as a birth-control measure: it looks as if Simon Forman, and surely the neighbourhood wise woman, might be able to recommend an abortifacient, such as marigolds or mandrake, but whether they worked is hard to tell.[6]

Sexual intercourse outside marriage just for the fun of it – or, if you prefer a more romantic formula, because of an overpowering passion – certainly happened, but it is difficult to spot, from this distance. The plays by Shakespeare that schoolchildren are compelled to read, thereby destroying their magic for years, are full of sexual innuendo, although the performance of sexual intercourse on stage was a treat in store for the future. It takes a Shakespearian scholar to identify the references that would have titillated an Elizabethan audience but which are now obscured by time and the changing resonances of words. But let me give just one instance. In *Henry V*, the French princess Katharine is trying to learn English. Her attendant had been to England, so she teaches Katharine a few words. It all looks perfectly proper, until you realise that Katharine's mispronunciation of 'neck' as 'nick' must have made the audience roll in the aisles, since 'nick' could be very obscene.[7]

Pornography was one of the many vices allegedly brought back from Italy by young men sent there to improve their education. I suspect that rude books were not beyond the capacity of the average English hack writer; it is just that the Italian ones, or references to them, have lasted better. In Ben Jonson's *Volpone*, Lady Politic Would-be is showing off her wide reading. She runs through the Italian poets:

> But, for a desperate wit, there's Aretino!
> Only, his pictures are a little obscene.[8]

And they certainly were. Aretino wrote sixteen pornographic sonnets, which were illustrated by Giulio Romano, depicting various positions of sexual intercourse. Their publication in 1520 so scandalised the Pope that Aretino had to leave Rome for Venice, where he produced *Ragionamenti*, in which two Roman courtesans purport to educate a young woman called Pippa in sexual technique. Aretino died in

1556, but his Sonnets, which became famous as *Postures*, outlived him for many years.[9] They were 'of late [1570] translated out of Italian into English, and sold in every shop in London'.[10] They were a familiar manual for prostitutes: 'they have Aretino's tables [pictures] at their fingers' ends'.[11]

Prostitution flourished. Despite the risk of sexually transmitted disease, it gave a woman a means of earning her living which was at least an alternative to the only other career opportunity open to most women, domestic service. Men have always been prepared to pay extra for deflowering a virgin; fortunately this once-and-for-all commercial asset could be revived as often as feasible. There was a sad story of a turnspit boy who tried the relevant lotion on his face, out of curiosity. When it dried, 'the boy's mouth and eyes [were] drawn so together and closed, that neither had he left an eye to look withal, and scarcely might ye turn your little finger in his mouth'.[12] His terrible predicament was cured by hot, fatty, meat broth.

Brothels operated outside the city limits. They had been officially closed down by Henry VIII in 1546, but they were legalised again a few years later by his son, Edward VI. The goodwill that attaches to premises takes a long time to disappear, and Bankside in Southwark was still generally recognised as the place to go. 'Trugginghouses' or 'whorehouses' could also be found in the poor quarters of Westminster and Shoreditch, Spitalfields beyond Bishops Gate, and parts of Whitefriars. (They were also called 'stews', but this can be misleading; the word could mean a perfectly proper steam bath in a fashionable Elizabethan house.) A 1584 broadsheet puts the charge in a brothel at 40s 'or better',[13] which seems improbably high.

There was a certain amount of amateur competition. In 1579 Alice Amos sued her neighbours Richard and Susan Symonds for defamation because Susan had called her a whore – an exceedingly serious insult to a woman, as bad as impugning a man's commercial probity. Alice and the Symondses all lived cheek by jowl in Boar's Head Alley off Fleet Street. Alice lived at the top of the house, with an outside staircase to her room, past the Symondses' rooms. The trouble began when Susan stuck her head out of her window and shouted at Alice, 'Thou art a whore. And I saw my husband stand between thy legs and thou didst put thy hand into his codpiece very rudely' – for which Susan blamed her neighbour, not her own husband. It got worse; from inside the house Richard Symonds shouted, 'Remember the quart of cream, remember the quart of cream. Yea thou art a whore indeed for I did occupy [have intercourse with] thee myself six times, for one mess [dish] of cream.' Unfortunately we don't know the court's decision, but it looks as if Alice had been unwise, in legal terms, to take her neighbours to court, and Richard would have done better, if his marriage were to survive, to keep his mouth shut.[14] (I strongly suspect that Richard used the short Anglo-Saxon word, rather than the stilted 'occupy'; the clerk of the court was taking a verbatim note of the evidence, but every now and then he diverged from strict accuracy in the interests of decency, and substituted the legalistic 'occupy' for the word Richard used.) In another case of slander for the same imputation, Margery Wright sued John Thomas, alleging that in the course of an argument in an alehouse in Holborn, in which Margery had cast aspersions on John's wife, he had replied, 'She was an honester woman than thou art, for she never occupied for a taffeta hat, as thou didst.'[15]

Homosexuality was viewed as an abhorrent divergence from the natural order, a crime punishable by death.[16] It was popularly imputed to Catholic priests and stage players, both of whom were outside the accepted social standards of the day. It was one of the reasons why Stubbes so disapproved of playhouses: not only might the players seduce the boys in the company, but some of the audience were no better. During the performance the occupants of the stools on the stage itself might 'with small cost, purchase the dear acquaintance of the boys'[17] and when the play is over 'every mate sorts to his mate, everyone brings another homeward of their way very friendly, and in their secret conclaves covertly they play the Sodomites or worse.'[18] Any sixteenth-century reference to Sodom implied what we would now call male homosexuality, but it would be rare for a reference to be more explicit, because of the threat of execution, and also because of the vagueness of the concept. The sixteenth-century label of sodomy could include bestiality (intercourse with animals) and sexual intercourse with evil spirits (in the person of the local Satanist) during witchcraft rituals. So it is not easy to delineate homosexuality in Elizabethan London.

Yet there are indications that it was tacitly accepted in London. Otherwise, the 'male stews' would have quickly been closed down. John Donne reproved a profligate young man who

... in rank itchy lust, desire and love
The nakedness and bareness to enjoy
Of thy plump muddy whore or prostitute boy.

Prosecutions for buggery were exceedingly rare, and were sometimes motivated by malice unrelated to any criminal behaviour.[19] In 1594 Nicholas Udall, then headmaster of Eton, was accused of a homosexual relationship with a former pupil, but survived.[20]

Marriage

Marriage involved a change of status. The woman moved from the power and responsibilty of her father, to that of her husband. The only women who were not treated as chattels in this way were widows, who were allowed to dispose of their own fates if they could. It was desirable for this change of status to be signalled in public, so that everyone should know that the new woman who had moved in round the corner was a respectable married lady, and so that her creditors knew they could press her husband to pay her debts.

This is a legalistic way of looking at marriage. The more normal way is to treat a wedding as an occasion for celebration. But before we get down to the cakes and ale, what was a valid marriage? As far as the Church was concerned, the only proper way was to have it publicised by the reading of banns, solemnised in church, before a congregation, by a parson, who would record it in a register and pocket his fee. The essence of the ceremony was the publicity given to it. The parties had to undertake that they knew of no reason, such as a previous marriage, or even a promise to marry someone else, why the ceremony should not proceed. Opportunities were also given to anyone else who had doubts about the capacity of either party, to say so, weeks before the service and again during it, before the parties exchanged their binding vows. This could be useful to a reluctant bridegroom. It was not unknown for a man to 'remember' a previous promise, even at the altar. The contract came into being when each party replied 'I do' to the question whether they took the other as their lawful wedded spouse. The parson's pronouncement that they were then married merely recognised the fact.

Although the union was blessed by the Church, and referred to as 'holy wedlock', marriage was not a sacrament of the Anglican Church, as it had been of the pre-Reformation Catholic Church. The parson would issue a 'testimony' or certificate of the ceremony, which the bride kept carefully. It was part of the equipment of wandering vagabond couples, who when asked awkward questions as to whether they were respectably married and deserving of help could produce 'a testimonial with the minister's name ... in a parish in some shire far away'.[21] It was probably forged anyway.

But there were other routes. A special licence could be bought from the Church authority, to avoid all that publicity, but it cost more than most people would afford – nearly 10s in fees, and, after 1571, a substantial bond guaranteeing that there were no impediments to the marriage.[22] A cheaper way was to dispense with the church service altogether. If each party took the other as his or her spouse, they were legally married, and if they chose slightly different words and said that they definitely *would* marry in the future, and followed that promise by sexual intercourse, they were equally bound.

Thomas Wythorne still had not found the ideal wife by the time he was 40, 'at the which year begins the first part of the old man's age', so he was, as it were, looking back through his address book, and he asked a friend to check on the availability of a certain widow. She seems to have promised at some stage to marry him in the future, but he had not taken the next step, leaving the poor woman in the air. 'She answered [the friend] that "it was no such promise ... she might break it again upon cause, and seeing that I took her not bianby [immediately] and dispatched the matter, she was determined never to marry"' – he had lost his chance.[23] During the interim between the promise and the consummation – provided it was not too long – the parties were regarded as legally committed, so that they could not contract another marriage.

Obviously it would be a rash bride who entrusted herself to a man for the rest of her life, if she had no means of proving that she was his wife. So witnesses were essential in practice, and the exchange of vows ('hand-fasting') was usually a family affair, with a certain amount of ceremony, often conducted by a parson, and accompanied by the giving of presents by the groom to his intended. The betrothal of a couple was sometimes celebrated with 'a great feast and superfluous banquet, and even the same night are the two handfasted persons brought and laid together ... weeks before they go to the church'. Theorists could argue that the words themselves, and if necessary the act, sufficed in law to make a valid marriage without any church service, when the parties 'did willingly take hands together, and either of them two did plight their faith and truth to the other, as man and wife, before god'.[24] This explains Thomas Wythorne's alarm one evening, when he was having a quiet drink with another widow and a man who happened to be a parson. They were all increasingly friendly, so much so that – and here is the conversation he set down afterwards in his diary –

> She said – Call ye me 'Mistress Elspeth' and why not 'wife'? Will ye not be my husband?
>
> He said – I did not know your mind certainly, in that matter, till now, and therefore I drink unto you, gentle wife, with all my heart.
>
> She said – I pledge you, good husband.
>
> The parson said – Be you so soon agreed? Come on, and it's make ye sure, that shall I. (And with those words he took her by the hand and reached to have taken mine also.)
>
> He said – no, soft, soft fire maketh sweet malt. Nay, I will woo a little while, before I be made sure, for we do see sometimes that they who do wed and marry in haste have time enough to repent them.
>
> The parson said – nay (and with that he did let go her hand) I do mean but merrily.
>
> He said – it may be so (but for all that I thought then that such a contract, made by a priest, and in such sort as it seemed that he would have done it, might have turned some one or other or both of us into some disquietness in the end).

So he made his excuses and left. But his narrow escape shows how easy it was to find yourself legally – or at least arguably – married.[25] 'I knew a wench married in an afternoon as she went to the garden for parsley to stuff a rabbit.'[26]

There was no prospect of divorce. A legal separation might be possible, but only for the husband, and only if he could prove adultery by his wife, and pay the legal expenses involved, and even then neither party could re-marry. Annulment, which treated the marriage as null and void from the beginning, was a more promising avenue. No marriage was binding if the parties were under age – fourteen for a boy and twelve for a girl. Since little girls were brought up as miniature women, this may not have been quite as brutal as marrying off a twelve-year-old daughter would be for us;

but in any case the usual age at marriage was more likely to be 25 or 26 for women, 27 or 28 for men.[27] Nor was it binding if both parties did not give their informed consent. A little thirteen-year-old girl was abducted by force and taken to a church in the middle of the night, where she 'said certain words after the priest which she neither then marked [understood] nor now remembered'.[28] Although the court's decision is unknown, it is hard to see how it could have found a valid marriage on those facts.

Another ground for annulment was that the parties were too closely related. Even if the parties had lived together and produced children, their marriage was treated as never having happened, so that the children were illegitimate. For example, a woman could not marry her dead husband's brother; it would be incest. This was the trouble that had made Henry VIII break away from the Church of Rome. It is usually, and inaccurately, referred to as a divorce, but he was asking the Pope to declare that his marriage to Katherine of Aragon had been null and void from its beginning because she had been the wife of his dead brother, Arthur. And this despite her many miscarriages, and the children she had borne him over 24 years, of whom only Mary survived. But had she been Arthur's wife? There had been a formal ceremony of betrothal, they had even been put to bed together, but then what happened? Had Arthur consummated their union? If – as Katherine swore – she was still a virgin when Arthur died, she had not become his wife, and was free to marry Henry: their marriage was lawful, and their daughter Mary was legitimate.

For Henry to succeed he had to satisfy the Pope that Arthur had had intercourse with Katherine, that they had therefore been legally married, and so as Arthur's widow she was not – now that Henry came to think of it – his legal wife and never had been. This explained why God was cross, and had shown his anger in smiting all Katherine's children by Henry except his daughter Mary, who was illegitimate. The Pope did not see it that way. It is fair to say that various political motives were at work, for all concerned. But Henry rebelliously left the bosom of the Church, set up the Church of England, and got what he wanted. I include this only to show how complicated matrimonial law could be. The state of Katherine's hymen when she married Henry VIII does seem, however, a remarkable foundation for the soaring edifice of the Church of England.

But assuming the parties have safely surmounted all these

difficulties, what next? Usually, a party. The beginning of married life was a fit occasion for celebration, but 'into this dish hath the devil put his foot'.[29] The party sometimes began before the happy couple even got to the church, and the drunken guests turned up half way through the sermon 'in all manner of pomp and pride, and gorgeousness of raiment and jewels. They come with a great noise of harps, lutes, kits [miniature violins], basens [a kind of drum] and drums', and went back to their drinking and feasting as soon as the service was over. After a while the party moved to somewhere they could dance, and 'there is such a lifting up and discovering of the damsel's clothes and of other women's apparel that a man might [if he were a reformer, like the writer] think all these dancers ... were sworn to the devil's dance. Then must the poor bride keep foot with all dancers, and refuse none, how scabbed, foul, drunken, rude and shameless so ever he be.'[30] Supper was even more scandalous. After more dancing the happy but exhausted couple was escorted to the matrimonial bed with rude songs.

Despite the convention that every guest contributed food or drink to the feast, 'as much is wasted in one day, as were sufficient for the two newly-married folks half a year to live upon'. By the 1570s Harrison was noting with relief that the 'heathenish rioting at bride-ales' was dimishing, but it had a long way to go. If the bridegroom was a yeoman in the lower ranks of a livery company, the happy couple also went the rounds of his fellow-yeomen 'to gather the goodwill of the company' in the shape of a small gift of money. This could develop into another riotous procession.

A grand wedding might go on for days. In July 1562 there was a wedding at which 'no manner of meats nor drinks that could be had for money ... were wanting [lacking]' and it was still going on the next day: 'after supper came three masques, one was in cloth of gold, the next was friars, and the third was nuns ... after, friars and nuns danced together'. A few months later a double wedding in exalted circles went on for 4 days, 'and every night great mummers and masques'.[31]

Then married life began in earnest. 'Women and horses must be well governed', according to Thomas Becon, whose book *The Christian State of Matrimony* came out in 1546 and ran to many editions. (The frontispiece depicts Eve rising out of Adam's side, just above his pelvis, while Adam looks deeply bored with the whole thing.) Apart from his conviction that women needed 'governing',

Becon's advice sounds surprisingly congenial to our ears:

> Marriage is a common participation of mind, body and goods ...
> [neither spouse should] deny his or her body to the other, because
> they are one body ... as concerning the bed, married folks may upon
> due occasion lie the one [apart] from the other, but [it must be] in
> the good consent of them both ... and only for a time, lest the devil
> be busy.

Here is another marriage guidance counsellor: 'As we do not handle
glasses like pots, because they are weaker vessels, but touch them
nicely and softly for fear of cracks, so a man must treat his wife with
gentleness and softness, not expecting that wisdom, nor that faith,
nor that patience, nor that strength, in the weaker vessel.'[32]

But things could go very wrong. In 1589 Simon White admitted
that he had beaten his wife, but no more than was reasonable. 'He
hath sundry times ... being thereto much provoked by the said
Elizabeth given her a blow upon the cheek with his hand ... he did
upon occasion chastise and correct her with a small beechen
wand.'[33] Simon Forman, the well-known necromancer, had 'married
[his wife] ... by chance, asking her a question in that behalf, the
which she took advantage of [like the widow who so nearly snared
Thomas Wythorne] and he would not go from his word', but he did
not trust her – she was, after all, only 16 – and 'she would not be
quiet till I gave her 2 or 3 boxes' (as in boxing).[34]

Widows had a hidden market value, if their husbands had been
established in a livery company, because their second husband could
expect to succeed to the first husband's position not only in the
matrimonial bed but in his livery company. Thus, apprentices could
jump the remaining years of their apprenticeship in one easy movement by marrying their master's widow. Although in theory it was
against the proper order of things, this seems very natural, when
you remember that the apprentice might be a man in his twenties,
and life was short. It is easy to imagine a household in which the
apprentice has grown up, and is well known to the mistress; in the
later years of his term he has become the husband's right-hand man,
and knows the trade or business thoroughly. When the husband
became old, or ill, the apprentice has probably carried the burden
of the trade or craft for him. Whom else would the widow turn to,
when her husband died?

In more aristocratic circles, widows were urged to remarry. 'Why, lady, do you think it profiteth at all the deceased ghost of him that loved you, (a young gentlewoman as you are, scarce exceeding 20 years) to live thus solitary?' This comes from a book of precedents for letters suitable for all occasions.[35] They are turgid in the extreme. This one purports to be written by a family friend, to a new widow, who clearly can expect no peace to grieve, as he wheels on 'a young gentleman, virtuous, discreet … the son and heir of a worshipful knight'. One is left wondering what the writer hoped to make out of it, let alone how this paragon of a bridegroom had escaped so long.

Servants

Employers often treated their maidservants as social equals. There was a maidservant who looked after her master's children 'while they sported about' in Finsbury Fields. There she met, so she said, a long-lost cousin. She brought him back with her, and her mistress welcomed him warmly, 'provided very good cheer, set all her plate on the cupboard for show, and beautified the house', and even invited him to stay the night. The next day he, and the silver, had gone.[36] A more paternal relationship may have been more usual. When Richard Stoneley's manservant married Mrs Stoneley's maidservant, Stoneley paid for the wedding feast and gave the happy couple 60s as well, and when two other servants married twelve years later he did it again. This time we have a fuller account; the parson and his wife came, and the parish clerk, and another couple and a friend of Stoneley's – a party of nine altogether. The wedding must have been on a fish day because they sat down to oysters and salmon and whiting, and a salt eel, with plenty of wine and beer.[37]

The starting day for a contract of employment was Lady Day, 25 March. The contract would be for a year, which could be extended by agreement. A little girl called Sicilia Clerke arrived from Norfolk when she was seven or eight, to take a job as a servant with Eliza Smith in London, for a year, and stayed for ten.[38] The going rate for a maidservant, paid in advance for the year, was 4 or 5 nobles, between 26s and 34s, not a lot in any currency, even taking into account that the girl was fed and lodged, and given shoes and some clothes; and there was, of course, no tax to pay, which bedevils the salaries of nannies nowadays.

Girls could also be apprenticed as domestic servants, which meant that they were not paid at all, but could present themselves after their term had ended, as properly trained young women. Christ's Hospital's records show how Agnes Squier [*sic*], who had been admitted to the Hospital when she was six, was sent out three years later 'to serve with James Cotts, silk weaver', but she was back six weeks later because her master was ill, and her ten-year apprenticeship indenture had to be cancelled. Ellin Parker, who had been admitted aged four, was apprenticed to a baker four years later, but her master 'with unreasonable correction abused her' and she came back. She was sent off to Evans Griffyn of Tunbridge 'for his own': that is, for adoption.

These girls were not intended to learn their masters' trades. They provided unpaid domestic service for seven or more years, starting very young as it seems to us. One of Dr Dee's maidservants left after twelve years, working for the first five 'upon apprenticeship' and for the next seven 'for wages'. He sent one of the girls off 'to Goodwife Tyndall's to learn to knit', but whether that was part of her apprenticeship training or during paid employment his diary does not say.[39] His wife was always complaining about her maids. Stubbes even suggested the power of prayer: 'Oh Lord our God, seeing thou hast ordained sundry degrees and states of men in this life, and among them hast appointed me to be a servant, give me grace ... to serve in my vocation faithfully.'[40] It may have helped. A more potent reminder of her lowly status may have been the whistle that was attached to her mistress's belt with other useful accessories such as tooth-picks and mirrors, to summon dogs – and servants.[41]

Childbirth

Procreative sexual intercourse within marriage was necessary if the family was to survive. For the nobility and gentry it could secure the succession to landed estates and family businesses. But for the average merchant or craftsman, was it so important that he should have children? And for his average wife, did she think her life would be blighted if she were childless? Much more was left to God, or providence, or sheer luck, then than now.

Whether conception could be prevented, or the foetus aborted, is hard to tell in the absence of reliable information about the practices of the wise women. These practices were passed down from woman to woman by word of mouth, women in general being not as keen on writing as men were. Judging from the number of herbal medicines recommended 'to bring down the terms' – that is, to re-start menstruation if it had ceased – amenorrhea was seen as a problem. Pregnancy is not the only cause for it, but it is the most obvious and usual. Some of these medicines may well have provoked miscarriage, by intention or by accident. We cannot know. Since one of the foundations of holy wedlock was the procreation of children, contraception – if it existed – was sinful, so it is no wonder that we hear little about it. There was certainly no equivalent to our modern, easily available contraceptive methods.

So why were Elizabethan women not as prolific as the Victorians? Perhaps this is an indication of their low vitality, frequently suffering minor infections that had to run their course; but this was the fate of everyone before the discovery of antibiotics. They married at about 25 or 26, when their most fertile time had passed. If they were breast-feeding their first child, the conception of the next would be delayed until the child was weaned, which might be long after its first birthday. Sexual intercourse during lactation was morally frowned on, and a resultant pregnancy in that time was in any event physiologically unlikely. It is also probable that menopause, the cessation of fertility, came sooner then than now.[42] Certainly 'our women through bearing of children do after forty begin to wrinkle apace', according to Harrison – a hint, surely, that by then their infertile old age had begun.[43] Fertility declines sharply after the age of thirty or so, and if a woman had filled the first five years of her wedded life with, say, two pregnancies, she might well have no more.

A woman may need to know at an early stage whether she is pregnant. 'If a woman doubting of the being with child feeleth or smelleth not the savour of garlic set by her bedside in the night, [it] doth then undoubtedly declare that she is conceived with child.'[44] But she might have a cold, or a defective sense of smell ... what then? Only when the foetus 'quickened' and the mother could feel it move in her womb, could she be sure she was pregnant. She can tell her women friends, and the local midwife. Meanwhile, she can sew and knit the baby's clothes, and watch her growing body for propitious signs. Boys were bound to affect her right side, since they, and it, were stronger. Therefore a baby boy would make her right eye brighter than her left, her right cheek redder, her right breast fuller.[45]

The obstetric knowledge current in English physicians' circles was unnervingly inaccurate.[46] Since, axiomatically, women were poor copies of men, it had to be possible to discern something like the male procreative apparatus in a woman's body, but her inferiority was demonstrated – if additional proof were needed – by her lack of testicles.[47]

No wonder pregnant women preferred to entrust themselves to other women. The midwife was a respected local figure, often the wife of a craftsman or small trader. Her religious orthodoxy had to be established to the satisfaction of the Church because if the baby was in danger of dying before a parson could arrive, it was she who had to baptise it. She was also important to the parish because if an unmarried mother were so obstinate as to refuse to disclose the name of the baby's father so that he could be forced to maintain her, the mother and her baby might become a charge on the parish. The midwife had a duty to extort the father's name while she had the mother at her mercy, during labour. The extent of the midwife's professional knowledge was not enquired into by anyone. It was probably as good as available anywhere, at the time.

Once labour had begun, the woman needed the encouragement of her friends. This was another aspect of the change of status brought about by marriage. An unmarried girl would not have been allowed to enter the birthing chamber, nor, of course, a man, even the father, but all the woman's married friends were welcome, childless or not, and they stayed on after the happy event for a month, during which they had to be provided with food and wine. The room must have been stifling, on a hot day, but it was at least cheerful. I will spare the reader a description of the birth, which proceeded in much the same way as now, the main differences being our insistence on cleanliness, the encouragement of the father's presence, and our increased ability to deal with complications, which in those days would have resulted in a dead baby and a severely stressed mother. Once a baby's cry announced its safe arrival, there was general rejoicing, and drinks for everyone, including the mother. The midwife could expect presents from the family, in cash or kind; a minor civil servant gave 5s to the midwife who safely delivered his grandchild – a handsome reward.[48]

The baby was washed, and wrapped in swaddling clothes. It was usual for the mother to feed her baby, but in well-to-do circles it might be breast fed by a hired wet-nurse. There is an enchanting contemporary description of such a mother visiting her baby.[49] She tells the nurse to

unswaddle him, undo his swaddling bands, give him his breakfast while I am here ... wash him before me, have you clean water? O my little heart! God bless thee, rub the crown of his head, wash his ears ... wash his face; lift up a little his hairs, is that not some dirt I see upon his forehead? ... His little cheeks are wet, I believe you did leave him alone to cry and weep ... How many teeth hath he? ... pull off his shirt, thou art pretty and fat my little darling, wash his arm-pits ... how he spreadeth his small fingers! His thumb and little finger are flea-bitten ... is there any fleas in your chamber? ... see how he beateth with his heels, do you kick, sirra? You have not washed the insides nor the soles of his feet, forget not to make clean his toes, the great toe and all, now swaddle him again, but first put on his biggin [cap] and his little band with an edge, where is his little pettycoat? give him his coat of changeable [shot] taffeta, and his satin sleeves. Where is his bib? Let him have his gathered apron with strings, and hang a muckinder [bib] to it. You need not yet to give him his coral with the small golden chain, for I believe it is better to let him sleep until the afternoon, give him some suck, I pray you take heed to wipe well the nipple of your dug before you put it in his mouth, for fear that there be any hair or other thing that may hurt him. You, maid, go fetch the child's cradle, make his bed ... put him in his cradle and rock him till he sleeps but bring him to me first that I may kiss him, God send thee good rest my little boykin.

This effusion of maternal love was ostensibly a vocabulary lesson for French readers but the philoprogenitive enthusiasm of the author seems to have overtaken his pedagogic intentions. It is so rare to have a contemporary description of a domestic scene that I make no apology for including it. The baby was still being breast fed despite having some teeth. His 'coral' was for him to chew on and help his teeth to erupt: a smooth piece of coral, mounted in gold in his case, quite probably with bells on the handle to amuse him. His clothes are remarkable. His 'little band with an edge' was a miniature ruff, decorated with lace or braid at the edge away from his face. One can only assume that it was softly folded, not starched. His petticoat and his separate sleeves copy adult clothes. 'Changeable taffeta' does not seem the most sensible fabric for babies, who are notoriously wet at both ends all the time – and as to that, the absence of any kind of nappy perhaps escaped the writer's mind. Safety pins had not yet been invented, but surely babies wore some kind of linen cloth, which must have been tied on in some way. The admirable Chinese way of addressing the problem by leaving the child's trousers open at the back had not percolated to Europe.

After a month of comparative peace and quiet, during which the father arranged the baby's christening, the mother emerged from the birthing room to resume her domestic duties. Her return to the community was signalled by attending church for a service of thanksgiving. She also gave a 'thank-you' party to her women friends, which could be a feast, if her husband's means ran to it.

Childhood and manners

Out of every hundred babies born alive, it has been estimated that perhaps 70 survived to their first birthday, but less than half saw their fifth.[50] By then a child ought to have learned how to behave in polite company. Children should, of course, be seen and not heard. They should humbly ask their parents' blessing when they get up and when they go to bed, and always take their caps off in the presence of their elders and betters.[51] This whole matter of head-gear presents problems we no longer have to worry about. Most of the time, gentlemen wore their hats indoors, even for dancing. But their company or their surroundings might compel them to show respect by taking their hats off. Erasmus advised young men to 'take off your hat and see that your hair is well combed', if you are 'seated with people of rank'.[52] The Benchers of Gray's Inn expressly forbade wearing 'any hat in the hall at dinner or supper time' in 1585.

One particular English habit was remarked on with enthusiasm by foreigners. When any man, including a foreigner, went to a citizen's house on a social visit or even a business call, the master's lady or daughter welcomed him and he 'has the right to take them by the arm to kiss them, which is the custom of the country, and if anyone does not do so it is regarded ... as ... ill breeding on his part'.[54] And this was not the air-kissing somewhere near the cheek, common nowadays, but a hearty kiss on the lips. 'They kiss each other a lot.'[55]

Some of the finer points of etiquette surrounded the natural functions. It is not surprising to find servitors who were following their master on foot, waiting bare-headed while he talked to someone; a little surprising that this respect was extended to his pausing to urinate, but definitely surprising to find them still standing there bare-headed, while their master's horse urinated.[56] (For those unfamiliar with equine habits, I'm told that a horse always stops to do this. A mare can walk and urinate simultaneously.) And 'it is impolite to greet someone who is urinating or defecating. A well-bred person should always avoid exposing without necessity the parts to which nature has attached modesty. If necessity compels this, it should be done with decency and reserve, even if no witness is present. For angels are always present', said Erasmus, and one would not wish to offend the angels.[57] But pissing – to use the Elizabethan term – was fairly widespread. The Mercers' livery company let out a corner property on condition that the tenant prevented 'naughty persons annoying our cellar by way of pissing in at the windows'.[58]

Farting, like pissing, should ideally be done when alone, if at all possible, but if it is not possible to withdraw, 'let a cough cover the sound', which is not the whole answer to the problem. In all this, one has to remember that there were few lavatories, public or private, to which one could withdraw. The unfortunate Earl of Oxford farted as he bowed before Queen Elizabeth one day. He was so mortified that he left the Court for seven years. On his re-appearance the Queen greeted him reassuringly. 'My Lord, I had forgotten the fart.'[59]

Belching at table was completely acceptable.[60] If you needed to spit or blow your nose, you should turn away from the company – unless, of course, you were the Queen, who expressed her disapproval of a courtier's dress by spitting on it.[61]

Sharing a bed did not necessarily have sexual overtones. 'If you share a bed with a comrade, lie quietly, do not toss with your body for this can lay yourself bare, or inconvenience your neighbour by pulling away the blankets.'[62]

Childhood was short. By the age of seven, a boy cast aside his petticoats and took to male breeches, with deep pleasure, no doubt. Children over seven came within the punitive provisions of the Act for Punishment of Rogues, Vagabonds and Sturdy Beggars, and boys were, with the rest of the male population up to sixty years old, liable for call-up in national emergency. In 1595, another year when a Spanish invasion seemed imminent, the parson of a London parish reminded his parishioners, from the pulpit, that they must have ready 'bows and arrows for themselves, their servants, and children from the age of seven years of age'.[63] In many families, a boy would leave the family home for an apprenticeship, after a few years of schooling, and he would rarely see his parents again unless they lived nearby and his master gave him permission. So the next stage in family life might well be the death of a parent.

Death and funerals

Elizabethan medicines rarely cured and, one suspects, frequently brought about the slow death of the patient by poisoning. In such cases the moribund sufferer had plenty of time to make his will, summon his family and compose an improving death-bed address.

For the rich and famous, death preceded their last status symbol. Funeral processions of varying degrees of grandeur threaded their way through the narrow streets. Queen Mary was buried in December 1558, nearly a month after her death, when Elizabeth was settled securely on the throne. Mary's body was taken from St James's Palace to Westminster Abbey in an elaborate procession, including all the appropriate dignitaries and a hundred poor men.[64] Her effigy lay on the coffin 'adorned with crimson velvet and her crown on her head, her sceptre on her hand, and many goodly rings on her fingers'. The next day she was buried with full Roman Catholic rites, in her grandfather's chapel. The gorgeous draperies of cloth of gold and velvet were immediately demolished by souvenir-seekers, 'every man [taking] a piece that could catch it'.[65]

The next year the Countess of Rutland died, and was buried in Shoreditch Church. Her funeral procession included 'thirty clerks [clerics] and priests singing, and many poor men and poor women in black gowns, sixty or more [she had probably been 60 when she died, the cortège would include as many poor people as the deceased had years, or more], mourners to the number of a hundred, and two heralds of arms, Master Garter and Master York. Then came the corpse. Before [it] a great banner of arms, and about her four goodly banerolls [smaller banners showing pedigrees] of divers arms.' After the sermon, 'a great dole of money, 2d a-piece' was distributed, 'and so to dinner'. The heralds wore their tabards, like the knaves in a pack of cards, stiff with gold and embroidery front and back.[66]

Two of their colleagues, Rouge-Cross and Clarenceux, took part in the funeral procession of Lady Hewet, whose husband had been Lord Mayor, in 1561. There were 'twenty four poor women in new gowns and twelve poor men, and ... forty in black', eight aldermen in black gowns, and the Lord Mayor and the rest of the aldermen, the two heralds, then the coffin, followed by the chief mourners, forty more women, all the senior members of the Clothworkers' Company, of which her husband had been a member, and two hundred more people.

The Earl of Sussex died at Bermondsey in 1583, and was to be buried at Newhall in Essex. His coffin was

> conveyed through the city of London ... first went before him forty five poor men in black gowns, then on horseback a hundred and twenty serving men in black coats, then twenty five in black gowns and cloaks ... heralds of arms and others which bare his helm, crest, sword, coat of arms and banners of arms, then the deceased, in a chariot covered with black velvet drawn by four goodly geldings.

It was followed by eight other coaches, the Lord Mayor and aldermen, the gentlemen of Gray's Inn, and the members of the Merchant Taylors' company in their livery. All this must have interrupted the traffic flow alarmingly. The Lord Mayor and most of the others went as far as the city limits, then turned back, leaving the cortège to plod through the countryside.[67]

The Lord Mayor went to Sir Philip Sidney's funeral too, with his aldermen, and the members of the Grocers' Company, and 300 citizens and 32 poor men, 'for he was so many years old'. Sidney was buried in St Paul's Church and 'they honoured him with a double volley of shot'.[68] If there was any danger that the procession might not be long enough, 'a competent number' of the Christ's Hospital children could be hired; they cost 20s, in 1577.[69]

The 'banners of arms' showing the heraldic arms of the deceased could be anything up to 7½ yards long, for a duke. A mere knight's banner was only four yards long. Guidons, the standard issue for esquires, were three yards long. As long as the wind blew, they must have made a wonderful sight, but when they drooped on the muddy ground they must have been seriously in the way of the mourners. If the deceased had no arms of his own at all, he could have as many scutcheons (diamond-shaped wooden shields) as he wanted. A gentleman of Gray's Inn who had been in that mortifying predicament was buried with six scutcheons of the arms of Gray's Inn.[70]

Meanwhile the church bells were tolling. 'Never send', as John Donne famously wrote, 'to know for whom the bell tolls; it tolls for thee.' More immediately, it gave notice to all within earshot that a parishioner had died. The coffin was carried as far as the church, where it was laid on the timber frame or 'hearse' waiting for it, and covered with a hearse-cloth. These were often provided on loan by the parish, or a livery company, and could be sumptuous. The Stationers' Company had one 'of cloth of gold powdered [scattered] with blue velvet and bordered with black velvet, embroidered and stained with blue, red, yellow and green'.[71] But even if the dead man had been a pauper, his parish would see that his funeral had some shred of dignity. 'To a sheet, to bury a poor man – 12d ... Laid out about the burial of a poor man that died in the wash way – 2s 8d.'[72] (This was in Lambeth, on the river bank. The wash way must have been connected with the river.) Many parishes had a re-usable coffin in which the shrouded body lay until it reached the graveside and was buried.[73]

It was still possible for most parishes to inter their parishioners within the church, if they were important – and rich – enough, or in the churchyard. The church of All Hallows Honey Lane found additional space in an ingenious way. Coffins were housed between the floor of the church and the ceiling of the cellar below, which was in separate ownership; an early example of a mezzanine floor.[74] If there was no more room in the parish ground, they were allowed to use the burial place attached to St Paul's. But in 1582 the Lord Mayor told the Privy Council that

> it had been thought good to restrain the burials in St Paul's Churchyard, which have been so many, and, by reason of former burials, so shallow, that scarcely any graves could be made without corpses being laid open. Some parishes have turned their churchyards into small tenements [lettable property] and had buried in St Paul's Churchyard. It has been determined to restrain from burial there all parishes having churchyards of their own ... The restrained parishes were to use the new burial place provided by Sir Thomas Rowe.[75]

This was a one-acre site near Bedlam, outside the walls, which Sir Thomas had originally intended for the use of poor people who could not afford the fees payable for burial in a churchyard, but his charitable intention seems to have been overridden by the City. All Hallows Honey Lane had been driven to use St Paul's Churchyard, despite its ingenious mezzanine, so presumably its parishioners had to make the trek out to the new burial place, after all.

Once the body had been committed to the earth, the mourners divided into the close family, and those present only out of duty or self-interest. Among the latter could be numbered the poor, who relied on a black gown, a good meal, a drink and sometimes even a small cash hand-out in return for their attendance. But the closer mourners began by commiserating with the bereaved, and usually went on to celebrate their own survival in the traditional way. When the youngest warden of the Carpenters' Company died, in 1579, his company laid out 58s 8d for his funeral feast of meat, capons, rabbits and sweetmeats.[76] Such gatherings were usually for men only. The Carpenters' Company clerk disapprovingly entered in his accounts for 1584 'for the livery *and their wives* [my italics] at the burial of Mistress Peacock which was her desire to have it so: £6 2s' – but in the next entry, with a sigh of relief, 'charges expended upon St Lawrence day and *no women there* [my italics] 24s 8d'.[77] One admirable lady left 40s for four women friends to 'make merry' at her funeral, even specifying where they were to spend it.[78]

CHAPTER II

Education

The first years

'The parents, especially the mother, must endeavour to speak to the child perfectly plain and distinct words, for as they be first informed to speak so they will continue ... and even from their infancy let the parents teach their children no fables ... but only that which is godly.'[1] One may agree with the advice against baby-talk, but it seems a bit hard to exclude 'fables' from the nursery in favour of religious themes. The author was a Protestant anxious to impart a devout way of life to married couples. He wrote at the end of Henry VIII's reign, but his book was still used in Elizabethan nurseries. Much of his advice, like the passage I have quoted, combines refreshing common sense with a religious fervour in tune with the times.

The first landmark for children is their first school, called then a 'petty school'. Harrison, writing in 1586, remarked gloomily that poor women 'are careless in the education of their children ... neither fearing God [nor] regarding either manners or obedience', but whatever their home background a petty school of some sort was open to most children.[2] Schools were under the general supervision of the Bishop of London, who issued licences when he was satisfied of the teacher's religious orthodoxy – irrespective of ability or knowledge. There was a marked increase in the number of licences granted, from 1570 onwards.[3]

Richard Mulcaster, a prominent educationalist, deplored the low standard and quick turnover of teachers, and pressed for a national curriculum, but he was ahead of his time. At what age should the child leave its mother's apron strings for school? 'Some are apt at four years and some not before five or seven years.'[4] The first lessons concentrated on reading: how else could a child equip itself to read holy books? For this all-important ability, writing was not needed, and many children never acquired the skill in writing that we treat as going hand in hand with reading. The child would be given an 'absey-book',[5] in which the alphabet was printed, or a horn book,[6] so called for the covering of transparent horn protecting the page. At the top of the page was the 'criss-cross row', the cross symbolising the pervasive importance of religion in education.

'When they can read both printed and written letters, and can well commit what they have learned to memory ... then let them learn to write, to cast a compte, to cypher, add, subtract, etc.'[7] 'Both printed and written letters' sounds fairly easy, but conceals a mine-field. Printed letters were in a heavy black font, crammed together and unwelcoming. Written letters would probably be in secretary hand, which had the disadvantage of having several variants for each letter. When it was written by a scribe with plenty of time and a good pen it could look elegant, especially when the tails of the letters were extended into those swirls and loops that decorated many an Elizabethan signature; but heaven help a child trying to decipher even carefully written secretary hand, or anyone trying to read a hastily scribbled note. Many common words were abbrevi-ated. Th was abbreviated to y, so that 'the' appears as 'ye', not of course to be confused with 'ye' as in 'God be with ye'. A squiggle or a line over a letter meant that some letters were missing, which are generally fairly easy to guess once you get the hang of it – but pity ye poor children.[8] Another writing system, court hand, was different again, but mercifully its use was mainly restricted to legal documents.

Figures

Now for 'casting an account, adding, subtracting, etc.' An extra-ordinary change was creeping in during the century without, apparently, any precipitating event: the change from Roman numerals to our system based on Hindu-Arabic numerals. We still use Roman numerals occasionally – *Henry IV Part II*, Act V, for instance – but can you quickly express in modern terms the sum total of the tax assessment of prosperous Londoners (the Subsidy roll) in 1589, lxxiiii^m iiii^c iii^{xx} xiii^{ll} vi^s 8^d? The small m means thousands, the small c hundreds, the double x means a score (i.e. twenty), and the ll stands for pounds (*libra* in Latin) and governs all the preceding amounts. Then the s means solidi or shillings and the arabic 8 with the d means 8 denarii or pence. The result is £74,473 6s 8d. But what a complicated business. How did people manipulate such figures? More realistically, how would an apprentice in a shop work out how much change to give?

The answer was, of course, by using a digital calculator. In his case, the apprentice would go to the nearest counting table or counter (not our kind of counter, which was a 'ware-bench') in the shop, and work it out by shuffling jetons or tokens – like tiddlywinks made of metal – on the horizontal lines marked on the counter. The bottom line was where the single units belonged. As soon as there were ten of them – the same number as he had fingers, so he was easily able to do that even if he was innumerate – they were taken off the board and one token put in the next row up, standing for ten. And so on. If he had a column of figures to add, he put the first one on the board and then put the next beside it and pushed it along to meet the first set of tokens, and went through the same exercise. Then he would have to put the next figure beside it, and plod through each successive figure. No doubt people could do it in a far shorter time than I have taken to explain it, when they were used to it, and it had the virtue of visible simplicity. I have not explained how to do multiplication or division because the book I was using became – as any book on the subject would have done, for me – incomprehensible, at that stage; but I am sure it was simple if you knew how.

There were plenty of counters about in merchants' shops and houses. Some of them had convenient drawers – 'tills' – in which to store the tokens. The reason why they cannot be found now is probably because, as I explained on page 61, they were such handy small pieces of furniture that they have long ago been turned into 'small Tudor oak tables, a convenient size for modern living' and lost their identity. In the unlikely circumstance that there was no counter available, you could use a 'counter cloth' or 'carpet for the counter', marked with lines, which could be spread on any flat surface, but clearly this was liable to ruck up and crumple and put your sums out. Still, handy for a travelling salesman, like taking your own lap-top.

Tokens came in sets or 'casts' of 100, sometimes 50. There were various conventions and systems. Some put the tokens on the line, some between the lines. Sometimes a token half way between the lines meant 50, or 500. Sometimes there were, as in writing, short-cuts that you had to know before you began. But all the systems were basically the same.[9]

A user's manual sets problems that illuminate Elizabethan thinking.[10]

'There is a galley upon the sea wherein be thirty merchants ... fifteen Christians and fifteen Zarasins [*sic*] ... there falleth great tempest ... [they jettison the cargo but] the galley is feeble or weak. The king says that half the merchants must be cast into [the] sea: how can you arrange things so that all the Christians survive?' (The answer depends on all the merchants standing on the heaving deck in a tidy row, to be counted.)

'A lover did enter into a garden for to gather apples for his lady, and unto the said garden be three gates, and in each gate is a porter, and when he shall issue after that he hath gathered the apples he must give the half of his apples and one to the first porter, and when he is at the second gate he must give unto him the half and one, and to the third porter the half and one, and when he is forth he hath no more than one apple to give to his lady paramour. I demand, how many apples had he gathered?' (The answer is 22.)

'A merchant has 100 francs in gold and he goeth unto a Changer' to convert it to coins of 2d, 3d, 4d, 5d, 6d, 8d, and 10d; interesting for the coins listed, and the existence of a Changer, a bureau de change.

'A young maiden beareth eggs to market for to sell, and there meeteth a young man that would play with her, in so much that he overthroweth and breaketh the eggs, every one, and will not pay for them.' The poor young maiden promptly took him to court, but neither she nor her mother knew how many eggs were involved. By a complicated formula the judge worked it out, and the young man had to pay.

'There is a cat at the foot of a tree the length of 300 feet. This cat goeth upward each day 17 feet and descendeth each night 12 feet.' How long till it reaches the top? (60 days.)

Lastly but irresistibly, 'a drunkard drinketh a barrel of beer in the space of 14 days, and when his wife drinks with him then they drink it out within 10 days. In what space will his wife drink that barrel alone?' (35 days.)

Schools

There were many schools scattered through London, some free, some fee-paying. Many of the great livery companies founded schools in Elizabeth's reign, or earlier. The Mercers founded a free grammar school in 1542, for 25 pupils, in part of the church that had belonged to the Hospital of St Thomas of Acre, a thirteenth-century crusader order – it must have made a very cold school.

The Merchant Taylors' school was established in 1561 'for the better education and bringing up of children in good manners and literature', in the romantic-sounding Manor of the Rose, in Suffolk Lane, bought for £500 by a former master of the company and presented to the school. Its foundation deed limited its intake to 250 children 'of all nations and countries indifferently', but they had to know the Anglican catechism, in English or Latin, and be able to 'read perfectly and write competently'. Although 100 boys could be the sons of rich parents, paying 5s a quarter, 100 were to be poor men's sons paying no fee, and the balance was tipped towards the poor by the remaining 50 boys being poor men's sons paying 2s 2d a quarter. All of them had to pay an entrance fee of 12d to the school cleaner.

The High Master was to be 'a man in body whole, sober, discrete, honest, virtuous and learned in good and clean Latin literature and also in Greek if such may be gotten'. He had an annual contract, a free house, twenty days' annual leave, and sick leave on full pay for 'sickness curable, or axes [agues]'. Below him was a Chief Usher and two under-ushers. Thus, when all the boys and all four teaching staff were present, each class could exceed 60. All four staff were paid £10 a year, but for many years the High Master's salary was supplemented by one of the company's masters, with another £10.

As well as his teaching duties, the Chief Usher was responsible for seeing that the boys did not get on to the roof, and that the school premises and the 'whole length of the street' were 'kept clean and sweet every Saturday', which involved supervising the cleaner to whom each boy had paid his 12d on entrance. One thinks, in modern terms, of the usual rubbish left by any children, but the main part of the cleaner's duties can be inferred from another rule of the school: 'unto their urine the scholars shall go to the places appointed them in the lane or street without [outside] the court', while 'for other causes, if need be, they shall go to the waterside'.

There were prayers three times a day, for which all boys knelt. The hours were 7–11, 1–5, except for Tuesdays and Thursdays when there was no school in the afternoon. In winter, when daylight had long gone by five o'clock, the school was lit by wax candles. Tallow candles were cheaper, but they were forbidden because they stank.

No food, drink, bottles or 'breakfasts' (snacks) were to be brought into school, 'nor drinking in the time of learning in no wise. If they need drink, let it be provided in some other place. Nor let them use no cock-fighting, tennis-play nor riding about of victoring [?] nor disputing abroad, which is but foolish babbling and loss of time.' The company and the 'learned men' appointed by it examined all the boys, and the teaching staff, every year, and the Bishop of London made regular visitations.

The company's first appointee as High Master, Richard Mulcaster, seems to have satisfied all their hopes. He stayed for 25 years, teaching the usual Latin and Greek, and Hebrew as well, necessary for reading the psalms in the original. Boys flocked to the school as soon as it opened, not only from London and the southern counties but from as far away as Yorkshire. Mulcaster came from the north himself, and despite years at Eton and Cambridge he still spoke with a north-country accent. Local accents were perfectly acceptable in most contexts, but unfortunately the ushers appointed by him also came from the north, and when the Bishop's visitors arrived in 1562, they found that 'being northern men born, [the ushers] had not taught the children to speak distinctly or to pronounce their words so well as they should'.

All went well for some years. In 1569 Mulcaster was reproved for exceeding the permitted number of boys by taking private pupils into his own house, and there were rumblings of disagreement between him and the Merchant Taylors, but they had made peace by 1579. In 1574 and 1576 plays he had written for the boys were presented before Queen Elizabeth, and in 1581–2 he published various educational books, but the £10 supplement to his salary had ceased, and Mulcaster was getting bored and tetchy. In 1585 he gave a year's notice, and he left in 1586. There is a vivid contemporary picture of his teaching methods: 'in a morning he would exactly and plainly construe and parse the lesson to his scholars, which done, he slept his hour (custom made him critical to proportion it [that is, he woke up when the hour was over]) in his desk in the school, but woe to the scholar that slept the while. Awaking he heard them accurately ... his temper was warm.'[11]

A school attached to St Paul's Cathedral had existed since the early twelfth century. John Colet, then the Dean of St Paul's, refounded the school in 1510, endowing it from his considerable personal fortune. It was to educate 153 boys – the number of fishes in the miraculous draught, according to tradition – 'of all nations and countries', who could already read and write. The High Master was to be appointed by the Mercers' Company. No fees were payable except for 4d on admission, 'to the poor scholar that sweeps the school'. The constitution was the model for the Merchant Taylors' school. The school survived throughout the century, but internal bickering became so serious that by 1596 its pupils were being taught by Mulcaster, who by now was running a private school in Milk Street. The position was sorted out that year, and Mulcaster was appointed High Master of St Paul's school at the age of 66. Perhaps he had lost his fiery temper by then; school life flowed calmly on, taking in its stride such episodes as a complaint from the verger of St Paul's to the Bishop of London that the masters of the school 'suffered their children to play in the churchyard, whereby the windows are broken, and well-disposed people in the church are disquieted at the time of divine service'.[12]

The other London cathedral, Westminster, had also had a school within its medieval organisation. When the Abbey surrendered itself to Henry VIII in 1540 he founded a grammar school there, and from 1560 its fortunes were improved by the active interest of Queen Elizabeth, who wanted it to rival her predecessor's foundation out at Eton. It provided the usual classical education, with an emphasis on Greek, for 120 or more boys, of whom 40 were 'Queen's scholars', paying no fees, and who were supervised individually by tutors who would look after them if they fell ill. Only boys aged over eight, who had already been at the school a year, could be elected to a scholarship, and they were supposed to be poor, but most were in fact the sons of London citizens who were not particularly poverty-stricken.

The Westminster boys' schooldays must have made many of them long for the fleshpots of home. They slept in the unheated stone building that had been the Abbey's granary. They were called at five o'clock to get up and dress, say their prayers – in Latin, of course – make their beds and sweep under them, comb their hair and wash their hands. At six the whole school met for prayers, and began lessons. By seven the High Master had arrived, and at eight he set a Latin passage for translation. Nicholas Udall, who was appointed High Master in 1560, had already made a name for himself at Eton as an enthusiastic flogger, to which he subjected any boy who was not neatly dressed, hands and nails clean, hair combed and free of nits. The boys must have been very hungry by breakfast time at eight o'clock. Then the day passed in lessons and prayers, broken only by dinner in the former monastic refectory, another stone-built medieval room, but at least it was heated, slightly, by an open wood fire in the middle of the room. All this time, the boys had to speak Latin; English was not allowed. At 6 p.m. they had supper, and another hour of lessons, before the day-boys dispersed. The scholars went to their dormitory at eight, but often worked at their books until midnight. Throughout the day, each boy's whereabouts were fixed and heaven help him if he was not where he should be.[13]

According to Stow, there had been other schools attached to monastic foundations which did not survive the depredations of Henry VIII, with one exception, the 'free school pertaining to the late dissolved hospital of St Anthony', in Threadneedle Street.[14] By 1560 it had as many as 200 pupils, who were poor men's children.[15] But when Stow was writing, at the end of the century, it was 'now decayed, and come to nothing, by taking that from it what thereunto belonged' – if Henry had left it alone, with its endowments, it would still have been famous.

Some schools were founded by private citizens. Nicholas Gibson, a Grocer, had founded a school for 60 boys in Ratcliffe, in 1536. Sir Roger Cholmeley's school at Highgate opened its doors in 1585. But perhaps the most interesting development was the two schools in Southwark built by the parishioners of Southwark themselves, the first for 100 youths in 1562, and nine years later another for 'children and younglings, as well of the rich as the poor'.[16] The impulse that had driven men for so many centuries to devote some of their wealth to good causes such as education by giving to the monasteries had found a new channel.

The specialist skill of teaching foreign languages requires well-written teaching aids.[17] Four such books have survived, written by two Frenchmen, Claudius Hollyband who came to London in 1566 and Peter Erondell who arrived about twenty years later. They describe scenes of everyday life, with a wealth of useful vocabulary. One has to beware of lists, in case the pedagogic passion for words had got the better of the writer's gift for description, but with that caveat each of the two writers gives an accurate, and enchanting, picture of everyday life.[18] Hollyband ran a school himself, for the sons of citizens. Erondell was a tutor in fairly grand households.

Hollyband's books give both the English and the French versions. His 'dialogues' describe the experiences of Elizabethan schoolboys. John is a new boy on his first day, going to Hollyband's own school. 'In Paul's Churchyard ... there is a Frenchman which teacheth both the tongues, in the morning till eleven the Latin tongue, and after dinner the French.' The boy's father asks what Hollyband's fees are – 'A shilling a week, a crown a month, a reall a quarter, forty shillings a year' – the first useful lesson. Either they get twelve weeks' holiday, or their fathers get a substantial discount for paying for a year at a time. 'Ciphering' is also taught, but we hear no more about it because the purpose of the book is to teach the French language.

John has arrived without the necessary equipment – the nightmare of any parent sending a boy to school for the first time – so his father goes off to buy a satchel, books, ink, quills, paper, an inkhorn and a penknife. John gets into a fight with another boy, a nasty telltale, and is told to 'untruss you, pull your hose down, dispatch', so down come his trunk hose and he is beaten on his bare bottom.

Peace reigns for a time while the boys learn their lessons, threatened with 'four blows with the rods' if they are not word perfect. John has not yet learned to read, so – 'take the table of the cross-row in thy left hand, and this festraw [originally a straw, by then a small pointer] wherewith thou shalt touch the letters one by one. Stand upright. Hold thy cap under thy arm ... Mark diligently how I move my mouth ...' Writing needs suitable paper and ink, and goose quills: 'cut off the feathers with a penknife, scrape away that which is tough', and soften the nib by spitting on it and rubbing it on your clothes. Then the lesson can begin: 'first I will give you the cross-row, then syllables, then joining hand [joined-up writing]'. The pupils produce several copies, but because thou hast gone about to change these letters into others, rasing [scraping, erasing] away some part with the point of thy knife, thou hast made the writing the fouler. It had been the less fault to have cancelled it with a little stroke of the pen. As much as you can, write with your head upright: for if one stand with his head downward, humours fall down to his forehead and into his eyes, whereof many infirmities do arise, and weakness of the sight.

At eleven they all kneel down and say their prayers, and go home for dinner. At twelve they are back, and embark on that favourite exercise of teachers, loathed by pupils, 'turn your lessons out of French into English, and then out of English into French'. It is getting dark: 'go fetch some light. Light the candle. Blow out that candle for the tallow stinketh. Snuff the other.' ('Snoof' in the original: it means to cut the burned wick so that the flame burns upright with less guttering.) At five o'clock they say their prayers and light their lanterns, and home they go.

But not all teachers were of Hollyband's calibre. Thomas Nashe wrote in 1588, 'I marvel how the masterless [unemployed] men ... such as paste up their papers on every post, for arithmetic and writing schools, escape eternity.'[19]

Christ's Hospital

After Henry VIII had abolished the monasteries, gaping holes showed in the social fabric of London which took time to mend. One was the treatment of poor orphans and foundlings. Edward VI asked the Lord Mayor to produce a plan

to take out of the streets all the fatherless children, and other poor men's children that were not able to keep them, and bring them to the late dissolved house of the Greyfriars ... where they should have meat, drink and clothes, lodging and officers to attend upon them ... the sucking children and such as for want of years were not able to learn should be kept in the country ... The late dissolved Greyfriars ... at that time stood void and empty, only a number of whores and rogues harboured there all night.[20]

The grey-robed Franciscan monks had founded their monastery in 1225, on a site given by a Mercer just within the wall, at the north-west edge of the city, by Newgate. More than 300 years later the complex of buildings included a majestic church, residential buildings and cloistered courtyards, but they were in poor repair.

The Lord Mayor acted fast. He gathered a committee of 30 aldermen 'and other grave citizens' to raise funds and assess demand. When their own funds were exhausted, they put collecting boxes all over London and in every parish church. They found 300 fatherless children and 350 'poor men overburdened with their children'. They arranged for the babies to be sent to wet-nurses in the country, and for 500 older children to be admitted to the Hospital.[21] A donor provided 500 straw mattresses and featherbeds, 500 blankets and 1,000 pairs of sheets.

They appointed a staff of 50, from the Honorary Treasurer Sir Thomas Rowe (later Lord Mayor himself) down to a sexton at £1 a year. The matron was paid £3 6s 8d, the 25 'sisters' (preserving the former conventual term) under her £2 each, all of them living in, with a living allowance as well. There were five administrative staff and an impressive muster of teaching staff. The 'grammar school master' was the highest-paid staff member, at a salary of £15 a year – more than the Merchant Taylors paid Mulcaster. His assistant got £10, but the writing master only £3 6s 8d, and the music teacher and two teachers for the small children or 'petties' a mere £2 13s 4d each. The surgeon was second only to the grammar school master, at £13 6s 8d. There was a brewer and a barber, a tailor and a general handyman ('mason scourer'; scourer then meant cleaner).

The deserted courts and cloisters came to life again. By 1599 when Platter visited, he was told that the Hospital held 700 young boys and girls:

> reading and writing are taught in special schools ... and they are kept there until they are fit for some craft or service ... they are all fine children ... they keep their hospital exceedingly clean – in the boys' long apartment are 140 beds in a row on either side, where they sleep two and two together, and by their beds they have low chests in which to keep their clothes. There are fewer girls, in a separate room.[22]

'The diet of the poor children harboured in Christ's Hospital in the City of London' was very reasonable, for the times.[23] They drank beer brewed on the premises, and their 'bread is wheaten bread, and is always of the goodness of the common wheaten bread sold to all

22. This intriguing picture by an anonymous artist, of Elizabeth receiving ambassadors, is valuable for its details of interior décor: the woven rush matting, the florid design glimpsed through the door – textile? wall painting? wallpaper? – and the pattern of curlicues on the wall of the audience chamber, which look like gilt leather, just coming into fashion (see page 54). The three ladies reclining on the floor look as if they are sitting on big cushions – or is it only their billowing skirts? (See page 64).

23. John Gerard published his *Grete Herbal*, including *The History of Plants*, in 1597.
The illustrations come from a Dutch herbal of 1590.

24. From Thomas Hill's *The Gardener's Labyrinth*, published in 1577. The Elizabethan gardener believed in raised beds and giving each plant space (see page 79).

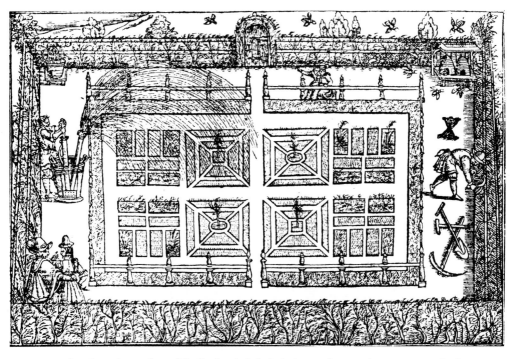

25. Another picture from *The Gardener's Labyrinth*. A man is pumping water over beds in a fine spray. Note the beehives in the corner.

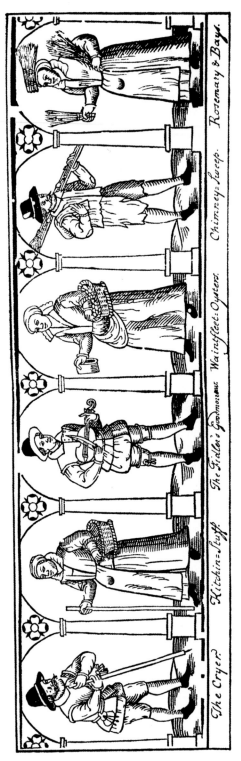

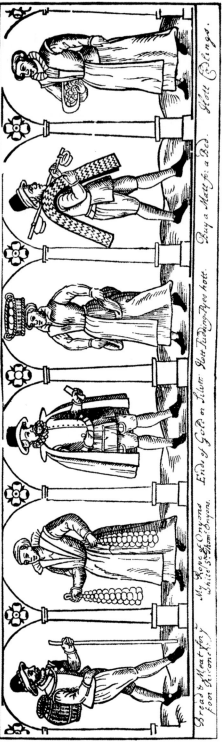

26. Street cries (see page 152). 'Kitchen stuff' (top row, 2nd from left), especially fat and dripping, had a saleable value. A man begs for 'bread and meat for the poor prisoners' (bottom, 1st from left) – the gaoler was under no obligation to feed his inmates (see page 253). The 'matt for a bed' (bottom, 5th from left) was the lowest layer in a bedstead, on top of which came several mattresses (see page 62).

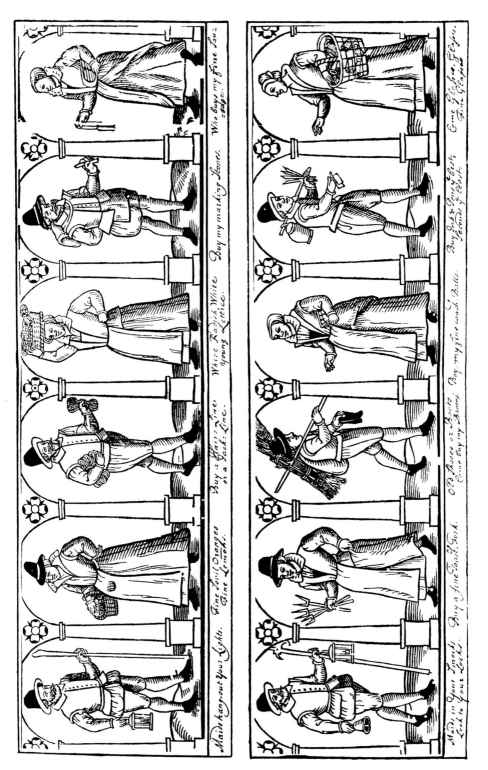

27. More street cries. There are two watchmen, each with a staff and lantern, one with a bell. Hair-lines and jack-lines (top, 3rd from left) could be ropes to repair bedsteads (see page 62) or to hang clothes to dry. There was a part-exchange trade in old footwear for new brooms (bottom, 3rd from left). Glass (bottom, 6th from left) was coming into fashion, replacing metal or wood for drinking vessels.

The labels within the sketch read:

tectum

porticus

sedilia

orchestra

ingressus

mimorum ædes

proscænium

planities fiue arena

28. Sketch – not wholly accurate, but unique – of the inside of
The Swan playhouse, by a foreign visitor in 1596.

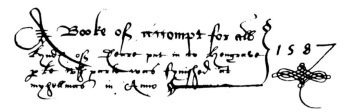

29. Elizabethan handwriting. This is an extract from the
Account Book of Hengrave Park, Suffolk. It reads: 'A Booke of
accompt for all kynd of Deare put in to Hengrave parke which
park was fynished at myhellmas in anno 1587.'

30. A scene from today's Globe Theatre.

31. The letters A to F of a model sixteenth-century alphabet, showing
possible variations in capital and lower-case letters.

32. (ABOVE) Stratford Grammar School, not changed much since the days of Shakespeare.

33. (LEFT) A school scene. All classes were taught in the same room. When one class was learning music, as at the top right here, concentration must have been even more difficult. Birching was frequent (see pages 197, 198). What books the school possessed were kept locked in a chest, such as the one behind the seated master.

citizens by the white bakers'. What else they ate depended on whether it was a fish day or a flesh day. Six ounces of bread came with dinner and supper, with a pint of 'flesh pottage' – half way between thick soup and thin stew[24] – at each meal on flesh days, and milk or 'pease pottage' with 2 ounces of butter or cheese, twice a day on fish days. Supper on Fridays was bread, only. There was no mention of fresh vegetables or fruit, but this was normal in those times. Although the children fed much better than they had in the streets, the appalling monotony of the food was broken only very rarely. At Christmas they had pies, at shrove tide they had 6 ounces of mutton each, their dinner on Good Friday was only a halfpenny loaf, but Easter day brought their annual treat – plum pottage.

The top limit of children admitted 'for lodging and learning' was supposed to be 250, the same as the Merchant Taylors' school, but in 1563, for instance, there were 331 crammed in somehow.[25] If they had no name when they came in, they were given one, often with a brutal lack of imagination. A baby girl left on the steps of an alderman's house was named Joan Steps. It was cruel to name a child Ellin Nomoreknown. Better to call her Jane Ytgodsentus (the 'yt' being the abbreviation for 'that'). Dorothy Butterydoor and Foster Cheapside told their own stories. Luckily a baby girl found 'in the common privy at the Queenhithe' was just called Joan Orphant, or Queenhithe. A girl's name emerged from, surely, a series of undecipherable drafts as Agara Zubabilime, which bears a faint resemblance to the Greek words for where she was found, in the market place, on someone's doorstep. One hopes she was able to marry early, and take her husband's name.

Beggars often used children as props, and if they were arrested they were sent to Bridewell and the children came into the Hospital, such as 'Elizabeth Thurston, 14, and Christian Taverner, 8, taken from Alice Griffin in Turneagain Lane a beggar, which Christian brought unto her within five days 22d, and for keeping these to begging she was sent to Bridewell'. Street-children scraping a precarious living often haunted St Paul's Cathedral looking for easy pickings. 'Antony Brown, 11, taken out of Paul's Church begging'. There was a trickle of abandoned children from 'Callice' (Calais) and Guynes, as the French wars dragged on. There were 'innocents' who needed protection, and blind and lame children who needed medical care. Sick children were referred to St Bartholomew's, and children discharged from St Bart's as cured were welcomed back. A ten-year-old from Yorkshire had somehow arrived in London by himself, an eight-year-old born in Wood Green had been brought to London by his uncle and 'left in the streets'. They were fed, sheltered, clothed, prayed for, educated, and prepared for life outside the Hospital.

Most of the girls became domestic servants, most of the boys were apprenticed to trades. Sometimes the boys ran away from their masters, sometimes their masters disappeared. John Hopkins had been admitted in 1563, when he was four. Five years later he was apprenticed to John Baggett, turner and silk weaver, but he came back to the only home he had known, 'for that he was misgoverned by his master'. Sometimes the children could learn a trade without leaving the Hospital. The City wanted to spread the knowledge and skills of foreign immigrant workers to Londoners, who were not always keen on learning from 'strangers'; what better trainees than the Christ's Hospital children? A foreign tapestry maker was employed at the Hospital from 1577, joining foreign craftsmen already teaching there. A few outstandingly intelligent boys were sent to university. Richard Cofe did so well that he became the sub-dean of Canterbury Cathedral in 1608. Anthony Dodd, taken in at seven years old in 1563, was 'preferred to the University of Oxford by the Goldsmiths Company' ten years later, and Thomas Colfe, born in Calais, and 'taken up in the street and sent in to this house by the Lord Mayor', was 'preferred to Oxford by the Salters Company' in 1578. By 1600 he was the Vicar of Burford.

Apprenticeship

The whole system of labour relations was regulated in 1563, by the Statute of Artificers, a consolidating statute repealing and re-enacting earlier legislation. There were, however, two major drawbacks to it: 'the Statute remaineth utterly unobserved' even ten years later, and in any case there was considerable doubt as to whether the Statute applied to London at all, or whether the old-established Custom of London excluded it.[26] Rather than analysing the Statute, it may be safer to look at actual contemporary records, especially those of the livery companies, to see how apprentices and their masters lived.[27]

Girls could be apprenticed to some trades, but this was rare, so I will call the apprentice 'he'. He might be the son of a Londoner, or he might have come many days' journey down from the Highlands of Scotland: the Fishmongers recruited 40 per cent of their apprentices from there.[28] The Carpenters' Company records for 1571 list 25 apprentices from Wales, Northumberland, Cumberland, Yorkshire and the home counties, as well as one from Ireland and several from London. Their fathers were smiths and tilers, bargemen and agricultural workers ('husbandmen') who were prepared to deprive themselves of their sons' earnings and help, for many years, and had scraped together the money to send their son away to better himself in London.[29]

Every father will have tried to get his boy bound to 'that master which is most excellent and cunning in that craft' in a trade that was likely to suit the boy's abilities.[30] This was a counsel of perfection, but it underlined the importance of making the right choice of master, since it was difficult to change once the agreement had been signed. There was no internet or trade journal to consult, the pecking order of masters was wholly a matter of personal reputation, which might be ascertained, perhaps, by some family or trade connection who had already made the journey to London and knew the ropes.

The apprentice's oath was formidable:

> His said master [he] faithfully shall serve, his secrets keep, his lawful commands everywhere gladly do. He shall not commit fornication nor contract matrimony within the said term. He shall not play at cards, dice, tables or any other lawful game. He shall not haunt taverns or playhouses nor absent himself from the master's service day or night unlawfully ...

For the master's part, 'his said apprentice [he] shall teach and instruct or cause to be taught and instructed, finding unto his said apprentice meat, drink, apparel, lodging and all other necessaries, according to the custom of the City of London'.[31] The Christ's Hospital boys, and parish apprentices, might be as young as nine when they were bound, but the more normal age was eighteen to twenty, so the boy will have had some education or work experience already. The average length of the term was $7\frac{1}{2}$ years, but the earliest it could be over was when the apprentice was 24, usually more. The Christ's Hospital boys had fifteen years to serve, which might be most of their lives, if the estimated expectation of life at birth – 25 – is taken into account.

As well as signing the Articles of Agreement with his master, the apprentice might be required to prove his literacy by writing out, and signing, an oath of loyalty to his master's livery company: 'I, John Hunter, apprentice with John Hill, ironmonger, promise by my faith and troth to be obedient unto the Master and Wardens of the fellowship of the Ironmongers ... in witness thereof I have written this with my own hand ...' So there he was, with about 1,250 other young men who came to London every year, securely tied up by law, and ready to serve and learn. His master could control his every move, and his only right of appeal lay to his master's livery company. No wonder 800 or more, three-fifths of them, dropped out or died, every year.[32] The Carpenters' records showed, in round figures, 40 per cent 'free' (i.e. qualified), 45 per cent 'gone', 15 per cent 'dead' and 1 per cent 'wed'.

An apprentice was instructed solely through watching his master. There were no textbooks, classes or manuals. A young and un-trained boy was more of a hindrance than a help, but he would gradually be trusted with the less difficult tasks. If he transgressed, retribution was painful and public. From a register kept by the Clothworkers' company: in 1574 Thomas Jones was 'punished in the Hall in the presence of divers other apprentices for example's sake' for 'slandering his master to whom he was bound for seven years from last September, viz. reporting that his master had and was laid [up] of the French pox'. The punishment was probably whipping. Hugh Shepperd was to be 'whipped at 8 a.m. tomorrow' for 'stubbornly using his master; disobedience'.[33] There is a sinister entry in the records of the Carpenters' Company's expenses for 1588: 'paid for 2 whips 6d, a pair of manakells [manacles] 16d'.[34]

But it was not all one-way. 'This day [18 November 1567] Matthew Calton promised to deliver to John Johnson his late apprentice a coat, a doublet, and a pair of hosen ... such as shall be whole and meet for an apprentice to wear.' 'This day [16 November 1570] Richard Hill promised to use his servants honestly as an honest man ought to do; and that they shall have three meals a day as other men's apprentices have.' In 1563 the Wardens of the Merchant Taylors' company 'committed Thomas Palmer to prison for that he hath broken Henry Bousfeld his apprentice's head without any just cause' and ordered another man to pay the surgeon's fee for 'healing [another] apprentice's head'.[35] In 1570 an apprentice complained to his master's company, the Carpenters, that 'his master doth not teach him the art of carpentry'; he was told to try to find someone who would.[36]

Apprentices were part of the life of London streets. A visiting Venetian merchant noted that 'one can see at the doors of many shops, and on the streets outside, bareheaded young men asking passers-by if they want anything', more usually expressed as a shout delivered with all the force of young lungs, 'What d' y' lack?'[37] Every apprentice was supposed to wear only the clothes provided by his master: a blue cloak in the summer, a long blue gown in the winter (hence blue was never worn by the fashionable), with an apron and a plain flat cap and loose white breeches – not for them the extravagance of bombasted trunk hose. Their coats and doublets of cloth or leather were not to be pinked or embroidered, their shoes had to be plain leather, and they could wear at their necks only a modest ruff, 1½ yards of a narrow folded frill – hardly worth calling a ruff, in those days. No swords, of course, or jewellery, but like any man they could carry a knife for general use, which sometimes found itself transmogrified into a serviceable dagger, and when they attended their masters at night they carried long clubs, as well as lanterns.[38] Those clubs must have been kept handy, because if an apprentice was involved in a brawl he had only to shout 'Clubs!' and fellow apprentices would run to help.

They were expected to help around the house, which was the master's business premises as well as his home. Only Mercers' apprentices could get out of the task of carrying water in those heavy tankards from the river, or the nearest conduit.[39] Is it surprising that these model young men occasionally got together in a peer group, created havoc, went to playhouses and even rioted? The Lord Mayor was always complaining about them. In 1592 he had to go out to Southwark in all his pomp because of 'a great disorder and tumult by apprentices of the Feltmakers out of Bermondsey and the Blackfriars, [who had] ... assembled themselves together under pretence of their meeting at a play'.[40]

The Inns of Court

The young gentlemen of the Inns of Court were comparatively well behaved. There were, as there are still, four Inns, Gray's Inn north of Holborn, Lincoln's Inn in Chancery Lane south of Holborn, and the two parts into which the Temple had been divided – Inner and Middle Temple – between the Strand and the river. In the sixteenth century, the legal profession was organised round the courts in Westminster, and the Inns were convenient places for lawyers and law students to stay in during term time. There were several other Inns annexed to the four main ones.

The members of each Inn lived a collegiate life centred on its Hall. In 1586 the biggest Inn was Gray's, with 356 members plus 257 in its two subordinate Inns. Lincoln's was next, with 200 members, again with two subordinate Inns of 120 members, then Middle and Inner Temples each with 200 members, with another 290 in subordinate Inns.[41] Not only were there no women members, but women were strictly forbidden in them, except for 'laundresses' (cleaners) who had to be under twelve or over forty, and thus present no temptation. The members met for breakfast, dinner and supper every day.[42]

Each Inn had a chapel, and members were expected to show their compliance with the Elizabethan religious settlement by taking Holy Communion there at least once a term. Perhaps the purchase of 'an hourglass for the chapel, 12d' signalled a time limit to sermons. Burghley wrote in 1579 to the Treasurer of Gray's Inn recommending him to 'have especial ... regard to the placing of such whose soundness in learning and honesty in conversation deserve ... preferment' – without mentioning such mundane matters as legal knowledge, or exams, which did not exist then.[43] In 1585, when Elizabeth's opposition to Catholic recusants had hardened, he wrote again: 'To our great grief we have understood that not only some seminary popish priests have been heretofore harboured in Gray's Inn but also have their assemblies and masses, and so perverted divers young gentlemen in so much as sundry of them ... do not ... frequent divine service', and the Inn teaching staff was told to keep a stern eye out for backsliders.

A typical Gray's Inn student would come from a prosperous London or country family, often in Wales or the northern counties – each Inn tended to have its own catchment area. He had probably studied the classics for a year or two at Oxford or Cambridge, before coming to London to complete his education. Few students intended to earn their living by practising law. For those who did, seven or eight years of hard work stretched before them, trailing from court to court to hear and see how things were done, borrowing the hand-written notes of their seniors, and debating points of law before their elders and betters in Hall. There were no textbooks. Even after call to the Bar, five more years had to pass before they could appear in the main courts at Westminster.[44] It must have been galling for them sometimes, to share the life of the Inn with the majority of its members, whose interest in the law was confined to acquiring enough knowledge of it to function adequately as a country Justice of the Peace, sometime in the distant future. Meanwhile there were more rewarding subjects to study, such as history and logic for the persistent scholar, and fencing, dancing and music, tilting and bowls for them all, and many friends to be made who might be useful in later life.

Pious Lady Bacon, whose son had joined the Inn intending to make a career of law, wrote to him in 1594: 'I trust that they will not mum nor masque nor sinfully revel at Gray's Inn', but the poor lady's trust was misplaced: mummers and masques and sinful revels were just what Gray's Inn was good at. That very Christmas a Prince of Purpoole[45] was elected and his Champion, imitating the royal Champion at the Queen's coronation, rode into Hall and proclaimed a long list of made-up titles, but 'then arose such a discordant tumult and crowd upon the stage ... [that] it was thought good not to offer anything of account saving dancing and revelling with gentlewomen; and after such sports [unspecified] a Comedy of Errors ... was played by the players ... Later in the reign of that Prince he and his followers performed a masque before the Queen', which she much enjoyed. The next year 100 marks (about £75, a substantial sum) was paid 'to the gentlemen for their sports and shows this Shrovetide at the Court before the Queen's Majesty'. Against that background, one can understand the entry in the accounts for 1570 'to the Carpenter for mending forms and tables in the Hall after the great show, and new-footing most of the trestles, 10s'.

Lincoln's Inn did not enjoy, as Gray's Inn did, the personal favour of the Queen, but its students could create a comparable amount of mayhem. In 1560 'Talbot fined 40s for drawing his sword and hurting Nugent, his chamber fellow [flatmate] Dilland fined 13s 4d for having a woman at night in Nugent's chamber.' This seems to have been a confused free-for-all. Another remarkable fracas took place in 1576: George Scrope was charged with striking one of the Benchers (the all-powerful Governors of the Inn, than whom few could be higher) in the Walks, because the Bencher 'had found fault with his study of astronomy, which he thought was more than he should have done'. One does get very touchy about one's research. But all went smoothly in 1567 when 'the gentlemen of the Middle Temple came here to dance the Post Revels with the gentlemen of this Inn'. This took place on 2 February, the Feast of the Purification of the Virgin Mary after Christ's birth, a Catholic tradition still, apparently, observed by the Inns of Court. Lincoln's Inn, too, had trouble with members who were suspected of being Catholics, 'to the evil example of others in their society'. They were threatened with expulsion, but they were allowed back when they repented and produced letters of support from Burghley and the Bishop of London.

Further education

Sir Thomas Gresham, the financier who had funded the Royal Exchange, died in 1579. His will provided that after the death of his widow his house should be used as a college, giving free daily lectures 'for all who chose to attend them'. Lady Gresham did not die for another seventeen years, but in 1597 teaching began (and still continues, although in different premises). Gresham provided a salary of £50 each, for seven lecturers, to teach divinity, astronomy, geometry, music, law, medicine and rhetoric. 'These lectures are [in the time of John Stow] read daily, Sundays excepted, in the term times, by every one upon his day, in the morning betwixt nine and ten, in Latin, in the afternoon, betwixt two and three, in English.' Teaching in English was unusual at that time, when all educated men conversed and wrote in Latin, for which their schooldays had thoroughly prepared them.

Private tuition and the foreign tour

It was normal for the sons of wealthy and titled families to be tutored at home, not mixing with *hoi polloi* in schools. High standards were set; whether they were reached is hard to tell. Roger Ascham, who had been Elizabeth's teacher, wrote *The Schoolmaster, or plain and perfect way of teaching children to understand, write and speak the Latin tongue, but specially purposed for the private bringing-up of youth in Gentlemen's and noblemen's houses* in 1570.[46] He sounds delightful. Unlike Mulcaster at the Merchant Taylors' school, he was anti-flogging. 'Gentleness is better than beating', which besides being cruel 'beats away the love of learning from children.' He warned parents against the solitary habits of academics, who can all too often be 'marred by overmuch study ... how solitary they be themselves, how unfit to live with others'. Ascham's idea of the well-brought up young man included more than book-learning. He should

> use and delight in all courtly exercises ... to ride comely, to run fair at the tilt or ring, to play at all weapons, to shoot fair in bow and surely in gun, to vault lustily, to run, to leap, to wrestle, to swim, to dance comely, to sing and play of instruments cunningly [skilfully], to hawk, to hunt, to play at tennis ...

It was still the custom for young men to spend some of their youth in other noble households, seeing how things were done. In Burghley's house, sometimes as many as twenty of them sat round his table, listening to his wise and learned conversation.

We think of the foreign tour as an eighteenth-century phenomenon, but it was firmly in place two centuries earlier. Harrison deplored 'the usual sending of noblemen's and mean [middle-class] gentlemen's sons into Italy, from whence they bring home nothing but ... atheism, infidelity, vicious conversation and ambitious and proud behaviour ... the affectation of foreign and strange words, presuming that to be the best English which is most corrupted with external terms of eloquence and ... many syllables.' Roger Ascham recommended a year's course of reading instead; it 'would do a young gentleman more good ... than three years travel abroad spent in Italy'.[47] But it would not be nearly so much fun, as appears from the exploits of young Thomas Cecil, Burghley's eldest son.

Thomas Cecil was determined to sow his wild oats, no matter how eminent and respectable his father was, so in 1561 his father sent him off on a foreign tour, aged nineteen, ostensibly to 'improve his education'. He went with another young man, Lord Hertford, one of Burghley's protégés, and to act as tutor and general minder Burghley sent his secretary, Thomas Windebank, who had been leading a quiet, scholarly life in Burghley's household until then. Reports of their travels duly arrived on Burghley's desk, where they joined the state papers relating, for instance, to the financing of a major loan to the Crown, and the arrangements for £25,000 in gold to be moved from the Tower to the Queen's palace at Westminster.[48] There is something very human in these exchanges of letters between Windebank, who was frequently desperate, and his employer, and between Thomas, who was incorrigible, and his father. Burghley sent his son off with 'A Memorial', telling him to do what Windebank told him, and above all to practise a daily routine of private prayer, public worship and Bible reading that would have taxed the most devout young man. I doubt if Thomas found time for much of it.[49]

When they got to Paris, they were looked after by the English Ambassador, naturally enough, but after only two weeks Windebank 'cannot send an estimate of their monthly expenses [which must have scandalised Burghley]. Mr Thomas has no great taste for the lute, but likes the cistern. He has been presented to the Queen of Scots.' Alarmed, Burghley fired off by return of post two letters, one to the tutor, 'relying on his discretion', and the other to his son, telling him to behave. It took Thomas some days to reply to his father. He had been 'more occupied in sightseeing than in his studies … he had been to the French King's court, and had watched a fight between a lion and three dogs – the dogs won'.

In August poor Windebank wrote to Burghley that it would be better if Thomas and Lord Hertford were separated, 'as well for the sake of avoiding the English tongue, as *for other reasons* [my italics]'. Hertford had contracted a secret marriage to Lady Katherine Grey, before he was sent on tour with Thomas. It may have been a love match, but it had red-hot political significance because she was in the line of possible succession to the throne. It is not clear how much Windebank knew, but he rightly suspected that Hertford was not a good influence on young Thomas.

Thereafter things quietened down a little. Burghley, like any anxious parent, told Thomas to keep an account of his money, and optimistically asked him to keep a detailed diary, and to write to him in Latin or French. Thomas seems to have managed at least one letter in French – which his father sent back to him, corrected. By the end of the year Burghley, who was not only responsible for the conduct of the government but also immersed in building himself a palatial house in Norfolk, told Thomas that 'children, as gifts of God, ought to be a comfort to their parents, but he is the contrary'. It goes almost without saying that Thomas and his tutor limped from monetary crisis to crisis, redeemed at the last moment by Windebank raising loans from English merchants abroad, and by

Thomas reprehensibly stealing money from Windebank's strongbox.

But other crises threatened them which were not so easy to solve. France was in a constant ferment, and the improving tours recommended by Burghley were not always possible. Burghley, surprisingly, suggested that they should go to Italy. Windebank was against that idea 'by reason of the enticement to pleasure and wantonness there', so they went to Germany instead, both of them thoroughly bored with each other's company and longing to be home. But 'Germany is not the place to acquire the accomplishments of a gentleman', so they came home, at last, in 1563. Thomas seems to have got his wild oats out of his system. He settled down to marriage and respectability, was created the first Earl of Exeter by James I, and died aged 80 in 1622.

CHAPTER 12

Amusements

Home entertainment

Elizabeth enjoyed card games such as gleek and primero, especially if she won. It could be expensive to play against her: Lord North lost £70 to her between 1576 and 1580.[1] Embroidery was safer, and more productive. Mary Queen of Scots turned out yard after yard of exquisite embroidery. Not every woman had her artistic skill, or her opportunity to fill the long years when the only possible alternative occupation was plotting, but most women could produce pleasant decorations for their homes, using commercial designs of flowers and birds and rather large insects – the object was to cover the canvas, at the cost of entomological accuracy.

The printing presses were turning out a spate of books and ballads.[2] Pliny's *The Secrets and Wonders of the World* described the dragons of Ethiopia. Dragons are mostly amiable – they have had a very bad press. But elephants, then known as 'oliphants', can be a different kettle of fish, and any child should know how to deal with them if she happened to meet two – tie their tails together and trip them up.[3]

There were books for more adult tastes, such as the obscene Italian books 'of late translated out of Italian into English, sold in every shop in London ... suffer these books to be read and they shall soon displace all books of godly learning'.[4] Roger Ascham, who wrote that in 1570, would have been horrified a few years later to see Boccaccio's *Amorous Fiametta* freely on sale in English, let alone Ariosto's *Orlando Furioso* translated by the Queen's godson, Thomas Harrington, no less. Aretino's *Postures* was even illustrated by notoriously obscene pictures.

But the publishing scene was not all filth. A translation from the Greek of Eusebius Pamphilius's *Auncient Ecclesiasticall Histories of the first Six Hundred Years after Christ* made interesting reading for some, as did Plutarch's *Lives* translated out of the original Greek into French, and then into English by Lord North, which hit the bookshops in 1577 and 1579. In 1590 the first part of Chapman's translation of Homer's *Iliad* suddenly made Homer available to less educated readers. The best-seller was undoubtedly Foxe's *Book of Martyrs*, published in 1563, and compulsive reading long after the fires kindled by Mary Tudor's persecution of Protestants had died down. Like Aretino's *Postures*, it was illustrated, but unlike those in Aretino, Foxe's blood-curdling pictures have survived.

The age of cheap pocket editions was yet to come, but almanacs could be bought for a penny or so and were always useful to have in the house, to consult for propitious dates for marrying, cutting your nails or even having a bath. There was also a steady stream of travel books, such as *The Voyage and Travaile of M. Caesar Frederick, Merchant of Venice, into the East India*, translated and published in 1588. *A Survey of France* bound, for some unknown reason, with a copy of Shakespeare's *Venus and Adonis* cost 12d, in 1593.[5] In Antwerp, where many London merchants had business, Mercator's new map of the British Isles was available in 1564.[6] Men began to collect maps:

> Some to beautify their halls, parlours, chambers, galleries or studies or libraries with ... some other[s] to view the large dominion of the Turk, the wide empire of the Muscovite, and the little morsel of ground where Christendom ... is certainly known ... some other[s] for their own journeys ... into far lands, or to understand other men's travels.[7]

And, of course, there were the plays, which could be read at home, but sometimes years after their performance on stage.[8] Marlowe's *Tamburlane the Great* was published in 1590, his *Dido Queen of Carthage* after his death, in 1594, probably in the same year as Shakespeare's plays began to be published.[9] Dekker's *The Shoemaker's Holiday* came out in 1599, followed by his *Pleasant Comedy of Old Fortunatus* the next year. Ben Jonson's *Every Man in his Humour* was published in 1601. During Elizabeth's reign 3,000 ballads poured off the presses and sold for a penny, most on popular subjects but a fair proportion on the new Protestant religion.[10] A ballad about the capture and execution of Campion, a prominent Catholic priest, was on the streets the day after his execution.

In theory, pamphlets were as subject to censorship as books and plays were, but despite every effort many escaped uncensored on to the streets of London. In 1564 Burghley gave special instructions to the Customs Officers ('customers') to admit five vats (large barrels) and two maundes (baskets) of books from the Frankfurt Fair, already going strong and still the fulcrum of a publisher's year, and the next year special searchers were appointed to seize all 'lewd and scandalous' imported books and deliver them to the Bishop of London. This was followed up by a proclamation that anyone who had any seditious books must immediately deliver them to the Bishop *without reading them* unless the Bishop licensed them, which does sound rather optimistic. In 1599 the Archbishop of Canterbury specified nine books of anti-government satires that were to be seized and burnt, and ordered that all books by Thomas Nashe must be 'taken and never printed hereafter', but the very next year Nashe's *Summer's Last Will and Testament* crept through the embargo.

As the opposition to Spain and Catholic influence grew, strict watch was kept for imported seditious literature, which usually emanated from Spain or its dependencies and was aimed at encouraging English Catholics and enlisting any discontented Protestants who might be persuaded to rebel against their monarch. In 1597, when a Spanish invasion looked all too possible, a port official informed Burghley that he had 'stayed a barrel of books from Zealand [then part of the Spanish Netherlands] and is keeping them in Her Majesty's storehouse although it is already full of the like. [He] hears that there should be another barrel consigned to a woollen draper of London which he will also stay when it has been found.'[11] Barrels sound an improbable packaging for books, but they were the standard way of carrying any goods. Loading them into ships was a familiar routine, whether they were full of wine or books. If a barrel in which your copy of, say, More's *Utopia* was transported had previously contained wine, a faint vinous memory would only enhance More's imaginative masterpiece.

But when the light became too poor for reading, and the candles were lit, music and dancing could begin. Any man of reasonable education would be expected to sight-read and sing part-songs, sometimes accompanied by a lute or more instruments. After 1575, when both Tallis and Byrd were granted patents to print music, the singers could gather round printed sheets, which revolutionised the

Elizabethan amateur music world. Most men could play a lute – one was available to the waiting queue of customers in any barber's shop, to while away the time. Someone was bound to be able to play dance tunes, to which they danced by the light of the fire and candles, in their brilliantly coloured, gem-studded costumes. Even old ladies and gentlemen over forty could take the floor in a pavane, their feet never leaving the floor – hence the general term, 'dance basse'. When the players struck up a quicker coranto or a galliard, or its even faster version, a lavolta, they left the floor to the young men, who took off their rapiers and cloaks and danced in their doublets, leaping and running and lifting their partners into the air. No wonder those dances were called 'haute dance'.[12] They all sound like healthy indoor exercise, but of course there were other views: a persistent reformer described 'the horrible vice of pestiferous dancing … what kissing and bussing [more kissing], what smouching and slabbering one of another, what filthy groping and unclean handling is not practised every where in these dancings?'[13]

Meanwhile the elderly sat round the fire and gossiped. Was the Queen really going to get married this time, and if so, to whom? Every time she had not been seen publicly for a week or so, she was always said to be pregnant and/or to have given birth, mostly by her long-time favourite the Earl of Leicester but sometimes more imaginatively. She had exchanged rings with her last suitor, the Duke of Alençon, 'who *as they say* is placed in the privy lodging' near Elizabeth's own rooms, when he came to court her.[14] It was rumoured that she was serious this time, which made a hot royal scandal that ran and ran until his death in 1584. Or the company might talk 'of the planets and the celestial signs with the constellations, and what their operations and workings were, and what effect they wrought'. Someone had perhaps brought with him Arcandam's *Most Excellent Booke to find the Fatal Destiny of Every man*, published in 1562. He would 'cast the nativity [horoscope] of some in the company, and then [he] would read unto them that which was said of them in the book, which sometimes did please some, and others it made to look down and bite their lips'.[15] How unsocial: the least an amateur fortune-teller can do is to prophesy only good things.[16]

When have the English not talked about the weather? But they had good cause, as the sixteenth century wore on. Summers were short and wet, winters savage. In 1561 the winds were so strong that an old woman and three cows died, near Charing Cross. It was bitterly cold in the winter of 1564, and the Thames froze over above the bridge so that anyone who felt inclined – the preceding summer had seen an appalling epidemic of plague that left people gloomy and apprehensive – could go and have fun on the frozen river. There were tempests causing 'much damage to houses' in 1567, and the next year 'through vehement rage and tempest of winds many vessels in the Thames, with two tilt-boats before Gravesend, were sunk and drowned'. On May Day 1573 a great muster was scheduled to take place at Greenwich in front of the Queen, when all the soldiers would show off 'many warlike feats', but it was rained off. Two feet of snow fell on London in 1577. There was an earthquake in 1589. 'The great clock-bell in the Palace of Westminster struck of itself … the gentlemen of the Temple, being at supper, were so much scared that they ran from their tables and out of the hall with their knives in their hands.'[17] Some thought the earthquake presaged the end of the world,[18] but it had not come ten years later, when another storm sank the ferry boat from Gravesend with the loss of nineteen passengers.

Then there were curiosities to be viewed and described. Had anyone managed to see the Eskimo children whom Sir Martin Frobisher had brought from his travels to the north-west passage to China? Their parents had already died in Bristol, but the children survived long enough to reach London, poor things.[19] Could it be true that four baby girls had been born at the same time, and all lived, although the mother died?[20] What, or who, exactly, was a hermaphrodite? Jonathan Best was one, although he had always been assumed to be a woman in man's clothes.[21] In Halifax, so a friend said, they had a queer way of executing criminals, by making them lie down and put their heads on a block so that a huge sharp knife poised in a framework above came down and sliced their heads off. Tidy, no doubt, but not an idea that was likely to catch on.[22] It was said that a large live camel could be seen in a house on London Bridge, and Mr Cope, who had travelled in the Indies, sometimes showed visitors his collection, including the horn and tail of a rhinoceros, a unicorn's tail and 'flies which glow at night in Virginia instead of lights, since there is often no day there for over a month'.[23]

Pets have a habit of monopolising the attention, surpassed only by children. Queen Elizabeth's household included a parrot in a cage and, horrifically, two unhousetrainable animals on long chains, a monkey and a 'musk cat'.[24] Inexplicably, this fondness for monkeys was shared by many of her subjects. How did the monkeys get on with the miniature spaniels, 'little and pretty ... for mincing mistresses to bear in their bosoms ... to succour with sleep and nourish with meat at board [table], to lie in their laps and lick their lips'?[25]

Free shows

There was a free concert at the Royal Exchange, every Sunday in the summer, at four o'clock, when 'the musicians of the City perform marvels of sound' from the galleries of the tower there, 'to the great contentment of all who hear'.[26]

One of the oddest free shows must have been the trial by combat of a lawsuit about the title to certain land. Each party chose a champion to fight his cause, and the court convened in Tothill Fields, where the Lord Chief Justice and his brethren sat on a platform at one side, while spectators occupied the stands round the other sides of the 21-foot-square arena. The champions duly arrived, but after some theatrical posturing by them someone noticed that one of the parties had not turned up, so the case was decided in favour of the other party. One of the champions,

> apparelled in a doublet and galleygaskin breeches all of crimson satin, a hat of black velvet with a feather, and band [ruff] ... challenged [the other champion] to play with him half a score of blows, to show some passtime to the Lord Chief Justice, and the others there assembled, but [the other champion] answered that he came to fight and would not play.

So the Lord Chief Justice 'commanded them both quietly to depart the field' and everyone went home.[27]

If there was nothing so extraordinary going on, it was worth keeping an eye on the Lord Mayor. He was easily recognised once you had seen him in the City, in his scarlet robes and heavy gold chain, always preceded by his swordbearer in a tall fur hat carrying the City sword upright in its pearl-encrusted scabbard. But he gave the City much more than that to look at. Every Sunday in August he and his aldermen went out to Finsbury Fields to judge the shooting and wrestling contests, culminating in the opening of the great St Bartholomew's Fair.[28] 'After this is over, a parcel of rabbits are turned loose among the crowd, which boys chase with great noise', and the fair got going, with all its rowdy sideshows.[29] A new mayor was elected every year. He and his aldermen took their elaborately decorated barges down to the Palace of Westminster for him to swear allegiance to the monarch, and his procession back to the Guildhall along the Strand and Fleet Street and through the City was a sumptuous parade of pageantry.

But the prime source of spectacle was the Queen, that past-mistress of public relations. Her accession was brilliantly stage-managed, in the grey November days after her half-sister Mary's death in 1558. She came in from Hatfield, to stay at first with Lord North in his mansion in the Charterhouse beyond the city walls. On 28 November 'the Queen removed to the Tower' to assume, as monarch, symbolic command of the Mint and the Armoury in the fortress where she had been a prisoner only four years earlier. She rode in through Cripplegate, down Bishopsgate Street and past Leadenhall, down Gracechurch Street and along Fenchurch Street to the Tower, and every street was hung with silks and tapestries, every window filled with cheering people.

> Before rode gentlemen and many knights and lords, and after came all the trumpets blowing, and then came all the heralds in array: and my Lord of Pembroke bore the Queen's sword, then came her Grace on horseback, in purple velvet with a scarf about her neck, and the Sergeant of Arms about her Grace: and next after rode Sir Robert Dudley, the master of her horse: and so the guard with halberds. And there was in certain places children with speeches, and [in] other places singing and playing ...

In January 1559 'the Queen came in a chariot from the Tower, with all the lords and ladies in crimson velvet, and their horses trapped [harnessed] with the same, and trumpeters in red gowns blowing, and all the heralds in their coat armour'. Her coronation procession the next day included all the usual brilliantly robed dignitaries, with the addition of the bishops in scarlet. That year 'there was great jousts at the Queen's palace', which anyone could watch if they could squeeze their way in.

In 1561 she went back to the Tower again to inspect the Mint. She came by water, but she left by road, making for Lord North's house again, at first through the streets then 'over the fields full of people' with all her trumpeters and heralds and lords and ladies. In July she set off on one of her progresses through the country. The streets along which her procession rode 'were hanged with cloth of arras [tapestry] and carpets and with silk, and Cheapside [was] hanged with cloth of gold and silver and velvet of all colours'. The Lord Mayor was there, carrying her sceptre, and Lord Hunsdon carrying her sword, and the whole gorgeous cavalcade went with her as far as Whitechapel, where they turned back. She came back early, that year, in September, through Enfield and Islington, making for St James's Palace, where no doubt she hoped for some more hunting. 'There was above 10,000 people to see her Grace, but it was night before her Grace came ...' All these accounts came from the diary of an ordinary Londoner who had been able to watch them.[30]

In 1584 the Queen came back from a progress rather later, in November, and her procession included '1,000 men with torches ready to give light on every side (for that the night drew on)'. She went to St Paul's in September 1588, to give thanks for the victory over the Armada. Although she was still a keen horsewoman, she preferred this time not to ride but to be carried in a 'chariot throne', no doubt so that her adoring people could see her better.[31]

Bear baiting, bull baiting and cock fighting

The Queen's palace of Whitehall could accommodate a royal baiting of bears and bulls, in the tiltyard, where it could be watched from a gallery. She gave the French ambassadors this treat, when they arrived in May 1559, 'and the Queen's grace and the ambassadors stood in the gallery looking [at] the pastime till six at night'.[32] The day after, the ambassadors and their suite went across the river to the rings on Bankside, like everyone else.

The French enjoyed animal baiting when they were at home. One of the best descriptions of it, however, was by a Venetian tourist, Alessandro Magno, who came to London in 1562.[33]

> Every Sunday everyone takes great pleasure in the training of the dogs. They pay 2d to stand and twice as much for a seat in the stands ... First they take into the ring a cheap horse ... and a monkey in the saddle. Then they attack the horse with 5 or 6 of the youngest dogs. Then they change the dogs for more experienced ones ... It is

wonderful to see the horses galloping along … with the monkey holding on tightly to the saddle and crying out frequently when he is bitten by the dogs. After they have entertained the audience for a while with this sport, which often results in the death of the horse, they lead him out and bring in bears – sometimes one at a time, sometimes all together. But this sport is not very pleasant to watch. At the end, they bring on a fierce bull and tie it with a rope about two paces long, to a stake fixed in the middle of the ring. This sport is the best one to see, and more dangerous for the dogs, than the others: many of them are wounded and die. This goes on until evening.[34]

Another foreign visitor's account adds a few details. The dogs,

great English mastiffs … although they were much struck and mauled by the bear, … did not give in, but had to be pulled off by sheer force, and their muzzles forced open with long sticks to which a broad iron piece was attached at the top. The bears' teeth were not sharp, so they could not injure the dogs; they have them broken short. [When a bull was brought in] one dog only was set on him at a time, which he speared with his horns and tossed in such masterly fashion that they could not get the better of him, and as the dogs fell to the floor again several men held sticks under them to break their fall, so that they would not be killed … Lastly they brought in an old blind bear which the boys hit with canes and sticks, but he knew how to untie his leash, and he ran back to his stall.[35]

An inventory of 1590 listed three bulls, five 'great' bears and four others, a horse and an 'ape'. The bears were well known to Londoners by name, such as George Stone, Harry Hunks (valued at £10) and Harry of T(h)ame (£8). Another was called Sackerson; a character in Shakespeare's *The Merry Wives of Windsor* boasts, improbably, that 'I have seen Sackerson loose 20 times, and have taken him by the chain'.[36] Even if any of the bears were as tame as that, it must have been a nerve-racking test for their keepers, and any onlookers, to bring them across the river to the royal tiltyard.

After all that savagery, farce:

A number of men and women came forward [into the ring] … dancing, conversing and fighting with each other … Right over the middle of the place a rose was fixed. This rose being set on fire by a rocket, suddenly lots of apples and pears fell out of it down upon the people standing below. While the people were scrambling for the apples some rockets were made to fall down upon them out of the rose, which caused a great fright but amused the spectators. After this, rockets and other fireworks came flying out of all corners, and that was the end of the play.[37]

A cock-pit had been added to the amenities of Whitehall by Henry VIII, as well as tennis courts and bowling alleys.[38] Ordinary Londoners resorted to the cock-pit near Smithfield, where for a penny you could watch the contest from the gallery, unless you intended to bet, when you paid more for a ring-side seat.

Stakes on a cock often amount to many thousands of crowns ... this entertainment usually lasts four or five hours ... The master ... told us that if one discovered that the cocks' beaks had been coated with garlic, one was fully entitled to kill them at once. He added, too, that it was nothing to give them brandy before they began to fight, adding what wonderful pleasure there was in watching them.[39]

Theatre-going

This is not an account of the theatre in the age of Shakespeare, or during the reign of Elizabeth. But I hope to describe how it felt to go to a play. Better than any description would be a visit to the New Globe Theatre, where present-day audiences can see, and feel, and hear, what Elizabethan audiences experienced.

Plays were still presented in the galleried courtyards of inns, which were squarely under the Lord Mayor's disapproving eye. After all, it was said that they led to

the inordinate haunting of great multitudes of people, specially youths ... occasion of [af]frays and quarrels, evil practices of incontinency ... having chambers and secret places adjoining to their open stages and galleries, inveigling and alluring maids, specially orphans and good Citizens' children under age, to privy [secret] and unmete [unsuitable] contracts ... withdrawing of the Queen's subjects from divine service on Sundays and holydays ...[40]

The City disapproved of plays, players and all that went with them, and the Lord Mayor would have closed them all down if he could, as 'the ordinary places of meeting for all vagrant persons and masterless men ... thieves [and] horsestealers'. There was an irascible exchange of correspondence between the Lord Mayor, whose view was that 'the players of plays ... were a very superfluous sort of men', and the Privy Council, who wanted them encouraged 'for honest recreation sake, in respect that Her Majesty sometimes took delight in those passtimes, and to give players practice'. The Lord Mayor was prepared to allow plays to be given on Sundays – the only day most people could go – but only after evening service, 'yet all the afternoon they took in hearers and filled the place with such as were thereby absent from churchtime'.[41]

The City authorities were no happier when Burbage built London's first purpose-built playhouse, which he called the Theatre, a mile outside the City's jurisdiction, in Shoreditch, in 1577, soon joined by a rival playhouse called the Curtain (so called after the name of the plot of land on which it was built – there were no curtains, as we know them, in Elizabethan theatres). Two playhouses on Bankside followed, also outside the City's jurisdiction: the Rose in 1587 and the Swan in 1595. The Fortune, opened in 1600, was a mile north of St Paul's on the western side of the City. In 1598 the management of the Theatre in Shoreditch ran into trouble with their ground landlord, so after the Christmas season the players themselves, with some help, dismantled the whole building, transported the iron work and timbers through the City and across the river – no mean feat in itself – and re-erected it, under its new name of 'the Globe', near the Rose and the Swan on Bankside, in less than a month, by January 1599. Fortunately, Burbage had been trained as a carpenter and could show his players how to number each component, knock out the timber pegs holding the frames together, and put the whole thing together again on its new site. But there must surely have been some brick footing to lay first, on the damp river bank.

Handbills distributed all over London could be consulted to find out what was on, where. Performances in the Bankside playhouses were during daylight, in the afternoon. For gentlemen and students at the Inns of Court their time was their own, but the apprentices and journeymen who came too were stealing time which they should have spent working for their masters, or listening to sermons. The scrum to reach your seat which still afflicts modern theatre-goers was worse in Elizabethan London:

You shall see such heaving and shoving ... to sit by women: such care for their garments, that they be not trod on ... such pillows to their backs ... such tickling ... such smiling, such winking, and such manning them home, that it is a right comedy to mark their behaviour ... not that any filthiness in deed is committed within the compass of that ground ... but that every wanton and his paramour ... are there first acquainted, and [they] cheapen [beat down the price of] the merchandise in that place, which they pay for elsewhere.[42]

In a full house, people were certainly crowded. One estimate is 18 inches per seat in the galleries – remember those padded trunkhose and voluminous skirts – with men being allowed 30 inches legroom, women only 24. The capacity in the pit, in both the Globe and the Fortune, was perhaps 600–800.[43] The six 'lords' rooms' over the playing area took only one or two people each. The plan of most playhouses was similar. As described by a foreign visitor,

they play on a raised platform, so that everyone has a good view. There are different galleries and places, however, where the seating is better and more comfortable and therefore more expensive. For whoever cares to stand below only pays one English penny, but if he wishes to sit he enters by another door and pays another penny, while if he desires to sit in the most comfortable seats, which are cushioned, where he not only sees everything well but can also be seen, he pays yet another English penny at another door. And during the performance food and drink are carried round the audience ... the actors are most expensively and elaborately costumed; for it is the English usage for eminent lords or knights to bequeath ... almost the best of their clothes to their serving men, which it is unseemly for the latter to wear [they would fall foul of the Statutes of Apparel if they did] so that they offer them ... for sale for a small sum to the actors.[44]

An actor's nightmare audience – spectators on the stage itself:

You may, with small cost, purchase the dear acquaintance of the boys: have a good stool for 6d ... get your match lighted [to smoke your toabcco pipe]; examine the playsuits' [costumes'] lace and perhaps win wagers upon laying it is [not gold but] copper. [After arriving late, just as the play begins,] creep from behind the arras with your ... three-footed stool in one hand ... Laugh aloud in the middle of the saddest scene of the terriblest tragedy ... by talking and laughing all the eyes in the galleries will leave ... the players and

only follow you … In the middle of the play … you rise with a
screwed and discontented face from your stool to be gone … and
being on your feet sneak not away like a coward but salute all your
gentle acquaintance that are spread either on the rushes [in the pit]
or on stools about you …[45]

The female characters were of course played by 'the boys', there
being no women actresses. We cannot leave these playhouses without a reminder of that unfortunate lady who was aiming for the
seclusion of the gallery via an unlit stairway, where lurking thieves
blew out the torch her page was carrying, leaving her in the dark
and, so they thought, at their mercy. She foiled their plan to snatch
the valuable embroidery on her dress, by hanging on to it rather
than her modesty when they assaulted her.[46]

As well as the round, galleried playhouses, there were others
shaped like a shoebox – where, incidentally, the acoustic may have
been much easier for the players – with two or sometimes three
galleries. Their capacity was less than the round playhouses, but
since they were enclosed and had to rely on artificial lighting
anyway, they were not limited to the hours of daylight. On the other
hand, the action had to pause from time to time, for the lamps to be
attended to. The choir school of St Paul's used a hall next to the
chapterhouse from 1575, with a capacity of less than two hundred,
and the children of the Chapel Royal had a hall theatre in
Blackfriars. Burbage tried his luck in Blackfriars in 1596, but the
local residents, who tended to be rich and respectable, petitioned
Parliament to close it because it would

> grow to be a very great annnoyance and trouble not only to the
> noblemen and gentlemen thereabout inhabiting but also … to all the
> inhabitants of the said precinct … by reason of the great resort and
> gathering together of all manner of vagrant and lewd persons … and
> besides, the same playhouse is so near the church that the noise of the
> drums and music will greatly disturb … the ministers and parishioners.

Despite all that, the audience at these playhouses was usually quieter
and more genteel than in the round theatres, where the audience
often joined in with comments and suggestions.

The playhouses were all dependent on the absence of plague. As
soon as it struck, all playhouses were closed and the players took to
the roads.

Sport

Archery was going out of fashion as a weapon of war, but Elizabeth still required all her male subjects aged between seven and sixty to possess bows and arrows and know how to use them. Boys between seven and seventeen were supposed to have a bow and two arrows, adult males a bow and four arrows.[47] There were 200 archery targets or 'butts' in Finsbury Fields, some of which can be seen on a map (see plate 17), north of the laundresses. The archers seem to be loosing off in all directions. There was another archery ground out at Mile End. In 1562, 35 men were prosecuted because they 'have without reasonable excuse neglected to provide themselves with bows and arrows and neglected to practise archery'.[48] But by the time John Stow was writing, in 1597, 'exercises in the long bow by citizens ... [are] now almost clean left off and forsaken ... our archers for want of room to shoot abroad [outside] creep into bowling alleys and ordinary dicing houses', which sounds most dangerous, unless they were just looking for a quiet drink. When Sir Thomas Ramsey, who had been Lord Mayor, died in 1590, the inventory of his household goods included a surprisingly modest six bows and arrows. In contrast, the inventory of the goods in the Earl of Leicester's house when he died in 1588 included 280 bows and arrows.[49]

Small-arms shooting was perhaps more fashionable for the young. Here more care was taken to prevent accidents. The Artillery Yard just to the east of Bishopsgate Street had a brick wall round it, and a clearly defined target at each end. The Earl of Essex had 421 light muskets or 'calivers' in his armoury.

Tennis was not quite the same as the Wimbledon version. 'The ball is used by noble men and gentlemen in tennis courts, and by people of meaner sort in the open fields and streets'.[50] Tennis balls were stuffed with the hair of poor women, a welcome means of raising money. Apart from the courts attached to great houses such as the Earl of Leicester's mansion on the river, there were some squeezed into the odd spaces left by the destruction of monastic buildings, such as the one in the former church of the Crutched Friars in Hart Street, sharing it with a carpenter's yard.

Football had no aristocratic supporters. In 1553 a prominent educationalist had condemned it as 'nothing but fury and external violence, whence proceedeth hurt, and consequently rancour and malice do remain with them that be wounded'.[51]

Bowls was played by every man. It would have been exceedingly disconcerting for a bowls player to coincide with an archer looking for a practice ground, but perhaps you were fairly safe in the Walks of Gray's Inn or the garden of your livery company.[52] There seem to have been privately owned sports complexes providing a choice of alleys. The Privy Council asked the Lord Mayor, in 1580, why he had refused building permission for a 'close[d] bowling alley for the recreation of honest citizens to bowl in, in foul weather'. The Mayor replied that the applicant already owned one, there was another next to it, three alleys in half an acre would be too many and, what was worse, the applicant 'also kept dicing, carding [card-playing] and table-play [gambling] which was resorted to by the worst and meanest persons ... while their families were in peril of starvation'. Please could he be allowed to close them all down, 'notwithstanding the Queen's licence'? No, said the Privy Council.[53]

Swimming was enjoyable in a hot summer, either in the Thames – which says a lot for the purity of its water – or in pools such as the Perilous Pond out past Finsbury. It was fed by a tepid spring, but it must have produced cold shivers in anyone remembering the 'divers youths swimming there who have been drowned'.[54]

Young men could also work off their energy with wrestling, and general free fights, and horsing around with girls, as observed by a startled young Venetian. 'Many of the young women gather outside Moorgate, and play with young lads, even though they do not know them. Often, during these games, the women are thrown to the ground by the young men, who only allow them to get up after they have kissed them. They kiss each other a lot.'[55]

The lottery

In 1567 'a great lottery [was] holden at London in [St] Paul's churchyard, at the west door'. The draw went on from 11 January to 1 May. The 400,000 tickets went on sale at 10s each, which was often shared between friends or by members of a livery company. Gray's Inn scraped together the huge sum of £1. The arrangements for buying tickets were complicated, but one interesting advantage was that any ticket-holder could travel to London, or to fifteen provincial cities, and stay there without further question for seven days, to oversee his progress in the draw, which may have been useful for other purposes in that era of internal travel restrictions. The glittering first prize, as advertised, was the huge amount of £5,000: £3,000 in cash and the rest in armour, plate and household linens and hangings – which would not be much use to someone without a grand house to put them in. One cannot help wondering whether all this armour and plate and linen came out of government stores. I have not come across any mention of anyone winning it, or anything like it. The Drapers' Company had put in £54, but all they won was some miscellaneous bits of armour.[56] Indeed, public enthusiasm fell short of what the authorities had hoped, since if all tickets had been sold they looked to make a profit of £100,000.

The next lottery, in 1585, was considerably slicker. The draw took only three days. The Privy Council leant on the Lord Mayor, to lean on the members of the livery companies both corporately and individually, to pay up. So the Merchant Taylors duly bought some tickets, and deputed three members to attend the draw at St Paul's, from 8 a.m. till noon – but their records have no mention of any win.[57]

Inns and taverns

Inns were strategically sited near markets such as Smithfield, and where the traveller to London might want to leave his horse and perhaps his coach, and make his way through the narrow streets on foot. The Cross Keys in Gracechurch Street, for example, had stabling enough to accommodate the '18 great horses, all pied-coloured' which arrived in London in 1561 as a present to the Queen from the King of Sweden.[58] Inns were considerable establishments. 'Every man may use his inn as his own house ... our inns are very well furnished with napery, bedding and tapestry.' The table linen was washed daily and 'each comer is sure to lie in clean sheets ... if his chamber be once appointed [he has booked in] he may carry the key with him'. The host was responsible for any loss sustained by a guest on his premises. The only snag was that if the staff chose to collude with highwaymen and the guest was robbed after he had left the inn, the landlord was not liable. Yet, after all this encomium, Harrison winds up his account by sourly remarking that 'of all in England there are no worse inns than in London'.[59]

Some glimpses from more favourable critics illuminate these inns.

Alessandro Magno found London inns 'very clean, and they treat well any who go there'. He stayed at an inn kept by an Italian, where he found the food palatable and the wine 'excellent'.[60] A young Swiss visitor, who was staying at an inn kept by a Frenchman in Mark Lane, admired London inns, although one cannot but suspect that he did not quite understand them.

> There are many inns, taverns and beer-gardens scattered about the city, where much amusement may be had with eating, drinking, fiddling and the rest, for instance in our hostelry, which was visited by players almost daily. And what is particularly curious is that the women as well as the men, in fact more often than they, will frequent the taverns or ale-houses for enjoyment [and, one cannot help adding, occasional prostitution, which this nice young man may not have noticed]. They count it a great honour to be taken there, and given wine with sugar to drink; and if one woman only is invited, then she will bring three or four other women along and they gaily toast each other; the husband afterwards thanks him who has given his wife such pleasure, for they deem it a real kindness.[61]

The musical entertainment he enjoyed was, however, authentic. There is another account of two young men, both musicians, in an inn one evening, where 'one of them showed his skill on the virginals, to the no little contentment of the hearers ... divers guests of the house came into the room to listen'.[62] And in taverns where there were no virginals, you could often meet a blind harper singing new ballads to familiar tunes. If you wanted to remember the words, there might be a copy on sale, or even stuck up on the wall, and if your reading was rather rusty, there was bound to be someone glad to show off and read the words aloud for you.[63] All taverns were supposed to be licensed, and they would advertise by their sign, or by a bush hanging over the door. But if they were trading without a licence they might rely on a red lattice or chequered pattern painted on the wall, instead.[64]

Recreational drugs

William Harrison was disappointed in nicotine. 'How do men extol the use of tobacco in my time, whereas in truth ... it is not found of so great efficiency as they write.'[65] Tobacco was at first thought to be good for you. The Spanish pharmacologist Nicolas Monardes praised it as a cure for anything from bad breath to kidney stones.[66] But smokers' wives must have noticed its negative effect on bad breath: 'It makes your breath stink like the piss of a fox'.[67] By 1577 it was being grown in England[68] and by the 1590s a small pipeful could be bought in a playhouse for 3d.[69]

A native of Brandenburg was much struck by English smoking habits, in 1598. At the playhouses and the animal-baiting rings 'and everywhere else, the English are constantly smoking the Nicotan weed [*Nicotiana*] which in America is called Tobaca'. Once they had got their clay pipes to draw, 'they draw the smoke into their mouths which they puff out again through their nostrils like smoke, along with it plenty of phlegm and defluxion from the head'.[70] (How revolting.) To 'drink' tobacco was to inhale.[71] A Swiss medical student, diligently writing up his experiences in London in 1599, gives a probably accurate description:

> In the alehouses tobacco or a species of wound-wort [possibly henbane] are also obtainable ... the powder is lit in a small pipe. The smoke is sucked into the mouth, and the saliva is allowed to run freely, after which a good draught of Spanish wine follows. This they regard as a curious [exceptional] medicine for defluctions, and as a pleasure, and the habit is so common with them, that they always carry the instrument [presumably the pipe] on them, and light up on all occasions, at the play, in the taverns or elsewhere, drinking as well as smoking together ... and it makes them riotous and merry, and rather drowsy, just as if they were drunk, though the effect soon passes – and they use it so abundantly because of the pleasure it gives, that their preachers cry out on them for their self-destruction and I am told the inside of one man's veins after death was found to be covered in soot just like a chimney ...[72]

– an interesting example of a clinical observation the significance of which had to wait for centuries to be recognised.

William Turner listed cannabis among the plants in his garden, as good for ear-ache. 'The hemp seed taken out of measure taketh men's wills from them.' Likewise 'the juice of the black poppy called opium ... swageth [dulls] ache and brings sleep ... but if a man taketh too much of it it is hurtful for it taketh away a man's memory and killeth him'. For an overdose, make him vomit and administer a 'sharp clyster' (enema) and wake him up by putting 'stinking things unto his nose'.[73]

CHAPTER 13

Networks and Boxes

'It is very hard', complained Philip Stubbes in 1583, 'to know who is noble, who is worshipful, who is a gentleman and who is not.'[1] And to be able to place someone in the right social rank was essential. Citizens ought to be categorised in tidy, recognisable boxes. Sometimes they might occupy different boxes, depending on what they were doing, and who was making the survey. Commercial and craft status involved the livery companies, religious affiliations were shown by the parish church, and civic duties and rights depended on the ward. The nightmare of the authorities was a 'masterless man' who owed no one allegiance.

The livery companies

Here was the organisation of the City of London, whirring like a huge dynamo, keeping all the wheels in the City turning. A man could not hope to amount to anything, in London, unless he belonged to a livery company. There were nearly 100 companies and trade associations in sixteenth-century London, many dating back to the twelfth century, but the twelve 'great companies' had most of the power and wealth. Their order of precedence had been fixed as long ago as 1516, and because they were such an integral part of City life I will give their precedence here:

> Mercers
> Grocers
> Drapers

Fishmongers
Goldsmiths
Skinners
Merchant Taylors
Haberdashers
Salters
Ironmongers
Vintners
Clothworkers

Some of these names may seem odd to modern eyes. The Mercers had controlled the wool trade and the export of cloth since 1347, and they imported the silks and velvets so beloved by those who could afford them. The Grocers (properly Grossers, because they dealt in bulk or, as the French said, *en gros*) controlled the import of spices and drugs, and they could trace their origins back to before 1189. The Drapers too could look back to the twelfth century; they concentrated on the wool cloth trade. The Fishmongers had a stranglehold on the diet of Englishmen, even after the Reformation when eating fish became a national, no longer a religious, duty. The Goldsmiths had sole responsibility for overseeing the quality of gold and silver articles, which had to be marked in their Hall ('hall-marked') before they could be sold. The Skinners dealt in the furs that all wealthy Londoners wore to show their high status.

The Merchant Taylors used to make tents, and the padded garments worn under armour, and when these markets began to fade they skilfully wedged themselves into yet another niche in the textile trade, having the last word on the measures for selling cloth in London and at the important fairs throughout England. The Haberdashers had a particular foothold in those essentials to any Elizabethan, pins, as well as making and selling hats and importing luxury articles from Italy. The Salters could count on their country-men's reliance on salt fish and salt meat. The Ironmongers supplied, and sometimes made, the bars and rods essential in building work, as well as iron rims for wheels. The Vintners controlled the import of wines, and had a supervisory function over inns and taverns. And the Clothworkers were the fourth of the great companies to depend on the textile trade, this time concentrating on the processes that cloth goes through between weaving and selling. The Carpenters regulated all dealing in timber and the construction of timber-framed buildings – that is, most of Elizabethan London – and the Stationers controlled the publication of books and ballads. The Bakers had to operate the Assize of Bread, producing loaves that satisfied the regulations, while the Butchers represented their members in objecting to any further inroads on meat eating, by further fish days, in the interests of the Navy.

As well as the many other companies whose senior members were entitled to wear distinctive dress ('livery'), there were two other important companies that did not adopt this custom: the Parish Clerks' Company, whose members were responsible for many civic duties including the compilation of the Bills of Mortality, and the Watermen and Lightermen of the river Thames, whose name speaks for itself.[2] Omission from the great companies did not mean that a company was insignificant.

Every aspect of life in sixteenth-century London was affected by at least one City company. As well as regulating training, and operating an effective closed shop, they were major property owners in the City, often acquiring land and buildings that had belonged to the pre-Reformation Church. The Goldsmiths were the richest. Then came the Skinners and the Fishmongers, followed by the Salters and Clothworkers, roughly equal. Despite their right to lead in any procession, the Mercers came only sixth in wealth.[3]

In essence, the organisation of all the companies was the same.[4] Each step in the ladder carried increasing privileges. The bottom rung was apprenticeship. The number of apprentices admitted by the Carpenters' Company varied between 50 and 70 a year, a fairly typical number. The Drapers and the Grocers admitted about twice as many, and the Merchant Taylors led the field, with an average annual number of 485 in the last decade of the century.[5] Most Carpenters' apprentices were between 14 and 24, some even as old as 29. Once a man was bound apprentice he was subject to the company's discipline, as well as to the daily supervision of his master, and offences against his master were punished by whippings administered in the company's hall.[6]

The drop-out rate during apprenticeship hovered around 40 or 50 per cent, especially when the apprentice reached the stage, about halfway through his term, when he was still earning only about 10s a month if he was lucky, but he felt he knew enough to be able to trade or practise profitably in his home town. It was a punishable offence to break an apprenticeship indenture in this way, but if the culprit managed to evade notice, little action seems to have been taken. It must have been maddening for a master to see his most promising pupils leave just as they were becoming useful to him.

But the fact remains that two out of every three men in their early thirties, in London, had been apprentices, who had spent more than a quarter of their lives in that status. They knew all their former fellow-apprentices, and probably knew the men who had been apprentices of other trades and had lived nearby, and when they were young had helped in a brawl or a football game. No doubt many forgot their youthful exploits as their beards grew longer and greyer, but their shared experience bonded them like an old school tie. They had all endured years of training in London, away from home, learning tolerance of their masters' quirks at work, and social skills in their masters' households, as well as what their master had to teach them.

Once the apprentice had successfully completed his term, he became a company man and a freeman of London, the next rung of the ladder up to riches and power. The status of freeman of the City was important, since only freemen could acquire property there. This was a jealously guarded right, leading to constant complaints that foreigners were trying to muscle into the market, and frequent requests to the Lord Mayor by various magnates, to admit to the 'estate' of freeman persons who had not properly qualified themselves through apprenticeship – they were normally refused.[7]

Within his company the new freeman joined the ranks of the yeomen, who were organised separately from the revered liverymen at the top of the pile. At this stage, again, some men left London and went back to their origins, but most stayed on. Three out of four male Londoners were members of a company.[8] Some of them left the rat-race, and settled for a quiet life as a paid journeyman. (The word is derived from the French *journée*, the length of a day, connoting someone who was paid by the day. In Elizabethan London a journeyman would be paid by the year, but rates were sometimes quoted as daily rates. The word has nothing to do with journeys.) Others put their energies into acquiring a wife and a shop, and becoming 'householders'.

Most masters gave their apprentices a helping hand at this stage, in the shape of a cash grant or loan, or the gift of tools. Many companies administered funds left by deceased members, which were lent to a newly qualified member at low or no interest, repayable once he was established. The Drapers had £3,000 to deploy in this way; they picked recipients by lot, and gave out anything from £20 to £56, repayable in 2–7 years.[9] An energetic man would not find it impossible to raise the necessary initial working capital of about £100, especially if his wife brought some money with her – she was often the daughter or widow of a man in the same company – or if he found a business partner to share the risks with him.[10] Members of the great companies, who often came from moneyed backgrounds, could take this step in a year or two. It took longer, perhaps more than three years, for members of the other companies, whose fathers were often simple countrymen. But becoming a respectable London householder was within the grasp of most of these young men.

If they made good in that 'estate', they might be chosen to move up to the next, and become entitled to wear the silk hood and fur-lined robes of a liveryman, of whom there were between 800 and 900 in the City.[11] After perhaps ten years, if they lived so long, they could take the next step and serve on their company's Court of Assistants. By then a member of a minor company might have 'translated' to one of the great companies. He would be entitled to call himself a merchant, one of the commercial aristocracy of London, with their fingers in every pie in the expanding commercial world.

In the years between 1561 and the end of the century, there were 13 to 24 'great merchants' – recognised as such by their brethren – in any year, and perhaps six times that number of 'lesser' merchants. According to Stow, 'the private riches of London rests chiefly in the hands of the merchants and retailers'. They probably all knew each other, or knew of each other, and deals could be arranged over a convivial meal in their livery company hall. These men earned their reputation by investing much time and effort in the administration of their company. About twenty of them served on their company's Court of Assistants. To be elected Warden of the Assistants meant further heavy calls on a man's time, and occasionally on his purse. Then for some, the ultimate accolade: election as master. This might not be always desirable; it was expensive and even more time con-suming. But from the ranks of the great companies' masters came the Lord Mayors of the City of London. So any humble apprentice, as he endured yet another painful and degrading whipping, could cherish the thought of one day being Lord Mayor.

Membership of a company was also the way into the developing regulated and joint-stock companies, such as the first joint-stock company, the Russian Company, incorporated in 1555, which traded not only to Moscow but to the lands beyond such as Persia; the powerful Merchant Adventurers, chartered in 1564; the Eastland Company, with a monopoly of the Baltic trade, chartered in 1579; the Levant Company (1581) and the East India Company (1600).

If in the end he did not make those heights, a liveryman could be sure that his company would look after him if he fell on hard times, and even shelter his widow if he had not been able to provide for her in his lifetime. All the companies owned and ran almshouses, scattered through London. But whether he had been rich or poor, his funeral and the feast given afterwards, for which the dead man had often earmarked a fund in his will, was attended by the whole company.

The Court of Assistants ran the company's affairs. These busy men, no doubt chafing to get back to their own businesses, dealt with everything, from large property holdings to personal minutiae. The Clothworkers ran some almshouses in Whitefriars, for any impoverished widows of Clothworkers or the few women members. Somehow, the windows of the almshouses had become too heavy for the old ladies to manage. The Court of Assistants gravely deliberated on this and reached a pragmatic decision: the windows had to be cut in half.[12]

The Carpenters were determined to preserve their control of the building trade. 'Foreign' carpenters – that is, non-members – had to apply for a licence every time they wanted to do any building work in London. Richard Bolt was licensed to employ 'two foreigns' to set up a garret in Chancery Lane. He was wise to apply in advance; another man was fined 10s 'for that a foreign did work in a house with him'. The court imposed fines on unlicensed jetties, and might issue a demolition order. The Merchant Taylors used their hall for plays and masques, up to 1573, but the Court of Assistants decided to stop this because 'lewd persons' always pushed into the best seats. A tenant of the Merchant Taylors proposed to sublet to a brazier (brass-founder), whose trade might constitute a nuisance because of the noise he would make. Nearby residents complained to the company, and the tenant was told to look for another subtenant. The Butchers even extended their jurisdiction to members' wives; a member was fined 12d 'for words spoken by his wife against Master

Austin', and another member had to pay the hefty amount of 5s 'for his wife's disobedience to the wardens'.[13]

But a company could operate in much higher spheres if necessary. The Vintners felt that their special privileges were threatened by certain proposed legislation. They mounted a discreet campaign, entertaining 'our friends in the Parliament House' to breakfasts and dinners, and slipping a retainer to the Recorder of London and hogsheads of wine to other officials. All was seemingly well until 1564, when they raised their sights to obtaining complete control of the wine trade. A cascade of presents flowed to those who might be helpful. The Lord Chief Justice accepted a modest £6 5s 4d 'for his friendship', but they did not dare to bribe Lord Burghley. Instead they made the delicate gesture of a present for his wife, of table linen worth nearly £40. The official cost of this campaign was only £22, yet somehow, when everything had been counted, it added up to £140. But it succeeded. One Saturday, after a very good lunch hosted by the Vintners, the members passed the desired legislation. Alas, having had Sunday to sober up, they reversed their decision on Monday morning. Nothing daunted, the Vintners returned to the fray. This time Leicester, who had had only two tuns of wine the first time round, got £90 in cash and £30 in wine, Lord Bacon the Lord Keeper got £11 worth of wine, and Lord Burghley himself – or was it addressed to his wife again? – a whole roll of velvet worth £30. Success. The legislation was still there, but the Vintners were specially exempt from it, and they got all that they wanted: a splendidly English solution.[14]

On the other hand, the Leathersellers had to confront Sir Edward Darcy, to whom the Queen had granted a monopoly that impinged on the company's rights. Again, the dispute was fought out in the highest of circles – all too literally, at one stage, when Darcy lost his temper and hit another man, in the presence of the Lord Mayor, and there ensued a general free-for-all, apprentices joining in with gusto. The proceedings dragged on. Three wardens of the company were gaoled for infringing Darcy's monopoly, but they were released on condition the company paid an extortionate fine of £4,000 – for merely exercising its rights. The monopoly was revoked in the end, but the Leathersellers had paid dear.[15]

The company court acted as arbitrators in disputes between members of the same company or, by agreement, between members of different companies. Plaintiffs were not prevented from resorting to the law courts, but if it was a case that could have been settled in a company court, the plaintiff would have to pay that company a fine. It would be a rare plaintiff who preferred the lengthy and tortuous proceedings of a law court to the company court, where the tribunal would have a specialist knowledge of the matter in dispute, and its decision would be made faster, and more cheaply, than in the law courts. Plaintiffs who were not members of a company could also use its court. Margery Story sued Thomas Taylor in the Merchant Taylors' court, in 1571, 'concerning a cassock made too little'; she was awarded 40s, and he kept the cassock.

The standard of living was rising, and the companies were buying tapestries and silver, table linen and furniture, padding their wooden benches with 'quishons with oliphants' (cushions embroidered with elephants, for the Cutlers' Company), and laying out new bowl- ing alleys in their gardens. Every now and then the Cutlers, and all the other companies, no doubt, were told by the Lord Mayor to attend some royal occasion 'attired in their best apparel'. The Drapers' Company records stipulate that only 'twenty of the chiefest *and comeliest* of the Company' were to go out to Mile End to greet the Queen, dressed in their 'best apparel and chains of gold'.[16]

It was not all hard work. In the last nineteen years of Elizabeth's reign the Cutlers found excuses for holding 58 feasts.[17] They patronised various inns, varying their custom from year to year to keep everyone on their toes. The Drapers could use their own kitchens. When they weren't having a slap-up feast (see page 161) there might be an excuse for a light 'banquet' of fruit and sturgeon and sweet wine, 'the price whereof was 24s'. Another time they had a small supper in the Red Bull, including oranges and lemons, and twelve blackbirds for 20d.

When the Merchant Taylors elected their master and wardens, they did it in style. They processed round their hall, with the City Waits playing, and the beadle carrying a silver baton and the clerk with a list of the members. Then 'the youngest Warden ... having one of the Election cups in his hand and his garland on his head', followed by all the other wardens, processed over the hearth – presumably it was in the middle of the hall, and all this took place in the summer – 'which is then finely set with flowers', until they got to the chief guest at the high table, where the master 'proffereth him his garland who cheerfully accepteth it and putteth it upon his head and after[wards] giving it again to the Master [who] setteth it upon so many of [the guests'] heads as he liketh at that table'. Then the garland goes the rounds of the past masters, and finally arrives at the new master for that year. The 'garland' was made of silver, not greenery, but even so it must have stood up to a lot of handling; there is no absolute guarantee that everyone was completely sober as they put it on and off. It would have been so much simpler just to announce the name of the new master – but not nearly such fun.[18]

Two threads run through all the companies' records: the Queen's repeated demands for men and money. She had no standing army, and England was constantly threatened with invasion, or obliged to support its continental allies. Elizabeth's solution was a compulsory call-up. Every community, whether a City company or a parish congregation, was assessed to a certain number of men, who had to parade, fully armed and ready for war, at regular intervals. Splendid though it sounds, one has faint doubts of the efficiency of this fighting force in battle. The Earl of Leicester wrote to Walsingham in 1586 about the City contingents, who had been complaining about the experienced officers put in command of them. 'I see their service will be little except [unless] they have their own captains, and having them, I look for none at all by them when we shall meet the enemy.'[19]

The Drapers provided 90 soldiers including two whifflers (men who cleared the way for a procession) in June 1559. They supplied twenty more the next year, with seven bowmen and eight harquebutters. In 1562, 63 of them had to go overseas, to Le Havre. The company had to pay for their arms and clothes, and even board wages. By 1574, not surprisingly perhaps, the company's store of armour was in need of repair. In 1577 the company employed a surgeon, for the first time, to accompany its quota of 175 trained men and drummers and an ensign, all costing the company nearly £40. The numbers kept mounting. In 1580 the company produced 260 trained men to attend the muster at Mile End. There is a disquieting note here: a tip of 5s to 'the messenger bringing books published by the Company of Archers on the use of the long bow' – a bit late, surely? In 1586 the company was told to raise 347 soldiers, their quota of the 4,000 men to defend London against invasion. The continued use of bows was again evidenced by an entry in 1588: 'for feathering, new casing and girdling 144 sheaves of arrows, £1 6s 8d'.

During Elizabeth's reign the Drapers, who were a rich company, spent £775 on soldiers and their equipment, which of course was money saved to the Treasury.[20] The Carpenters, not a rich company, spent less. The total cost to them of the 1559 muster at Greenwich was 46s 5d, the same price as 'making the bowling alley', so it was cheap at the price. It included paying an armourer 8d 'to help arm the men' – could they not get into their armour without professional help? – and 'bread and drink for the men, 16d.' The 1560 muster at Westminster, 'before the Queen's grace', only cost 35s 10d, including eleven soldiers, two whifflers and three shirts of mail at 15d each. Either the Butchers enjoyed some kind of exemption, or their historian did not think musters were worth noting, with the sole exception of an entry in 1601 – 'received of Aveny Wood for being spared [excused] to be a wiffler, 40s'.[21] The editor of the Merchant Taylors' records may have taken much the same view; I cannot believe that the first time they were asked for armed soldiers was in 1577, when the Lord Mayor asked for '200 men, armed, dwelling within the City, to be provided by the more wealthy and able persons of this company'. This is a confirmation that the men whom the companies produced were not necessarily members of the company themselves; they could have been hired off the streets. The company was assessed to 395 men for the London defence force in 1585. Normal musters lasted only two or three days, except when the force went abroad, reluctantly. The standard of training would not have met with the approval of a modern sergeant-major, even though all males between the ages of 7 and 60 were supposed to keep themselves in training for just such a call.

In 1579 the Merchant Taylors were asked to supply 40 'men in blue jerkins to serve in Her Majesty's ships' – the royal attention was turning towards the cost of the Navy. The Leathersellers, not a rich company, had to pay £24 towards the cost of six warships and a pinnace, even after the 1588 victory over the Armada.

Not content with demanding warships and a ready-made army, Elizabeth milked the companies for money. The Drapers found themselves lending £4,000 to her, allegedly for six months; over the years the company parted with nearly £7,000 in this way.

Parishes

Another classification of Londoners was by where they lived, which would affect what they could expect and what they must do. For ecclesiastical purposes the unit was the parish, of which there were about 110 in the City. (Although this number should be finite, it varied slightly as one parish was divided in two, or another created, or abolished, after the dissolution of the monasteries.) Parishes varied widely in size and in prosperity. St Mary Colechurch in Cheapside, with about 50 households, was a fairly typical size for an inner-City parish.[22] Their boundaries had mostly been established in the twelfth and thirteenth centuries, and whatever reason for parochial limits had existed then had long been lost by the sixteenth century.

Each parish had to find from its congregation men prepared to take various offices. After the incumbent, the clerk was the most important official. A church in Eastcheap paid its clerk 15s in 1558, plus incidentals such as 'paid at divers times for my own drinking 12d' and 'writing of a deed and a will 3s 4d'.[23] Lambeth parish church was paying their clerk £6 12s 8d by 1585.[24]

Part of a parish clerk's job was to keep records of all christenings, weddings and funerals in the church, which had been compulsory since 1538, when Parliament passed an Act that was widely resented because it seemed to be laying the groundwork for some kind of taxation, which no Londoner ever likes paying. The constant reminders of this duty show how widely it was ignored. In 1598 the Archbishop of Canterbury, backed by the Queen, ordered that all such parish records that had been made since Elizabeth's accession in 1558 were to be copied into parchment registers – more work for the clerk. The extent to which this, like the earlier registers, was done is hard to judge, since so many have been destroyed by fire and war. But the chapel of the Tower of London has a register that makes chilling reading. The clerk obviously got bored with laboriously copying out 'hanged, drawn and quartered' time after time, so he abbreviated it to 'h d q'.

After the clerk in importance came the two churchwardens, who were responsible for administering the church finances and maintaining its fabric. The 'people's warden' was appointed by an 'open vestry' – an annual general meeting of all the parishioners, although normally only the hard core who were interested came – and the other by the incumbent. They gave their time without pay. When the new Poor Law came in, in 1601, they were assisted by Poor Law overseers.[25] These literate, numerate, public-spirited men were surely accessible to a serious enquirer, as a fund of information on the parishioners. As everyone left the church on a Sunday morning, what would be easier than to murmur to a churchwarden, 'I'm looking for a reliable supplier of hay, or bricks, or firewood – is so-and-so all right, would you say?'[9]

The Lambeth churchwardens took their duties seriously. In 1565 they 'laid out at the King's Head when we were chosen church-wardens, 4s 4d', and paper and ink, and 'writing out the Register Book of Christenings weddings and burials for the whole year' cost 3s 4d. In the next year, '24 persons at the King's Head when the churchwardens were chosen, 14s ... our breakfast when we made up these our accounts, 2s'. By 1597 the cost of choosing churchwardens at the King's Head had fallen to 5s. In 1603 one of them had a better idea, and gave the assembled company drinks at his own house: 6s. He happened to be the supplier of the Communion wine. Then there were walk-on parts for sidesmen, who assisted the churchwardens and were not paid, a beadle, and the sexton, who had to see that graves were dug and who was paid. At St Michael Cornhill it was the sexton, not the bellringers, who rang the curfew every night at eight.

The parishes too had to contribute their quota of armed men. The system worked in the same way as for the livery companies, and the Earl of Leicester's comment on the men supplied by the companies no doubt applied at least as much to the parish contingents. Every church had its stock of armour, which gave rise to constant worries. The meticulous accounts of the Lambeth churchwardens drew a clear, if sometimes hilarious, picture. In 1583, for instance, they paid 2s 6d 'unto 2 men for wearing the armour at the muster for 2 days'. In 1584 they paid '2 men to wear the 2 corselets [breastplates] at the muster and training of men at Streatham, 2s 8d' and two months later another 4s for two days' training at Croydon. They had peace and quiet for four years, then in 1588, the year of the Armada, there were five separate musters, totalling twelve days and costing Lambeth 33s. The musters must have been quite exhausting. The armour needed 'new riveting, 7d', and two men had to be paid 14d 'for going to Croydon to fetch the church armour after the breaking up of the camp', the brave warriors being apparently too tired to carry it back themselves.

How effective these gallant fighters and their armour would have been in war is hard to tell, especially if those wretched rivets gave way at the crucial moment.

Wards

The third way of classifying Londoners was by ward. Stow found it natural to describe London ward by ward in his *Survey* (which makes it a hard read until you can visualise the boundaries of each ward as he goes). There were 26, including since 1550 the borough of Southwark, which you would have thought would be called Southwark ward, but just to make it difficult Southwark was included in a new ward called Bridge Without: that is, outside, or on the other side of, London Bridge. A ward included several parishes, between four and eight. It elected an alderman, who held the office for life and was ex officio a member of the Lord Mayor's Court of Common Council, which administered the by-laws and street regulations. There were about 200 other Common Council men.

The Court of Aldermen, undiluted by other members, controlled the City's finances, ran its affairs generally, executed Elizabeth's orders conveyed to it by the Privy Council, and occasionally did battle, especially in the matter of playhouses, which the City was always trying to rein in, despite the royal favours they enjoyed.[26] The Court of Aldermen was astoundingly efficient. It was they who disseminated the royal view that 'no blue starch shall be used or worn by any of Her Majesty's subjects', by ordering the beadles of the various parishes within their jurisdiction to visit every single house to acquaint its occupants with their Queen's views. More importantly, the aldermen were entrusted, in 1593, to make 'with as great secrecy as may be … diligent search … within all parts in your ward' for foreigners, who were increasingly alarming City freemen by what was seen as unfair competition. The order required all this detailed information to be returned within four days, which demonstrates at least faith in the aldermen's power to deliver it.

The Lord Mayor's staff, based in the Guildhall, included sheriffs, the coroner, the City clerk, a common sergeant, and such exotic office-bearers as four common hunt esquires and four water bailiffs with an under water-bailiff, three sergeant carvers needed for all the feasts the Lord Mayor had to give, three meal weighers, four yeomen of the waterside and two yeomen of the wood wharves.[27]

Each alderman had two or three assistants or deputies, who took most of the administrative work of the ward off his shoulders while he was busy at the Guildhall. The ward also appointed various officials, such as constables, watchmen and scavengers, who kept the local government machinery functioning within the ward. The rich ward of Faringdon Within had twenty-seven constables and eighteen scavengers, its neighbour Faringdon Without had fourteen constables and eighteen scavengers, but the poorest ward, Lime Street, had only four of each. The constables were supposed to supervise the watchmen, who were supposed to patrol the streets all night, armed with a staff and a lantern, calling out at intervals that – if it was the case – 'All's well', with a weather report and a guess at the probable time.

Constables and watchmen were all notoriously inefficient. In Shakespeare's *Much Ado about Nothing*, Dogberry, the constable, gives the watch their orders, in what he thinks to be proper legal language: 'You shall comprehend all vagrom men; you are to bid any man stand, in the prince's name.' When the watch reasonably asks what to do if the vagrant won't 'stand', 'Why then take no note of him, but let him go ... The watch ought to offend no man, and it is an offence to stay a man against his will ...' So the watchmen decide to 'go sit here upon the church-bench till two, and then all go to bed'.[28] In *Measure for Measure* there's another comic constable, who had been in office for more than seven years; the men in his ward 'are glad to choose me for them; I do it for some piece of money'.[29]

Constables were supposed to organise the 'hue and cry', the pursuit of a suspected thief by a posse of public-spirited – and fleet-footed – citizens. But the citizens tended to say, 'God restore your loss! I have other business at this time' and opt out.[30] Another of the constables' duties was to whip miscreants 'till the back be bloody'; perhaps they were better at that.

Servitors and retainers

Before the Wars of the Roses a land-owning magnate had been able to impose his will on his neighbours by the hundreds of armed retainers in his pay. These private armies had been discouraged by the Tudors, but medieval habits persisted, even though warlike intent had gone. The Earl of Shrewsbury brought 100 men with him when he came to town, and his friend Lord Talbot went to pay him a social call with 60 horsemen. The Earl of Oxford came up to London in 1562 with 140 mounted retainers, all demonstrating their allegiance to him by wearing his livery.

These men were not like the huge staffs of indoor and outdoor servants that a rich Victorian kept, who each had a useful function, even if it was only to look after fellow-servants higher up the pecking order. According to Harrison, writing as late as the 1580s, these Elizabethan men congregated in 'great swarms of idle serving men ... No nation cherisheth such store of them as we do here in England, in the hope of which maintenance many give themselves to idleness, that otherwise would be brought [forced] to labour and to live in order, like subjects.' Instead of working, a servitor 'carried a buckler [shield] at his back which hung by the hilt or pummel of his sword which hung before him', and swaggered about the streets looking for trouble. It was surprising how rarely they found it. 'Seldom [was] any man hurt, for thrusting was not then in use.' The sword was a weapon that needed space in which to take a swing at your enemy. Thrusting or stabbing, the 'deadly fight of rapier and dagger' which was gradually displacing sword play, was much more likely to be fatal, in crowded streets and tavern brawls. But the message had changed: tiresome though they might be, these men were not likely to threaten the stability of the state.

The idea of retainers lived on. The employer of a servitor could be identified – the usual passion of the Elizabethans for categorising people – by the livery worn by him, and a licence had to be obtained from the Crown, to maintain liveried retainers. Elizabeth licensed Burghley to keep household retainers in 1561, 'each of them to wear a livery badge'.[31] In 1582 a man called Johnson wrote to Walsingham that he 'desires to have his honour's cloth for a livery this year, for it is a great comfort to be known to be one of his servants'.[32] Walsingham was perhaps the most powerful Crown servant after Burghley, and we do not know who Johnson was, but clearly he thought it would help him, to be able to dress so that everyone would know he had a powerful backer.

The various companies of players shared Johnson's view. Under an Act of 1572, 'all common players ... not belonging to any baron of this realm or [to] any other person of greater degree ... shall be adjudged and deemed rogues, vagabonds and sturdy [i.e. able to work] beggars' to be punished severely. But 'belonging to' did not mean 'being employed or paid by'. James Burbage, the principal owner-manager of the time, promptly wrote to the Earl of Leicester on behalf of his company, asking him to 'retain us as your household servants ... not that we mean to crave any further stipend or benefit at your Lordship's hands but [except] our liveries as we have had, and also your honour's licence to certify that we are your household servants when we shall have occasion to travel amongst our friends as we do usually once a year'. He got his wish, and the company became known as Lord Leicester's men. Two years later he did even better, when the Queen herself gave the company her royal licence to present plays,

> as well for the recreation of our loving subjects, as for our solace and pleasure when we shall think good to see them ... within our City of London and ... throughout our realm, provided that the said ... stage plays be by our Master of the Revels ... before seen and allowed [i.e. they had passed the censor] and that the same be not ... shown in the time of common prayer, or in the time of great and common plague in our City of London.

The Lord Mayor must have ground his teeth with rage. Other companies were able to find similar sponsors, and became known as Sussex's, Warwick's, Essex's and Oxford's companies, but none achieved Burbage's success with the Queen.[33]

CHAPTER 14

Crime, Punishment
and the Law

The underworld

The nave of St Paul's Cathedral was a general meeting place, like an Italian piazza with a roof. It was packed with men doing business deals, prostitutes touting for customers, servants looking for jobs, innocent sightseers and criminals. You should avoid a 'courtesy man' or confidence trickster, and a 'cheater or fingerer', well-dressed and persuasive, who pick on innocent 'young gentlemen which are sent to London to study the laws' and lure them into crooked card games.[1] You might be accosted by a 'whipjack', with a sad story of shipwreck, or a 'demander for glimmer', begging because her home was burned down and she was destitute, so she said.[2]

There is a sad story of a country gentleman who came to London to look for a wife. To dress the part, he invested £57 in a gold chain, and went off to Paul's, where of course he was immediately spotted. An apparent well-wisher persuaded him to take his chain off and put it in his sleeve, for safety. Soon after, there was a fracas, at the end of which the well-wisher and the chain had gone.[3] Another countryman gazing about him was spotted by a gang of three. The first man pretended to recognise him and invited him to have a drink. If the countryman had the sense to refuse, and looked like a good prospect, the next man in the gang took over. There was still a third man in reserve, and it needed a strong-minded countryman to resist three successive approaches. Off they all went to the tavern, for a friendly card game – with the inevitable result.

There were pickpockets and sneak thieves everywhere, in Paul's and the Royal Exchange and round about the playhouses and animal-baiting rings, and during church services, and even at the law courts themselves, where 'the term-time is their harvest', especially in cases involving unsophisticated country folk too intent on following the sophistries of the law to look after their own property. Ballad singers collected crowds; their confederates watched the crowds. If trade was slack, one of the gang would warn the crowd to 'look to their purses ... which made them often feel where their purses were, either in sleeve, hose or at girdle, to know whether they be safe or no', an invaluable guide to a skilful thief.[4]

Just like honest craftsmen, thieves had their company, which handled their contributory pension fund. Many of them lived in the ruinous buildings of the Savoy. Others favoured Islington, especially in winter when the brick kilns there provided warmth. There was a training school for pickpockets and cutpurses near Billingsgate, run by

> Wotton, a gentleman born and [formerly] a merchant of good credit ... there were hung up two devices; the one was a pocket, the other a purse. The pocket had in it certain counters and was hung about with hawks' bells and over the top did hang a little sacring-bell [the bell formerly rung in church, at the elevation of the host]; and he that could take out a counter without any noise was allowed to be a *public foister*; and he that could take a piece of silver out of the purse without the noise of any of the bells, he was adjudged a *judicial nipper*.[5]

Criminal law enforcement

There was an ugly moment in 1589 when Drake's ships came home from Portugal without the prizes they had hoped for. Hundreds of disgruntled sailors and soldiers made for London, where they threatened to loot St Bartholomew's Fair. The authorities took fright and mobilised 2,000 militiamen, and the soldiers and sailors and 'masterless men' – those bogeys of the Elizabethans – had to go home quickly or risk execution.[6]

Normally the enforcement of law was the function of the energetic constables we have seen in Chapter 13, aided by professional informers. The emphasis on rank so typical of Elizabethan society applied here: the reward for information about the perpetrators of certain crimes varied from £40 to £100, depending on the rank of the informant. This cosy *modus vivendi* was abruptly disturbed by William Fleetwood, the City's Recorder between 1571 and 1591. He would galvanise the local magistrates into joining him in person in a search for criminals, district by district and usually at night, rounding them up by the hundred and consigning them to Bridewell for summary punishment or to prison for a more formal trial. 'Upon Friday last we sat at the Justice Hall in Newgate [the forerunner of the Old Bailey] from 7 in the morning until 7 at night, where were condemned certain horse-stealers, cutpurses and suchlike to the number of 10, whereof 9 were executed ... upon Saturday in the morning.' There were no complaints of the law's delay where Fleetwood was concerned.

Minor offences

Justices had power to impose fines, and to consign an offender for a limited time to the house of correction at Bridewell to labour on the treadmill, grinding corn for the poor, or to pick oakum for the use of the Navy. Offences against the current idea of public decency were punished by a kind of naming and shaming that cost the state nothing. On 19 January 1560, Machyn saw a baker 'ride in a cart for fornication, divers times proved'. The baker probably had to bear the jeers of the crowd, as he was carried through the crowded streets wearing a placard detailing his offences. Two months later Machyn saw 'a woman that was bawd [procuress] to a girl of 11 years old, and brought her to a stranger', being carted, this time 'with a basin tingling before' to make sure no one ignored her. The landlady of the Bell in Gracechurch Street and another tavern landlady were both carted for being bawds and whores, and a brother and sister were carted for incest. A variant on carting was to tie the offender on to his horse, facing backwards, with the account of his crimes for all to see.

A servant girl got off lightly for 'giving her masters and her household poison'; she was pilloried twice, both her ears were cut off, and she was branded on the forehead, but as long as she did not die of septicaemia she survived. A man was pilloried for making a 'fray in St Paul's church, and his ear nailed to the post, and after[wards] cut off', and another man who had arranged a contract killing was pilloried twice, losing an ear each time. A woman was 'set in the stocks at Newgate Market with certain files and other instruments which she brought to Newgate [prison] to file the irons off [her husband's] legs'. I cannot believe she attracted much public opprobrium for such wifely devotion, and the worst thing about being stocked was the mud and missiles the crowd threw, if it disapproved of the offence.

A surprisingly lenient sentence was imposed on an ex-inmate of Bedlam, 'for he said he was Christ', and another man who 'said he was the same Peter that did follow Christ'. Perhaps they were so wrapped up in their religious mania that whipping seemed quite natural to them. A much more serious offence was forging the handwriting of Lord Robert Dudley, for which a man was 'whipped about Westminster and through London and over London Bridge and Southwark', a truly purgatorial journey when you remember that the constable had to whip hard enough to make the poor man's back bloody.

More serious punishments

'To use torment ... or question by pain and torture ... is with us greatly abhorred.'[7] Abhorrent to William Harrison it might be, but it happened. If you were a Catholic priest, there were seven different kinds of torture waiting for you in the Tower of London.[8] The Pit was a hole 20 feet deep, totally dark. The Little Ease was a cave too small to stand upright in. The Rack 'by means of rollers and other machinery tears a man's limbs asunder' – not literally: at its most extreme it would snap the ligaments, causing excruciating pain. The Scavenger's Daughter was an iron band that compressed the head and feet into a circle; iron gauntlets crushed the hands, fetters were loaded on the arms, and irons were fitted to the feet. These were the standard torture methods, for which an official order had to be obtained. Sidelines such as needles pushed under the nails were left to the discretion of the 'examiners'. In 1592 the government was jittery about the mounting anti-foreigner feeling, especially the threatening handbills that were appearing everywhere. The Privy Council ordered the City to find out where they were coming from, using torture 'if necessary'.[9]

Slavery, too, was un-English, but like torture it happened. There were three galleys in the Navy in 1562, to which prisoners could be consigned from 1598 if they looked strong enough to row.

A curiously varied bunch of crimes was punishable by death. Buggery had been a capital offence since 1540, so were murder, manslaughter, treason, rape, felony, sodomy, stealing hawks, witchcraft, desertion in the field, highway robbery and letting out of ponds.[10] Capital punishment was usually by hanging. A contemporary estimate was that 300 executions a year were carried out, making it almost worth employing a regular hangman; but in practice a butcher was detailed to act as executioner.[11] The criminal was seated in a cart with one end of a rope round his neck, the other tied to the gallows. When the cart moved on, he was left hanging. To hasten his end, his friends mercifully pulled on his legs.[12]

In 1588, the Armada year, when Elizabeth was anxious to eradicate any pro-Catholic sympathy, 11 priests were hanged, two at Mile End, two in Lincoln's Inn Fields, one each at Clerkenwell and the Theatre, and the rest at Tyburn.[13] They were hanged for threatening Elizabeth's rule, which was treason, not burned for heresy. Sometimes the jury ordered another location, such as the scene of the crime.

> A new pair of gallows [was] set up [outside] the west door of Paul's, and between 9 and 10 of the clock afore noon [two murderers] were brought thither by the sheriffs and there hanged till 4 at afternoon: and so the hangman cut them down and carried them into St Gregory churchyard and there was a grave made and so they were stripped of all and tumbled naked into the grave.[14]

They were lucky: some wilful murderers were 'hanged alive in chains' and left there 'till [their] bones consume to nothing'.

For heinous crimes such as treason, hanging alone was not enough. Here is where the butcher's professional skills were useful. The prisoner was cut down while still alive, and disembowelled, the heart burned, the head cut off and the body divided into four pieces for distribution around the City. Somehow the blood is still chilled by the matter-of-fact picture of an average Londoner who met some notorious Catholic recusant priests on their way to their deaths. 'After morning prayer, [he was] riding through Cheapside, [when] there came one Edmund Campion [and others] drawn upon hurdles to Tyburn.'[15] A special ritual awaited pirates; they were hanged at Wapping 'at the low water mark, there to remain till three tides had overflown them'.[16] This really seems rather futile – they died of hanging, not drowning; polluting for the fish and not good for the tourist trade coming up-river on the Long Ferry.

Poisoners were burned at the stake, or 'boiled to death in water or lead, although the party [intended victim] died not of the practice'.[17] On 1 March 1590 'a wench was burned in St George's Field ... for poisoning of her mistress and others'.[18] Heretics were still burned alive, although the nature of heresy had changed since poor Catholic Mary had tried to save her subjects' souls by burning their Protestant bodies. In 1572 'two Dutchmen anabaptists were burnt in Smithfield who died in great horror with roaring and crying'. Sometimes heretics were merely deported.[19] In 1585, 53 seminary priests were deported to France.[20] Suicide was still a crime, but since the criminal had escaped, punishment had to be inflicted on the corpse. In 1588 a coroner ordered that a suicide's body 'should be carried from her ... house to some cross way near the town's end and there ... have a stake driven through her breast and so be buried with the stake to be seen, for a memorial that others going by, seeing the same, might take heed'.[21]

Criminal trials were fast. If an accused person could get a word in edgeways in this judicial quickmarch, there were various escape routes. A woman could 'plead her belly', alleging that she was pregnant. It would not be lawful to kill her unborn child as well as its mother, so her execution was delayed until she was no longer pregnant, and with any luck she might be discharged, or lost in the system, in the interim. A man might be able to claim benefit of clergy. He did not have to be a clergyman, he only had to be able to read. This was an ancient rule that had survived the Reformation. Before the spread of literacy, anyone who could read at all was likely to be a priest or cleric, and if found guilty of a crime he was handed over to the Church authorities for punishment. They might impose a lesser sentence, such as branding on the hand, for a crime that the civil authorities regarded as a capital offence, so it was well worth trying, especially because the test was merely to read one verse of a psalm. But you could only use this once. On 8 March 1560, eleven criminals were hanged: one was a priest, 'for cutting of a purse of 3s, but he was burnt in the hand afore, or else his book would have saved him'.[22] (Benefit of clergy was not abolished until 1847, but the list of offences for which it could *not* be claimed grew longer and longer.) Sometimes a royal pardon came before the sentence was carried out – sometimes at the last minute, or even later, and always unpredictably.

The notorious *peine forte et dure* did not deflect punishment, but had the merit of preventing the goods of the accused person from becoming the property of the Crown in the event of a guilty verdict, and for that reason alone some brave men who wanted to save their families from penury deliberately chose not to plead either guilty or not guilty at their trial, but to remain silent. They died, slowly and painfully, lying under huge stones and starving, allowed only a little stale bread and a sip of foul water at intervals, until death came.[23]

Imprisonment is absent from this list of punishments. Prisons were used for holding accused persons before their trial, and for some minor offences, but their main function was in the administration of the civil, not the criminal, law.

The civil law

Before your case came to court it was well worth your while to mobilise any influence you could muster. A book of model letters includes one to a judge 'wherein is recommended the cause and speedy furtherance of justice – "I have been informed by this bearer, being a poor tenant of mine, of a certain cause [lawsuit] of his depending [pending] before you in her Majesty's Court of King's Bench." ' The letter goes on to explain that the other side keeps getting the case adjourned, and so 'I have thought good upon his humble suit to move your lordship in his behalf' and please will the judge not grant any more adjournments.[24] The letter does not quite ask the judge to find in favour of the writer's tenant – perhaps that would be a bit risky in a published book – but a little careful tinkering should produce an appropriate draft. Thomas Wotton, a prosperous citizen,[25] was in the habit of writing to Burghley, Walsingham and others to ask for favourable judgements for his friends. He wrote to Sir Edward Hoby, a judge on assize, 'I do nevertheless towards this man in this matter entreat you to be as good as by the rules of justice you may conveniently be', which should not strain anyone's conscience.[26]

Once the hearing began, the court was likely to use a lot of archaic French words, pronounced in the inimitable English way so that a Frenchman could not understand them either. This was a hangover from the Norman Conquest – the law tends toward conservatism – which was not finally put to rest until 1650.[27] The other language of the courts was Latin, which should have presented no problems to an educated man. The three principal civil courts were all held in Westminster Hall, which, spacious though it was, cannot have made it easy to follow the proceedings if an advocate in an adjacent court had a loud voice. The Court of Star Chamber and the Court of Chancery, which sat elsewhere, had made the transition into the vernacular already; documents and arguments were in English and their procedure was more flexible.

If you were adjudged to owe money that you could not pay, you were sent to prison until you did. There were prisons scattered all over London – some worse than others, but all bad. They were kept by private individuals, who had no duty to feed prisoners or to look after them in any way. Two extremes can be seen, in the men traversing the London streets begging for 'food for the poor prisoners', with a box on their backs for food scraps, and on the other hand the diary kept by an Exchequer official, Richard Stoneley, who seems to have got into some temporary difficulty with his official accounts and was consigned to the Fleet prison in 1596.[28] He paid 15s a week rent for his 'chamber', and regularly entertained his wife and daughter, and friends, to meals, which – being in the habit of keeping records and having nothing else to record – he set out in detail, with their costs. Dinner could be a calf's head, roast veal, boiled beef, a woodcock, cheese and fruit, with plenty of claret and dry white wine ('canary sack'). A typical supper was a lettuce salad, roast mutton, roast lamb and three pigeons. He was, like so many prisoners, worried about what was happening in the outside world, so 'to the Warden of the Fleet [prison] for half a day abroad, 10d', and later 'this day I went to my house in Aldersgate Street … being the first time I came there since my confinement, [I] had with me Thomas Roche the Warden's man with Roper my friend'. That cost him 2s 8d. 'For one week's liberty abroad by the Warden's agreement, 3s 4d: to John King my keeper for going with me abroad this week, 2s 6d'. It is endearing to see 'to a decayed gentleman in the Fleet to relieve him, 12d', although one feels Stoneley could have made it more.

Imprisonment for debt provided no way for the debtor to raise any money, and weighed on the consciences of decent citizens. The only way out, for a poor man, was through charity. The records of

St Aldgate's parish contain many instances, such as the case of John Kiste 'who heretofore hath been an owner of good shipping and of good wealth, and is now by sundry losses fallen into utter decay and poverty, and being also greatly indebted is committed to the Marshalsea [prison], where he remaineth in great misery, likely to perish unless he may be relieved with the benevolence of charitable persons'. The parish raised 2s 3d, but a similar appeal was made in all the other City parishes, so we will never know whether John Kiste was released, or died in prison. A pathetic plea came from another prison, in 1580. The addressee is unknown:

> In all lamentable manner, most humbly beseech your good worship, we the miserable multitude of very poor and distressed prisoners in the hole of Wood Street Compter, in number 50 poor men, or thereabouts, lying upon the bare boards, still languishing in great need, cold and misery, who by reason of this dangerous and troublesome time be almost famished ... and hunger-starved to death: others very sore and diseased for want of relief and sustenance by reason of the great number which daily increases, do in all humbleness ... beseech your good Worship even for God's sake to pity our poor lamentable and distressed cases ...[29]

One more contemporary picture, from Philip Stubbes:

> The Lawyers they go ruffling in their silks, velvets and chains of gold ... It grieveth me (walking in the streets) [to hear] the pitiful cries and miserable complaints of poor prisoners in durance for debt and like so to continue all their life, destitute of liberty, meat, drink ... and clothing to their backs, lying in filthy straw and loathsome dung, worse than any dog ...[30]

A more cheerful scene: the 'bawdy courts'. Surprisingly, these were the ecclesiastical courts, which unlike the civil and common law courts recognised the separate existence of women, who suddenly step into the limelight. In the 1570s the plaintiffs in half the cases brought before these courts, involving questions of marriage and sexual assaults, were women, and so were half the witnesses. The court sat in the long chapel in St Paul's Cathedral, and 'going to Paul's' or to 'the bawdy court' meant invoking that court's jurisdiction. Most cases were settled at an early stage, but some went as far as taking evidence from witnesses. Their testimony was carefully recorded by the clerk to the court, whose vocabulary was probably widened as he wrote down the evidence word for word. 'Whore', 'knave' and 'cuckold' were commonplace enough, but the clerk's pen faltered on the many colloquialisms for sexual intercourse, which he rendered as 'occupying' – a word these litigious ladies certainly never used for it.

In 1587 John Lysbie, the parson of St Margaret Pattens, was alleged by a parishioner to have 'had thy pleasure and use of me, and in occupying me thou didst use me more ruffianlike than honestly'. A year later he was in trouble again, this time as a complainant. Another parishioner, Richard Baker, had insulted him in words 'tending towards the peril of his life if they had been true', which looks like an imputation of buggery, at that time a capital offence. In that case, unlike many of the others, we know the result, a curious one to modern minds. Richard Baker was ordered to provide Lysbie's wife and servant with paying work, sewing hose for him – he must have been a shopkeeper selling such things, and the Lysbie household needed the money. Presumably he apologised, as well.[31]

Statutes, proclamations and the Custom of London

We are so accustomed to the stream of legislation issuing from Parliament that it is startling to see how few laws were enacted during the whole of Elizabeth's long reign. She found the comments of her loyal Members of Parliament on her private life, in particular on her duty to marry, infuriating and unnecessary, so she did without Parliament as far as possible – a habit adopted by her successors with such enthusiasm that it led to the Civil War in the next century. The proper function of Parliament, in her view, was to provide money for governmental purposes, and this she found elsewhere, as far as possible, especially in the City. But there were questions that needed the assent of the nation, signified by the Commons and the Lords, including the bishops. The powers of the Crown had to be recognised under the Act of Supremacy. Labour relations and the apprenticeship system needed tightening up: the comprehensive Statute of Artificers of 1563 was a masterpiece of legislation, but it did not apply to the City, and in any case suffered the fate of much idealistic legislation in not being fully applied. From 1576 onwards the problems of unemployment and poverty were addressed in a series of Acts.

What surprises anyone looking for statute law in the Elizabethan era is not only its absence, but how it was replaced by direct rule from the throne through the monarch's Privy Council. For example, when Elizabeth came to the throne she was determined to avoid religious faction, so she made clear to her subjects what she expected them to do, by the exercise of her personal power as monarch – not through Parliament. She was faced with an incipient currency crisis caused by successive debasements of the coinage resorted to by every ruler since Henry VIII. She, or rather her adviser Burghley, dealt with it decisively in 1560 by calling in and re-coining all silver and gold coins in circulation, putting business transactions on a sounder footing than for many years and incidentally netting the Crown a considerable profit. The injection of 26,000 pounds of Spanish gold must have helped the country's economic state perhaps as much as the rectification of the existing currency. The changeover to the new currency was enforced by the livery companies on behalf of the Queen: their representatives were to 'walk in every market, with a white rod in their hands', to see that only the new currency was changing hands.[32] It was essential that this complicated exercise should go through quickly and smoothly,[33] so in March 1562 a new offence was created by proclamation: 'no man should dare to speak of [the] falling of money but they should be put in prison three months and after had to the pillory'.

The Custom of London had evolved over centuries, as the City grew in power until it was almost an autocracy within the realm. It provided a complete civil code, governing every relationship between its citizens. How should the relationship of master and servant or apprentice be regulated? If a tenant improved the premises during his occupation, what compensation was he entitled to on the termination of his lease? When a man died, how should his property be divided between the members of his family? For all such questions, an answer could be found in the Custom of London.

CHAPTER 15

The Poor

The welfare system

If you slipped through all the networks, what happened to you? Good Christians have always recognised their duty to give to the poor. But 'was there ever, in any age, the like number of poor people as there are at the present [1582], begging in the streets of the City and wandering in the fields so idly, being ready to attempt any mischief upon any light occasion?'[1] Philip Stubbes lamented, the next year, that 'the poor lie in the streets upon pallets of straw ... or else in the mire and dirt'.[2] Something surely had to be done. But if it was, the problem would only get worse. London was already faced with relieving not only its own poor but 'the poor that from every quarter of the realm do flock to it'.[3]

The monasteries used to look after the poor, but Henry VIII had stopped that when he wound them up and appropriated their wealth. He dealt with the resultant crisis in poverty management by generously allowing the impotent poor to beg, at no expense to the state, as long as they had a licence. (Four words that constantly crop up in this subject need to be clarified before we go any further. 'Impotent' just meant unable to work, disabled; 'sturdy' was the opposite, able to work; it was often linked with 'idle', refusing to work although able-bodied; and 'vagabond', which nowadays has a romantic overtone, should be read as 'vagrant'.) By 1552 the problem was of such a scale that the parochial poor rate was introduced to supplement individual begging. Parliament required every parish to appoint collectors, to 'gently ask' all the parishioners who could afford it, to give alms for the poor. Their self-assessments

were entered in a register and they were reminded in church the
next week, if they failed to pay up.

In 1563 the 'gentle asking' turned into a general statutory obligation backed by imprisonment if a proper payment was refused. But
still the poor insisted on being poor, and annoying prosperous
citizens. In 1569 the City attacked the problem by ordering 'all idle
persons and begging people, whether men, women or children, or
other masterless vagrants' to be sorted into categories and stowed
out of sight in institutions. The able-bodied beggars and vagrants
were to go to Bridewell where they would, willy-nilly, receive work
experience. The sick and impotent were to go to St Bartholomew's
and St Thomas's hospitals, orphans and foundlings to Christ's
Hospital. Hopeful economic immigrants were to be stopped at the
City gates and sent on their way.[4]

The example set by London was followed by a general Act of 1572
'for the punishment of vagabonds and for the relief of the poor and
impotent', elaborated by later Acts in Elizabeth's reign, which formed
the basis of the national poor law until 1834. From 1576 Overseers
of the Poor were to be appointed, and the Justices of the Peace,
Elizabeth's workhorses, were to register all 'poor, aged and impotent
persons' born in their districts, or living there for the last three years,
and get them housed, at the cost of the other residents.[5]

Four years later an Act for the Setting on of the Poor on Work and
for the Avoiding of Idleness was passed. The parents of illegitimate
children were to be traced and compelled to maintain their off-
spring. 'To the intent Youth may be accustomed and brought up in
labour and work', raw materials such as flax and wool were to be
issued to poor people on benefit, for them to spin; they would be
paid 'according to the desert of the work' – a botched job meant no
money, and nothing produced at all meant the newly established
house of correction. The Act took for granted that anyone would
have sufficient basic skill at spinning and other handwork to produce
a marketable result.

One of the foundations of the system was that a poor person
should stay in his or her own parish and be content with what was
available there, and not resort to economic migration. Harrison
described the system in place by 1597:

> With us the poor is commonly divided into three sorts, so that some
> are poor by impotency, [such] as the fatherless child, the aged, blind,

and lame, and the diseased person that is judged to be incurable: the
second [sort] are poor by casualty [mischance], [such] as the
wounded soldier, the decayed householder, and the sick person
visited with grievous and painful diseases; the third [sort] consisteth
of thriftless poor, [such] as the rioter that hath consumed all, the
vagabond that will abide nowhere ... and finally the rogue and
strumpet ...

If the first two sorts do not stay quietly at home and 'live within the
limits of their allowance (as each one will do that is godly and well
disposed) ... they are adjudged to be parcel of the third sort and so,
instead of courteous refreshing at home, are often corrected with
sharp execution and whip of justice abroad'.[6]

If this tidy system worked, why was Stubbes complaining so bitterly?
And how was it that William Fleetwood, the energetic Recorder of
London, could describe to Burghley in 1582 a most successful sweep
he had organised, which netted over 100 'rogues', of whom only
twelve came from London, the rest from all over England and Wales?
Was there perhaps a gap between the theory and the practice? It is
difficult to weigh Harrison's complacency against Stubbes' complaints, to tell how effective the system was in practice, but in theory
responsibility for helping the poor was finally transferred from the
Church to the state acting through local authorities.

Emergencies and single payments

No system can accommodate sudden crises. The meticulous accounts
kept by the churchwardens of Lambeth parish church show many
payments for emergencies not provided for by Harrison's tidy
demarcation.[7] 'A sheet to bury a poor man, 12d ... a sheet and for
bearers to carry a poor Irish woman to church, which died in
Fawkes Hall [Vauxhall, within Lambeth parish], 20d; for victuals for
her children, 14d; for the grave making and for the clerk, 6d; for
burying one of her children, 6d ...' The parish was not always so
open-handed. 'To conveying away a child that was brought to the
parish, 12d ... for two warrants for the remove of certain poor folks
that new came into the parish, 22d'; when it decently could, or
perhaps when those particular churchwardens felt particularly
parsimonious, a parish was not above shrugging off calls on its poor

box, to the next parish. This may explain the entry in the accounts of the churchwardens of St Michael Cornhill: 'Paid for carrying away a poor boy that lay under a stall, 2d.'[8]

But again, the parish could be generous. There are frequent payments for babies found in the parish, who were not consigned to Christ's Hospital. 'Paid to a poor woman that was delivered of a child in the Royal Exchange, 4s' – she certainly picked the right spot to go into labour – and 'paid to the poor woman that were brought abed in the alley, 3s, paid to Nicholas Payne for keeping of the said poor woman in his house, 3s 4d'. 'Paid for things necessary for a maiden child taken up about the conduit in Cornhill, 13s 3d, for nursing the said child 9 weeks, 12s.' The parish of St Botolph Without Aldgate had eleven foundling children on its books at one time. It had a regular arrangement with a joiner out at Hatfield Broad Oak, in Essex, who fostered several children, and even saw to their schooling, at 3d a week each. He had to 'bring the said children up to London that the Parish might see the said children' at regular intervals.[9]

Things were not always so easy for a woman in labour looking for an advantageous lying-in place in which to have her baby, and leave it: 'paid to a beadle and a woman for finding out of the mother of a child left in the parish, 4s 6d' – she had not covered her tracks well enough. And poor Mary Parry, a sailor's wife who lived in another parish,

> being sick was taken into the house of Reynold Burnett, a labouring man who lived in Hog Lane ... where [he] had, by the report of the neighbours, the sum of 14s [from the parish where she had fallen ill] to keep her in her sickness, and the said woman being on the point of death he carried her to the cage [temporary lock-up] in east Smithfield, where she died. He ... did gather certain money to bury her with, but the corpse being brought to the grave he paid the sexton 4 farthings.[10]

– and pocketed the rest. The 1593 accounts of the same parish tell a human story: 'paid to myself William Harrison [one of the churchwardens] by order of the vestry ... to the end I should keep, maintain and bring up orphan Michaell [she was a little girl], a foundling of this parish, and for that I should for ever discharge the parish of her, £6 13s 4d' – in other words, he adopted her.

Begging licences

Harrison thought the poor should be able to live 'within the limits of their allowance'. But he probably had not tried it himself; and the visibility of the rich, especially in London, never makes the lot of the poor any easier to bear. Surely there was a case for a slight transference of wealth, from the rich to the poor; the rich only needed an invitation to donate – such must have been the reasoning of many an enterprising beggar. But to be found begging without a licence was to risk prosecution, so first equip yourself with a licence.

The easiest way was to buy a forged one. This, of course, was as punishable as not having one at all, but the forgery might pass a cursory examination. One well-known begging gambit was to use a forged licence to wheedle money out of market women, saying it was for a hospital, which these good women with a little cash in their purses were often glad to give to.[11] In the progressive tightening-up of the system, from 1572 onwards, not only was anyone who could 'give no reckoning how he or she does lawfully get his or her living' to be treated as a vagrant, but all the colourful street people, such as men with performing bears, and jugglers, and fortune tellers, and pedlars, and street players had to get licences signed by two Justices of the Peace – an almost impossible task for them, one imagines, and unlikely to be free of charge. Scholars from Oxford and Cambridge had to get begging licences from their university. Discharged prisoners and mariners must have the proper documents to allow them to beg their way home. Otherwise they were all to be rounded up and sent to Bridewell. Common labourers refusing to work for reasonable wages should join them there – this was long before the days of trade unions.

Licences were also issued by the church authorities, such as the Bishop of London. They specified the area and the period covered. The area was usually limited to the London parishes, sometimes extending to adjacent areas within the Bishop's jurisdiction. The period varied between six months and two years. Where we would expect some sort of pension, an Elizabethan ex-serviceman had to beg: John Hammond, gentleman, 'being in great extremity and poverty and in respect of divers his good services done unto her Majesty as well in Ireland as in the Low Countries', got 3s 2d one Sunday, from St Botolph Without Aldgate parish church, which will have been noted on his licence.

Sunday after Sunday collections were made for men 'captived by infidels' or 'by the Turk', who were being held until their ransom was paid. William Hulls even managed to spy for England during his captivity by the Turks, and identify 'sundry traitors conspiring against our sovereign lady the Queen'. His captors 'most tyrannously' cut off his left arm because he refused to convert to Islam. His licence was unusual in that it applied country-wide, but it still seems a cumbersome way to raise a ransom of £70.

A sad story of student debt from the same parish:

> Thomas Awsten son to John Awsten, citizen and haberdasher of London, who hath bestowed his time hitherto in learning and hath in the University of Oxford proceded Bachelor of Arts, the charge whereof, as also of books and other things necessary for such a scholar such as he, being already by the charge of his late degree become indebted, and his father by pirates robbed and impoverished is unable to bear ...

This heart-rending tale realised 3s 8d, but one hopes that when other parishes' contributions came in, poor young Thomas became solvent.

Private charities

The impulse that had led medieval men to devote part of their wealth to charity through the Church still inspired post-Reformation merchants, but the machinery had to be different. Often the donor, who had come up from the countryside decades earlier to be bound apprentice and had made his fortune as a merchant, sent some of his fortune home again, to endow a school or an almshouse. But the poor of London outside his door usually benefited too. His widow might in her turn supplement his bequests, with more charitable giving of her own. It was normal for anyone with any substantial estate to devote some of it to charitable purposes, particularly the relief of poverty.

After the demise of the monastic system it was advisable to bring such bequests within the framework of legally recognised charities, which was formalised in the Charitable Uses Act of 1601. The list of charitable objects in the Act illustrates the problems of the day which a benevolent testator might consider: 'the relief of aged, impotent and poor people; the maintenance of sick and maimed soldiers and mariners ... the repair of ... churches, sea banks and highways ... education and preferment of orphans ... marriages of poor maids ... the relief or redemption of prisoners or captives'.

A livery company provided an efficient and permanent channel between the donor and the poor people who were to benefit. A typical arrangement was made by Sir Martin Bowes, Goldsmith and merchant, who died in 1566 leaving over £2,500 to charities, of which half was for the relief of poverty. This fund was vested in the Goldsmiths jointly with individual trustees who could exercise some personal discretion in allotting the payments. These immensely wealthy men were not above providing for small details in their wills. William Lambe, a member of the Clothworkers' Company, who died in 1580, left almost the whole of his fortune – £5,695 – to charity, including £6 to buy 120 pails so that 60 poor women could earn their livings as water-carriers. Robert Fleming, who died in 1568, was a member of the Salters' Company. Among his bequests to charity were £67 to the Fishmongers, to use the income to help poor people who relied on fish trimmings for their food, and a similar amount to the Butchers, for poor people who came to their shambles for meat refuse.[12]

As well as the munificence of rich men like Lambe, there were all kinds of small parochial charities, which might be good for a dole of bread, or coal, or even a cash handout.[13] If, as a poor person, you could get yourself into a rich man's funeral procession – the churchwardens and their beadle probably knew who should apply and where – you could pick up a black gown for wearing in the procession, and a square meal after the funeral. Gray's Inn gave out free food at the gates, three times a week, 'due consideration [to be] had to the poorer sort of aged and impotent persons', and no doubt other large establishments still followed this medieval custom.[14]

The sick poor

St Bartholomew's Hospital was founded by a monk, Rahere, in 1123, as part of a priory that survived for more than 400 years until Henry VIII.[15] It escaped his rapacity by the skin of its teeth, when the Lord Mayor persuaded Henry to transfer it to the City of London. Henry signed the Letters Patent two weeks before he died, in 1547. What the City got was a rambling complex of ex-monastic buildings, interspersed with green spaces, just outside the walls, looking on to Smithfield. What a generous gift. But instead of the expected provision for 100 poor people, there was only 'such as sufficed three or four harlots then lying in childbed'. The properties that had been granted with the hospital buildings, which should have produced a substantial endowment income, turned out to be 'some in great decay and some rotten ruinous', which was a blow for the City authorities, and some of the buildings in the hospital complex were already leased to secure tenants on unprofitable terms.

Undismayed, the governors set about getting the buildings into usable shape, and in 1552 issued a press release justifying their actions so far, and explaining their plans for the future.[16] The administrative machinery they had put in place was impressive, the more so since it was created from scratch. There were twelve honorary governors appointed by the Lord Mayor, who held office for two years only. They were charged to 'set apart [all your other business] as much as you possibly may: you shall endeavour to attend only upon the needful doings of this house, with such a loving and careful diligence as shall become the faithful ministers of God whom ye chiefly in this vocation are appointed to serve'. This was written during the ultra-Protestant reign of Edward VI, but even after Mary had come and gone, and the smoke of the Protestant martyrs had cleared from Smithfield, there remained this ethos of devout service.

The president, always an alderman, had general control of the running of the hospital. The other governors, some aldermen, some 'commoners' but all able and public-spirited businessmen, took on specific functions. The treasurer had to produce annual, audited accounts; four surveyors saw that the hospital's property was kept in good order and the tenants paid their rents and observed the conditions of their leases; four almoners kept records of admissions and discharges, and ensured that 'peace and quietness' reigned in the hospital. They undertook 'in your proper persons [to] visit [the patients] once every week at the least', to check that patients were getting their food and drink, and being kept 'sweet' (i.e. clean), an unusual condition for those days, especially for the poor. Lastly there were two 'scrutineers' responsible for fund-raising, and recording gifts and legacies.

The paid staff were the hospitaller, the chief executive, who was

34. The Earl of Leicester, c. 1575–80. By now codpieces were less noticeable. His doublet is still cut with a peasecod belly (see page 126). His beard and splendid moustache must have made his ruff even more uncomfortable.

35. 'Elizabeth Vernon, Countess of Southampton, at her toilet.' She is combing
her hair – hairbrushes were not yet used. Her carefully ironed ruff is pinned to the
curtain to keep it safe until she is ready to use it.

36. (LEFT) Detail, showing her jewel box, with several pieces awaiting her choice. The pincushion is filled with pins of different sizes (see pages 125, 133).

37. (BELOW) Lord Cobham and his family, painted by Hans Eworth in 1567. He wears a turndown collar, the two women wear ruffs and so do all the children, even the one-year-old twins (see pages 134, 183). Household pets such as monkeys and parrots were frequent, but I do not know whether it was usual to let them wander over the table at meal times, as here.

38. An engraving, c. 1570, of monkeys 'aping' the fashion for starched ruffs (see page 125 for the whole process). A satisfied customer stands in the middle of the workshop having his finished ruff adjusted.

39. An engraving of 1590 showing women dressing for a masque. Padded rolls are being tied round their waists under their skirts, to create the same outline as the lighter farthingales stiffened with reed or whalebone.

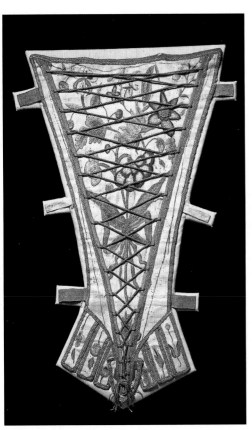

40. A sixteenth-century stomacher. The tabs down the sides were pinned or tied under the edges of the gown, the larger ones at the foot were arranged over the skirt waist.

41. Once the ruff had been seen to, there was not much ironing to do. Table linen and bed linen were folded neatly and pressed flat, in a press like this.

42. This sixteenth-century woodcut shows animal-baiting in Nuremberg. It will have been much the same in London, except that the animal-baiting houses were round, like playhouses. The bear is not cuddling the dog, but squeezing it to death.

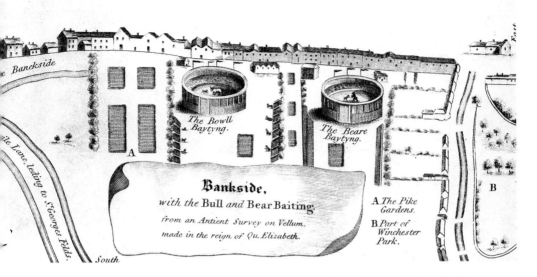

43. Bull-baiting and bear-baiting on Bankside. The rectangles marked A are described as the Pike-Ponds, for keeping the royal pike. B, part of Winchester Park, belonged to the Bishop of Winchester.

44. These serene old gentlemen are enjoying a game of primero. The cards look so modern, but were not so easy to play with as modern cards, which have rounded corners and smooth surfaces. The stakes are high – gold and silver coins lie on the table.

45. Miniature by Nicholas Hilliard of *A Young Man among Roses*, probably the Earl of Essex, in 1587. The legs are so beautiful – see page 126 – that one hardly notices the ugly peasecod belly. The cloak slung over one shoulder was a fashionable fad.

responsible for seeing that supplies were accounted for, admissions and discharges recorded, and even that any valuables or money brought in by the patients were noted and safeguarded, using any spare time for visiting and preaching to the patients; the renter clerk had to keep four carefully described books of account; and the steward or butler had to order and account for all provisions. If he saw anything going wrong in any other staff member's department, he was to tell one or two of the governors 'and to none other person nor further to meddle therein' – how wise.

The matron was 'the chief governess ... of this house'. She received patients from the hospitaller, and found them beds 'in such convenient places within this house as [she] shall think mete [suitable]'. She had to make sure that the nursing staff 'do their duty to the poor, as well in making of their beds and keeping their wards as also in washing and purging their unclean clothes'. The patients' bedding was one of her many concerns. Her contract, too, had that odd, wise, provision about whistle-blowing.

The twelve sisters – the nursing staff: their name was a survival from monastic times – were directly under the matron's command. Their first duty was to show themselves 'gentle, diligent and obedient' to the matron. Then 'you shall also faithfully and charitably serve and help the poor in all their griefs and diseases, as well by keeping them sweet and clean as in giving them their meats and drinks after the most ... comfortable manner. Also you shall use unto them good and honest talk such as may comfort and amend them ...' Fortunately when the hospital was divided from the rest of the priory buildings, which were sold off, it had managed to retain a share in the water supply of the priory, which came from the pure hills of Canonbury. This relieved the hospital from dependence on London water, so that keeping the patients 'sweet' was that much easier.

In their spare moments the sisters could spin the flax and wool issued by the matron, which would be woven by an outside contractor into sheets and blankets for the hospital. The hum of spinning wheels must have made a soothing noise in the wards. But the governors seem to have been uneasy about these women. They were to 'avoid, abhor and detest drunkenness' and 'so much as in you shall lie, ye shall avoid and shun the conversation and company of all men', which does seem asking a lot. For all that, they were paid 16d a week, rising to 18d in 1580.

Needless to say, no alcohol was allowed, although there was constant trouble with tenants of properties inside the hospital grounds who persisted in selling strong ale and beer to the patients. If a sister spotted anything going wrong, she could tell the matron or – perhaps if she needed to inform on matron herself – one or two of the governors, but 'neither shall you talk or meddle therein any further.' The governors themselves had been subjected to a sustained whispering campaign, which had prompted this public statement of the hospital's constitution, but it's still impressive to see such careful, explicit provisions for whistle-blowing.

There were three salaried surgeons ('chirurgiens', pronounced 'surgeon') on whose diagnosis depended the fate of every poor person hoping to be admitted. If the case was judged by two of them to be curable, the patient was admitted. No mention is made in the rules of bed shortages – presumably the matron had to admit them and stow them somewhere, on the equivalent of trolleys if necessary. Incurable cases were sent away, and any offer of a bribe had to be reported to the almoners. It looks as if the surgeons were 'on call' but did not have to attend the hospital full time.

For the patients, the hospital porter must have been a menacing figure, because after just one warning he could put in the stocks anyone swearing or blaspheming or showing contempt to the matron or any other officer, or refusing to go to bed at the proper time. There were eight beadles, who lent dignity to the governors' meetings, and otherwise patrolled the City and liberties looking for anyone infected with a 'loathly grief or disease, which [who] shall happen to lie in any notable place of this City, to the annoyance and infection of the passers-by, and slander of this house', sensitive as it was to its public image. They did not have to do anything themselves about such a horrid sight, such as moving the sufferer out of public view, or even bringing him into the hospital – they just had to tell the almoners.

The last staff member in the rules was the 'visitor of Newgate', who had no medical function at all. His anomalous duties included visiting and preaching to all the prisoners in Newgate, offering to arbitrate between them in civil cases such as imprisonment for debt, and in the surely surreal case of someone imprisoned in Newgate with money to spare, do some fund-raising for the hospital.

Admissions were on Mondays only. The authorised capacity was 100 inpatients. In 1588 this was increased to 120, but the actual number of patients somehow crammed into the hospital by then was 180. Bed occupancy seems to have been short: 442 patients on average were discharged as cured every year.[17] There were prayers twice a day, when those patients who could, had to kneel by their beds, and the bed-bound had to listen devoutly. Discharged patients had to kneel in the hospital's great hall and formally thank God and the hospital for curing them. They were given enough money to get them home, and clothes if they needed them, and a vital document – a passport authorising them to travel home without being treated as a vagrant.

The running costs of the hospital for 1552 amounted to £798 2s, met by 'King Henry's endowment' and the City equally, with a deficit of £120 paid by donations by 'certain merciful citizens'. The costs were carefully divided between foreseeable costs such as salaries and patients' food ('100 persons at 2d the person for every day'), and 'uncertain' costs such as

> for shirts, smocks and other apparel for the poor, needful either at their coming in or departure: for sugar and spices for caudles for the sick, flax for sheets and weaving of the same, soltwiche [?] cloth for winding sheets [shrouds], bowls, brooms, baskets, incense [this must have been for fumigating the wards], juniper ashes to buck [wash] their clothes, and also money given to the poor at their departure, which is measured according to their journey and need.

All that came to £60. The salary costs were comparable with those at Christ's Hospital. The surgeons did rather better, £20 each instead of £13 6s 8d, but the nursing staff were paid much the same in both places.

The treatment that the patients received was standard for the time. Probably rest, absence of lice, regular food and temporary freedom from the anxiety of poverty did them at least as much good as the medications to which they were subjected. The hospital's journals contain some interesting entries. In June 1558 a 'kettle' was bought 'for the surgeons to seethe [boil] and boil their necessaries in': an early autoclave? In 1555 the surgeons had asked for a 'hot house' for the patients 'to sweat in', which seems to have been built; it was listed in 1571. This was surprisingly advanced. Sweating chambers, which were like Turkish baths, were favoured by the rich, but these seem to have been viewed as therapeutic, and at least they got the patients clean for the first time in their lives, and eased the burden on the nurses of keeping their patients 'sweet'.

The prestige of the hospital attracted some eminent men. A resident physician had been added to the medical staff by 1572. Until 1580 he was Roderigo Lopez, a Portuguese who had found asylum in England from the Inquisition. He was appointed chief physician to the Queen in 1586, but he unfortunately upset Essex, who accused him of plotting to poison the Queen, and he was executed on shamefully flimsy charges, backed by evidence obtained by torture, in 1594.[18] One of his colleagues was Timothy Bright, a protégé of Walsingham, who was appointed to St Bartholomew's in 1585, where he continued his medical researches into melancholy. Unfortunately he was obsessed with inventing the first system of shorthand, 'Characterie', which was not at all 'short' and was soon overtaken by better systems. Meanwhile, however, the governors of the hospital, perhaps mindful of their own duty to concentrate on hospital business to the exclusion of private matters, sacked him for 'neglecting his duty about the poor of this house' and he went off to be a parson instead.[19] The surgeon William Clowes (see below) was appointed to the staff in 1575. Among his many specialities was the care of syphilis, and he was able to boast that 'in the hospital of St Bartholomew in London there has been cured of this disease by me and three others, within five years, to the number of 1,000 and more'.[20]

The fate of those whom the surgeons diagnosed as incurable is less known. They probably applied to St Thomas's Hospital over the river, if they could get there. (Unfortunately the records of St Thomas's Hospital are not so accessible as those of St Bartholomew's.) The hospital of St Thomas the Apostle had been founded in 1213 in Southwark as an almshouse, by the Prior of Bermondsey. Like St Bartholomew's, it was refounded after the Dissolution, this time by Edward VI, in 1551, for 'the curing and sustenation of ... poor, sick and weak people'. By 1553 St Thomas's was ready for 300 'aged, lame and sore' patients, falling to 200 in 1587, but still more than St Bartholomew's. Its running costs were £900, and it was discharging as 'cured' 400 patients a year. One thing you could be sure of, there, was incongruously fine linen: Edward VI ordered that all the pre-Reformation church linen should be sent there, except surplices and Communion tablecloths, 'which linen did great service'.[21] There were six surgeons on its staff, each paid £15 a year, one physician paid £13 6s 8d, and between 15 and 25 sisters. They seem to have been perhaps less 'obedient to matron' than their colleagues in St

Bartholomew's – or else the historians of the two institutions chose different details to immortalise. Margaret Allen was sacked in 1563 'for that she would not do her duty in her office but run to the tavern and neglect her office', and Ann Reader was sacked for the same failing, after three warnings.[22]

Not all of the patients flourished there; just like the first children admitted to Christ's Hospital, 'being taken from the dunghill, when they came to sweet and clean keeping and to a pure diet, [they] died right down, and so likewise the poor aged and other in the hospital died'.[23] The hospital had been handsomely – but still inadequately – endowed, and it also received individual payments from the parish where a patient lived, as in the case of Francis Pemberton, 'a poor boy born in this parish and now being in St Thomas Spittle in Southwark and having his leg cut off'. The parish made a lump sum payment of 6s, and an allowance of 12d a week during his stay.[24]

The demarcation between the two great hospitals for the sick poor is not clear. Harrison assumed that 'the aged, blind and lame, and the diseased person that is judged to be incurable' could find a home somewhere, and as we have seen, St Bartholomew's turned away anyone its surgeons did not think they could cure, so presumably St Thomas's took them, as well as curable patients. Thus, there was a splendid, comprehensive, welfare system in place. Yet –

> Why do the streets yet swarm with beggars, that no man can stand or stay in any church or street but presently 10 or 12 beggars come breathing in his face, many of them having their plague sores and other contagious diseases running on them? … What is the cause that so many little pretty children, boys and girls, do wander up and down the streets, loiter in Pauls, and lie under hedges and stalls in the night?[25]

I have no answer.

CHAPTER 16

Religion, Superstition, Witchcraft and Magic

A baby girl born in 1520, while the Pope was still the head of the Church in England, was still under 40 when Elizabeth succeeded her sister Mary. This child had grown up during Henry's religious tantrums, his son Edward's devout Protestantism and his daughter Mary's equally devout Catholicism.[1] She must have wondered what would happen under the new queen. The importance of this question to ordinary people, and the pervasive importance of religion, are difficult to imagine, for a twenty-first-century person in a preponderantly secular society.

Elizabeth was a widely read and intelligent woman with a highly developed political sense. During the sometimes dangerous years before she came to the throne, she must have considered carefully what line she would adopt on the subject of religion. Her subjects urgently needed religious peace more than any more doctrinal switches. Mary died on 17 November 1558. The transfer of power to Elizabeth went smoothly. Mary's body was buried with full Catholic rites, on 14 December. At the end of December, Elizabeth issued a holding proclamation on religious matters, until 'consultation may be had by parliament'.[2]

Her first parliament assembled on 23 January 1559. First on the agenda was the Act of Supremacy, the next was the Act of Uniformity. It was quickly clear that there would be no continuance of Mary's Catholicism: the clock would be turned back to Edward's Protestantism. Mary had managed to retrieve some of the monastic foundations so abruptly diverted to secular hands by her father. This was promptly reversed, and although the monks and nuns were offered life pensions and the chance to stay on if they would take the oath prescribed by the Act of Uniformity, that summer 'the friars of Greenwich went away ... the black friars [Dominicans] went away ... the priests and nuns of Sion House went away, and the Charter-house'.[3] England was no longer Catholic. Parliament went home, and did not meet again for four years.

The Elizabethan religious settlement

The full title of the Act of Supremacy is 'an Act restoring to the Crown the ancient jurisdiction over the state ecclesiastical and spiritual, and abolishing all foreign power repugnant to the same', which it did, in 24 detailed sections. Every lay and ecclesiastical official and every university graduate (later applied to every teacher) had to swear an oath 'that the Queen's Highness is the only supreme governor of this realm ... as well in all spiritual or ecclesiastical things ... as temporal, and that no foreign prince ... prelate ... or potentate hath any jurisdiction ... within this realm'. Refusal to swear was severely punished.

So much for the Pope. As to what English people were to believe, the Act for the Uniformity of Common Prayer and Divine Service in the Church and the Administration of the Sacraments, passed by a majority of only three votes, revived Edward VI's Book of Common Prayer, with minimal amendments. Divergence from it, or objections to it, could be punished in persistent cases by life imprisonment. Everyone had to attend their parish church to hear the prescribed service every Sunday – fine for non-attendance, 12d.

So what exactly were English people supposed to believe? This can be found, if you have the same edition of the Book of Common Prayer as I have, towards the end of it, under Articles of Religion. There are 39 of them, some more obscure than others. Original sin, free-will and predestination – favourite subjects for discussion in some circles – are defined in fairly inscrutable terms. All the sacraments are swept away, except for baptism and Communion. Transubstantiation, another much-debated doctrine, is dismissed: it 'cannot be proved by holy writ; but it is repugnant to the plain words of scripture ... and hath given occasion to many superstitions.'

(When pressed for her own views on transubstantiation, Elizabeth replied:

> His was the word that made it,
> He took the bread and brake it,
> And what that word did make it,
> That I believe, and take it –

which means as much, or as little, as you like.)

Every now and then something emerges clearly, such as that 'the Romish doctrine concerning Purgatory, Pardons, Worshipping and Adoration, as well of Images and Reliques, and also invocation of Saints, is a fond thing vainly invented' – the Roman Church had made a scandalous amount of money out of all that, but it had to stop. Only licensed clergy might preach, but there were homilies available that could be read to the congregation 'diligently and distinctly, that they may be understood of the people'. The flavour of the whole exercise can be savoured in the titles of these 21 homilies. Most of them deal with such predictable matters as good works and prayer, but every now and then the congregation had to sit through pointedly practical addresses on 'the repairing and keeping clean of churches', 'against excess of Apparel' and 'against Idleness'.

Early in 1559 the Queen issued injunctions to tidy up any loose ends. Licensed preachers had to give quarterly sermons reminding their congregation that 'the Queen's power within her realm ... is the highest power under God', and monthly sermons condemning pilgrimages and prayer beads as 'maledictions of God'. All shrines and paintings had to be destroyed 'so that there remain no memory of the same', and instead, the churchwardens had to provide a 'comely and honest pulpit'. Every parish had to buy a large Bible, in English, and a copy of Erasmus's *Paraphrases upon the Gospels*, as well as the Book of Common Prayer, and put them in the church for people to read 'out of the time of common service'. One can imagine how the unfortunate churchwardens struggled with old habits and new rules.

The familiar images and wall paintings had to go. 'All images, shrines, tabernacles, rood lofts and monuments of idolatry are removed, taken down and defaced.'[4] Between 1559 and 1561 the Church of St Margaret Moses spent 12d on 'a new service book' – the new Book of Common Prayer. A carpenter charged 13s 5d for 'taking down the rood loft', but the materials were sold for 22s and 'all the old copes and vestments, with the alb' fetched £5 10s, so the church made an overall profit from the changeover.[5] St Michael Cornhill paid out 11s for 'taking down the rood'.[6] St Andrew Hubbard got rid of its rood in 1560, at a cost of 6s, but it took another four years to pay a plasterer 3s 6d for three days' work in 'whiting [whitewashing] the chapel and the choir'.[7] Whitewashing was not always permanent, for which many a historian rejoices. There was a painting of the Passion, in Chichester Cathedral, that was duly whitewashed, but 'well-wishers' gently rubbed the whitewash away until 'it is almost as bright as ever it was'.[8]

There were bonfires everywhere, burning the images that had been so dear for so long. 'All the roods and Marys and Johns, and many other of the church goods, both copes, crosses ... banners ... and banner-stays with much other gear' were burned in the streets.[9] Lincoln's Inn took down the altar in its chapel in 1559, and seems to have moved the altar stone into the garden. This may have been a cautious move, in case it was wanted again, but by 1571 it seemed safe to sell it, for 5s.[10] The only things that remained from the old days were the gloriously coloured medieval windows, which 'for want of sufficient store of new stuff ... by little and little [are] suffered to decay, [so] that white glass may be provided and set up in their rooms [instead]'.[11] Sunlight threw the old colours on to newly whitewashed walls.

Absence from your parish church on Sunday was seen as a sign that you were a recusant, a Roman Catholic who supported Spain and the Pope, and were prepared to betray your lawful queen, so it raised questions of temporal loyalty as well as religious affiliation, and was tried as treason, not heresy.

Dissidents

It seemed as if the uproar emanating from both Protestants and Catholics might die away, as time went on, the older generation died out and the new religion was no longer novel, and people came to enjoy their ability to understand and take part in the service. But this calm was broken by the arrival of Catholic Mary Queen of Scots in 1568, and the papal Bull excommunicating Elizabeth, in 1570. In 1571 the importation of any papal Bull was made high treason, therefore punishable by hanging, disembowelling and quartering. Ten years later the same penalty was applied to Catholic proselytisers. Anyone saying or hearing mass could be fined heavily and imprisoned, and the fine for non-attendance at a 'usual place of common prayer' was increased to £20 per month, enough to deter anyone but the most devoted – and the richest – Catholic supporters.

But Catholic dissension was growing. A seminary, or training college, had been founded for English Catholics, at Douay[12] across the Channel, in the year of Elizabeth's accession, 1558. By 1574 a flood of 'seminary priests' was secretly infiltrating England. The most notorious was Edmund Campion, who was captured, tortured and executed under the Treason Acts in 1580. The tolerance that Elizabeth had imposed at the beginning of her reign was replaced, inexorably, by bloodshed and martyrdom. By the end of her reign 166 priests had died as traitors, and others had been banished or imprisoned. Camden wrote percipiently, 100 years later: 'Such were the times that the Queen (who was never of opinion that men's consciences were to be forced) complained many times that she was driven by necessity to take these courses unless she would suffer the ruin of herself and her subjects upon some men's pretence of conscience and the Catholic religion.'[13]

There was a running battle between the Queen and some of her bishops and clergy who inclined to the more extreme Protestant views of Edward VI's advisers, but they were never able to invoke the bogey of foreign intervention, comparable with the enmity of Catholic Spain. The main issue between the opposing sides was the matter of freedom of speech in the pulpit. Elizabeth profoundly distrusted the extempore inspiration that might lead a passionate preacher to advocate who knew what, in the heat of the moment – he might even go so far as to doubt her supremacy over the Church. She insisted that all clerics must toe her party line. Any doubt of her authority was dispelled with a splendid flash of Tudor temper when she prorogued Parliament in 1585. Having referred to fault-finders and slanderers 'to myself and the Church, whose over-ruler God hath made me', she turned on the assembled bishops with the words, 'All of which, if you my Lords of the Clergy do not amend, I mean to depose you.'[14] So they knew where they stood.

Continuity

The parish church had seen many changes, but through them all it had been the familiar place to go every Sunday, to worship God, and meet your neighbours, or sit and think, or even just sit, in your accustomed pew – and now several churches were installing special pews for the poor.[15] The colourful images and vestments, the sacrus bell and the mystery and the incense – they had given way to the Ten Commandments painted up for all to read; and the place was the duller for it. At least the bells from the old times had escaped destruction. Indeed, their peals were more elaborate than they ever had been,[16] and sometimes went on longer than altogether necessary, when 'a number of them that have got a glass in their hands ... go up into some belfry and ring the bells for hours together, for the sake of exercise'.[17] But the sense of participating, the encouragement to read the Bible, and saying the prayers and the creed in English – this must have been rewarding for those who took their religion seriously, as people did in those days. And the penalties for striking out independently and flaunting the old Catholic ways, or the new Puritan thinking, were too serious. For the ordinary people, as long as they turned up for the service and behaved decently, everyone was satisfied. Most people conformed.

The sermons at Paul's Cross

If your thirst for sermons was unsatisfied in your parish church, you could try the ones at the cross in the churchyard of St Paul's. From those 'Dialogues' we have looked at before:

> *Father*: ... we will go to hear the sermon at Paul's Cross ... there preacheth no body but is of choice, and of great learning.
>
> *Gossip* [friend]: I do think that they be the best sermons that men may hear in all the rest of the realm of England ... men do see all Sundays and holy days a great and noble company in Pauls Churchyard ... where shall we sit? All is full. All the forms be occupied ...
>
> [After the sermon] *Father*: now the sermon is almost ended: let us rise and get out first, let us not tarry for the press.[18]

Since at least 1241, Londoners had convened at a cross in the northeast part of the churchyard.[19] If you remember that until the Fire of 1666, St Paul's was a huge Norman cathedral, it is easier to imagine the setting. Covered galleries had been built on the exterior walls of the north transept and the choir, where the great and the good sat in comfort, looking down on the preacher. He stood in a ground-level pulpit with a roof that had a cross on top of it, and a low wall round it. Just like members of the audience sitting on the stage at a play, some favoured members of the congregation could sit within this wall. But everyone else had to stand, or squash together on benches, in the space between the pulpit and the cathedral walls. There could be several thousand people there, and on a hot day the place stank so badly that 'many a man taketh his death [there]'. If it rained, the sermon was given in the 'shrouds' – the crypt. The sermons attracted not only Londoners – not all of whom had attended their parish churches, despite the rules – but tourists from the country and abroad. The Queen came only once, on the last of the days of thanksgiving for the victory over the Armada. The occasion belonged to Londoners.

Women could check on the fashions worn by the ladies of the Lord Mayor and aldermen and the great nobles and merchants who occupied the galleries. Men could exchange the latest commercial and other gossip in undertones. Sometimes the sermon was totally inaudible, which must have made those hard benches even harder as the sand ran through the hour-glass for a second time, and made the task of the two brightest Christ's Hospital boys, who were supposed to take notes of the sermon, impossible. Sometimes you could hear the latest report on current affairs, or the newest government spin, or an official notice that all feasts in the Guildhall and the livery companies' halls were cancelled because of the plague. The Bishop of London wrote to Burghley to ask whether the King of Navarre was really dead, as was rumoured – he needed to know, for his sermon in three days' time; and 'if there be any other matter which you wish to be uttered there for the present state I would be pleased to know it in time'.

Government opposition to Catholicism was constantly hammered home. The Lord Mayor's jaundiced view of actors also got regular airings despite the royal favour enjoyed by players. During an epidemic of plague the preacher put the matter succinctly, if ungrammatically: 'The cause of plagues is sin, if you look to it well: and the cause of sin are plays: therefore the cause of plagues are plays.'

Sometimes you could see Londoners doing penance there for quite interesting sins. In November 1561 Henry Machyn, a respectable and well-known purveyor of funeral furnishings, had to kneel throughout the sermon, in the presence of the Bishop of London and a French preacher, Veron, as penance for passing on the gossip about Veron having been 'taken with a wench'.[20] (Who knew whether it was true or not? But it was certainly well publicised by then.) There was a scandal when Closse, an academic from Cambridge, accused the Lord Mayor, to his face, of fraud. Closse was given a chance to recant, but he did it again. Eventually an official statement was issued vindicating the Lord Mayor and discrediting Closse. It must have been fun while it lasted. One of the more trite sermons explained that 'God made some rich, and some poor, [so] that two excellent virtues might flourish in the world, charity in the rich and patience in the poor', which was thoughtful of Him.

Superstition

As the images went up in smoke, the Protestants jeered at them as superstitious, but many an old-fashioned, uneducated, devout Londoner must have been heart-broken as she watched the bonfire consuming the statue of Mary that had comforted her and her mother and her grandmother in their prayers. The miraculous Rood of Grace that had been found in the Thames in 1117, having been dropped from heaven, had been venerated in Bermondsey Abbey for centuries. It was saved, and re-erected on Horsley Down common, but a Protestant mob destroyed it in 1559. Sometimes an adherent to the old faith managed to remove an image and hide it until better days might come. This accounted for the findings of 'black virgins', many years later, which had spent the intervening period hidden in a dung heap where the wood had turned black.

The new religion appealed especially to people with the intelligence to take on new ideas and, above all, the ability to read. But people, especially the unsophisticated, have always wanted to find additional ways of interrogating or placating the inscrutable powers that be, and neither the Renaissance nor the Reformation stopped them. Thomas Nashe, born in 1567, reminisced in 1588:

> I have heard aged mumping beldams as they sat warming their knees
> over a coal ... bid young folks beware on what day they pared their
> nails, [and] tell what luck everyone should have by the day of the
> week he was born on [and] show how many years a man should live
> by the number of wrinkles on his forehead ...[21]

Henslow, the theatre manager and impresario, kept a diary between
1592 and 1609, mainly as a record of various business payments, but
he sometimes jotted down odd things that might come in useful,
such as 'to make a fowl fall dead: picture it in paper and when it is
making let one say "m. a. n. to thee"'.[22] It is hard to tell where
superstition begins and folk medicine ends; perhaps the superstition
that medicinal baths were not advisable during leap years straddled
both.[23]

Witchcraft and magic

Were there witches? Many learned men said there were, including
James I when he succeeded Elizabeth. They were certainly mentioned in the Old Testament, which could not be mistaken: but
then, was the translation accurate? The Witchcraft Act was passed
in 1563, imposing the death penalty on those guilty of 'invocations
or conjurations of evil ... spirits', and of killing by witchcraft.[24]

The debate rumbled on. The county of Essex, which enjoyed the
services of an energetic witch-hunter, was a hotbed of witches. There
were fewer in London. Simon Forman believed in them, and gave
several spells to get rid of them, such as burning a smock or shirt
belonging to the bewitched person and soaked in his or her urine.[25] In
1584 Reginald Scot published his *Discoverie of Witchcraft*. He attributed
the popular belief in witchcraft to the human need to blame someone
or something – other than God or oneself – for calamities:

> The fables of witchcraft have taken so fast hold and deep root in the
> heart of man that few or none can nowadays with patience endure
> the hand and correction of God ... One sort of such as are said to
> be witches are women which be commonly old, lame, blear-eyed,
> pale, foul, and full of wrinkles; poor, sullen, superstitious and papists
> ... lean and deformed ... doting [senile], scolds.

Deleting the reference to papists and adding a steeple hat and a broomstick, could there be a closer description of the witch in fairy stories? These pitiable old women deluded themselves and their enemies. One of them

> confessed at the time of her death that she had raised all the tempests and procured all the frosts and hard weather that happened in the winter of 1565 [when the Thames froze over, the cold was so extreme] and many grave and wise men believed her ... this melancholy humour (as the best physicians affirm) is the cause of all their ... incredible confessions

It was not only 'grave and wise men' who believed such improbabilities. Elizabeth herself gave Essex a magic ring to protect him from highway robbery and the dangers of travel: it is hard to know whether she was serious.[26] But 'everyone knew' – those potent words introducing an unproved statement – that a piece of unicorn's horn in a ring would protect against poison,[27] that mandrake [mandragora] roots scream when they are taken out of the ground, and that 'they grow under gallows, from the seed [semen] of man that falleth from him that is hanged'. Some unscrupulous villains turned this popular conviction to commercial profit. They made models like miniature men and women, which mandrake roots were said to resemble, 'to mock the poor people with, and to rob them both of their wit and their money'[28]

There were rich pickings at any gathering of ordinary people, for conjurors who could make things appear and disappear at will, and seem to pierce their own bodies yet remain alive.[29] Reginald Scot explained just how it was done. To end with, here are two harmless anecdotes from his book: 'if a butcher ... cheapens [bargains for] a bullock but if he buy him not, he saith "God save him." If he do forget it, and the ... bullock chance to die, the fault is imputed to the chapman [in the context, the bargaining butcher].' And 'it is a common jest among the watermen of the Thames, to show the parish church of Stone [a small Kentish village visible from the river] to the passengers, calling it the lantern of Kent, affirrning, and that not untruly, that the said church is as light [meaning in weight and not in brightness] at midnight as at noonday'.

Epilogue

By now you may have been able, sometimes, to think yourself back to the life of an ordinary Londoner in the half-century of Elizabeth's reign. Now, much more difficult, imagine his or her view of the future. How might a sixteenth-century person have seen the future?

For example, birth and death are immutable. The Lord gives, and a baby is born in blood and agony: and the Lord taketh away, so the cradle just filled is empty again. There is no other way. Man is the master, of course: the Bible says so. A woman needs a husband to defend her in this wicked cruel world, and sometimes husbands can be quite likeable. She bears the children and runs the home; he earns their living. None of that is likely to change – how could it?

God is at last settled in His right place in the community. A society needs God, and both society and God need to know how to deal with each other. No society, surely, could function otherwise. More could be learned about His wonderful creation, but extended study of the Bible should produce the answers to most problems.

On the everyday front, women hide their legs in long skirts, which get muddy and bedraggled in the rain. But this is natural. Men do sometimes change their fashions, showing or hiding their legs, but perhaps they need the opportunity to change their image, just for fun, having serious hard-working lives otherwise. If you want to know the latest news, there are ballads and broadsheets and those sermons at Paul's. Every child can learn to read, and many of them can write as well.

On national affairs, the great victory over the Spaniards in 1588 demonstrated, if proof were needed, that God loves England. The new countries that are being discovered should be glad that England has arrived, to do them good. At home, the Queen has been wonderful. It is interesting to follow, if you can, the debates in Parliament, where some men seem to want more power than she is prepared to give them. This is new, and it is bound to settle down in time. After all, even though she is only a woman, she has done her best to overcome that disadvantage, and it is obvious that whoever takes the throne after her, for the measurable future, will follow the lines she has laid down.

It has been a good idea to keep all the men in practice with their bows and arrows. The principle of mustering to defend your country in times of crisis will have to continue until that golden age comes that will make armies and navies unnecessary, but it might be possible to improve the administration.

Taxes are too high, but then they always are, and at least the poor are being looked after, and the sick can call on the nation's medical advisers. Medical care can go no further. The humours are as immutable as the stars; it is just a matter of interpreting them correctly.

So on the whole the future looks good.

Appendix I: Words and Pronunciation

Below are some of the words that have changed their meanings, or which have dropped out of use altogether, or are now spelt so differently that the Elizabethan way would be a pity to lose. Most come from the notes I made as I went along. I have not given their sources, as it would be tedious for the reader. As to pronunciation, in the absence of tape recorders how can we tell? But I have used a rhyming dictionary first published in 1570.[1] A safe bet is that what we would have heard in the streets and playhouses of Elizabethan London would sound to us now almost self-consciously rural and regional.

Words

artificially skilfully
auntes ants
bachelor member of a livery company, below a liveryman – it did not mean unmarried
bare-faced a timber joint with one shoulder, normally having two
Bathellmuw day St Bartholomew's Day, 24 August
beam weighbridge, official weighing scales
bridge jetty, landing-place (as well as our bridge)
broche, broach spit, as in cooking
buck (n.) a male deer; (v.) to launder
caliver light musket
cheap (v.) to bargain, try to beat down price
coffin large chest or container, not necessarily for corpse
corselet breast-plate
counter abacus
crowner's quest coroner's inquest
customer customs official
doddypol fool
drinkpenny tip, pourboire

Ellyngtun Islington

estrich ostrich

French marbles (slang) venereal disease

Fystret Fish Street

galoche overshoe

garble (v.) to control the quality of imported drugs and spices, a right exercised exclusively by the Grocers' Company

glass house glass works, factory

gorgyusle gorgeously

gossip friend, esp. female; godparent

hairs (as we would say) hair

herbs plants, or vegetables, fruit and flowers

hot codlings baked apples

huddipick coward

ingluvious gluttonous

jetty or jutty protruding storey of house

knille knell – bell tolling to mark a death; hence 'pit and knille' – cost of grave and knell

lewd immoral, worthless, not necessarily obscene

maiden female of any age from babyhood on

man male of any age from babyhood on

mowchatowe moustache

quickinge stoole ducking stool for scolds

quishon cushion

oliphant, oliphaunt elephant

pilgarlic bald and/or unlucky

promoter common informer

sewer storm-water drain

shot tavern bill

singlewoman prostitute

smell-feast (slang) uninvited guest

stairs landing-place, jetty

Steelyard the London premises of the Hanseatic merchants: from High German *Stälhof*, warehouse

stewed prunes (slang) laxative, and/or prostitute, offered in taverns

stranger foreigner or non-Londoner

table gaming table or notebook

tabling house cooked-food shop

tippler ale and beer retailer (not drinker)

turkey-stone turquoise

ware-bench counter in a shop, in our sense

whiffler, waffler steward of a procession

whittled drunk

Winchester geese south bank prostitutes: the Bishop of Winchester owned much of the south bank where the brothels were

Pronunciation

In many cases the stress fell on a different syllable, e.g. délectable, inéxcusable, cáthedral, perséverance, debónair, parént, villánie, flagón. It looks as if in all those *–ough* words that trap foreigners, such as bough, cough, plough, slough, trough, through, rough and tough, the *–ou* was pronounced *–ow*; also *–oo* and *–ou*, in blood, flood, soul, wound, pour, smooth. Plague rhymed with wage. The *–ant* in ant, infant, pant, plant, oliphant, servant and ignorant was pronounced as in *vaunt*.

Appendix II: Currency, Wages and Prices

One always wants to know how much things cost in the past. I have not suggested any kind of formula, because the normal 'shopping basket of consumer goods' of an Elizabethan was so completely different from ours. Their lives were simpler – no mortgage, no commuter's season ticket, no car, no washing machine, no hi-fi, no foreign holidays, no insurance. I hope the examples below will at least provide a scale. Perhaps the wage of a skilled tradesman such as a carpenter – 1s 2d a day – is helpful to bear in mind. The rich were very rich, and there was not much to invest in – no stocks and shares in our sense, no banks, no yachts. They could put their money into trading ventures to foreign countries, or spend it on clothes, jewels, feasts and, within the constraints of London, houses.

Currency

Elizabeth inherited a debased currency. She reformed it early in her reign. From November 1560, the coins in circulation were:

Gold coins, 23 carats and more:

Sovereign	worth 30 shillings
Ryal or rose noble	15s
Angel	10s
½ angel, angelet	5s
¼ angel	2s 6d

Gold coins, 22 carats:

Sovereign	20s
½ sovereign	10s
Crown	5s
½ crown	2s 6d

Silver coins:

Crown, ½ crown, shilling, 6d ('tester'), 4d ('groat'), 3d, 2d, 1½d, 1d, ¾d and ½d.

There were no copper or brass coins; nor, of course, were there any bank notes, there being no banks.

There were also foreign coins in circulation, such as:

French crown   6s
Spanish ducat   6s 8d
Dutch florin   2s

Sums were often reckoned in marks, which represented 13s 4d, and were 'money of account', not real coins. You will often see this odd amount – or even half of it, 6s 8d – in accounts.[1]

Wages and prices

A penny would always buy a loaf, but the weight of the loaf varied. It would buy admission to a circular playhouse as a 'groundling', or to the plays at Merchant Taylors' hall, or hire a two-oar wherry to cross the river.

2d	admission to a gallery in a circular playhouse; the cost per person on the London/Gravesend ferry
3d	a small pipe of tobacco at a playhouse
4d	would hire a woman to wash the dishes and a boy to turn the spits, for a feast, or buy a pair of spectacles, or 2 ounces of ginger
5d	the horse ferry at Fulham, across the river and back
6d	would buy a quart of claret, or holly and ivy to decorate the church at Christmas, or a medical handbook, or a bag of nuts at a playhouse
7d	a day was the pay of an unskilled labourer in 1560
8d–1s	a week was the cost of keeping an abandoned baby; 8d would buy two dozen eggs, or seven almanacs, or a quart of strawberries in season, or hire a two-man wherry from London to Greenwich with the tide
1s	a pair of shoes for a poor man, or pay a carpenter's mate for a day, or the daily board of a Westminster schoolboy in time of plague, or buy admission to watch a royal tournament
1s 2d	would pay a carpenter or a joiner for a day, exclusive of food and drink
1s 3d	a shirt of mail
1s 4d	the weekly pension paid to widows in the Merchant Taylors' almshouses
1s 8d	would buy a dozen blackbirds, or keep a patient in Bedlam for a week
2s	would pay two sawyers for a day, or buy a shirt for a poor man, or hire a stool on the stage of a playhouse, or buy four tobacco pipes, or hire a wherry between London and Gravesend
3s	1lb of pepper
4s 6d	a man's bow
5s	would pay for making two coats and two pairs of gaskins (breeches), or buy an ounce of tobacco
5s 4d	would hire a gardener to mow the grass for four days, or buy a beef

	joint weighing 56lb
6s	plus candles and soap would hire a wet-nurse for a month, or buy 1,000 great farthingale pins
7s	would hire a horse for six days
8s	a pair of fashionable summer boots
10s	a month might be paid to apprentices; it would hire a tilt-boat with four oars and a steersman to Windsor and back
10s	the annual pension of a Carpenter's widow
12s	a swan
12s 3d	a 10-lb sugar loaf
15s	a week in a tolerable room in the Fleet prison
20s	would hire some Christ's Hospital children for a funeral, or a barge for a state occasion
26s 8d	would buy an untrimmed beaver hat, or two dozen damask napkins
£3	a year was the wage of a maidservant
£3 6s 8d	the annual salary of the matron of Christ's Hospital
£5	the controlled annual wage of a clothworker
£6	the annual controlled wage of a blacksmith and a butcher, and the annual pension paid by the Merchant Taylors to John Stow, and the fee charged by Forman in a typical case (£3 down, the rest 30 days after recovery)
£10	the top fee of a barrister, or the value of two coaches and two coach horses, or the controlled annual wage of a brewer
£15	the annual salary of the grammar school master in Christ's Hospital
£20	the value of one of the Earl of Leicester's cloaks
£25	the value of one of Leicester's suits of armour
£30	each was the annual salary of the surgeons at St Bartholomew's Hospital
£40	the cost of a year in an Inn of Court
£177	the value of Leicester's plain silver, not counting his parcel-gilt silver
£2,030	the income of St Bartholomew's Hospital in 1558–9 (its expenditure in that year was £1,970)
£3,000	the cost of Leicester's funeral
£8,000	the valuation of his estate
£9,535	the Queen's annual expenditure on her wardrobe

Appendix III: An Elizabethan Invoice

The Accompt of Frauncis Bacon Esquire of Money laide out & disbursed for Graies Inne Walkes taken & agreed upon the xxiiii of Aprill An° Eliz: xlii^{do}.

Imprimis to the carpenter for the stayres & rayles	viii^{li} x^s
Item for lxxi elmes at ix^d a piece	xlix^s vi^d
For viii Birche trees at xviii^d the tree	xii^s
For xvi cherrye trees at xii^d the tree	xvi^s
For cclxxxvi bundles of poles & stakes at iiii^d ob the bundle	v^{li} vii^s iii^d
For iii^m iiii^c great oziers at xiii^d the C	xxxix^s viii^d
For xx^m of quicke setts at iii^s viii^d the M	iii^{li} xiii^s iiii^d
For small Bindinge oziers	xxxv^s i^d
For i^m vi^c of woodbines at vi^d the C	viii^s
For iii^m vii^c of eglantyne at xii the C	xxxvii^s
For cxxv standerds of roses	xii^s vi^d
For xx^m of privye at ii^s the M	xl^s
For pincks violetts & primroses	vii^s
For cuttinges of vynes	ii^s vi^d
For car: wharfinge & toll of all the stuffe & for barrowes trestles brooms &c	xii^s iiii^d
For the principall gardiner & his mans wages at 3^s per diem xxix daies & a halfe	iiii^{li} viii^s vi^d
For other gardiners at xviii^d the daie clxi days	xii^{li} i^s vi^d
For gardiners at xvi^d the daie lxxvi daies	v^{li} iiii^s
For labourers at xii^d per diem cxxvi daies & a halfe	vii^{li} vi^s vi^d
For other wages	xiiii^s
Sm̃a total:	lx^{li} vi^s viiii^d
Rec: of the Steward	xl^{li}
Sic rem: claro computant:	xx^{li} vi^s viiii^d

W^{ch} twenty pounds six shillings eight pence is the 28th of Aprill 1600 paidd by me Robte Coates for my Mr. John Brograve Esquire to Frauncis Bacon Esquire

(Excerpt from ed. R. J. Fletcher, *The Pension Book of Grays Inn, Vol. 1: 1569–1669*, London 1901, reproduced by kind permission of the Benchers of the Honourable Society of Gray's Inn.)

The date in the heading uses the regnal year, Anno Elizabeth 42,[do] the 42nd year after she came to the throne. This was often used in legal documents. The date at the end uses the system familiar to us, anno domini (the year of our Lord) 1600.

Bacon had built a mount in the Inn's gardens, known as the Walks, in 1598 – see Chapter 5 – and this must have been the final account of the cost of constructing it and redesigning the Walks. The carpenter had spent £8 10s on the 'stairs and rails' – the stepped path round the mount, with handrails. The 286 bundles of poles and stakes at 4½d a bundle, costing £5 7s 3d, must have been used to stabilise the soil of the mount, with the possible addition of 3,400 'great osiers' – willow withies – and a quantity of small 'binding oziers'. C stood for 100, M for 1,000. The 125 'standerds of roses' may have been standard rose bushes, or perhaps rooted cuttings. The 20,000 'priveye' were privets, not privies. The cost of this substantial work included 'brooms &c', to clear up afterwards. The 'principal gardiner' brought his own 'man'; they were together paid 3s a day, a considerable wage for those days, compared to 'other gardiners at 18d the day' and 'others' at only 16d per day. They could be relied on to know what they were doing, but they needed the 'labourers at 12d' for the heavy work. The work was spread over two years. The principal gardiner was there for only 29½ days, leaving the 'other gardiners' to get on with the work, but there is no indication of how long it took them; 156 days could mean 2 men for 78 days each, or more men, for shorter times. Gardening in this climate is dependent on suitable weather. When work was impossible, the gardeners and labourers got no pay.

The ~ over the m in 'Sma' means that some letters have been omitted; the whole word is Summa. The Steward had already paid £40, leaving £20 6s 8d 'rem' or, as we would say, outstanding, which was duly paid to Bacon on 28 April.

The manuscript original of the account is faded now, which makes the task of deciphering it almost impossible. In particular, the numbers were no doubt clear to the Gray' s Inn clerks, but they look nothing like the tidy 'cclxxxvi' used by the 1901 editor. The symbol for 100 looks more like a hot-cross bun – a circle with a cross in it – than a c.

Notes

Preface (pp xiii–xvii)

1 John Stow, *A Survey of London* (originally published London, 1598), Oxford, 1908. This edition, edited by C. L. Kingsford, gives much additional information in the notes and is the one I have used. An Everyman edition with notes by H. B. Wheatley was published in 1912. Reissued in 1997 by Sutton Publishing, Stroud, Glos., with an introduction by Antonia Fraser.

2 This has suffered from successive editing: the best edition to use is the one edited by Georges Edelen and published as part of the Folger Shakespeare Library in 1968, republished in paperback in 1994, Toronto, Ontario, Canada.

3 C. Barron, C. Coleman and C. Gobbi (eds), 'The London Journal of Alessandro Magno 1562', *The London Journal*, vol. 9, no. 2, 1983.

4 W. B. Rye, *London as Seen by Foreigners*, London, 1865.

5 Ibid.

6 Ibid.

7 Ibid.

8 Ibid.

9 P. Razzell (ed.), *The Journals of Two Travellers in Elizabethan and Early Stuart England*, London, 1995.

10 Peter Finch, *John Dee: The World of an Elizabethan Magus*, New York, 1989; Edward Fenton (ed.), *The Diaries of John Dee*, Charlbury, Oxon, 1998.

11 Barbara Traister, *The Notorious Astrological Physician of London*, Chicago, 2001; Judith Cook, *Dr Simon Forman, a Most Notorious Physician*, London, 2001.

12 J. M. Osborn (ed.), *The Autobiography of Thomas Wythorne*, Oxford, 1961.

13 J. G. Nichols (ed.), *The Diary of Henry Machyn 1550–63*, London, 1848.

14 In the Douce collection in the Bodleian Library, Oxford.

15 I read the accounts and minute books of the Bakers, the Butchers, the Carpenters, the Cutlers, the Drapers, the Merchant Taylors, the Stationers, the Vintners and the Watermen.

16 C. L. Kingsford, 'Essex House formerly Leicester House and Exeter Inn' *Archeologia*, vol. XXIII, 1923. Gladys Scott Thomson, *Two Centuries of Family History*, London, 1930.

17 Surrey Record Society, *Lambeth Churchwardens' Accounts*, London, 1943. The

accounts of St Botolph Without Aldgate were edited by Thomas Rogers, *Chronicles from Aldgate*, London, 1971.

18 Irene Scouloudi, 'Returns of Strangers in the Metropolis, 1593, 1627, 1635, *1639*', Huguenot Society of London, vol. LVII, 1985.

19 Derek Keene and Vanessa Harding, *Historical Gazetteer of London Before the Great Fire*, London, 1994.

20 Phillip Stubbes, *The Anatomy of Abuses*, London, 1583.

Prologue (pp. xviii–xxiv)

1 I have drawn on Stephen Inwood's *History of London*, London, 1998, for this brutally curtailed summary.

2 A. L. Beier and Roger Finlay (eds), *The Making of the Metropolis, London 1500–1700*, Harlow, Essex, 1986. These figures are estimates, in the absence of any census. See also E. A. Wrigley and R. S. Schofield, *The Population History of England 1541–1871*, London, 1981.

Chapter 1: The River (pp. 5–19)

1 John Stow, *A Survey of London*, London, 1598.

2 George Turberville, *Epitaphs, Epigrams, Songs and Sonnets*, London, 1567.

3 Edmund Spenser, *Prothalamium*, London, 1596.

4 Michael Drayton, 'Song to Beta' in *The Shepherd's Garland*, 1593. All three poems are in *The Oxford Book of Sixteenth Century Verse*, Oxford, 1932.

5 This is the figure given me by Captain Potter of MV *Princess Pocahontas*, which takes visitors on day excursions between Gravesend and London every week. Captain Potter's knowledge of the river is encyclopedic. The only statement of his which I did not altogether accept was that Thames water flows in his veins, not blood.

6 This is an early example of my reliance on Ben Weinreb and Christopher Hibbert, *The London Encyclopedia*, London, 1983, revised edn 1995. I acknowledge my debt to this fount of knowledge here, but I shall not do so for individual mentions, from now on.

7 Stow, op. cit.

8 Peter Razzell (ed.), *The Journals of Two Travellers in Elizabethan and Early Stuart England*, London, 1995.

9 My other main source of information about the river was Henry Humpherus, *History of the Origin and Progress of the Company of Watermen and Lightermen of the River Thames*, vol. I: *1514–1829*, London, 1859, reissued London, 1999.

10 From the preamble to an Act of 1555: that is, during the reign of King Philip and Queen Mary. It may come as a shock to see King Philip's name preceding that of his wife. He was crowned king consort.

11 W. B. Rye, *England as Seen by Foreigners*, London, 1865.

12 Razzell, op. cit. The woods and pleasant hamlets have gone; the abiding impression is of flat marshes stretching along either bank, being industriously filled with London's household refuse, and punctuated by sewage disposal units.

13 H. M. Colvin and S. Foister (eds), *The Panorama of London circa 1544* (publication

no. 151, London Topographical Society), London, 1996. The slight hill behind the palace, now crowned by the Observatory, is the first break in the uniformly flat landscape from Gravesend.

14 Humpherus, op. cit.

15 Colvin and Foister (eds), op. cit.

16 The well-known inn, the Prospect of Whitby in Rotherhithe, was one such. It can trace its beginnings back to 1520. Its name comes from its view over the boats carrying coal from Whitby and other north-east mining ports, to London. I owe this information to that mine of river lore, Captain Potter (see note 5).

17 Stow, op. cit.

18 *Remembrancia 1579–1664*, London, 1878; an invaluable summary of the City's records.

19 The Customs House is approximately on that site, now.

20 Razzell (ed.), op. cit.

21 C. Barron, C. Coleman and C. Gobbi (eds), 'The London Journal of Alessandro Magno 1562', *The London Journal*, vol. 9, no. 2, 1983.

22 I am told that this description makes tolerable sense, and also that it is on the same principle as a bicycle's gears, which I never understood. It all depends on pulleys, but Alessandro's sketch does not show any. He was clearly impressed.

23 The river is rarely straight. The bend at Whitehall means that it flows from south to north, but any Londoner knows that the Kent bank on its east is still 'south of the river'.

24 The New Globe can be seen from the river, but it looks surprisingly unimpressive, more like a canvas mock-up. It is better approached by land.

25 Statement by William Smith, Rouge Dragon Poursuivant, quoted in Rye, op. cit. In the Embankment Gardens there is a water gate dating from 1626, marooned on dry land. By an exercise of imagination it is just possible to flood the space between it and the river, and see the water lapping at it at high tide. How far the river extended on the opposite bank is problematic.

26 William Harrison, *Description of England*, London, 1577. I used the edition by Furnival, London, 1877, in which he collated the two editions of Harrison, 1577 and 1587.

27 Humpherus, op. cit.

28 Harrison, op. cit.

29 Ibid.

30 Humpherus, op. cit.

31 Ibid.

32 Stow, op. cit.

33 Humpherus, op. cit.

34 Ibid.

35 J. G. Nichols (ed.), *The Diary of Henry Machyn 1550–1563*, London, 1848.

36 Ibid.

37 Ibid.

38 An eyewitness account by a German visitor Paul Hentzner, who was able to inspect it at close quarters as it lay at its berth near the Bankside theatres. 'It is kept upon dry ground and sheltered from the weather' – but not, one

immediately thinks in these days, from terrorists.

39 Humpherus, op. cit.

40 Shakespeare, *Antony and Cleopatra*, Act II, scene 2. The Nile has the unique advantage of a steady current taking boats north to the Mediterranean with their sails furled, and a steady wind blowing them south under full sail, so the rowers' task was not too onerous in the right season.

41 Thomas Platter, in Razzell (ed.), op. cit.

42 *Lambeth Churchwardens' Accounts 1504–1645*, published by the Surrey Record Society, London, 1950. This was one of the fascinating contemporary records that the congenial and endlessly helpful staff at the London Metropolitan Archives produced for me.

43 Humpherus, op. cit.

44 Bower Marsh (ed.), *The Records of the Worshipful Company of Carpenters, Vol. IV: Wardens' Account Book 1546–1571*, Oxford, 1916.

45 Arthur Pearce, *History of the Butchers' Company*, London, 1929.

46 Ibid.

47 Barron et al. (eds), op. cit.

48 Platter in Razzell (ed.), op. cit.

49 Rye, op. cit.

50 Humpherus, op. cit.

51 Ibid.

52 Razzell (ed.), op. cit.

53 Barron et al. (eds), op. cit.

54 Harrison, op. cit. Until 40 years ago, the river still provided employment for 5,000 watermen and lightermen (see note 5).

55 An Act touching Watermen and Bargemen on the River Thames.

56 Humpherus, op. cit.

57 Ibid.

58 *Court Minutes of the Surrey and Kent Sewer Commissioners*, London, 1909: another treasure trove for which I am indebted to the London Metropolitan Archives staff.

59 Paul Hentzner, who came to England in 1598. His description of England then was translated from Latin to English by Horace Walpole in 1757. Included in Rye, op. cit.

60 *Remembrancia*, op. cit.

61 Ibid.

62 Harrison, op. cit. The water was fresh for seven miles downstream from London Bridge. Fishes are not that particular about a taste of salt in the water, so the occasional sea fish mingled with freshwater fish. I owe this information to Mike Aspinall, the kind librarian of the Docklands Museum.

63 Humpherus, op. cit.

64 Barron et al. (eds), op. cit. It is always difficult to tell when a foreign tourist is retailing some tall story kept strictly for tourists, or recording something he has seen himself. I would not like to offer a swan any 'needful meat' myself. My small son was feeding bread to a goose in Regent's Park once, and I turned to see his hand disappearing into the goose's mouth. He had forgotten to let go.

65 Trans. G. von Bülow, 'Journey through England and Scotland by Leopold von

Weddel 1584–5', *Transactions of the Royal Historical Society*, New Series, vol. IX, 1895.
66 Hentzner in Rye, op. cit.
67 Harrison, op. cit. It is sad that the only swans I saw between Gravesend and Lambeth were a few at Gravesend.
68 Ibid.
69 Bryant Lillywhite, *London Signs*, London, 1972.
70 Razzell (ed.), op. cit.

Chapter 2: The Main Streets, Water Supply and Sewerage (pp. 20–41)

1 John Stow, *A Survey of London*, London, 1598. I have used the edition by C. L. Kingsford, Oxford, 1908. For the whole of this chapter I have gratefully relied on Ben Weinreb and Christopher Hibbert (eds), *The London Encyclopedia*, London, 1983, and John Richardson, *The Annals of London*, London, 2000, with Juliet Gardiner and N. Wenborn (eds), *The History Today Companion to British History*, London, 1995, to keep me straight on the dates of kings, etc.
2 G. Beard, *Upholsterers and Interior Furnishing in England 1530–1840*, London, 1997.
3 Howard Colvin and Susan Foister (eds), *The Panorama of London circa 1544 by Antonis van den Wingaerde*, London, 1966.
4 Stow, op. cit.
5 These arches vary between twenty and nineteen, depending on who is counting and whether the smallest one nearest the north shore is to be included or treated as an abutment.
6 Colvin and Foister (eds), op. cit.
7 William Harrison, *Description of England*, London, 1877.
8 Thomas Platter in Peter Razzell (ed.), *The Journals of Two Travellers in Elizabethan and Early Stuart England*, London, 1995.
9 The author's *Dr Johnson's London*, London, 2000.
10 Henry Humpherus, *History of the Origin and Progress of the Company of Watermen and Lightermen of the River Thames*, vol. 1: *1514–1829*, London, 1959, reissued London, 1999.
11 *Christ's Hospital Admissions*, published by authority of the Council of Almoners of Christ's Hospital, London, 1937.
12 Stow, op. cit.
13 John Stow, *The Annals of England*, London, 1592.
14 Shakespeare, *The Merry Wives of Windsor*, Act II, scene 3.
15 Reddaway, 'Elizabethan London – Goldsmith's Row in Cheapside 1558–1645', *Guildhall Miscellany*, vol. II, no. 5, October 1863.
16 It was not finally ended until the Post Office Act of 1815.
17 C. Barron, C. Coleman and C. Gobbi (eds), 'The London Journal of Alessandro Magno' in *The London Journal*, vol. 9, no. 3, 1983. Knapped or broken flint makes a hard surface. I have met it between Dar es Salaam and Tanga, in Tanganyika as it was then. One could go at a fair speed on it – until a sharp flint punctured your tyre or your sump or your brake-fluid hose, or all three. But this would not have been a worry to sixteenth-century Londoners.
18 Harrison, op. cit.

19 John Schofield, *The Building of London from the Conquest to the Great Fire*, London, 1984.

20 D. M. Bergeron, *English Civic Pageantry 1558–1642*, London, 1971.

21 J. G. Nichols (ed.), *The Diary of Henry Machyn 1550–1563*, London, 1848.

22 R. J. Fletcher (ed.), *The Pension Book of Gray's Inn*, London, 1901. 'Pension' meant the governing body of benchers.

23 W. P. Baildon (ed.), *The Records of … Lincoln's Inn, vol. II*, London, 1897.

24 *Archeologia*, vol XL, 1831.

25 'Extracts from the Book of Household Charges by Lord North 1575', *Archeologia*, vol. XXXII, 1847.

26 *Archeologia*, vol XL, 1831.

27 A. V. Judge (ed.), *The Elizabethan Underworld*, London, 1930.

28 Gladys Scott Thomson, *Two Centuries of Family History*, London, 1930, giving the inventory of the household goods of the Earl of Bedford, who died in 1585.

29 Alison Weir, *Elizabeth the Queen*, London, 1998.

30 Scott Thomson, op. cit.

31 C. L. Kingsford, 'Essex House formerly Leicester House and Exeter Inn', *Archeologia*, vol. LXXI, 1921.

32 Anon., *A Health to the Gentlemanly Profession of Serving Men*, London, 1598.

33 Henry Humpherus, *History of the Origin and Progress of the Company of Watermen and Lightermen of the River Thames*, London, 1859.

34 Stow, *Survey*, op. cit.

35 M. St Clare Byrne, *Elizabethan Life in Town and Country*, London, 1925.

36 C. Barron et al. (eds), 'The London journal of Alessandro Magno 1562', *The London Journal*, vol. 9, no. 2, 1983.

37 T. R. Forbes (eds), *Chronicle from Aldgate*, London, 1971.

38 Nichols (ed.), op. cit.

39 W. H. Overall and H. C. Overall (eds), *Remembrancia AD 1579–1664*, London, 1878, in which notes from the original City records for the period 1579–1664 are set out under alphabetical headings.

40 From 'A brief London chronicle 1547–1564', in C. L. Kingsford (ed.), 'Two London chronicles from the collections of John Stow', *Camden Miscellany*, vol. XII, London, 1910.

41 Presumably the sheep, geese, fruitgrowers' carts, etc. were somehow kept out of Her Majesty's way, just as successive police officers listening intently on their mobile telephones to the Queen's progress from Buckingham Palace to Liverpool Street en route for Sandringham produce, as if by a miracle, a clear route for the royal car, by stopping all the other traffic, so that she must wonder why people complain about traffic jams.

42 Nichols (ed.), op. cit.

43 Barron et al. (eds), op. cit. I am told that geldings and stallions have to stand still to urinate whereas mares can keep going.

44 Excerpts from the diary of Richard Stoneley, in the Douce Collection, Bodleian Library, Oxford.

45 W. K. Jordan, *The Charities of London 1480–1660*, London, 1960. When I lived in Gray's Inn in the 1960s there was a small dairy just off Lamb's Conduit

Street kept – as traditionally so many London dairies were – by a charming Welsh couple. They said that there was a vestige of the conduit at the back of their shop, and I much regret never having accepted their invitation to see it.

46 Nichols (ed.), op. cit.

47 Dorothy Hartley, *Water in England*, London, 1964. Lead pipes that were constantly full of water were 'so well coated with a green deposit that the water hardly reached the metal', so although the 'green deposit' – she did not suggest what it was – might make the water taste foul, at least you did not get lead poisoning.

48 Nichols (ed.), op. cit.

49 Stow, *Survey*, op. cit.

50 For this and for much information about London's water supply, I am indebted to that immense work of scholarly research, Derek Keene and Vanessa Harding, *Historical Gazetteer of London before the Great Fire*, London, 1994.

51 M. St Clare Byrne (ed.), *The Elizabethan Home*, 3rd edn, London, 1949.

52 Stow, *Annals*, op. cit.

53 I am grateful to Dr Forsyth of the Museum of London, for the information on Bulmer's system.

54 *Remembrancia*, op. cit.

55 S. V. Morgan (ed.), *John Howes's Manuscript, 1582*, London, 1904.

56 *Remembrancia*, op. cit. The power of search was conferred by an Act of Henry VIII.

57 I am grateful to Dr Stephen Porter of English Heritage for this information, and for making available to me copies of the plans of the system, and of an interesting article on it in *Archeologia*, vol. XL, 1902.

58 Arthur Pearce, *History of the Butcher's Company*, London, 1929.

59 Shakespeare, *The Merry Wives of Windsor*, Act III, scene 5.

60 Baildon (ed.), op. cit.

61 *Christ's Hospital Admissions*, Vol. I: *1554–99*, London, 1937.

62 R. Reynolds, *Cleanliness and Godliness*, London, 1946.

63 A. Boorde, *Compendious Regiment of Health*, London, 1547.

64 J. Imray, *The Charities of Richard Whittington*, London, 1968. The Long House was rebuilt after the Great Fire but with a meagre twelve seats.

Chapter 3: The Buildings (pp. 42–50)

1 An (unnamed) contemporary historian quoted by John Schofield, *The Building of London from the Conquest to the Great Fire*, London, 1984.

2 Clare Williams (ed.), *Thomas Platter's Travels in England 1599*, London, 1932.

3 I am grateful to Dr Malcolm Airs of Oxford University Department of Continuing Education for giving me a personal and instructive seminar. He also recommended a small book by Richard Harris, *Discovering Timber-framed Buildings*, Princes Risborough, 1978, which despite its format – it is one of the excellent 'Discovering' series – conveys more information than many larger tomes I have read.

4 At this point the reader may be asking why I have not used as an example the timbered houses looking on to Holborn at Staple Inn. It is because, alas, they

'are now almost completely rebuilt' (Edward Jones and Christopher Woodward, *The Archiecture of London*, London, 1983) – and not very well at that.

5 Andrew Gurr, *The Shakespearian Stage*, Cambridge, 1980.

6 Bower Marsh (ed.), *Records of the Worshipful Company of Carpenters*, London, 1915.

7 William Harrison, *Description of England*, London, 1587.

8 Lawrence Stone, 'Social mobility in England 1500–1700', *Past and Present*, 1966.

9 Anthony Quiney, *The Traditional Buildings of England*, London, 1990. The author pinpoints the beginning of accurate joints from 1120, when Crusaders returning from the Near East brought Euclid's *Elements* with them, including the theorem of Pythagoras that the square on the hypotenuse of a right-angled triangle is equal to the sum of the squares on the other two sides. This made obvious to medieval carpenters something that will be equally obvious to you: that is, the useful knack of making right-angled triangles.

10 Schofield, op. cit.

11 Per Dr Malcolm Airs (see note 3).

12 *Lambeth Churchwardens' Accounts 1504–1645*, Surrey Records Society, London, 1950.

13 Schofield, op. cit.

14 *Lambeth Churchwardens' Accounts*, op. cit.

15 Derek Keene and Vanessa Harding, *Historical Gazetteer of London Before the Great Fire*, London, 1994: an astounding piece of scholarship.

16 Ibid.

17 Ibid.

18 Ibid.

19 Ibid.

20 Ibid.

21 Ibid.

22 Walter Besant, *London in the Time of the Tudors*, London, 1904, gives a list of the religious houses in London at the time of the dissolution:

Charterhouse	Austin [Augustinian] friars
Greyfriars	St Bartholomew's
Blackfriars	Halliwell
Holy Trinity	Minoresses
Eastminster	
St Helen's	
Crutched Friars	
White Friars	

The point he is making, by contrasting the number of bequests to them between 1250 and 1540, is that most of them were declining by that time, anyway. What I deduce from his list is that there were many more ex-monastic properties on the market than I had realised.

23 John Stow, *A Survey of London*, London, 1598.

24 See Schofield, op. cit., for a fascinating and detailed description of the conversion.

25 Ibid.

26 The Masons were, of course, freemen of London, but the arcane mysteries of

Freemasonry were a later development.

27 Stow, op. cit.
28 Ann Saunders (ed.) *The Royal Exchange*, London Topographical Society, publication no. 152, London, 1997.
29 Keene and Harding, op. cit.
30 Schofield, op. cit.
31 Keene and Harding, op. cit.
32 St Andrew Undershaft was so called, according to Stow, because a maypole 'higher than the church steeple' used to be stored along its eaves, until it was demolished as a heathen idol after an inflammatory sermon at St Paul's cross.
33 The astonishing thing about Crosby Hall is that part of it still exists. It survived on its site on Bishopsgate, gradually losing status, until it was demolished in 1908, but after urgent intervention by the City the hammer-beam roof timbers and oriel windows were saved and installed in a Tudor-style building called Crosby Hall, in Chelsea, used as a hostel for the British Federation of University Women. In 1988 it was bought by a millionaire and incorporated in his re-created 'Tudor' palace on Cheyne Walk, next to Battersea Bridge.
34 Stow, op. cit.
35 S. W. Rawlins (ed.), *Visitation of London 1568*, London, 1963.
36 Stow, op. cit.
37 Names taken at random from Keene and Harding, op. cit.

Chapter 4: Interiors and Furniture (pp. 51–67)

1 Barbara Traister, *The Notorious Astrological Physician of London*, London, 2001.
2 Shakespeare, *The Merry Wives of Windsor*, Act IV, scene 5.
3 There is a fragment of it in the V. & A.'s British Galleries. It looks like something by Burne-Jones or Rossetti, it is so curved and subtly coloured.
4 Here I must again thank Dr Saunders of the Prints and Drawings Department of the Victoria and Albert Museum, for her expertise and enthusiasm.
5 Tessa Watt, *Cheap Print and Popular Piety 1550–1640*, Cambridge, 1991.
6 C. L. Kingsford, 'On some London houses of the early Tudor period', *Archeologia*, vol. LXXI, 1921.
7 Shakespeare, *Henry VI Part II*, Act II, scene 1: Falstaff commended the 'story of the Prodigal in water-work' (i.e. painted on to cloth), rather than Mistress Quickly's tapestry.
8 Derek Keene and Vanessa Harding, *Historical Gazetteer of London Before the Great Fire*, London, 1994. They give one example of painted cloth being held to be as much a landlord's fixture as the wainscoting.
9 'O Sir, you have overthrown Alisander the conqueror! You will be scraped out of the painted cloth for this' – Shakespeare, *Love's Labour's Lost*, Act V, scene 2.
10 Anthony Wells-Cole, *Art and Decoration in Elizabethan and Jacobean England*, London, 1997.
11 In the anonymous picture of Elizabeth receiving ambassadors, the background walls are a dark green patterned with a typical gilt leather design. I do not know, of course, whether whatever room she was supposed to be in was

so decorated. See plate 22.

12 Gladys Scott Thomson, *Two Centuries of Family History*, London, 1930.

13 Bess's interior decorating is splendidly illustrated in Santina M. Levey, *An Elizabethan Inheritance: The Hardwick Hall Textiles*, London, 1998, a National Trust publication. I have reluctantly spent little space on Bess, because she was (a) very rich and (b) not in London. But she either set, or followed, the fashion, even though she lived in Derbyshire.

14 C. M. Clode, *Memorials of the Merchant Taylors*, London, 1874. If 'olne' is a version of 'ell', which seems a reasonable assumption, the Flemish ell measured 27 inches. For a fascinating summary of the various systems of measurement current in Europe in the sixteenth century, see Janet Arnold, *Patterns of Fashion: The Cut and Construction of Clothes for Men and Women c.1560–1620*, London, 1985. The English ell was 45 inches.

15 Levey, op. cit.

16 Keene and Harding, op. cit.

17 M. Jourdain, *English Decoration and Furniture of the Early Renaissance 1500–1650*, London, 1924.

18 J. G. Nichols (ed.), *The Diary of Henry Machyn 1550–63*, London, 1848.

19 R. J. Fletcher (ed.), *The Pension Book of Gray's Inn*, Vol. I: *1569–1669*, London, 1901.

20 'Extracts from the Book of Household Charges by Lord North 1575', *Archeologia*, vol. XXXII, 1847.

21 Shakespeare, *Romeo and Juliet*, Act I, scene 4.

22 Thomas Tusser, *Five Hundred Good Points of Husbandry*, London, 1573.

23 I was warned about this by a kind and knowledgeable expert who shall remain anonymous. Many a prized family heirloom is in fact a 'Tudor-bethan' Victorian reproduction.

24 Levey, op. cit.

25 C. L. Kingsford, 'Essex House formerly Leicester House and Exeter Inn', *Archeologia*, vol. XXIII, 1923.

26 'Excerpts from Richard Stoneley's Diary in the Douce Collection', Douce manuscript in the Bodleian Library, Oxford. For guilloches, see R. Edwards, *The Shorter Dictionary of English Furniture*, London, 1964.

27 Edwards, op. cit.

28 Kingsford, *Archeologia*, vol. XXIII, op. cit.

29 J. Ainsworth (ed.), *Records of the Carpenters' Company*, London, 1939.

30 Fletcher (ed.), op. cit.

31 Nichols, op. cit.

32 When I was a civil servant, up to 1987, the cupboards where one kept such papers as would not go into filing cabinets were called 'presses'. I think that usage has ceased by now.

33 There is a famous milky drink which used to claim that it would 'avoid night starvation'. The French thought this was hilarious; only the English ate so poorly that they feared dying of hunger overnight.

34 Edwards, op. cit.

35 F. P. Barnard, *The Casting-Counter and the Counting Board*, Oxford, 1916.

36 Shakespeare, *Twelfth Night*, Act III, scene 2.

37 Calendar of State Papers, 15 January 1585.
38 Thomson, op. cit.
39 J. Arnold, *Queen Elizabeth's Wardrobe Unlock'd*, London, 1988.
40 Norman Moore, *The History of St Bartholomew's Hospital*, London, 1918.
41 Arnold, op. cit.
42 Stoneley, op. cit.
43 M. St Clare Byrne (ed.), *The Elizabethan Home*, 3rd edn, London, 1949.
44 Edwards, op. cit. For a charmed moment I thought the Italians were using them for their own siestas, but they were, of course, for their employer.
45 Shakespeare, *Richard III*, Act III, scene 7, and *Twelfth Night*, Act II, scene 5.
46 C. Welch, *History of the Cutlers' Company*, London, 1923.
47 William Harrison, *Description of England*, London, 1587.
48 Welch, op. cit.
49 Bower Marsh (ed.), op. cit.
50 The Goldsmiths' Company had never been asked before, but very charmingly could not help. Nor could the V. & A., or any of the books of reference I consulted.

Chapter 5: Gardens and Open Spaces (pp. 68–83)

1 Print by Wenceslaus Hollar.
2 Gray's Inn Pension Book Accounts, 'Disbursed 1598–1600. The Account of Francis Bacon ... of money laide out & disbursed for Grays Inn Walks.' Bacon was a bencher of the Inn. See Appendix III.
3 J. G. Nichols (ed.), *The Diary of Henry Machyn*, London, 1848.
4 W. P. Baildon (ed.), *The Records of the Honourable Society of Lincoln's Inn*, Vol. II, London, 1897.
5 John Schofield, *The London Surveys of Ralph Treswell*, London, 1987.
6 Francis Bacon, *Essays*, London, 1598. I used the Everyman edition of 1972.
7 Ash grows like mad once it takes root, which it does all too easily as anyone living near an ash tree knows. Willow also roots, which is part of its charm for modern garden designers. Perhaps Thomas Hill, from whose *The Gardener's Labyrinth*, London, 1577, this advice is taken, meant the gardener to use only dead wood; but that would have made it too brittle to bend into an arbour shape. A puzzle.
8 Hill, op. cit.
9 Ibid.
10 Schofield, op. cit.
11 Ibid.
12 Derek Keene and Vanessa Harding (eds), *Historical Gazetteer of London Before the Great Fire*, London, 1994.
13 Ibid.
14 Phillip Stubbes, *The Anatomy of Abuses*, London, 1583. He disapproved of so many things, in such detail, that he is an invaluable source.
15 There is a faint echo of the habits that Stubbes so disapproved of, in Dekker, *The Honest Whore, Part I*, which appeared in 1604. Viola is trying to get her brother to pretend to be her lover, to make her husband jealous. She says he

should call her his cousin. He replies that he will call her coz: 'that's the gulling [slang] word between the citizens' wives and the mad-caps that man 'em to the garden'.

16 John Stow, *A Survey of London*, London, 1598. Italics added.

17 J. Norden, *Speculum Britanniae*, London, 1593.

18 Mireille Galinou, *The Glorious History of London's Parks and Gardens*, London, 1990.

19 A. Prockter and R. Taylor, *The A to Z of Elizabethan London*, London, 1979.

20 R. J. Fletcher (ed.), *The Pension Book of Gray's Inn, Vol I: 1569–1669*, London, 1901.

21 W. E. Prest, *The Inns of Court under Elizabeth I and the Early Stuarts 1590–1640*, London, 1972.

22 Shakespeare, *Henry VI Part I*, Act II, scene 4.

23 Prockter and Taylor, op. cit.

24 Stow, op. cit.

25 Baildon (ed.), op. cit.

26 A. H. Johnson, *The History of the Worshipful Company of the Drapers of London*, Oxford, 1915.

27 Ibid.

28 Bower Marsh (ed.), *Records of the Worshipful Company of Carpenters*, Oxford, 1916.

29 Galinou, op. cit.

30 I owe the information on the Clothworkers to their kind archivist, David Wickham.

31 C. M. Clode, *Memorials of the Merchant Taylors*, London, 1874.

32 Galinou, op. cit.

33 Ibid. I have taken the liberty of substituting for Miss Galinou's 'garden house' a 'banqueting house', as in Bacon.

34 Keene and Harding, op. cit. In 1566 part of St Mary le Bow's churchyard was leased, *with the buildings on it*.

35 Derek Keene, *Social and Economic Study of Medieval London*, London, 1987.

36 Ibid.

37 One of the charms of the City, especially on a Sunday, is the little courtyards and gardens where one can sit and think and eat one's lunch. They often mark the site of churches destroyed long ago by war or fire.

38 Galinou, op. cit.

39 John Harvey, *Early Nurserymen*, London, 1974, stated that both dates and pomegranates had been grown in England since Chaucer's time, but an article by the same author in *Garden History*, vol. 17, no. 2, autumn 1989, stated that 'an ancient kind of small red plum now known as French Prune or Prune d'Agen, was meant by "Date",' which sounds much more likely.

40 Maggie Campbell-Culver, *The Origin of Plants*, London, 2001. I have drawn heavily on this marvellous book for this section.

41 This exotic-looking climber that grows in Oxford cottage gardens as long as they are slightly sheltered, has three stigmas (the nails of the crucifixion), five stamens (the wounds), a corona standing in for the crown of thorns, and ten petals and sepals which do – just – for the disciples, if you miss out Judas and

– less understandably – Peter. You may prefer the American name, Maypops.

42 Lena Cowen Orlin, *Elizabethan Households, An Anthology*, Washington, DC, 1995.

43 Calendar of State Papers Domestic, 27 8 and 10 9, 1566, 25 3 and 8 4, 1567.

44 William Harrison, *Description of England*, London, 1587.

45 John Gerard, *Herbal*, London, 1597.

46 *Genealogists' Magazine*, vol. 14, March 1963.

47 I had been trying to find the answer to this conundrum, in all kinds of places. There have been so many various locations of 'Gerard's garden' by so many writers that I was grateful to friends in the Institute of Historical Research for pointing me in the direction of the Local Archives of the parish of St Andrew's, Holborn, housed in Holborn Public Library, where the helpful staff found for me Caroline Barron's *The Parish of St Andrew Holborn*, published in London in 1979, which finally produced the answer.

48 R. H. Jeffers, *The Friends of John Gerard*, Connecticut, 1967. De l'Obel's copy is in the Museum of Natural History in Connecticut.

49 Harvey, op. cit.

50 Harrison, op. cit.

51 Excerpts from Richard Stoneley's Diary in the Douce Collection in the Bodleian Library, Oxford. Stoneley was a minor civil servant. It is always possible that this was an office expense, but it was presumably the going rate. His entry reads 'For gardening twenty days 28s 6d'. It roughly fits the 10s 8d paid by the Carpenters' Company 'to the gardeners for four days work' in 1571, as long as there were only two gardeners. The next charge in the Carpenters' account book was 'for drink for the gardeners 12d'. It all mounted up.

52 Sometimes called Parish Garden, but Paris is correct – and nothing to do with the capital of France. It had once belonged to Robert de Paris. Jane Seymour, one of Elizabeth's many stepmothers, had also owned it.

53 Platter in Peter Razzell (ed.), *The Journal of Two Travellers in Elizabethan and Early Stuart England*, London, 1995.

Chapter 6: Health, Illness and Medicine (pp. 89–109)

1 Steve Rappaport, *Worlds Within Worlds: Structures of Life in Sixteenth Century London*, Cambridge, 1989, using the records of various livery companies – that is, males. Women nowadays live longer than men, but I do not know whether or to what extent that applied in the sixteenth century, in London.

2 Margaret Pelling, *The Common Lot: Sickness, Medical Occupation and the Urban Poor in Early Modern England*, London, 1998.

3 Quoted in Charles Webster (ed.), *Health, Medicine and Mortality in the Sixteenth Century*, Cambridge, 1979 – a man, again.

4 M. Osborn (ed.), *Autobiography of Thomas Wythorne*, Oxford, 1961.

5 R. H. Adams, *The Parish Clerks of London*, London, 1971. The Bills were continued, with increasing sophistication, until 1859, although by then everyone knew that as a reliable source they were almost useless; but they were the only source there was.

6 John Stow, *The Annals of England*, London, 1592.

7 W. W. Greg (ed.), *A Companion to Arber*, Oxford, 1967.

8 Richard Stoneley, a minor civil servant. His diaries came to the notice of that magpie antiquarian Douce, and he copied out the bits that interested him. Luckily his writing is mostly legible, and his interests seem to have been much the same as mine: that is, the minutiae of everyday life, the price of fish, etc. Douce Collection in the Bodleian Library, Oxford.

9 All they had to do was to say 'plague' or 'not plague'. The series stopped in 1595 and began again in the bad plague year of 1603. The returns became more sophisticated as time went on. In 1625 they were done on printed forms: for examples see the author's *Restoration London*, London, 1997, and *Dr Johnson's London*, London, 2000.

10 Adams, op. cit.

11 *Lambeth Churchwardens' Accounts 1504–1645*, Surrey Records Society, London, 1950.

12 For this, and for so much more in the history of medicine, I am indebted to Roy Porter, in particular *The Greatest Benefit to Mankind*, London, 1997.

13 Paul Slack, 'Mortality crises and epidemic diseases in England 1485–1610', in Webster (ed.), op. cit.

14 The parish of St Botolph Without [outside] Aldgate stretched from the Tower of London north to near Bishopsgate, outside the wall. At 45 acres, ¼ square mile, it was one of the largest London parishes. It was served by a succession of parish clerks who saw it as their duty to record every fact likely to interest a social historian. Providentially, their records have been preserved. Equally providentially they have been analysed: Thomas Rogers, *Chronicle from Aldgate*, London, 1971.

15 Thomas Phaire, *The Regiment of Life, wherein is added a Treatise of the Pestilence, with the Book of Children*, London, 1560.

16 Porter, op. cit.

17 Rappaport, op. cit.

18 In 1397 Ragusa, now Dubrovnik, had increased the period of compulsory isolation to 40 days – *quarantenaria* – hence the word 'quarantine': Porter, op. cit.

19 W. H. Overall and H. C. Overall (eds), *Remembrancia AD 1579–1664*, London, 1878.

20 Adams, op. cit.

21 Norman Moore, *The History of St Bartholomew's Hospital*, London, 1918, and Irene Scouloudis, *Return of Strangers in the Metropolis*, London, 1985. I am not sure whether St Bart's and the City between them built at least one plague house.

22 Osborn (ed.), op. cit.

23 For the following account I am indebted to Alison Weir, *Elizabeth the Queen*, London, 1998.

24 Ibid.

25 T. D. Whittet, 'The History of Pharmacy in British Hospitals,' in F. N. L. Poynter (ed.), *The Evolution of Pharmacy in Britain*, London, 1965.

26 Moore, op. cit.

27 *Cochlearia officinalis*. Richard Mabey, *Flora Britannica*, London, 1996. Presumably

the banks of the Thames, tidal at London, could supply fresh scurvy grass.

28 The significance of lemons was known: E. S. Donno (ed.), *An Elizabethan in 1582: The Diary of Richard Madox*, London, 1976. Madox was a sailor who went to Brazil. By the time the ship got to Sierra Leone, before the long transatlantic haul, the crew was already suffering from scurvy, but the lemons they were able to buy or find on shore 'have scoured their mouths, fastened their teeth and purified their blood'. When they reached Guinea a fellow-mariner 'found many lemons growing whereof we brought great store aboard … almost forty of our men [are] sick with scurvy … God be praised we see some of them amend.'

29 B. H. Traister, *The Notorious Astrological Physician of London*, London and Chicago, 2001.

30 Phaire, op. cit.

31 Shakespeare, *Hamlet*, Act I, scene 1: 'the nights are wholesome; then no planets strike'. This is suggested by Thomas Forbes: 'By what disease or casualty: the changing face of death in London' in Webster (ed.), op. cit.

32 T. Rogers (ed.), op. cit.

33 Stoneley, in the Douce Collection, op. cit.

34 Andrew Boorde, *A Compendyous Regyment or a Dyetarie of Healthe*, London, 1547.

35 Shakespeare, *Twelfth Night*, Act III, scene 4.

36 John Hollybush, *A Most Excellent and Perfect Homish Apothecary or Homely Physic Book for all the Griefs and Diseases of the Body*, London, 1561; and see note 54.

37 The following account is taken from Patricia Allderidge, 'Management and mismanagement at Bedlam 1547–1633', in Webster (ed.), op. cit.

38 John Awdeley, *The Fraternity of Vagabonds*, London, 1561, included in A. V. Judge, *The Elizabethan Underworld*, London, 1930.

39 The measurements come from Allderidge, op. cit.

40 Shakespeare, *The Comedy of Errors*, Act I, scene 1, 'feeling my pulse, cries out, I was possessed'.

41 Shakespeare, *Henry IV Part II*, Act I, scene 2.

42 Shakespeare, *Twelfth Night*, Act III, scene 4.

43 Traister, op. cit.

44 Poynter (ed.), op. cit.

45 A report in the *Independent* newspaper on 16 October 2000 of a lecture by Dr Bert Keizer describes sixteenth-century medicine better than I can hope to do:

> 'Looking back into history, it would appear that people have always been pretty good at the simpler tasks of medicine, such as dealing with fractures and wounds. As to the many other ailments, there was an extensive use of herbs and less pleasant concoctions which occasionally hit a target people didn't even know existed. Apart from that there was a lot of vomiting, purging, cupping, praying, blessing, sacrificing, laying on of hands, going on a pilgrimage, showing it to the moon, magnetising, mesmerising, or hypnotising, and then all of a sudden we arrived in the nineteenth century [when Modern Medicine began] … in many cases we

get stuck after diagnosis, for we cannot treat a stroke, or Alzheimer's, or Parkinson's disease, or multiple sclerosis, or motor neurone disease, or schizophrenia, or osteoporosis, or nicotine addiction, or most famously and least believed of all we cannot cure cancer.'

I do not know whether some of these diseases are new to our times. Perhaps – with the exception of nicotine addiction – they always existed. but the message remains: it doesn't always help if all you know is the name of what ails you.

46 Stoneley, in the Douce Collection op. cit. (see note 8). His voice is extraordinarily vivid, perhaps because unlike Samuel Pepys he really had no presentiment that anyone else would ever read it.

47 Moulton Thomas, *This is the Mirrour or the Glasse of Health*, London, 1561.

48 Traister, op. cit.

49 This theory was not just a fee-spinning device of the Elizabethan apothecary. Avicenna, 980–1037, the great medieval physician, had advocated it. It was still going strong in the 1920s. Colin Gunn, 'A history of some pharmaceutical presentations' in Poynter (ed.), op. cit. *Evolution of Pharmacy in Britain*, London, 1965.

50 Phaire, op. cit.

51 Stoneley, in the Douce Collection, op. cit.

52 Peter Razzell (ed.), *The Journals of Two Travellers in Elizabethan and Early Stuart England*, London, 1995.

53 Poynter (ed.), *Selected Writings of William Clowes 1544–1604*, London, 1948.

54 John Hollybush, op. cit., described his book as a translation of a book in German by Arnold Bichman printed in Collen (Cologne), but this may have been a boast, to add status. By his title Hollybush meant a do-it-yourself medical dictionary such as many of us have on our shelves. Culpeper's *English Physician* in the next century is a better-known example.

55 For its heyday in the reign of Charles II, see the author's *Restoration London*, London, 1997.

56 Poynter (ed.), *Clowes*, op. cit.

57 For a comprehensible and fascinating account of the ancient Greeks' medical theories, Roy Porter, op. cit., is unbeatable.

58 Phaire, op. cit.

59 This, like so many other things in medicine, began with the Greeks, whose name for testicle is *orchis*. Perhaps Greek orchids looked different from English ones, it being almost certain that Greek testicles looked the same as English ones.

60 Moulton Thomas, op. cit.

61 Act II, scene 2.

62 Traister, op. cit.

63 P. French, *John Dee: The World of an Elizabethan Magus*, New York, 1989.

64 Margaret Pelling and Charles Webster, 'Medical practitioners', in Webster (ed.), op. cit.

65 S. W. Rawlins (ed.), *Visitation of London 1568*, London, 1963. I have excluded entries describing someone as 'Doctor' because this may refer simply to a man with a degree, not a medically qualified doctor.

66 Scouloudi, op. cit.
67 Ibid.
68 Porter, op. cit.
69 For the information on Clowes and much of the background to the Elizabethan medical profession I am indebted to Dr Margaret Pelling. See also Poynter (ed.), *Selected Writings of William Clowes*, op. cit. I have also read with enjoyment most of Clowes' books.
70 Traister, op. cit.
71 *Romeo and Juliet*, Act V, scene 1.
72 For the weapon salve in its heyday, see the author's *Restoration London*, op. cit.
73 Poynter (ed.), *Clowes*, op. cit.
74 These medical stories invite personal reminiscences. I will inflict on you only a parallel experience in a small hospital in Tanganyika, whither I was taken with a fractured forearm. The procedure had to be done in the X-ray department, a small mud hut that was very hot, so that progress could be checked. Two large men were summoned and told to pull, one on my hand and the other on my elbow. Unfortunately we were all so sweaty that they kept slipping off. But the surgeon, a foreign gentleman who had been struck off in his native country as an abortionist, did it beautifully and I am very grateful.

Chapter 7: Foreigners (pp. 110-122)

1 Calendar of State Papers, 16 9 1567.
2 See note 12 below for the source of the three maids. It is possible that 'in his home lodging three maids, Blackamoors' meant some status – orphans? refugees? – other than the usual domestic service.
3 T. R. Forbes, *Chronicle from Aldgate*, London, 1971.
4 James Walvin, *Black and White*, London, 1973.
5 References in *Othello* to the dramatis personae, Act I, scene 1; Act III, scene 3.
6 W. B. Rye, *England as Seen by Foreigners*, London, 1865.
7 Ibid.
8 Shakespeare, *Troilus and Cressida*, Act II, scene 2.
9 Peter Razzell (ed.), *The Journals of Two Travellers in Elizabethan and Early Stuart England*, London, 1995.
10 The English/Kiswahili one I used when I went to Tanganyika in the 1950s began, as I remember, 'Hang the carcase on a tree. I will have the liver for dinner.' I never had occasion to use that phrase, but it sounded more topical than the opening phrase in the book it replaced, which began 'The Sultan's men have stolen our turbans'.
11 Rye, op. cit.
12 S. W. Rawlins (ed.), *Visitation of London 1568*, London, 1964. Visitation here means, roughly, census.
13 R. H. Tawney and Eileen Power (eds), *Tudor Economic Documents*, London, 1924.
14 The following are taken from L. H. Yungblut, *Strangers Settled Here Among Us*, London, 1996, from which I have also taken the probable average.

Date of census	Total number of aliens
1562	4,543; 1,674 since 1558, of whom only 712 had religious reasons
October 1565	(Westminster omitted. Figures not given.)
March 1567	3,324, of whom 388 had come in the last two years
December 1567	(Westminster omitted.) 3,758, of whom 1,059 had come in the last two years
March 1568	9,302, of whom 77% were 'Dutch', 18% French
July 1568	461 since March, of whom 259 had religious reasons
May–December 1571	6,513
April–May 1583	(Westminster and Southwark omitted.) 4,141

15 W. H. Overall and H. C. Overall (eds), *Remembrancia AD 1579–1664*, London, 1878.

16 I am indebted throughout this section to Irene Scouloudi, *Returns of Strangers in the Metropolis, 1593, 1627, 1635, and 1639*, published by the Huguenot Society of London as vol. LVII, 1985.

17 Yungblut, op. cit.

18 Scouloudi, op. cit. This tall order was issued on 6 March 1593, returns to be in *four days later*, another testimony to the efficiency of London government, even if – I do not know when the returns actually came in – they were a bit late. The returns analysed by Scouloudi are a fascinating picture of London life, albeit in foreigners' households. There is, of course, no comparable picture of the households of native English Londoners.

19 A. L. Beier and Roger Finlay (eds), *The Making of the Metropolis 1500–1700*, London, 1986.

20 Scouloudi, op. cit.

21 The Steelyard was the London headquarters of the Hanseatic merchants.

22 Scouloudi, op. cit.

23 Andrew Pettegree, *Foreign Protestant Communities in Sixteenth Century London*, Oxford, 1986.

Chapter 8: Clothes and Beauty (pp. 123-147)

1 Janet Arnold, 'Three examples of late sixteenth and early seventeenth century neckwear' in *Waffen und Kostümkinde*, 1977. Here I must acknowledge again the kindness of Jenny Tiramani, Master of Design of the new Globe Theatre. Among the garments that Ms Tiramani allowed me to handle were several ruffs.

2 C. Barron et al. (eds), 'The London Journal of Alessandro Magno 1562', *The London Journal*, vol. 9, no. 2, 1983.

3 Until my visit to the Globe I had relied mainly on C. and P. Cunnington, *Handbook of English Costume in the Sixteenth Century*, London, 1954, which remains a mine of information on all aspects of Elizabethan costume, and Janet Arnold's two books (see notes 4 and 18).

4 Elizabeth liked people to give her presents of items of dress. Matching sets of ruffs and cuffs were ideal, because they did not have to fit. One set contained

6 yards in the ruff, 2 yards in each cuff. Janet Arnold, *Queen Elizabeth's Wardrobe Unlock'd*, London, 1971.

5 Dekker, *The Honest Whore Part I*, Act III, scene 1.

6 Henry Humpherus, *History of the Origin and Progress of the Company of Watermen and Lightermen of the River Thames*, vol. I: *1514–1829*, London, 1859, reissued London 1999.

7 Norman Moore, *The History of St Bartholomew's Hospital*, London, 1918.

8 Sometimes called more simply a 'poker', as in Dekker, *The Honest Whore Part I*, Act II, scene 1. If anyone still uses a poker, the end of it conveys far more accurately than my description, the business end of a poking stick. Dekker is as usual cheerfully obscene. The comic potential of poking sticks is obvious.

9 Phillip Stubbes, *The Anatomy of Abuses*, London, 1583.

10 John Stow, *The Annals of England*, London, 1592.

11 Smalt was a pigment made from cobalt in ground glass, sometimes seen as that vivid blue background in miniature paintings of the time. It was lasting, unlike blue vegetable dyes such as woad or indigo.

12 In 1591 blue starch seems to have been the trademark of prostitutes: 'these streetwalkers ... in ruffs of the largest size ... gloried richly with blue starch'. R. Greene, *A Notable Discovery of Cosenage*, London, 1591.

13 T. R. Forbes, *Chronicle from Aldgate*, London, 1971.

14 Arnold, op. cit.

15 Anon., pamphlet, *A Health to the Gentlemanly Profession of Serving Men*, London, 1598.

16 Where no reference is given, I have used the books by Janet Arnold or the Cunningtons, or the seminar that Jenny Tiramani so kindly gave me.

17 William Harrison, *Description of England*, London, 1587.

18 Anyone wanting to see how these garments were made must consult Janet Arnold's comprehensive *Patterns of Fashion: The Cut and Construction of Clothes for Men and Women c.1560–1620*, London, 1985, a fascinating combination of erudition and practicality.

19 Shakespeare, *Romeo and Juliet*, Act II, scene 4.

20 Shakespeare, *Much Ado About Nothing*, Act II, scene 1.

21 Dekker, *The Honest Whore*, Act II, scene 1.

22 Stubbes, op. cit.

23 Shakespeare, *Troilus and Cressida*, Act IV, scene 4: Troilus says to Cressida, 'Wear this sleeve' and she answers 'and you this glove'.

24 There is a superlative suit of jousting armour in the British Gallery in the Victoria and Albert Museum.

25 C. L. Kingsford, 'Essex House formerly Leicester House and Exeter Inn', *Archeologia*, vol. XXIII, 1923, which contains the inventory of the Earl's possessions when he died in 1588.

26 Ibid.

27 Shakespeare, *King John*, Act IV, scene 3.

28 B. H. Traister, *The Notorious Astrological Physician of London*, London, 2001.

29 Calendar of State Papers Domestic, 9 5 1567.

30 If you draw diagonals across the well-known portrait of Henry VIII with his three heirs, they cross exactly on Henry's codpiece, on which the succession to

the throne was so poignantly dependent.

31 And yet, see Dekker, *The Shoemaker's Holiday*, Act V, scene 2: 'my codpiece point is ready to fly in pieces every time I think upon Mistress Rose'. Jenny Tiramani of the new Globe could not enlighten me on codpieces, since she justifiably has never made one, Shakespeare's plays coinciding with the demise of the codpiece. My other costume guru, Janet Arnold, gives diagrams and cutting designs for codpieces in her *Patterns of Fashion*, from which I realised that they did not, as I had always assumed, contain the penis.

32 Shakespeare, *The Two Gentlemen of Verona*, Act II, scene 7. This curious use seems to have been normal – see also Dekker, *The Honest Whore*, Act IV, scene 2: 'you are a sweet youth to wear a codpiece, and have no pins to stick on't'.

33 James Osborn (ed.), *Autobiography of Thomas Wythorne*, Oxford, 1961.

34 Alex Werner, *London Bodies*, London, 1998.

35 Harrison, op. cit. In the days when nylon stockings were almost unobtainable, one sometimes resorted to drawing a mock seam line up one's bare legs, but this too was very difficult. I never thought of using a plumb-line.

36 Long ago when I was a student of Gray's Inn, members of the Inn put on a Shakespeare play, to an audience of the great and the good. I am ashamed to say that the only detail I remember from the dress rehearsal I was privileged to watch was the sight of senior male members of the bar furtively hitching up their tights.

37 Shakespeare, *Twelfth Night*, Act III, scene 2.

38 Shakespeare, *Hamlet*, Act II, scene 1.

39 Arnold, *Queen Elizabeth's Wardrobe Unlock'd*, op. cit.

40 I. Archer, C. Barron and V. Harding (eds), *Hugh Alley's Complaint: The Markets of London in 1598*, London, 1988.

41 Quoted in Arnold, *Queen Elizabeth's Wardrobe Unlock'd*, op. cit. Italics added.

42 The French word for brassière is, surprisingly, not brassière but *soutien-gorge*. When Queen Elizabeth, the late Queen Mother, accompanied her shy and reserved husband George VI to Paris, the French loved her, and promptly nicknamed her la Soutien-Georges.

43 Stephen Gosson, *School of Abuse*, London, 1579; T. Nashe, *Christ's Tears over Jerusalem*, London, 1593.

44 'Farthingale' is derived from the Spanish word for smooth twigs from coppiced willows, *verdugos*: Arnold, *Queen Elizabeth's Wardrobe Unlock'd*, op. cit.

45 In Shakespeare's *The Two Gentlemen of Verona*, the comic character Launce has a long conversation with his dog which includes: 'When didst thou see me heave up my leg and make water against a gentlewoman's farthingale?' I don't know whether this was a real hazard.

46 Shakespeare, *Othello*, Act IV, scene 3.

47 This need for pins, which were not cheap, gave rise to the special allowance to married women by their husbands called 'pin money'.

48 Werner, op. cit.

49 Puke brown sounded so improbable that I was glad to recognise it in an account of the Mercers' Company's feast to celebrate the election of one of its members to be Lord Mayor: all members were to wear, throughout the feast, their 'pewke' gowns and their crimson satin hoods.

50 Shakespeare, *Love's Labour's Lost*, Act IV, scene 3.

51 J. G. Nichols (ed.), *The Diary of Henry Machyn 1550–1563*, London, 1848.

52 W. H. Overall and H. C. Overall (eds), *Remembrancia AD 1579–1664*, London, 1878.

53 R. J. Fletcher (ed.), *The Pension Book of Gray's Inn, Vol. I: 1569–1669*, London, 1901.

54 Shakespeare, *The Taming of the Shrew*, Act IV, scene 3.

55 The doublet and hose that Jenny Tiramani showed me were of scarlet silk velvet, sewn by hand in minute stitches. No wonder the costumes at the Globe look so magnificent. Although they are heavy, they are all made of natural fibres so are more comfortable than, say, nylon velvet would be.

56 Act IV, scene 2. There is a reference in *The Taming of the Shrew*, Act III, scene 2, to 'a pair of old breeches thrice-turned', which does sound a bit optimistic.

57 Excerpts from Richard Stoneley's Diary in the Douce Collection in the Bodleian Library, Oxford.

58 See Thomas Dekker, *The Shoemaker's Holiday*, Act III, scene 3, 'let me have a pair of shoes, cork ... wooden heel too'. I am not clear about these 'cork shoes'. Obviously the cork had to have something between it and the ground, to protect it, hence I have called it an inner sole. But think of a cork bathmat. If the sole were thick enough to be noticeable, it would not bend. It would bend if it was only a thin layer, but then it would not be effective. A thick rigid layer must have made the wearer walk like a duck with rheumatism. During the last war, when clothing including shoes was rationed, there were wooden shoes on the market with rigid soles hinged under the instep, which necessitated a whole new way of walking, since they were not always curved like clogs.

59 Barron et. al., op. cit.

60 Stoneley, in the Douce Collection, op. cit.

61 Kingsford, op. cit.

62 Arnold, *Queen Elizabeth's Wardrobe Unlock'd*, op. cit.

63 M. St Clare Byrne (ed.), *The Elizabethan Home discovered in two dialogues by Claudius Hollyband and Peter Erondell*, 3rd edn, London, 1949.

64 Kingsford, op. cit. It is somehow moving to see the detailed inventory of Leicester's belongings. He had 26 sets of doublets and hose, starting with '4 doublets of satin embroidered with gold and silver, with hose to them, old and worn', his newer ones being the '4 doublets of satin laid on with gold and silver lace, and hose suitable [matching]', which even if new were worth less than half the other 'worn' ones. A contemporary account of the death of his stepson Essex, which the Librarian of the Tower of London very kindly copied for me, described his dress for the scaffold: a 'black wrought velvet gown and a satin suit of the same colour' and a hat and ruff. He took off his hat at an early stage, then the gown and the ruff, and his doublet 'under which he had a red waistcoat embroidered before with a border of gold'.

65 Arnold, *Wardrobe Unlock'd*, op. cit.

66 Diana Scarisbrick, *Tudor and Jacobean Jewellery*, London, 1995, on which I have based much of the following section.

67 H. Kelsey, *Sir Francis Drake: The Queen's Pirate*, New York, 1998.

68 Thomas Phaire, *A Treatise of the Pestilence*, London, 1560.

69 Traister, op. cit.

70 This comes from an 'epigram' by the Elizabethan wit Harington, quoted in Andrew Gurr, *Playgoing in Shakespeare's London*, Cambridge, 1987. Maybe it is not true; but it was too good a story to miss.

71 Arnold, *Wardrobe Unlock'd*, op. cit. One can only hope that whatever the donor was hoping to achieve succeeded; he sounds rather regretful.

72 Arnold, *Wardrobe Unlock'd*, op. cit.

73 John Schofield (ed.), *The London Surveys of Ralph Tresswell*, London, 1987. Tresswell surveyed various properties in London and his plans have survived. Most of them were made between 1607 and his death in 1616, but his meticulous description of each property shows that they had changed very little for decades.

74 Andrew Boorde, *Compendious Regiment of Health*, London, 1547.

75 Stoneley, in the Douce Collection, op. cit.

76 M. St Clare Byrne (ed.), op. cit.

77 Ibid., the Erondell dialogue called 'The French garden'.

78 William Turner, *Herbal*, London, 1568.

79 Thomas Hill, *The Gardener's Labyrinth*, London, 1577.

80 Thomas Raynall, *The Birth of Mankind otherwise named The Woman's Book*, London, 1634 – there were earlier editions.

81 Thomas Dekker, *The Honest Whore*, Act II, stage directions, scene 1.

82 Traister, op. cit.

83 Turner, op. cit.

84 Ibid.

85 Ben Johnson, *Sejanus*, Act I, scene 1.

86 W. P. Baildon (ed.), *The Records of the Honourable Society of Lincoln's Inn*, London, 1897.

87 Thomas Hill, *The Profitable Art of Gardening*, London, 1568.

88 John Hollybush, *A Most Excellent and Perfect Homish Apothecary ...* London, 1561.

89 Ben Johnson, *Volpone*, London, 1616 (acted in 1605).

Chapter 9: Food and Drink (pp. 146–168)

1 A. Pearce, *History of the Butcher's Company*, London, 1929.

2 W. H. Overall and H. C. Overall (eds), *Remembrancia AD 1579–1664*, London, 1878.

3 C. Barron, C. Coleman and C. Gobbi (eds), 'The London Journal of Alessandro Magno 1562', *The London Journal*, vol. 9, no. 2, 1983.

4 I. Archer, C. Barron and V. Harding (eds), *Hugh Alley's Complaint: The Markets of London in 1598*, London, 1988. Hugh Alley had ideas about reforming the market system. His pamphlet is delightfully illustrated with naif but vivid drawings.

5 Ibid.

6 John Norden, *Surveyor's Dialogue*, London, 1608 – five years after Elizabeth's death, but I have assumed it was in place before.

7 Ibid.

8   Pearce, op. cit.

9   *Remembrancia AD 1579–1664*, op. cit.

10 Barron et al. (eds), op. cit.

11 Silvia Thrupp, *A Short History of the Worshipful Company of Bakers of London*, London, 1933.

12 These are taken from John Stow, *A Survey of London*, Oxford, 1908.

13 Derek Keene and Vanessa Harding, *Historical Gazetteer of London Before the Great Fire*, London, 1994.

14 There were, for example, three properties at the east end of Cheapside, called the Half Moon, the Bell and the Fox, probably parts of one house, originally. None appears to have been a shop. Keene and Harding, op. cit.

15 Bryant Lillywhite, *London Signs*, London, 1972.

16 W. B. Rye, *England as Seen by Foreigners*, London, 1865.

17 Barron et al. (eds), op. cit.

18 Samuel Pepys was a great collector of prints. He owned several sets of London 'Cries' and also some foreign ones. The earliest set in his collection (reproduced as plates 26 and 27 in this book) includes the 'food' ones I have mentioned here, all of which are women, and some others. They are clearly a set, and they seem to me to depict the dress of 1550–1600. The most prosperous character, who is inviting offers of 'ends of gold and silver', is wearing a small ruff, and the details of the other clothes are consistent with the period I suggest. There has been inconclusive academic discussion about their date, summarised by Richard Luckett, Pepys Librarian, in his Introduction to *The Cryes of London: The Collection in the Pepys Library at Magdalen College, Cambridge*, Leeds, 1994. I have treated the set of *Cryes* to which I have referred as belonging to the second half of the sixteenth century. If my attribution is wrong, I suggest that they represent a well-established custom that was operating at that time, even if the prints were made later.

    For convenience I list here the other characters in the set: the Cryer, and two watchmen each with their lantern; a man begging for 'bread and meat for poor prisoners'; a woman asking for 'kitchen stuff' (food refuse, for resale); women selling drinking glasses, washballs and toast forks; men selling bed-mats, clothes lines, marking stones, pens and ink, and brooms and old shoes; and men offering services, such as a chimney sweep and a fiddler. All these happen to have made their way into the series, and Pepys's collection, and immortality. There is nothing to say that they were the only street vendors around at the time. It is interesting to see how much the same *Cryes*, in different clothes, survived well into the next century, not only in London but in Paris, Rome and Bologna too.

19 J. G. Nichols, *The Diary of Henry Machyn 1550–63*, London, 1848.

20 W. H. Overall (ed.), *Accounts of the Churchwardens of the Parish of St Michael, Cornhill*, London (no date).

21 Hubert Hall, *Society in the Elizabethan Age*, London, 1902. This is a history of the Darrell family of Wiltshire, one of whom came to London in 1589 and kept careful accounts, transcribed by Hall.

22 Pearce, op. cit.

23 *Remembrancia*, op. cit.

24 Shakespeare, *Henry IV Part II*, Act II, scene 4.

25 Lena Cowen Orlin, *Elizabethan Households: An Anthology*, Washington, DC, 1995.

26 Shakespeare, *The Merry Wives of Windsor*, Act I, scene 4.

27 R. J. Fletcher (ed.), *The Pension Book of Gray's Inn, Vol. I. 1569–1669*, London, 1901. Gray's Inn's cook had at his disposal seven sword spits 12 feet long, two round ones the same length, and two 'little bird spits' 7 feet long, but he was catering for over 200 men. I have assumed that domestic ones would be designed in the same way, but on a smaller scale.

28 William Harrison, *Description of England*, London, 1587.

29 M. St Clare Byrne, *The Elizabethan Home discovered in two dialogues by Claudius Hollyband and Peter Erondell*, 3rd edn, London, 1949.

30 Thrupp, op. cit.

31 Pearce, op. cit.

32 Thomas Dawson, *The Good Housewifes Jewel*, London, 1596/7.

33 Andrew Appleby, 'Diet in sixteenth-century England: sources, problems, possibilities', in Charles Webster (ed.), *Health, Medicine and Mortality in the Sixteenth Century*, Cambridge, 1979. The authority for this statement is the accounts of the Star Chamber. Appleby remarked that a sixteenth-century aristocrat – such as would sit in that court – was more physically active than a rich businessman in our century, which may have reduced the risk of arterial/coronary disease caused by a high-fat diet.

34 T. Nashe, *Pierce Penilesse*, London, 1592.

35 Jacques Bellot, *The Englishe Scholemaister*, London, 1580.

36 Ibid., under the heading, 'The Poesye or Nosegay of Love'.

37 All these recipes, including the carp, come from Dawson, op. cit.

38 Robin Howe, *Mrs Groundes-Peace's Old Cookery Notebook*, London, 1971, quoting *The Good Huswives Handmaid*, c.1597.

39 William Harrison, *Description of England*, 1587.

40 Andrew Boorde, *The Compendious Regiment of Health*, London, 1547.

41 Hall, op. cit.

42 James Osborn (ed.), *Autobiography of Thomas Wythorne*, Oxford, 1961. Wythorne came to London in 1545, aged seventeen.

43 Harrison, op. cit.

44 Ibid.

45 Thomas Nashe, *The Anatomy of Absurdity*, 1588.

46 Thomas Hill, *The Profitable Art of Gardening*, London, 1568.

47 Barron et al. (eds), op. cit.

48 St Clare Byrne, op. cit.

49 Dawson, op. cit.

50 Calendar of State Papers Domestic 1559 (no day or month).

51 A. H. Johnson, *The History of the Worshipful Company of the Drapers of London*, Oxford, 1915.

52 Nichols (ed.), op. cit.

53 Bower Marsh (ed.), *Records of the Worshipful Company of Carpenters*, Oxford, 1916.

54 Nichols (ed.), op. cit.

55 Johnson, op. cit.

56 Shakespeare, *Henry IV Part II*, Act V, scene 3.

57 Robin Howe (ed.), op. cit.

58 St Clare Byrne (ed.), op. cit. It is fair to say that this happy family scene at table was written by a Frenchman, who may not have known the niceties of the English food vocabulary.

59 Ben Jonson, *Volpone*, Act IV, scene 1.

60 Pontius Pilate's hand-washing gesture was not so outlandish as it may now seem. And we never learned the admirable eastern habit of keeping one hand – the left – for dirty jobs (hence, cack-handed) – and the right for honourable functions such as eating.

61 C. L. Kingsford, 'Essex House Formerly Leicester House and Exeter Inn', *Archeologia*, vol. LXX, 1923.

62 Gladys Scott Thompson, *Two Centuries of Family History*, London, 1930.

63 St Clare Byrne (ed.), op. cit.

64 Osborne (ed.), op. cit.

65 Alexander Barclay, *Eclogues*, 1570.

66 St Clare Byrne (ed.), op. cit.

67 Ibid.

68 Osborne (ed.), op. cit.

69 Stephen Perlin in 1558, quoted in Walter Besant, *London in the Time of the Tudors*, London, 1904. The words I have omitted were laborious attempts by Perlin to render the English phonetically.

70 Boorde, op. cit.

71 That wonderful wine merchant Berry Bros and Rudd, whose combined forces produced this translation.

72 Boorde, op. cit.

73 St Clare Byrne (ed.), op. cit.

74 R. Greene, *The Third and Last Part of Cony-catching*, London, 1592.

75 Paul Hentzner, of Brandenburg, in W. B. Rye, *England as Seen by Foreigners*, London, 1865.

76 Boorde, op. cit. I am not convinced that an ale-drinker avoids a beer belly.

77 Barron et al. (eds), op. cit.

78 Nashe, *The Anatomy of Absurdity*, op. cit.

79 Inquiry of the Privy Council and reply of the Lord Mayor concerning the food supply of the City of London, quoted in R. H. Tawney (ed.), *Tudor Economic Documents*, London, 1924.

80 Ibid.

81 Perlin in Rye, op. cit.

82 Boorde, op. cit.

83 Irene Scouloudi, *Returns of Strangers in the Metropolis*, London, 1985.

84 Boorde, op. cit. He also suggests that you should add distilled waters such as strawberry or dandelion water, instead of just water. The man obviously had no palate, though the result may have been delicious.

85 Harrison, op. cit.

86 Boorde, op. cit.

87 Charles Welch, *History of the Cutlers' Company*, London, 1923.

88 Platter in Rye, op. cit.

89 Shakespeare, *The Taming of the Shrew*, Act I, scene 2.

90 Nashe, *Pierce Penilesse*, op. cit.

91 J. Payne Collier (ed.), *The Egerton Papers*, London, 1840.

Chapter 10: Sex, Marriage, Family Life and Death (pp. 169–189)

1 R. Ascham, *The Schoolmaster*, London, 1570.

2 William Harrison, *Description of England*, London, 1587.

3 Thomas Hill, *The Profitable Art of Gardening*, London, 1568.

4 Ibid.

5 Ibid.

6 B. H. Traister, *The Notorious Astrological Physician of London*, London, 2001.

7 Helge Kökeritz, *Shakespeare's Pronunciation*, New Haven, Conn., 1960.

8 Ben Jonson, *Volpone*, Act III, scene 4.

9 Montgomery Hyde, *A History of Pornography*, London, 1964.

10 Ascham, op. cit.

11 Robert Greene, *The Black Book's Messenger*, London, 1592.

12 Gilbert Walker, *A Manifest detection of the Most Vile and Detestable Use of Dice-play, and other practices like the Same*, London, 1552.

13 Anon., *A Mirror for Magistrates*, 1584.

14 Laura Gowing, *Domestic Dangers: Women, Words and Sex in Early Modern London*, Oxford, 1996. The records of the evidence in some of these cases have survived, which can present fascinating vignettes of real life, but the separate records of the decisions are lost.

15 Ibid. *And* she was breaking the laws against over-rich apparel, if she wore her taffeta hat.

16 This section is largely based on Alan Bray, *Homosexuality in Renaissance England*, 2nd edn, New York, 1995.

17 Thomas Dekker, *The Gull's Horn-book*, London, 1609.

18 Phillip Stubbes, *The Anatomy of Abuses*, London, 1583.

19 My husband practised at the Divorce Bar. In the 1960s he told me that an allegation that a husband was a bugger – grounds for at least a profitable settlement for the wife if he were to avoid public scandal – was being replaced by allegations that he was a tax fraud, which had more clout as a blackmailing weapon.

20 Bray, op. cit.

21 Thomas Harman, *A Caveat for Common Cursitors*, London, 1566.

22 R. B. Outhwaite, *Clandestine Marriage in England, 1500–1850*, London, 1995.

23 James Osborne (ed.), *Autobiography of Thomas Wythorne*, Oxford, 1961.

24 A 1573 case quoted in Outhwaite, op. cit.

25 Osborne (ed.), op. cit.

26 Shakespeare, *The Taming of the Shrew*, Act IV, scene 3.

27 David Cressy, *Birth, Marriage and Death … in Tudor and Stuart England*, Oxford, 1997.

28 Gowing, op. cit.

29 Thomas Becon, *The Christian State of Matrimony*, London, 1546.

30 Ibid.

31 J. G. Nichols (ed.), *The Diary of Henry Machyn 1550–63*, London, 1848.

32 G. Eland (ed.), *Thomas Wotton's Letter Book 1574–86*, London, 1960.

33 L. L. Giese (ed.), *Consistory Court Depositions 1586–1611*, London, 1995.

34 B. H. Traister, *The Notorious Astrological Physician of London*, London, 2001.

35 Angell Daye, *The English Secretary*, London, 1586.

36 R. Greene, *The Third and Last Part of Cony-catching*, London, 1592.

37 Excerpts from Richard Stoneley's Diary in the Douce Collection in the Bodleian Library, Oxford.

38 Gowing, op. cit.

39 E. Fenton (ed.), *The Diaries of Dr Dee*, Charlbury, Oxon, 1996.

40 Phillip Stubbes, *A Perfect Pathway to Felicity*, London, 1592.

41 Diane Scarisbrick, *Tudor and Jacobean Jewellery*, London, 1995.

42 Peter Laslett, *The World We Have Lost – Further Explored*, 2nd edn, Cambridge, 1971.

43 William Harrison, *Description of England*, London, 1587.

44 Hill, op. cit.

45 Roesslin, *The Birth of Mankind otherwise named the Woman's Book*, translated into English in 1540 by Thomas Raynall, physician, quoted in Cressy, op. cit.

46 In Paris, the respected surgeon Ambroise Paré (1510–90) was giving courses for midwives, but his example was not followed in London.

47 Thomas Raynall, *The Birth of Mankind*, London, 1634. There had been earlier editions.

48 Richard Stoneley's diary, op. cit.

49 M. St Clare Byrne (ed.), *The Elizabethan Home discovered in two dialogues by Claudius Hollyband and Peter Erondell*, 3rd edn, London, 1949.

50 Thomas Forbes, 'By what disease or casualty: the changing face of death in London', in C. Webster (ed.), *Health, Medicine and Mortality in the Sixteenth Century*, Cambridge, 1979.

51 M. St Clare Byrne, op. cit.

52 See note 6.

53 R. J. Fletcher (ed.), *The Pension Book of Gray's Inn*, vol. I: *1569–1669*, London, 1901.

54 Samuel Kielchil, who was in London between September and November 1585. W. B. Rye, *England as Seen by Foreigners*, London, 1865.

55 C. Barron, C. Coleman and C. Gobbi (eds), 'The London Journal of Alessandro Magno 1562', *The London Journal*, vol. 9, no. 2, 1983.

56 Ibid.

57 Erasmus wrote *De Civilitate morum puerilicum* (Polite Manners for Boys) in 1530. It was translated into English in 1532 and reprinted many times: Norbert Elias, *The Civilising Process: The History of Manners*, translated from the German by Edmund Jephcott, Oxford, 1978. It was a pity that Samuel Pepys had not read it when he memorably entertained Lady Sandwich in his drawing room when she was 'doing something on the pot'.

58 Derek Keene and Vanessa Harding, *Historical Gazetteer of London Before the Great Fire*, London, 1994.

59 Alison Weir, *Elizabeth the Queen*, London, 1998.

60 Perlin in W. B. Rye, *England as Seen by Foreigners*, London, 1865.

61 Weir, op. cit.

62 Erasmus again.

63 T. R. Forbes, *Chronicle from Aldgate*, London, 1971.

64 The decision to conduct the funeral in Westminster Abbey and not St Paul's meant 'a great saving of expense': Calendar of State Papers Domestic, 19 12 1558.

65 Nichols (ed.), op. cit.

66 During the funeral of the late Queen Mother, in 2002, many people watching on television were surprised by the recital, by a herald, of her titles and pedigree, not realising the historic precedents for this.

67 John Stow, *The Annals of England*, London, 1592.

68 Ibid.

69 E. H. Pearce, *Annals of Christ's Hospital*, London, 1908.

70 Nichols (ed.), op. cit. Machyn took a professional interest in funerals, since he purveyed the necessary furnishings.

71 Ibid.

72 *Lambeth Churchwardens' Accounts 1504–1645*, Surrey Record Society, London, 1943.

73 Cressy, op. cit. St Alphage in London paid 5s for such a coffin, in 1569. Professor Cressy makes the point that the word 'coffin' then meant simply a large chest. I could remind the reader that it was also used for the pastry container in which a joint was baked: a general-purpose word.

74 Keene and Harding, op. cit.

75 W. H. Overall and H. C. Overall (eds.) *Remembrancia AD 1579–1664*, London, 1878.

76 J. Ainsworth (ed.), *Carpenters' Company Wardens' Account Book 1571–91*, London, 1937.

77 Ibid. Italics added.

78 Surrey Record Society, *Surrey Wills Part II Archdeaconry Court*, London, 1916.

Chapter 11: Education (pp. 190–211)

1 Thomas Becon, *The Christian State of Matrimony*, London, 1546; twelve years before Elizabeth's accession, but regularly reprinted.

2 William Harrison, *Description of England*, London, 1587.

3 J. P. Anglin, 'The expansion of literacy: opportunities for the study of the three Rs in the London diocese of Elizabeth I', *Guildhall Studies in London History*, vol. IV, no. 2, 1980. Sixty-eight licences were granted in the decade 1570–9, 211 in the next decade, and the figure was still rising.

4 Becon, op. cit.

5 Shakespeare, *King John*, Act I, scene 1.

6 These horn 'books' were just like the wooden-handled information sheets shaped like ping-pong bats, covered with transparent plastic, which you still see sometimes in tourist sites. They work, and worked, perfectly.

7 Becon, op. cit.

8 Black-letter is legible, with difficulty. Some of the secretary hand can be deciphered, court hand is impossible. I used, with gratitude, Lionel Munby,

Reading Tudor and Stuart Handwriting, Chichester, 1988.

9 I learned my accounting from Anon., *An Introduction of Algerisme to Learn to reckon with the penne or with the Counters, in Whole numbers or Broken*, London, 1581, and F. P. Barnard, *The Casting-Counter and the Counting-Board*, Oxford, 1916.

10 *Algerisme*, op. cit.

11 The whole account of the Merchant Taylors' school is taken from H. B. Wilson, *The History of Merchant Tailors' School*, London, 1812.

12 M. F. J. McDonnell, *History of St Paul's School*, London, 1909.

13 John Sargeant, *Annals of Westminster School*, London, 1898.

14 John Stow, *A Survey of London*, London, 1598.

15 W. K. Jordan, *The Charities of London 1480–1660*, London, 1960.

16 Ibid.

17 I became very aware of this when I tried to teach English to Swahili-speaking young adults who had managed to emerge from the Tanganyikan educational system, in the 1950s, without any grasp of English. I could find nothing in my own experience or in the public library that had any relevance to their lives. Christopher Robin? Toad of Toad Hall? Alice, anywhere? Hardly.

18 They were edited by M. St Clare Byrne, *The Elizabethan Home discovered in two dialogues by Claudius Hollyband and Peter Erondell*, 3rd edn, London, 1949. Hollyband is the more down-to-earth, Erondell portrayed a higher social life, but both aimed at the mercantile class.

19 T. Nashe, *Pierce Penilesse*, London, 1592.

20 This account of the Hospital is taken from a manuscript written by John Howes in 1582, *A brief Note of the Order and Manner of Proceedings in the first erection of the three Royal Hospitals of Christ, Bridewell and St Thomas the Apostle*, edited by S. V. Morgan, London, 1904, and made available to me by the kindness of the librarian of Christ's Hospital, where I also read some of the original records. I hope that in this description of Christ's Hospital I shall make amends for a serious error I committed in *Dr Johnson's London* as to the date of the Hospital's foundation, which was pointed out to me by several old boys, in time for it to be corrected in later impressions.

21 'Hospital' here means shelter or asylum – as in asylum seekers – not a place for medical treatment, though some hospitals such as St Bartholomew's Hospital did offer medical care. Christ's Hospital was an orphanage, but its primary function was educational.

22 Platter in W. B. Rye, *England as Seen by Foreigners*, London, 1865.

23 The librarian of Christ's Hospital (see note 20) kindly sent me a copy of this manuscript, and another kind librarian in Duke Humfrey's library in Oxford helped me to decipher it.

24 Thomas Dawson in his the *Good Huswife's Jewel* published in 1596 gives two recipes for 'pottage' based on chicken stewed with violet leaves, either with the chicken meat left in, or after it had been strained away. Remove the violet leaves and substitute stringy meat for chicken, and maybe the poor children's diet was not unlike Dawson's recipes.

25 *Christ's Hospital Admissions, Vol. I: 1554–99*, published by authority of the Council of Almoners of Christ's Hospital, London, 1937.

26 From a *Memorandum on the Statute of Artificers* cited in R. H. Tawney and E.

Power (eds), *Tudor Economic Documents*, London, 1924.

27 The Statute can be found in Tawney, op. cit. It has a distinct flavour of 'and pigs might fly'.

28 Laurence Stone, 'Social mobility in England 1500–1700', *Past and Present*, no. 33, 1966.

29 Bower Marsh (ed.), *Records of the Worshipful Company of Carpenters, Vol. III: Court Book*, Oxford, 1915.

30 Becon, op. cit.

31 From Steve Rappaport, *Worlds Within Worlds: Structures of Life in Sixteenth Century London*, Cambridge, 1989.

32 The most famous apprentice of all, Dick Whittington (?–1423), left his master and was on his way home when he famously heard the bells of London telling him to 'turn again, Whittington, thrice Mayor of London'.

33 A copy was lent to me by the kind archivist of the company, David Wickham.

34 J. Ainsworth (ed.), *Carpenters' Company's Wardens' Account Book 1571–91*, London, 1937.

35 C. M. Clode, *Memorials of the Merchant Taylors*, London, 1874.

36 Ibid.

37 C. Barron, C. Coleman and C. Gobbi (eds), 'The London Journal of Alessandro Magno 1562', *The London Journal*, vol. 9, no. 2, 1983.

38 H. Humpherus, *History of the Origin and Progress of the Company of Watermen and Lightermen of the River Thames*, London, 1859, reissued 1999; Harrison, op. cit.

39 Harrison, op. cit.

40 W. H. Overall and H. C. Overall (eds), *Remembrancia AD 1579–1664*, London, 1878.

41 For those interested in legal history, the subordinate Inns were:

> Barnards and Staple Inns, under Gray's Inn
> Thavies and Furnivals Inns, under Lincoln's Inn
> Clements and Cliffords Inns, under the Inner Temple
> The New Inn, under the Middle Temple.

As it happens, the records of Gray's Inn and Lincoln's Inn have survived best, while the records of the two Temples for the sixteenth century are sparse; which explains my emphasis on the first two. My own membership of Gray's Inn may explain, if it does not justify, my references to Gray's more often than to the other Inns. Statements in the text without any other source may be taken as referring, depending on the context, to Gray's Inn's or Lincoln's Inn's records. No doubt all four Inns led much the same kind of corporate life. R. J. Fletcher (ed.), *The Pension Book of Gray's Inn, Vol. I: 1569–1669*, London, 1901, gives the number of Gray's Inn members as 200, compared to the figure in W. P. Baildon (ed.), *The Records of the Honourable Society of Lincoln's Inn 1422–1586*, London, 1897, but they concur in stating that Gray's Inn was the biggest.

42 Members were expected to be friendly, and to get to know each other. One man complained to Queen Elizabeth that he had not been elected a Reader, a form of professional advancement, but the Inn explained that 'in his conversation he is not sociable'. Nowadays every student has to eat a certain number of dinners in hall, as well as passing exams, before he or she can be

called to the Bar and allowed to practise. When the Bar was smaller, this was not as silly as it sounds. Anyone whose standards of probity fell short of professional standards would soon be known, and shunned.

43 Fletcher (ed.), op. cit.

44 David Barnard, 'The Elizabethan law student', *Graya*, no. 83, 1979–80.

45 Purpoole was the ancient manor in which Gray's Inn stood.

46 Usually known as R. Ascham, *The Schoolmaster*, 1570.

47 Ibid.

48 I have used entries in the Calendar of State Papers Domestic, for various dates between May 1561 and January 1563. Some passages were quoted verbatim in the Calendar, other passages are as summarised by the Victorian editor, Robert Lemon, in 1856. I suspect that his reaction to this human interest story was the same as mine.

49 Louis Wright (ed.), *Advice to a Son: Precepts of Lord Burghley [and others]*, New York, 1961.

Chapter 12: Amusements (pp. 212–229)

1 'Extracts from the Book of Household Charges by Lord North', *Archeologia*, vol. XXXII, 1847.

2 The compass of this book is too small to include a comprehensive study of Elizabethan literature. I must leave that to scholars. With books, and particularly with plays, I try to imagine what the man and woman in the street might be buying and reading. This is not easy, and if I do not do justice to it, forgive me.

3 M. St Clare Byrne, *Elizabethan Life in Town and Country*, revised edn, London, 1961.

4 Roger Ascham, *The Schoolmaster*, London, 1570.

5 Excerpts from Richard Stoneley's Diary in the Douce Collection, Bodleian Library, Oxford.

6 Nicholas Crane, *Mercator, the Man who Mapped the Planet*, London, 2002.

7 John Dee, quoted in Crane, ibid.

8 See note 2.

9 The Register of the Stationers' Company shows that before 1603 the following had been registered:

Henry VI Parts 1, 2 and 3 (1594 and 1595, probably)
Titus Andronicus (1594)
Richard III (1597)
Love's Labour's Lost (1598)
Romeo and Juliet (1597, probably)
Richard II (1597)
Merchant of Venice (1598)
Henry IV Part 1 (1598)
Henry IV Part 2 (1600)
Midsummer Night's Dream (1600)
Henry V (1600, probably)

Much Ado about Nothing (1600)
Hamlet (1602)
Merry Wives of Windsor (1602)

I have taken these dates from F. E. Halliday, *A Shakespeare Companion*, London, 1952. I have marked 'probably' against those dates which are not certain. Various dates are given by other authorities.

10 Tessa Watt, *Cheap Print and Popular Piety*, Cambridge, 1991.

11 W. W. Greg (ed.), *A Companion to Arber [transcript of the Registers of the Company of Stationers of London 1554–1640]*, Oxford, 1967.

12 Byrne, op. cit.

13 Phillip Stubbes, *The Anatomy of Abuses*, London, 1583.

14 Stoneley, op. cit. Italics added.

15 James Osborn (ed.), *The Autobiography of Thomas Wythorne*, Oxford, 1961.

16 Many years ago I agreed to tell fortunes, crystal ball and all, at a party in a social centre in the east end of London. I was, I fear, unscrupulous. I first gathered all available gossip. When a small, very work-worn hand was given me, I told its owner that soon her hard work would be lessened, since I reckoned that she would become entitled to the state pension. She looked so happy. My next customer was a Cheltenham-educated but foolish girl who was worrying us all by threatening to run away with a fair-haired lorry-driver's mate, who was exceedingly nervous at the prospect. I foresaw for her a period of strain and a journey overseas, and eventual happiness with a dark stranger. I was both ashamed and relieved to see that she clearly took me seriously. Some time later, I checked. All was well, she was at a finishing school in Switzerland, and the lorry-driver's mate had been promoted. But it did make me realise the power of 'predictions'.

17 Z. Grey, *A Chronicle and Historical Account of the Most Memorable Earthquakes*, Cambridge, 1750. Most of the other references come from John Stow, *The Annals of England*, London, 1592.

18 Stubbes, op. cit.

19 W. B. Rye, *England as Seen by Foreigners*, London, 1865.

20 Stow, op. cit.

21 W. H. Overall and H. C. Overall (eds), *Remembrancia AD 1579–1664*, London, 1878.

22 William Harrison, *Description of England*, London, 1587.

23 This is Platter, who was sometimes a little credulous. P. Razzell (ed.), *The Journals of Two Travellers in Elizabethan and Early Stuart England*, London, 1995.

24 Janet Arnold, *Queen Elizabeth's Wardrobe Unlock'd*, London, 1988.

25 Harrison, op. cit.

26 Ann Saunders (ed.), *The Royal Exchange*, London, 1997, quoting from L. Grenade, *Les Singularités de Londres*, 1576.

27 Stow, op. cit.

28 J. G. Nichols (ed.), *The Diary of Henry Machyn 1550–63*, London, 1848.

29 Hentzner in Rye, op. cit.

30 Nichols (ed.), op. cit.

31 Stow, op. cit.

32 The ambassadors were a splendid bunch of men: Charles Cardinal of Lorraine, Anne Duke of Montmorency, Jacques Marquis de Fronsac, the Bishop of Orleans and a chevalier. Machyn, whose account this is taken from, particularly noted their 'gorgeous apparel'.

33 C. Barron, C. Coleman and C. Gobbi (eds), 'The London Journal of Alessandro Magno 1562', *The London Journal*, vol. 9, no. 3, 1983.

34 The *Independent* newspaper printed on 4 January 2001 a description of bear baiting in Pakistan, where, according to the reporter, the sport had been outlawed but was still being performed, with the connivance of the authorities. The details tally almost exactly with bear baiting in London in the sixteenth century. In 1554, during the reign of Mary Tudor and her husband Philip of Spain, London *almost* saw a Spanish bullfight. 'A great preparation was made in Smithfield for the Spaniards to bait the bull after the manner of Spain ... and a great frame for a house was new set up there.' But for some unspecified reason it was cancelled. C. L. Kingsford (ed.), *Two London Chronicles in the Collections of John Stow*, Camden Miscellany, vol. XII, 1910.

35 Platter, in Razzell (ed.), op. cit.

36 Act I, scene 1.

37 Trans. von Bülow, 'Journey through England and Scotland by Leopold von Wedel 1584–5', *Transactions of the Royal Historical Society*, New Series, vol. IX, 1895.

38 John Stow, *A Survey of London*, London, 1598.

39 Razzell (ed.), op. cit.

40 Quoted in Andrew Gurr, *The Shakespearian Stage 1574–1642*, Cambridge, 1980. For much in this section I am indebted to this book and another by Gurr, *Playgoing in Shakespeare's London*, Cambridge, 1987.

41 W. H. Overall and H. C. Overall (eds), *Remembrancia AD 1579–1664*, London, 1878.

42 S. Gosson, *The School of Abuse*, London, 1579.

43 Gurr, *Playgoing*, op. cit.

44 Razzell (ed.), op. cit. Platter was here in 1599. Italics added.

45 Dekker, *The Gull's Horn-book*, London, 1609 – but I doubt if Elizabethan audiences were different from this early Jacobean description.

46 See page 143.

47 *Remembrancia*, op. cit.

48 Ibid.

49 C. L. Kingsford, 'Essex House formerly Leicester House and Exeter Inn', *Archeologia*, vol. LXXIII, 1923.

50 Stow, *Survey*, op. cit.

51 Thomas Elyot, *The Book Named the Governor*, London, 1553.

52 R. J. Fletcher (ed.), *The Pension Book of Gray's Inn, Vol. I: 1569–1669*, London, 1901. It is pleasant to record that the Inn has recently (summer 2002) revived the playing of croquet, which must surely be related to bowls.

53 *Remembrancia*, op. cit.

54 Stow, *Survey*, op. cit. In 1743 the Pond was renamed the Peerless Pool and relaunched as a lido.

55 C. Barron et al. (eds), op. cit.

56 A. H. Johnson, *The History of the Worshipful Company of the Drapers of London*, Oxford, 1915.

57 C. M. Clode, *Memorials of the Merchant Taylors*, London, 1874.

58 Nichols (ed.), op. cit.

59 Harrison, op. cit.

60 Barron et al., op. cit.

61 Razzell (ed.), op. cit.

62 R. Greene, *The Third and Last Part of Cony-catching*, London, 1592.

63 T. Watt, *Cheap Print and Popular Piety 1550–1640*, Cambridge, 1991.

64 P. Clark, *The English Alehouse: A Social History 1200–1830*, London, 1983.

65 Harrison, op. cit.

66 Roy Porter, *The Greatest Benefit to Mankind*, London, 1997.

67 Dekker, *The Honest Whore*, Act II, scene 1.

68 Stow, *Annals*, op. cit.

69 Gurr, *Stage*, op. cit.

70 Hentzner in Rye, op. cit.

71 Hutton, *The Black Dog of Newgate*, 1596, quoted in Judge, *The Elizabethan Underworld*, London, 1930.

72 Platter in Razzell (ed.), op. cit.

73 W. Turner, *Herbal*, London, 1568.

Chapter 13: Networks and Boxes (pp. 230–245)

1 Phillip Stubbes, *The Anatomy of Abuses*, London, 1583.

2 See the fascinating account of these and all the other companies now extant, in Ben Weinreb and Christopher Hibbert (eds), *The London Encyclopedia*, 2nd edn, London, 1983.

3 S. W. Rawlins (ed.), *Visitation of London 1568*, London, 1964.

4 I read some of the records of eight companies – not all the great ones – as transcribed by later antiquarians from the originals, which are written in scripts that only a trained eye can decipher, and histories of others. The Carpenters' records that I read, which are unusually full and accessible, were *Vol. III, Court Book 1533–73* and *Vol. IV, Wardens' Account Books 1546–71*, both edited by Bower Marsh, Oxford, 1915, and *Vol. V, Wardens' Account Book 1571–9* and *Vol. VI, Wardens' Account Books 1571–91*, both edited by Ainsworth, London, 1937.

5 Steve Rappaport, *Worlds Within Worlds: Structures of Life in Sixteenth Century London*, Cambridge, 1989.

6 The training of apprentices is set out in more detail in Chapter 11, Education.

7 W. H. Overall and H. C. Overall (eds), *Remembrancia AD 1579–1664*, London, 1878.

8 I. Gadd and A. Wallis (eds), *Guilds, Society and Economy in London 1430–1800*, London, 2002.

9 A. H. Johnson, *The History of the Worshipful Company of the Drapers of London*, Oxford, 1915.

10 W. K. Jordan, *The Charities of London 1480–1660*, London, 1960.

11 Rappaport, op. cit.

12 From information kindly supplied by David Wickham, the company's archivist and a mine of such information.

13 A. Pearce, *History of the Butchers' Company*, London, 1929.

14 Edwin Green, 'The Vintners' Lobby 1552–68', *Guildhall Studies in London History*, no. 2, 1974.

15 P. Hunting, *The Leathersellers' Company: A History*, London, 1994.

16 Johnson, op. cit. Italics added. She quite often asked for only the 'comeliest' men to greet her.

17 C. Welch, *History of the Cutlers' Company*, London, 1923.

18 The editors of *Guilds, Society and Economy in London 1450–1800*, op. cit., make the interesting suggestion that these 'derivative processions, ceremonies, fur-and-velvet pomp and circumstance that even the newest companies adopted were … driven by [a] sense of insecurity' – that the companies might meet the same fate as the monasteries and be dissolved by royal fiat. The effect of Henry's dissolution of the monasteries lingered on in unsuspected corners.

19 Johnson, op. cit.

20 Ibid.

21 Pearce, op. cit.

22 Derek Keene and Vanessa Harding, *Historical Gazetteer of London Before the Great Fire*, London, 1994.

23 C. Burges (ed.), 'The church records of St Andrew Hubbard, Eastcheap 1450–1570', *London Record Society*, vol. XXXIV, 1999. This parish was of Anglo-Saxon origin.

24 *Lambeth Churchwardens' Accounts 1504–1645*, Surrey Records Society, London, 1950.

25 R. Adams, *The Parish Clerks of London*, London, 1971.

26 M. St Clare Byrne, *Elizabethan Life in Town and Country*, London, 1925. Her explanation is a great deal clearer than the contemporary account by Stow, so I have adopted it.

27 John Stow, *A Survey of London*, London, 1597.

28 Act III, scene 3.

29 Act II, scene 1.

30 William Harrison, *Description of England*, London, 1587.

31 Calendar of State Papers Domestic.

32 Ibid., 12 5 1582.

33 Andrew Gurr, *The Sheakespearian Stage 1574–1642*, Cambridge, 1980.

Chapter 14: Crime, Punishment and the Law (pp. 246–256)

1 I. J. Awdeley, *The Fraternity of Vagabonds*, London, 1561.

2 T. Harman, *A Caveat for Common Cursitors*, London, 1560.

3 R. Greene, *The Third and Last Part of Cony-catching*, London, 1592. A cony was in this context a thief.

4 R. Greene, *The Second Part of Cony-catching*, London, 1591.

5 Fleetwood, the Recorder of the City of London, writing to Burghley on 14 January 1582, quoted in R. H. Tawney and E. Power (eds), *Tudor Economic*

Documents, London, 1924.

6 Judge, *The Elizabethan Underworld*, London, 1930.

7 William Harrison, *Description of England*, London, 1577.

8 The following account comes from B. A. Harrison (ed.), *A Tudor Journal: The Diary of a Priest in the Tower 1580–85*, London, 2000.

9 I. Scouloudi, *Returns of Strangers in the Metropolis*, London, 1985.

10 Harrison, op. cit.

11 Hentzner in W. B. Rye, *England as Seen by Foreigners*, London, 1865.

12 Kielchil in Rye, op. cit. He was in London in 1585.

13 John Stow, *The Annals of England*, London, 1592.

14 J. G. Nichols (ed.), *The Diary of Henry Machyn 1550–63*, London, 1848.

15 Campion was the most prominent Jesuit priest of the time. A few days earlier he had traversed Cheapside in the opposite direction, on his way to the Tower, 'with a paper upon his hat written "This is Campion the Chief Captain of the Jesuits"'. Excerpts from Richard Stoneley's Diary in the Douce Collection, Bodleian Library, Oxford.

16 John Stow, *A Survey of London*, London, 1597.

17 Harrison, op. cit.

18 Stow, *Annals*, op. cit.

19 Ibid.

20 Ibid.

21 T. R. Forbes, 'By what disease of casualty: the changing face of death in London' in Charles Webster (ed.), *Health, Medicine and Mortality in the Sixteenth Century*, Cambridge, 1979. This gruesome ritual was not abolished until 1823.

22 Nichols (ed.), op. cit.

23 The words were a survival of the law French that was used in English law courts. The plea gradually became obsolete, but it was not formally abolished until 1772.

24 Angel Daye, *The English Secretorie*, London, 1586.

25 So far as I know, not the man who ran the school for thieves (see p. 247 above).

26 Eland (ed.), *Thomas Wotton's Letter Book 1574–86*, London, 1960.

27 Baker, *Manual of Law French*, London, 1990.

28 Stoneley, op. cit.

29 Quoted in W. K. Jordan, *The Charities of London 1480–1660*, London, 1960.

30 Phillip Stubbes, *The Anatomy of Abuses*, London, 1583.

31 L. Gowing, *Domestic Dangers: Women, Words and Sex in Early Modern London*, Oxford, 1996.

32 Nichols (ed.), op. cit.

33 To estimate the size of the problem, 'discreet persons were sent on a fixed day to all the butchers' shops of London, who, under colour of settling a wager as to the proportion of the good, bad and indifferent money in actual circulation, were to persuade the butchers to allow them to count over and divide into categories one day's take of their shop-tills'. 'The Tudors and the currency 1526–60', *Transactions of the Royal Historical Society*, New Series, vol. IX.

Chapter 15: The Poor (pp. 257–269)

1 S. V. Morgan (ed.), *John Howes's Manuscript 1582*, London, 1904.
2 Phillip Stubbes, *The Anatomy of Abuses*, London, 1583.
3 John Stow, *A Survey of London*, London, 1598.
4 T. R. Forbes (ed.), *Chronicles from Aldgate*, London, 1971.
5 An Act for the Punishment of Vagabonds and for Relief of the Poor and Impotent, 1572.
6 William Harrison, *Description of England*, London, 1587.
7 *Surrey Record Society*, no. 44, London, 1943.
8 W. H. Overall and H. C. Overall (eds), *Remembrancia AD 1579–1664*, London, 1878.
9 Ibid.
10 Forbes (ed.), op. cit.
11 J. Awdeley, *The Fraternity of Vagabonds*, London, 1561.
12 W. K. Jordan, *The Charities of London 1480–1660*, London, 1960.
13 When I was studying at the London School of Economics in Aldwych in the 1940s, there were printed handbills on lamp posts inviting applications to a charity that had been established long ago to provide marriage portions for maidservants in the parish who had served the same master for – I don't remember the qualifying period, but I do remember the regret with which, hopelessly unqualified but very broke, we read the notices. Most of these small charities have long been amalgamated into larger charities with more economic administration costs.
14 R. J. Fletcher (ed.), *The Pension Book of Gray's Inn*, vol. I: *1569–1669*, London, 1901.
15 This wonderful institution was in danger of being closed because so few people live in its district compared to earlier times before the spread of London. It is very good news that the present (2002–3) plan is to make it a specialist cancer and cardiac centre. I am indebted to its archivist, Marion Rea, for her help, and for allowing me to see its archives.
16 *The Order of the Hospital of St Bartholomews in West-Smithfield in London*, London, 1552, now available from St Bartholomew's Hospital, with a Preface, 1997. It makes fascinating reading, especially against the background of the present National Health Service. The unfortunate governors met a campaign of slander and back-biting. They had had to spend nearly £1,000 on repair bills to get the premises habitable at all, and were still lumbered with charges such as pensions which Henry had promised to various people before he died. I also consulted Norman Moore, *The History of St Bart's Hospital*, London, 1918, for the subsequent history of Bart's.
17 John Howes, *Familiar and Friendly Discourses*, London, 1582 and 1587.
18 A. and V. Palmer, *Who's Who in Shakespeare's England*, London, 2000.
19 Ibid.
20 F. N. L. Poynter (ed.), *Selected Writings of William Clowes*, London, 1948.
21 Howes, op. cit.
22 C. Graves, *The Story of St Thomas's*, London, 1947.
23 Howes, op. cit.

24 Forbes (ed.), op. cit.

25 Howes, op. cit. 2nd Discourse, 1587.

Chapter 16: Religion, Superstition, Witchcraft and Magic
(pp. 270–279)

1 The primary meaning of 'catholic' is 'universal'. In the Apostles' Creed which is part of the Anglican liturgy, 'the holy Catholic church' means the Anglican Church. But according to the *Oxford Concise Dictionary*, when the initial letter is capitalised it can mean 'of the Roman Catholic religion'. I have followed that usage here.

2 P. Prothero (ed.), *Select Statutes and other Constitutional Documents*, 4th edn, London, 1913.

3 J. G. Nichols (ed.), *The Diary of Henry Machyn 1550–63*, London, 1848.

4 William Harrison, *Description of England*, London, 1587. The rood was the crucifix over the nave of the church, confronting the congregation. Christ is flanked by his mother Mary on one side and his friend John on the other.

5 G. Huelin, 'The Churchwardens Account Book of St Margaret Moses 1547–97', *Guildhall Studies in London History*, vol. I, 1973.

6 W. H. and H. C. Overall (eds), *Accounts of the Churchwardens of the Parish of St Michael Cornhill*, London (undated).

7 P. Burgess (ed.), 'The church records of St Andrew Hubbard Eastcheap, 1450–1570', *London Record Society*, vol. XXXIV, 1999.

8 E. Duffy, *The Stripping of the Altars*, London, 1992.

9 Nichols (ed.), op. cit.

10 W. P. Baildon (ed.), *The Records of the Honourable Society of Lincoln's Inn, Vol. I: 1422–1586*, London, 1897.

11 Harrison, op. cit.

12 Pronounced Dow-ey by English speakers: between Amiens and Lille.

13 Camden, *Annals of Queen Elizabeth*, London, 1675, quoted in W. T. MacCaffrey, *Elizabeth I*, London, 1993; a most helpful work.

14 Quoted in Prothero (ed.), op. cit.

15 For example, St Andrew's Holborn, 'at the lower end of the church'. C. Barron (ed.), *The Parish of St Andrew Holborn*, London, 1979.

16 R. Woodger, 'Post Reformation Mixed Gothic in Huntingdonshire Church Towers and its Campanological Associations', *Architectural Journal*, vol. 141, 1984; an enlightening account of the general change in campanology, 1550–80.

17 Hentzner in W. B. Rye (ed.), *England as Seen by Foreigners*, London, 1865.

18 M. St Clare Byrne (ed.), *The Elizabethan Home discovered in two dialogues by Claudius Hollyband and Peter Erondell*, 3rd edn, London, 1949.

19 M. Maclure, *The Paul's Cross Sermons 1534–1642*, Toronto, 1958, on which the rest of this section is based. The sermons stopped in 1633 and the cross was demolished ten years later.

20 Nichols (ed.), op. cit.

21 R. Nashe, *Pierce Pennilesse*, London, 1592.

22 W. W. Greg (ed.), *Henslowe's Diary*, London, 1904.

23 M. Pelling and C. Webster, 'Medical practitioners' in Charles Webster (ed.), *Health, Medicine and Mortality in the Sixteenth Century*, Cambridge, 1979.

24 A law against something does not prove that it exists. There was a Witchcraft Ordinance in Tanganyika in the 1950s, but it was passed, and occasionally invoked, to punish malefactors who persuaded their victims of their evil powers, and led them to commit suicide, so strong was the victims' belief that they had been bewitched. But the legislators did not necessarily believe in witchcraft when they passed the ordinance. A modern example of witchcraft comes from my days as a student of Gray's Inn in the late 1940s. Many students came from Nigeria. One of them kept failing his exams, although he was very intelligent and had worked hard. The Under-Treasurer of the time asked him, gently, what was wrong. The man replied that a witchdoctor in his home town had put a spell on him preventing him from passing, no matter how hard he tried. The Under-Treasurer took a moment to consider, then making himself as impressive as possible told the young student that *his* spell was stronger, and that he would pass – and he did.

25 B. H. Traister, *The Notorious Astrological Physician of London, Simon Forman*, London, 2001.

26 Diana Scarisbrick, *Jewellery in Britain 1066–1837*, Norwich, 1994.

27 Ibid.

28 William Turner, *Herbal*, London, 1568.

29 'Conjuring' meant, in Elizabethan legal language, invoking spirits. I use it here in its modern sense.

Appendix I: Words and Pronunciation (pp. 282–284)

1 Peter Levins, *Manipulum Vocabulorum*, London, 1570, ed. Wheatley, London, 1867.

Appendix II: Currency, Wages and Prices (pp. 285–287)

1 M. St Clare Byrne, *Elizabethan Life in Town and Country*, revised edn, London, 1961.

Index

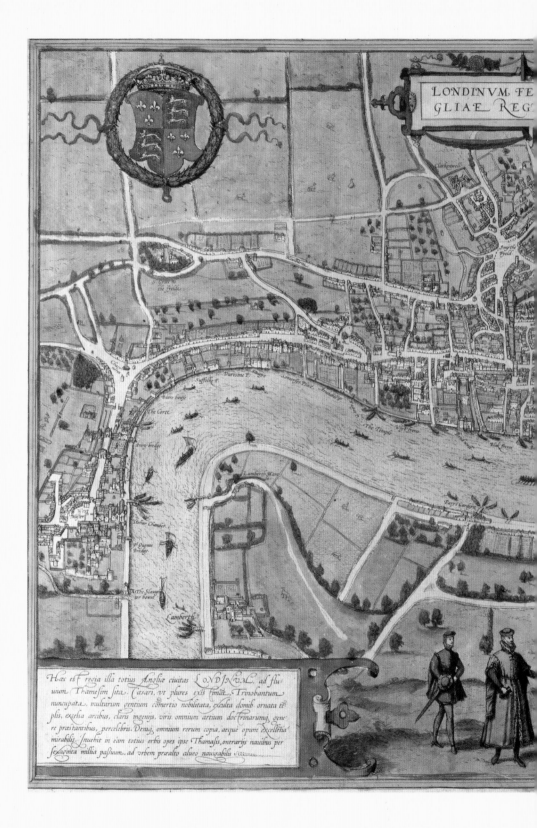